# EXISTENTIALISM NOW

# EXISTENTIALISM NOW

## 21 QUOTES FOR THE 21ST CENTURY

*Nik Farrell Fox*

BLOOMSBURY ACADEMIC
NEW YORK • LONDON • OXFORD • NEW DELHI • SYDNEY

BLOOMSBURY ACADEMIC
Bloomsbury Publishing Plc, 50 Bedford Square, London, WC1B 3DP, UK
Bloomsbury Publishing Inc, 1359 Broadway, New York, NY 10018, USA
Bloomsbury Publishing Ireland, 29 Earlsfort Terrace, Dublin 2, D02 AY28, Ireland

BLOOMSBURY, BLOOMSBURY ACADEMIC and the Diana logo are trademarks of Bloomsbury Publishing Plc

First published in Great Britain 2026



Cover design: Ben Anslow



A catalogue record for this book is available from the British Library.

A catalog record for this book is available from the Library of Congress.

ISBN: HB: 978-1-3504-3542-1
PB: 978-1-3504-3543-8
ePDF: 978-1-3504-3544-5
eBook: 978-1-3504-3545-2

Typeset by Lumina Datamatics Ltd
Printed and bound in Great Britain

For product safety related questions contact productsafety@bloomsbury.com.

To find out more about our authors and books visit www.bloomsbury.com and sign up for our newsletters.

*To*

*Anne and Howard*

*my beloved mum and eldest brother whose presence and absence manifest day by day. This book is dedicated to their vibrant death*

*The book becomes almost human*. Every writer is surprised each time a book, as soon as it is separated from him, begins to take on a life of its own . . . Perhaps he almost forgets the book; perhaps he rises above the views expressed in it; perhaps he no longer understands it and has lost those wings on which he soared when he wrote that book. Meanwhile, it goes about finding its readers, kindles life, pleases, horrifies, spawns new works, and becomes the soul of others' resolutions and actions.

(Nietzsche, *Human, All Too Human*)

Philosophical systems are living thoughts. It is by seeking in the written word in order to revive these thoughts within ourselves that we may hope to hear them deliver their message

(Émile Boutroux, *Historical Studies in Philosophy*)

# CONTENTS

# ACKNOWLEDGEMENTS

"To think is to thank" (as Heidegger said), and my gratitude goes to all the invaluable interconnections I encountered in the writing of this book:

Firstly, to Bloomsbury Academic (Liza Thompson, Miraya McCoy, Ben Piggott) who took my idea and ran with it. Such enthusiasm was vital fuel in the daily writing of the book. Suggestions made by (anonymous) reviewers were very insightful and significantly informed the final manuscript—any shortcomings in the text are, of course, entirely of my own agency.

On an academic level, I thank my colleague and friend Dr. Joss Winn whose zeal for Heidegger inspired me tremendously and aided my footing on the difficult terrain of the German philosopher's recondite thinking by working through the secondary literature with great celerity. Inspired by Rousseau's "Reveries," walking, philosophizing and drinking coffee together were felicitous and thought-provoking occasions.

Also, I acknowledge a debt to Alfred Betschart. Just when you imagine you know everything there is to know about Sartre (also Beauvoir, Heidegger, Jaspers, Marcel, or Nietzsche, for that matter!), a conversation with Alfred soon dispels complacency. He is an indomitable scholar and a font of knowledge. Thanks also to John H. Gillespie at *Sartre Studies International*, to Jonathan Webber and Kate Kirkpatrick at the *UK Sartre Society*, and to two of Sartre's most eminent Gallic ambassadors, Annie Cohen-Solal and François Noudelmann, whose labors and passion are a great inspiration to those who wish to keep the Beauvoir-Sartre ball rolling with momentum in the twenty-first century.

Finally, my deepest heartfelt thanks go to my family, past and present, for all their wondrous love and support (especially Rachel, *la renarde*, and Harvey, who first introduced me to Nietzsche all those moons ago) and most of all, for enduring my acquired habit of summarizing every discussion with a Nietzsche, Beauvoir or Sartre quotation *ex cathedra*. It's a hard habit to shake (and must be very frustrating for the interlocutor), but one I greatly encourage in others by reading this book and recycling many of the quotations within to suit the topic in hand!

# ABBREVIATIONS OF EXISTENTIALIST WORKS

Beauvoir

| | |
|---|---|
| **ASD** | *All Said and Done* |
| **EA** | *The Ethics of Ambiguity* |
| **FC** | *Force of Circumstance* |
| **FS** | *Adieux: A Farewell to Sartre* |
| **FW** | *Feminist Writings* |
| **MDD** | *Memoirs of a Dutiful Daughter* |
| **MPPS** | "Merleau-Ponty et le pseudo-Sartrisme" |
| **OA** | *Old Age* |
| **PC** | *Pyrrhus et Cinéas* |
| **PL** | *The Prime of Life* |
| **PW** | *Philosophical Writings* |
| **SS** | *The Second Sex* |

Fanon

| | |
|---|---|
| **BSWM** | *Black Skin, White Masks* |
| **WE** | *The Damned of the Earth* |

Heidegger

| | |
|---|---|
| **BPP** | *The Basic Problems of Phenomenology* |
| **BT** | *Being and Time* |
| **BW** | *Basic Writings* |
| **DT** | *Discourse on Thinking* |
| **EB** | *Existence and Being* |
| **EP** | *The End of Philosophy* |
| **GA** | *Martin Heidegger's Gesamtausgabe* |
| **HJ** | *Heidegger-Jahrbuch, Vol.4* |
| **IM** | *Introduction to Metaphysics* |
| **OG** | "Only a God Can Save Us" |
| **PLT** | *Poetry, Language, Thought* |
| **WCT** | *What is Called Thinking?* |

Kierkegaard

| | |
|---|---|
| **CA** | *The Concept of Anxiety* |
| **CUP** | *Concluding Unscientific Postscript* |
| **EO** | *Either/Or* |
| **FT** | *Fear and Trembling* |

**PF** *Philosophical Fragments*
**PJ** *Papers and Journals: A Selection*
**SD** *The Sickness Unto Death*
**WL** *Works of Love*

Marcel

**AW** *Awakenings*
**BH** *Being and Having*
**CF** *Creative Fidelity*
**EB** *Existential Background of Human Dignity*
**EO** "Existence et objectivité"
**EPC** *Essai de philosophie concrète*
**HV** *Homo Viator*
**MB** *The Mystery of Being*
**MP** *Music and Philosophy*
**PE** *The Philosophy of Existence*
**PEX** *The Philosophy of Existentialism*
**TW** *Tragic Wisdom and Beyond*

Merleau-Ponty

**AD** *Adventures of the Dialectic*
**HT** *Humanism and Terror*
**PP** *Phenomenology of Perception*
**PW** *The Prose of the World*
**S** *Signs*
**SNS** *Sense and Non-Sense*
**VI** *The Visible and the Invisible*

Nietzsche

**A** *The Antichrist*
**AOM** "Assorted Maxims and Opinions"
**BGE** *Beyond Good and Evil*
**BT** *The Birth of Tragedy*
**CW** *The Case of Wagner*
**D** *Daybreak*
**EH** *Ecce Homo*
**G.S** "The Greek State"
**HH** *Human, All Too Human*
**JS** *The Joyous Science*
**KSB** *Sämtliche Briefe, Kritische Studienausgabe*
**KSW** *Sämtliche Werke, Kritische Studienausgabe*
**LN** *Writings from the Late Notebooks*
**OGM** *On the Genealogy of Morals*
**PTAG** "Philosophy in the Tragic Age of the Greeks"
**TI** *Twilight of the Idols*
**UM** *Untimely Meditations*

| | |
|---|---|
| WP | *The Will to Power* |
| WS | *The Wanderer and his Shadow* |
| Z | *Thus Spoke Zarathustra* |

Sartre

| | |
|---|---|
| BN | *Being and Nothingness* |
| BO | *Black Orpheus* |
| CDR | *Critique of Dialectical Reason, Vol.1* |
| CDR2 | *Critique of Dialectical Reason, Vol.2* |
| CM | *Cahiers pour une morale* |
| EH | *Existentialism is a Humanism* |
| EJ | *Ecrits de jeunesse* |
| EM | *L'espoir maintenant* |
| FI | *The Family Idiot, Vol.1* |
| FI2 | *The Family Idiot, Vol.2* |
| FI3 | *The Family Idiot, Vol.3* |
| FI4 | *The Family Idiot, Vol.4* |
| FI5 | *The Family Idiot, Vol.5* |
| HN | *Hope Now* |
| I | *The Imagination* |
| IF] | *L'idiot de la famille, Vol.3* |
| IM | *The Imaginary* |
| IT | "Itinerary of a Thought" |
| N | *Nausea* |
| SG | *Saint Genet* |
| SM | *Search for a Method* |
| STE | *Sketch for a Theory of the Emotions* |
| TE | *The Transcendence of the Ego* |
| W | *Words* |
| WD | *The War Diaries of Jean-Paul Sartre* |
| WL | *What is Literature?* |

For simplicity of referencing, I use the following conventions in the text:

Nietzsche's works are listed by part/section/subsection

| | |
|---|---|
| BT 9 | *The Birth of Tragedy*, section 9 |
| Z 3.12.2 | *Thus Spoke Zarathustra*, part 1, "Of Old and New Law-Tables," section 2 |
| GM P3 | *On the Genealogy of Morals*, "Preface," section 3 |
| Z P2 | *Thus Spoke Zarathustra*, "Prologue," section 2 |
| UM 3.1 | *Untimely Meditations*, "Schopenhauer as Educator," section 1 |

All other works are listed by volume and/or page

| | |
|---|---|
| CDR2: 22 | *The Critique of Dialectical Reason*, volume 2, page 22 |
| EA 18 | *The Ethics of Ambiguity*, page 18 |
| GA2: 20 | *Gesamtausgabe*, volume 2, page 20 |

# PREFACE

According to Nietzsche, a person "who has completely lost his way in a forest, but strives with uncommon energy to get out of it in whatever direction sometimes discovers a new, unknown way" (HH 231). *Existentialism Now* tracks the pathways trodden by existentialist philosophers as we venture through the dense forest of their conceptual thinking. It shows the common trails they forge as well as the tributary paths that lead off in their own singular way. I use leading quotations from existentialism as *pathmarks* or points of orientation to consider topics that have a strong contemporary resonance—*ecology*, *age*, *race*, *gender*, *class*, *death*, *art*, *love*, *music*, *humanism*, *animals*, *violence*, *religion*, *science*, *technology*, *reason*, *emotion*, *consciousness*, *the body*, *interconnectedness*, *anxiety*, *politics*, *freedom*, and *individuality*. Each chapter corresponds to a specific topic and charts the path made by existentialists as they endeavored philosophically to discover a "new, unknown way."

*Existentialism Now* has two purposes. First, *curatorial*—to bring key existentialist concepts and phrases together side by side, many of which have seeped into our everyday lexicon and colored our collective psyche as "untranslatable locutions" (Sartre) or as "inconspicuous furrows in language" (Heidegger). Second, my aim in this book is *propaedeutical*, that is, to assemble key existentialist concepts as entry points and marking posts that enable others to venture further into the lush forest of existentialist thinking. This is a response to Beauvoir's plea in "Existentialism and Popular Wisdom" (1945) to present existentialism in a form that is digestible but one that overcomes misleading popularizations, goes beyond a simple introduction, and yet engages with the concepts in a way that does justice to the complexity of existentialism's philosophical depth. I offer these quotations purposively as vital components of a developing *Existential Posthumanist Manifesto*[1] and as trigger points for active reconceptualization.

This book is inspired in part by Jonathan Webber's excellent *Rethinking Existentialism* (2018) which was concerned with updating our view of existentialism and showing the ways that, in its most sophisticated form, existentialism prefigures or informs contemporary developments in psychology, political theory, and ethics. With this same purpose in common, *Existentialism Now* takes an alternate approach by spreading the net to include a wider range of thinkers beyond the French "phenomenological quartet" of Sartre, Beauvoir, Fanon, and Merleau-Ponty in defining what constitutes existentialism. As well as these four, I add Kierkegaard, Nietzsche, Heidegger, Jaspers, and Marcel into the mix and take a more genealogical view for the sake of context. While I agree with Webber's central thesis that existentialism reaches its most elevated expression and canonical form in the works of the French existentialists, I also judge that French existentialism is unthinkable without German *Existenz* philosophy (Jaspers, Heidegger) which was itself influenced strongly by Kierkegaard's *existential turn* and Nietzsche's *Lebensphilosophie*. My aim in this book is to show the several pathways that existentialism took from the rich beginnings of Kierkegaard's and Nietzsche's thinking whose philosophical insights greatly inform and anticipate the work of Heidegger and the French existentialists.

Where possible, *Existentialism Now* attempts to strike a felicitous balance between exposition and reproduction. That is, to guide the reader toward valid interpretations of key existentialist concepts while allowing the texts (and the elegant writing of the existentialists) to speak for themselves as much as possible.

# Introduction

## *Composting Existentialism in the Twenty-First Century*

The *existentialist offensive* ignited with spectacular fulgurations in 1945 in Europe and the United States and marked the beginning of the celebrity status of its most famous protagonists, Jean-Paul Sartre and Simone de Beauvoir. They appeared on the pages of *Vogue*, *Harper's Bazaar*, and *Atlantic Monthly* attracting a host of European and international press coverage. *Time* magazine christened Sartre the "literary lion of Paris" while Beauvoir was given acolyte status, described in *Samedi Soir*, a postwar tabloid in France, as "la grande Sartreuse" and "Notre Dame de Sartre."[1]

Down the years, "excrementalism" (as François Mauriac caustically labeled it in the 1950s),[2] has been regularly presented in ways that vulgarize its key messages in the form of what Thomas Flynn (2006: 105) disparagingly calls "weekend existentialism." Ascribed stereotypically to the cliques of Bohemia, chic café dwellers, avant-garde jazz musicians, and mystical tyro philosophers, existentialism is probably the most misunderstood and caricatured of philosophical movements. Attacked by the political Right and Left in equal measure, it is associated with an absolute notion of individual freedom (if Sartre is the target) or with an authoritarian conservatism (if Heidegger or Nietzsche are under the microscope). This was certainly how the neo-Marxist German philosopher Herbert Marcuse viewed it, criticizing Sartre's *Being and Nothingness* as an apology for bourgeois liberalism and individualism[3] while condemning existentialist thinking in its authoritarian Heideggerian form. Shortly after Heidegger's controversial Rectorial Address to Freiburg University in 1933 in support of Hitler's cultural program, Marcuse concluded:

> Existentialism collapses in the moment when its political theory is realized. The total-authoritarian state which it yearned for gives the lie to all its truths. Existentialism accompanies its collapse with a self-abasement that is unique in Intellectual history . . . it ends philosophically with the radical denial of its own origins [the historical concretion of individual existence]; the struggle against reason drives it blindly into the arms of the reigning powers. (1968: 40)

Existentialism's reception by Anglo-American philosophers[4] was also guarded, lukewarm, or just plain hostile. Gilbert Ryle expressed some admiration for Heidegger's philosophy as an "advance" in phenomenology but added that it was "an advance towards disaster" which will terminate either in a "self-ruinous subjectivism" or a "windy mysticism." A. J. Ayer begrudgingly acknowledged existentialism's importance and devoted several essays to it but complained about its incipient "metaphysical pessimism." In the Oxford circle of philosophers who embraced it in some form or other, the reception was always qualified. Iris Murdoch warned of existentialism's "intellectual snobbery" fueled by a spirit of elitist individualism that informed its critique of the crowd (Kierkegaard), the herd (Nietzsche), the They (Heidegger), or inauthenticity (Beauvoir/Sartre). Although Mary Warnock praises existentialist philosophers for their anti-Cartesian methodology, her final judgment is damning—"Existentialism, however attractive its doctrines of individual freedom may be, has come to an end as a philosophical movement." This is the result, she adds, of its "subjective anti-scientific dogmatism" and its futile attempt to reveal the ultimate meaning of existence.[5]

As we will see, these judgments are generally, and sometimes wildly, misplaced. Contrary to charges of intellectual snobbery, for instance, existentialism is, at heart, a democratizing philosophy of the *everyday* for *everyone* that gives special significance to common activities of all ages and classes. For Heidegger, the point of philosophizing was "to 'see' all things more simply, more vividly and in a more sustained manner" (GA29/30: 35). He wished his thinking to "open up the vastness of the sky" but at the same time "be rooted in the dark of the earth."[6] But this is not always an easy task, he acknowledged, since philosophy is the opposite of all comfort and assurance: "It is turbulence, the turbulence into which man is spun, so as in this way alone to comprehend *Dasein* without delusion" (GA29/30: 29). Famously, Beauvoir recounts how, when Raymond Aron pointed at his glass on an evening together at the Bec de Gaz, and told Sartre he could theorize about it, "Sartre turned pale with emotion at this. Here was just the thing he had been longing to achieve for years—to describe objects just as he saw and touched them, and extract philosophy from the process" (PL 135). The method of phenomenology expounded by Husserl would enable concrete descriptions of self and world that would return philosophy to a deeper apprehension of *things themselves*. According to Beauvoir:

> [Sartre] was interested in everything and never took anything for granted. Confronted with an object, he would look it straight in the face instead of trying to explain it away with a myth, a word, an impression, or a pre-conceived idea: he wouldn't let it go until he had grasped all its ins and outs and all its multiple significations . . . The freshness and dogged tenacity of his perceptions grasped the very essence of things in all their lively profusion. (MDD 340)

In a bid to "look reality in the face" (MDD 337), as Beauvoir wrote, and "to bring philosophy right down to earth" (MDD 344), existentialism generated new ways of apprehending everyday life. *Thinking* about things "all the time" (MDD 337), existentialists philosophized about a cornucopia of things from the perception of ordinary objects like beer glasses, underwear, trees, crabs, moustaches, and chairs, to sex, seduction, love, sadism, masochism, friendship, boxing, skiing, city walks, travel, eating, smoking, jazz, painting, sculpture and literature, boredom, and insomnia. "[L]ife itself has become a problem" (JS P3), said Nietzsche, and so must be interrogated, examined, and scrutinized more severely than previously.

Like Sartre, Heidegger was wooed by Husserl's philosophy and it was his former mentor's way of viewing the world that "put phenomenological eyes in my head" (GA63: 5). Here, perception is not just the passive reception of objects through sense experience but a "productive seeing" or "bringing-into-view" of things that "draws something forth" (GA45) through "the activating intellect" that unconceals and activates the world around it. Things do not just exist out there in the world, standing over against us as independent objects, but are significant to us, impinging and intruding on our lives as meaningful realities. Heidegger's early lectures repeatedly insist that every encounter with a thing is an encounter with something meaningful, stating in a lecture course of 1921–1922: "The category of meaningfulness indicates how objects are in life according to the basic sense of their content and how and as what they hold themselves and comport themselves in a world" (GA61: 92). Thus, even drinking a cup of tea is "always caught in meaningfulness" (GA58: 104–5) since "everything comes at us loaded with meaning, all over the place and all the time" (GA56/57: 72).

Rarely for a philosophical school of thought, French existentialism simultaneously enjoyed both elite academic pedigree and a broad public audience, finding new channels of cultural transmission that philosophy had hitherto not reached. Marcel, Sartre, and Beauvoir disseminated their ideas into public life, writing novels, plays, autobiographies, travelogues, political essays, and journalistic pieces, alongside, and as practical developments, of their philosophical works. Sartre and Beauvoir frequented jazz clubs (they met and befriended Miles Davis and Charlie Parker), Sartre wrote a screenplay for John Huston's *The Freud Scenario* and made a film for television showing him in interview. A twentieth-century Abelard and Héloïse, Sartre and Beauvoir were celebrated and photographed in newspapers around the world as philosophy's most famous couple and their relationship was held in the glare of the international media spotlight. With exposure of this kind, Western culture has become infused with existentialist ideas. Much of contemporary art, film, literature, and music is said to have been inspired by existentialism,[7] and key existentialist concepts, such as *authenticity*, *anxiety*, and *bad faith*, have seeped into everyday vocabulary used as keywords to explain who we are and as semantic markers to frame contemporary experience.

With fame and exposure, however, came defamation and caricature. From the moment of its inception, as Beauvoir records with considerable irritation in *The Force of Circumstance*, existentialism was subject to "absurd objections" and lampooned "as nihilist philosophy, wilfully pessimistic, frivolous, licentious, despairing and ignoble" (FC 76). Its popularity gave force to a flagrant vulgarization of its key tenets. More so than other philosophies, existentialism was apocryphally simplified and condensed to such a degree that its wider philosophical purpose was often obscured. As Beauvoir opined:

> No one would dream of demanding that the system of Kant or Hegel be dispensed in three sentences; existentialism does not lend itself to popularization any easier. A philosophical theory, like a physics or mathematical theory, is accessible only to the initiated. Indeed, it is indispensable to be familiar with the long tradition on which it rests if one wants to grasp both the foundations and the originality of the new doctrine. (PW 324)

When it came to Sartre's philosophy, in particular, Beauvoir noticed how vulgarization was commonplace (and sometimes openly vituperative) even from those close to him, like his fellow existentialists. As time has passed, this situation has not greatly improved. Referring to *Being and Nothingness*, Sebastian Gardner (2009: 36) writes, for instance:

> All great structures of thought in the history of philosophy achieve a kind of pictorial, visionary force, and consequently allow themselves to be reduced for purposes of rapid reference to a cluster of images and bold slogans. B & N is no exception, and in the course of its reception and the conversion of existentialism into a diffuse cultural movement, Sartre's early philosophy has been subjected to exceptional simplification, not to say vulgarization.

## TO BE OR NOT TO BE AN EXISTENTIALIST

Imposing a strict classification on who is or isn't an existentialist is a thorny issue. As one of existentialism's first American interpreters, Walter Kaufmann quipped—existentialism represents a heterogeneous set of revolts against traditional philosophy more dissimilar than alike to the extent that "a bewildered outsider might well conclude that the only thing [existentialists] have in common is a marked aversion for each other."[8] Although they agreed on freedom, responsibility, and action, they also disagreed about a great deal—the possibility of ethics and love, pessimism or optimism, whether God exists. It is in this sense perhaps more appropriate to talk about existentialism*s* rather than existentialism in order to do justice to their pluralism.[9]

However, differences aside, existentialists share a core of common concerns—the priority of *concrete personal "lived" experience*, *authenticity*, *individuality*, *awareness of death*, and the *creative determination of values*. They provide a distinctive view of the world characterized by *estrangement* and *ambiguity* but also by a positive sense of *freedom* and *care* that stresses the intimacy of the relationship between human beings and their world, as well as their powers of reflection, self-interpretation, evaluation, and choice. Thus, it is useful to view existentialism as a series of overlapping traits or family resemblances shared by a cluster of thinkers that appear in two main chronological waves. The first forms in the nineteenth century in the philosophies of Friedrich Nietzsche (1844–1900) and Søren Kierkegaard (1813–1855) who are commonly regarded as the founding fathers of existentialism. They both mount a revolt against traditional rationalist philosophy and against the prioritizing of abstract logical systems of thought over the subjective experience of living individuals. After them came Martin Heidegger (1889–1976) and Karl Jaspers (1883–1969), proponents of German *Existenz* philosophy and the phenomenological method. Many of the key themes they spotlight—*contingency*, *freedom*, *historicity*, *moral responsibility*, *mood*, *subjective truth*—explicitly follow Nietzsche and Kierkegaard in articulating the "impending calamity" (Jaspers) of devaluing existence. These themes were taken up and absorbed in the Second Wave of existentialism that blossomed in the 'existentialist offensive' in France after 1945, elucidated in the writings of Gabriel Marcel (1889–1973), Jean-Paul Sartre (1905–1980), Simone de Beauvoir (1908–1986), Frantz Fanon (1925–1961), and Maurice Merleau-Ponty (1908–1961).

The path common to all existentialists is one that leads away from the "abstract"—"monotonous, empty, undialectical, and even dead"—toward the "concrete"—"real, fulfilled . . . and alive."[10] Condensing this into a shorthand list, Kate Kirkpatrick (2024: 184) outlines ten main theses that are regularly associated with existentialism:

1. the becoming *thesis*: we have no fixed essence or nature, and our life is a perpetual becoming
2. *the Stoic freedom thesis*: we have inalienable metaphysical freedom to choose our actions
3. *the situated freedom thesis*: we still have the alienable freedom to choose, but not all situations confer the same possibility for expressing it
4. *the ontological individualism thesis*: the relation of human subjects to one another is contingent; social relations can be reduced to relations between separate individuals
5. *the ontological interdependence thesis*: to be human is to be intersubjective; the relation of humans to each other is essential
6. *the not-a-thing thesis*: humans are not objects, and it is fallacious to treat them as such
7. *the action thesis*: our actions make us who we are
8. *the projects thesis*: our character is constituted by the projects we undertake and value
9. *the sedimentation thesis*: our character is the result of actions, habits, and projects that accrete over time
10. *the metaethical thesis*: freedom is the primary value and the foundation for other values

As Kirkpatrick acknowledges, not all of these can be held consistently and it should become clear throughout this book which of these pertain to which particular thinker, as well as the recognition of which are vulgarizations and which are firmly identifiable views. Alongside these ten theses, there are also other significant themes, as we will see, that further epitomize existentialist philosophy, most notably, *the social other*, *bad faith*, *alienation*, *authenticity*, *historicity*, *nihilism*, *embodiment*, and *aestheticism*, on top of other, more posthumanist themes that are sometimes left out of definitions of existentialism, such as *a creative collective ethics*, *intersubjective freedom*, *political commitment*, and *dialectical thinking*.

Of course, there is plasticity to any strict classification of who is or isn't an existentialist. Kierkegaard and Nietzsche were existentialists *avant la lettre*, and some Nietzsche scholars, for instance, still pose the question—Is Nietzsche an existentialist?—though apart from a few dissenters, most judge his work to be unequivocally so.[11] In an effort to distance his work from French existentialism, Heidegger disowned the existentialist label and later repudiated his existentialist classic *Being and Time* after his 'turn' away from humanism and subjectivity in the 1940s. However, Heidegger's influence on existentialism was hugely significant with the bestowing of many key themes such as *inauthenticity*, *the They*, *everydayness*, the *ready-to-hand*, existential moods such as *angst*, joy, and boredom, *fallenness*, *the not-yet*, and our *being-towards-death* that drew upon Nietzsche and Kierkegaard and in turn strongly influenced the French existentialists.[12]

## A DOUBLE RELATION

Gabriel Marcel's essay "Existence and Objectivity" (1925) signposted the main lines of development in French existentialism. Reacting to idealism, political individualism and collectivism and various determinisms (materialist, psychological, sociological, and theological), he argued in favor of a concrete investigation of the experience of the living person, "the existential index" (EO 176). Marcel set much of the agenda for the postwar generation of existentialists in a series of interviews he gave in the 1940s on the theme of "What is Existentialism?." Advancing his own form of theistic existentialism, he was publicly critical of Sartre's atheistic philosophy which he described as a "diabolical debasement of the human" and as "a form of metaphysics which denies or refuses grace" (HV 183). He was also less than complimentary about Heidegger's *Existenz* philosophy.[13]

Heidegger's opinion of other existentialist philosophers was mixed and is in many ways indicative of the *double relation* existentialists shared with their forebears and peers. He repudiated and yet was beguiled by Nietzsche, a fascination that led him to devote four volumes and 1200 pages (published in 1961) to Nietzsche's philosophy. From 1936–41, he delivered four lecture courses and composed at least six other lectures or essays that situate Nietzsche's work in the context of the history of Being. Initially, he presents Nietzsche as a diagnostician and visionary of European nihilism where the *Übermensch* embodies an authentic overcoming of nihilism in relation to the *Führerprinzip*. At the end of 1930s, however, the Nietzschean *Übermensch* is seen as the *consummation* rather than the overcoming of metaphysics, the agent of subjective domination and control as the "will to will." Nietzsche's "reversal of Platonism," according to which "the sensuous becomes the true world and the supra-sensuous becomes the untrue world," Heidegger argues, "is thoroughly caught in metaphysics."[14]

This stance of *double relation* was also adopted with Sartre. When in 1946 the French philosopher Jean Beaufret contacted Heidegger with a view to establishing a dialogue and *entente cordiale* between French and German existentialism, his intentions backfired. Heidegger took exception to a comparison with Sartre and dissociated himself from humanist existentialism altogether in his *Letter on Humanism* (1947). He condemned Sartre (as he had done Nietzsche) and cast them both to the flames as "grand metaphysicians," charging Sartre for not recognizing "the essential importance of the historical in being" and not opening his thought to "a productive dialogue with Marxism" (GA9: 340).[15] Reportedly, he took little interest in Sartre and much is often made of the fact to support this that he cut open only forty pages of *Being and Nothingness* before giving it away to Hans-Georg Gadamer. But Heidegger was more enthusiastic about Sartre's philosophy than is often supposed. Many of their disagreements were in effect "mock battles" over small technicalities concerning philosophical jargon.[16] In the autumn of 1945, a young Frenchman Frédéric de Towarnicki visited Heidegger in Freiburg in an attempt to arrange a meeting between the two existentialist philosophers and so boost Heidegger's philosophical profile in France. Heidegger was interested in meeting Sartre and a rendezvous was scheduled in Baden-Baden but never materialized.[17] According to Towarnicki (who gives a much more positive spin on the Heidegger-Sartre relation), he lent Heidegger a copy of *Being and Nothingness* that Heidegger started to read eagerly, expressing a liking for Sartre's finesse of presentation, especially his 'phenomenology of skiing' in which Sartre differentiated the technique and experience of a Savoyard skier from that of the Norwegian method as resulting in their different perceptions of slope. Heidegger was a keen skier and had wanted to philosophize about it in a published work but had not done so. In 1993, Towarnicki published a letter from Heidegger to Sartre written in October 1945 in which the German philosopher is full of praise for his lucid French interpreter:

> Here for the first time I encountered an independent thinker who, from the foundations up, has experienced the area out of which I think. Your work shows such an immediate comprehension of my philosophy as I have never before encountered. (Towarnicki 1993: 83–5)

Heidegger proposes a "joint venture" of philosophizing with Sartre, expressing "the wish, together with you, of bringing thinking back to a point from which it can be experienced as a basic event of history and bringing present-day man back into an original relation with Being." He concludes his letter by presenting them both as "Dioscuri of Being-thinking," one who attacks the matter on the side of Being and the other from the side of Nothingness. Working together, Heidegger expresses confidence they can provide "the crucial experience" that awakens "how abysmally deep in essential nothingness the wealth of Being is concealed." Unusually for Heidegger, he makes concessions and bends to Sartre's criticisms, accepting Sartre's shift of "emphasis on the Being-for-one-another," as well as Sartre's critique of the "explication of death" in *Being and Time*.[18] Despite his well-publicized damning critique of Sartre in *Letter on Humanism*, in a note dated October 5, 1945, published in the appendix of his Kant book, Heidegger offers a different opinion, crediting him as an independent thinker who had properly comprehended *Being and Time* "for the first time" (GA3: 251): "Effect on Sartre crucial; only from there *Being and Time* understood." Curiously, Heidegger contradicts himself further in a lecture course at Freiburg in 1952 (on February 13, precisely twenty-five years after *Being and Time* was published) when he states that "Sartre . . . has completely misunderstood" (GA83: 650) his concept of "Being-in-the-world in his 1927 work.[19]

Against the general trend of attack-and-retreat, Sartre and Beauvoir were more deferential to other existentialists than they were to them. Sartre bought a copy of *Being and Time* in 1933 but didn't begin to read it in depth until the Summer of 1939 and found it to be "providential" because it taught him the meaning of authenticity and historicity at the time when the war made these notions indispensable in comprehending the reality of the situation: "I can rediscover Heidegger's assumption of his destiny as a German, in that wretched Germany of the postwar years, in order to help assume my destiny as a Frenchman in the France of '40'" (WD 187). Sartre and Beauvoir were critical of aspects of Heidegger's work while still acknowledging the importance of its main themes. When Sartre's essay "Legend of Truth" was published along with a French translation of Heidegger's "What is Metaphysics?" in the review *Bifur*, they failed to see the interest in it and hardly understood a word (PL 92). After reading *Being and Time*, which "was not, in his opinion, very closely argued, but packed with suggestive ideas" Sartre credited Heidegger for supplying a phenomenological method "of reconciling objective with subjective" (PL 355). In *Existentialism is a Humanism* (EH 15), Sartre endorses him as a fellow existentialist. Indeed, Sartre's *Being and Nothingness* is in many ways a mapping out of Heidegger's fundamental ontology and constitutes, in Safranski's (2002: 347) words, "an ingenious continuation" of the phenomenological analysis of Dasein in *Being and Time* in which he moves "being-with-others" (under exposed by Heidegger) into the center.[20]

After the war, Sartre's interest in Heidegger waned. In *Notebooks for an Ethics* (1947/8), he describes Husserl and Heidegger as "small-time philosophers" in comparison with Hegel and Marx (NE 61). Although most references in the *Critique* are to the "early Heidegger," in one passage he addresses Heidegger's later thinking, accusing the German philosopher of fatalism and misanthropy: "But any philosophy which subordinates the human to what is other than man, whether it be an existentialist or Marxist idealism has hatred of man as both its basis and its consequence. History has proved this in both cases" (CDR 181). In an interview in May 1975, Sartre told a group of students who wondered whether as a Nazi one could take Heidegger seriously as a philosopher: "I would reproach him, but rather for a lack of seriousness. His attitude showed a compliance with the regime in power in order to continue teaching his courses more than an awareness of any value that Nazism claimed to have" (1981a: 32).

In Occupied France, Sartre had been criticized for taking an interest in a Nazi philosopher like Heidegger, but his turn away from Heidegger after the war was mainly philosophically motivated due to Heidegger's growing anti-humanism and his abandonment of the notions of freedom and subjectivity. The impact of the Second World War had precipitated a change in emphasis from their early work in *Being and Time* and *Being and Nothingness* to more of a deterministic or situated perspective—in Heidegger's case to the "thrownness" of our historical condition and in Sartre's to the force of social, historical, and material factors in the form of a "practico-inert" reality. Contrary to what Heidegger claimed in *Letter on Humanism* though, it is Sartre and not he who embarked upon a "productive dialogue with Marxism" as a crucial element in grounding his later existentialism.

## A COLLECTIVE GENETICS

According to Alfred Betschart (2024), the study of Sartre's existentialism has reached its fourth stage of development, the genetical stage. In the (first) prophetic stage, the founders and authors of the Holy Scriptures formulate their statements while in the (second) scriptural stage, the canons of the Holy Scriptures are defined. In the (third) exegetical stage, these canons are subjected to an exegesis in which the respective meta-narratives are formulated, leading to the formation of various denominations, factions, and interpretative schools. In the (fourth) genetical stage, the results of the previous three stages are scrutinized and deconstructed.

Occupying this fourth stage of critical reflection, the time has come to "deconstruct Sartre" (Betschart 2022) and assemble "an altogether other Sartre" (Noudelmann 2021) or a "New Sartre" (Farrell Fox 2003) from the straw man erected in previous meta-narratives. In many accounts of existentialism, Sartre is cast in Manichean fashion as the serpent and his philosophy in *Being and Nothingness* as the forbidden fruit that no unwary visitor should touch. It has been commonplace to paint a vulgar picture of Sartre, a disfiguring of his image that was prevalent in the times when he was alive, but also persists posthumously into the present.[21] Vexed by this, Annie Cohen-Solal asks with some poignancy and alarm in 2023—"Who's Still Afraid of Sartre?"—documenting how "[f]or decades now, allegations, rumours and misquotes have been concocted . . . [and] ever increasing verbal vilification has become a kind of national sport in France." Eighty years or so previously, Beauvoir had similarly thrown her hands in despair about the false portrayal of Sartre as a "Hyena with a fountain pen, enemy of mankind, filth pedlar, tool of the bourgeoisie, gravedigger" (FC 653). While such condemnations were understandable coming from political ideologues and philosophical opponents, it was the guerrilla attacks from other existentialists that irked her most. When criticized by fellow traveler Maurice Merleau-Ponty,[22] she stoutly leapt to Sartre's defense in her essay "Merleau-Ponty et le pseudo-sartrisme" (1954) accusing Merleau-Ponty of badly misrepresenting Sartre's philosophy, in particular his portrayal of the Sartrean individual as a "sovereign demiurge." In *Force of Circumstance*, she recounts how she had become exasperated by serious vulgarizations of Sartre's philosophy and rejected Merleau-Ponty's "pseudo-Sartrism," in which "he remodelled [Sartre's] philosophy in a most fantastic way" that would only prompt others to "give Sartrism its death blow":

> Sartre's ideas were already so ill understood that it seemed to me deplorable that they should be distorted even further. It was so often forgotten that in *Being and Nothingness* man is not just an abstract point of view, but an embodied presence, so often man's relation with the other was reduced to a manner of the *regard* alone! (FC 331)

Dispelling Merleau-Ponty's false labeling of the Sartrean Other as "an intruder," she reports how "I wanted to re-establish the truth; Sartre *applied the dialectical method* in a great many domains; his philosophy was not a philosophy of the subject." Insisting that Sartre's work contains the essential ingredients to construct a theory of social structures, she surmises Merleau-Ponty is the victim of "a strange delirium" in thinking Sartre does not provide an account of "mediations" or intersubjective realities.[23]

Beauvoir had good reason to defend Sartre for Merleau-Ponty borrowed heavily from him, "stealing his clothes" and developing his fundamental insights without due acknowledgment.[24] There are many areas—the body, intersubjectivity, language, freedom, and dialectical reason—in which their philosophies closely intersect. When we look at the diachronic evolution of Sartre's philosophy and correct some of its more misunderstood elements, Beauvoir's exasperation at the "strange delirium" of "pseudo-Sartrism" that has enveloped Sartrean interpretation from the outset is easy to appreciate. There are times, as Beauvoir wrote, that "[a]s he searched, Sartre sometimes groped blindly," but his philosophy constantly evolved, opened up new pathways of comprehension and "always remained open" (FC 117), both prefiguring subsequent philosophical investigation and modifying itself in the light of further discovery. Like Nietzsche, Heidegger, and other existentialists, Sartre philosophized "with doors left open" (D P5), never ceasing to call himself into question.

An important part of the process of rethinking the Sartre narrative involves looking more closely at an "alternative genealogy" of early existentialism, one that ascribes other influences in Sartre's and Beauvoir's thinking than "the three H's" (Hegel, Husserl, Heidegger), but also one that thinks about existentialism in terms of a "collective enterprise."[25] Rather than as separate discrete philosophers with divergent methods and agendas, it is more accurate to view the French existentialists, (Beauvoir, Sartre, Merleau-Ponty, and Fanon) as a phenomenological quartet, developing their ideas in tandem through critical collective discussion and modification within a shared aesthetic and political epistemological matrix. The mature existentialism they espouse is very much the product of a "collective genetics," an evolving community of thought in which each participant influences the other. In the case of Beauvoir and Sartre, for instance, she was Sartre's confidante, stern editor, and profound critic while he was her reader, philosophical ear, and advisor: "Generally Sartre proposed a "theory," which I would criticize and modify; sometimes I rejected it altogether, and prevailed upon him to revise it" until we "reached some agreement" (PL144). She recollects, for instance, how she spent hours on end reading and re-reading his *Critique of Dialectical Reason*, "grop[ing] my way along many dark tunnels" while "transported by a feeling of pleasure" (FC 487) as she contemplated its ingenious philosophical maneuvering and wondered how to present it with greater clarity and precision. Almost without exception, they scrutinized every essay, play, novel, and philosophical tract produced by the other one. "So assiduously have we always criticized, corrected or ratified each other's thought," she wrote, that "we might almost be said to think in common" (FC 659).

The French existentialists all tread a common path that champions the pursuit of intersubjective freedom and ethical reciprocity, but also understands the individual's perspective as comprehensively shaped through the sedimentation of culturally mediated ideas, which form the collective unconscious or the "objective spirit" of society.[26] Throughout their philosophizing, they moved closely step by step in a recursive form of thinking where one reacted to and further developed the insights of the other. Beauvoir's key concept of the *Social Other* in *The Second Sex* (1949), for instance, grew from the seeds of their earlier work and was in turn given a further development by Fanon in *Black Skin, White Masks* (1952) and Sartre in the *Critique of Dialectical Reason* (1960). As a "Singular Universal," she pays her debts to Sartre and Merleau-Ponty but is beholden to neither. *The Second Sex* is very much an intellectual *ménage à trois*, where, as Debra Bergoffen (2009: 17) puts it, "the angles of Sartre's and Merleau-Ponty's thoughts are triangulated through the cutting edges of Beauvoir's thinking." As Beauvoir states:

> We have a common store of memories, knowledge and images behind us; our attempts to grasp the world are undertaken with the same tools, set within the same framework, guided by the same touchstones . . . we share "the same inner path." (FC 659)

## POSTHUMANIST EXISTENTIALISM

As Frederic Jameson (1995) recognized over thirty years ago, existentialism lies as a "hidden origin" of postmodernist and posthumanist thinking, inaugurating new approaches and pathways that many others would follow, sometimes venturing further and sometimes exploring auxiliary paths that lead to new discoveries. Donna Haraway (2016) urges us in the posthuman age to become composters by repurposing the old in order to make new things grow. This is proposed as a generous methodology for analyzing and acting in the present times, one that is "self-reflexive," "experimental," and "intersectional." More importantly, it is a methodology with a transformative mandate that connects theory with praxis. Utilizing an "integrative approach," Haraway's composting recommends a "regime of disposability" where theoretical weaknesses are ironed out, amended, or discarded.[27] It signifies a dialectical process of change and *becoming*, a time, in Nietzsche's words, for "daring birds" (D 575), "experimenting imitators" and "daredevil copyists" (HH 221) to breathe new life into old ideas. Existentialists regularly insisted that their thinking was "open-ended." "Fixed ideas are like cramp, for instance in the foot," Kierkegaard wrote in his journal, and "the best remedy is to step on them" (PJ 97). Posthumanist existentialism, by drawing on the insights of subsequent philosophers, like Derrida, Deleuze, and Guattari who further developed existentialism's "affective turn" in philosophy, is in many respects a fulfillment of this promise by correcting some of existentialism's shortcomings, as well as bringing out a number of its suppressed or parenthetical elements.[28]

Becoming "posthuman right now" according to Francesca Ferrando (2023), requires an *existential* approach that confers existential dignity to all beings. This deconstructs any discrimination based on human-indexed differences and conceives existence in terms of affinities, assemblages, and co-emergences in which diversification is prized as "the spark of existence." Annexed to flourishing and existential commitment, and echoing Sartre's dictum "existence precedes essence," 'posthuman' in this existential sense means realizing that the human condition is neither our destiny nor our nature, but "a spatio-temporal manifestation of unlimited material and poietic possibilities."[29] Comprehending the extension of the resonances, impacts, and effects of our being in the world in an age of ecological fragility, posthumanist existentialism values a practical and applied way of existing where humans can embark on a path of self-enquiry and self-discovery through understanding the interconnectedness of the self, a path first established by the German and French existentialists.[30]

## THE SPIRIT OF THE AGE

Presently, existentialism exists in a "strange purgatory" between being remembered and being forgotten.[31] Its key concepts and ideas sparkle like fireflies in our everyday discourse and imagination, and yet in academic circles it remains an outlier-of-sorts. Continuing Freud's project of transforming "hysterical human misery into normal human unhappiness," existentialism unmasks modernity by exposing the influences of inherited intellectual paradigms that have a latent hold on our present ways of thinking, being, and speaking.[32] But its eye is firmly set on the future, on what is desirable, possible, and preferable to the errors, injustices, and missed opportunities of the past. Contemplating the future direction of humanity fifty years or so ago, Simone de Beauvoir posed the pressing question "*what is the historical meaning of the moment?*"

> Is it a period before a war? Are we on the eve of vast revolutions that will do away with the system? Will the young people of today see the coming of a true socialism; or the triumph of a technocracy that will perpetuate capitalism; or a form of society unlike anything I can imagine? (ASD 49)

Beauvoir's sentiments echo amplified in the present. The first quarter of the twenty-first century has thrown up strange, disconcerting, and collapsarian times. In the "objective spirit" of our compressed global consciousness, the prospect of total ecological meltdown threatens the planet like a Damoclean sword in a new Anthropocene age where we have become acutely conscious of the human impact upon the rest of life on earth. With alarm, we are warned of pandemics of potentially deadly viruses, both biological and digital, that could decimate social infrastructure and jeopardize life. The media engine churns with narratives of Race and Gender Wars while class divisions deepen as inequalities become further entrenched. We have become witness to the exponential growth of sophisticated networks of technological control and the specter of Artificial Intelligence that threaten to degrade existing modes of human intersubjectivity and communication. In political terms, authoritarianism is on a conspicuous rise just as it was a hundred years ago in the 1920s/1930s before crystallizing into State Fascism. Where do we go from here? How to escape a rabbit hole of anxiety, insecurity, and despair in which, as Beauvoir decried, "the future has no face. We feel unemployed, useless, abashed" (FC 463).

Existentialists agonized how to change our world for the better, philosophizing about past, present, and future, about historical progress and regression, and the meaning of our material, psychological, and social existence from the macro-level of the universe to the micro-level of everyday commonplace things and situations. Moreover, they asked what kind of *we* could be spoken of in any collective journey when divisions seem to run so deep. How, indeed, do we define a common humanity while recognizing diversity and without reinforcing otherness and exclusivity? Existentialism emphasizes the close entanglement of philosophy and history. Philosophy is a response to our embeddedness in the objective spirit of the world and both a product and critique of its time. In Heidegger's view, philosophy should be "in control of its time,"[33] a process of critical reflection for the perplexing times in which we live that provides therapeutic insights on our contemporary experiences of mental anxiety, isolation, digital saturation and technocratic subjugation. Indeed, existentialism's earthly phenomenology has significant implications for our relation to contemporary technology. Directing us toward the immediate and real physicality of bodies and things, existentialism precipitates a countermovement away from a disconnection with the physical world's "immediate corporeal presence."[34] In today's "algorithmic capitalism," we are assailed with virtual-reality worlds that provide diversion from, and a distortion of, the actual concrete sensorial world, a continual digital flow of images that precipitate spirals of mental anxiety and "existential distress."

Existentialism flourished as a healing balm to soothe this existential threat to humankind and all living things. As Jacques Guicharnaud (1962: 16–18), one of the "Left-Bank Existentialists" who gathered around the cafés of 1940s Paris recorded, Sartre and Beauvoir brought philosophy "down to earth for us," making "our lives intelligible to us" in a time of existential despair. Ever accommodating and open to philosophical critique, they were not "masters on the prowl for disciples" but "awakeners" who were intent on deciphering existential truths and ambiguities. In today's world, their summons to a clear consciousness is still valid—to express the mysteries and realities of a world in comprehensible terms with an animating sense of ethical meaning at a time when human history is seemingly spinning in a whirl of nihilism, despair, and self-destruction. In such a world, as Nietzsche prescribed, what is required first of all is "[t]remendous self-examination: becoming conscious of oneself, not as individuals but as mankind. Let us reflect, let us think back; let us follow the highways and byways"! (WP 585). But this is just a prelude to action—"[w]hat I really need is to get clear about *what I must do*," Kierkegaard wrote, "not what I must know, except insofar as knowledge must precede every act" (2007: 19). Hence, while it is quite true "that life must be understood backwards," we must not forget the other principle—"that it must be lived forwards" (PJ 161).

## OF THAT "WHICH IS TO COME"—THE EXISTENTIALIST FUTURE

Speaking about her teacher and the legacy of his work, Hannah Arendt remarked how Heidegger brought thinking "to life again," replenishing the present with the "treasures of the past":

> Thinking has come to life again; the cultural treasures of the past, believed to be dead, are being made to speak, in the course of which it turns out that they propose things altogether different from the familiar, worn-out trivialities they had been presumed to say. There exists a teacher; one can perhaps learn to think (1971: 51)

Although they are pathologists of the past, existentialists wish to present themselves as seers and philologists of the future, as messengers and crafters of the yet-to-come. "The light of the stars," Nietzsche prognosticates, "requires time; deeds, though done, still require time to be seen and heard" (JS 125). His own thinking, a series of "thoughts out of season," belonged to the future when "perhaps a few . . . [will] have eyes to see what has been done through me."[35] Speaking not as "a man" but as "dynamite" he predicts that "[o]ne day my name will be associated with the memory of something tremendous—a crisis without equal on earth, the most profound collision of conscience" (EH14.1). "*Seeing with New Eyes*" (D 433) and questioning sedimented patterns of thought, the philosopher is "a storm pregnant with new lightnings" (BGE 292) that can electrify future minds. Philosophers *are commanders and law-givers*: "they say "thus it *shall* be!," as it is they who determine the Wherefore and Whither of mankind" (BGE 211). Great thinkers and poets, Heidegger avers, "go ahead and make ready." They act as emissaries and harbingers of the future who prepare and disseminate future thinking with "the unobtrusive sowing of sowers" (GA5: 210).

As a lantern in the dark like the one held by Nietzsche's madman (JS 125), the tragic wisdom of the existentialists provides a glimmering light through which we can discern the shape and form of the things around us. For sure, existentialism has seeped into the collective unconscious of our age and vocabularies, but it is rarely brought fully into view through a purifying reflection in order to serve as a lightning rod for powering the possibilities of the historical present. After all, Sartre foretold, it would only be in *our present century* (after the Owl of Minerva has taken flight) that we would be fully in position to properly appreciate existentialism's riches:

> It's in the twenty-first [century] that one will be able to judge the lives belonging to the twentieth and give them their place . . . I do try to project my vision of myself into the twenty-first century . . . The knowledge that I possess and that characterizes me is also future and will characterize me in the future. Thus I am and thus I shall be, even though I have lost my consciousness. (FS 427–8)

Casting aside vulgarizations and dead dogma, we can be enthusiastic about existentialism's philosophical promise as a set of critical concepts and ideas pregnant with the future. New updated translations of two of the Holy Books of the existentialist scripture,[36] Beauvoir's *The Second Sex* (by Constance Borde and Sheila Malovany-Chevallier in 2009) and Sartre's *Being and Nothingness* (by Sarah Richmond in 2018) have elicited a timely reconsideration of our interpretation of these iconic existentialist works and suggest new openings in unlocking their thinking. Nietzsche scholarship is waxing and branching out into new areas of concern with an ever keener eye cast toward his middle works (*Human, All-Too Human*, *Daybreak*, *The Joyous Science*, and *Thus Spoke Zarathustra*) that portray a more "gentle" and liberal thinker than the fire-and-brimstone, "snarling dog" polemicist of the later works.[37] This new focus on Nietzsche as a *deconstructionist of power* and *creative ethicist* has helped bridge the divide between postmodernist and existentialist interpretations of his work and present a different face to the German philosopher, one more attuned to the political orientations of the French existentialists, Sartre, Beauvoir, and Fanon, who followed in his wake.

The publication of Heidegger's *Black Notebooks* in 2014 has "caused an earthquake," as Peter Trawny (2019: 2) says, in the reception of his thought and prompted a renewed concern for analyzing the extent to which his "spiritual National Socialism" infects his philosophical project. In Richard Wolin's (2022: 26, 45) judgment, interpretations of Heidegger's work tend to represent an "exculpatory consensus" in which his political allegiances to National Socialism are consistently downplayed, misconstrued, or disregarded. For decades, the public has been presented with a "misleading, politically sanitized" image of Heidegger's thought—"a bowdlerized version in which Heidegger's protofascist political allegiances have been extensively airbrushed." This includes editorial miscues and distortions, as well as postwar fabrications in which he rewrote entire passages of earlier works. Despite his disclaimer of practicing "spiritual resistance" to the Nazi Party between 1934 and 1944,[38] Heidegger's numerous critics argue that his "Nazi experience" stood in an essential relation to his philosophical project, dimensions of a philosophical life that mutually inform one another as "communicating vessels." His existential approach has a direct bearing on his future political orientation eliciting a "double reading" of *Being and Time* as a work of first philosophy and as a work of its time that provides a "transcendental grounding" for his political conduct of the 1930s.[39]

In confronting Heidegger, we come face to face with the horrors and abysses of history. But, before consigning him to history's poison cabinet, we should remember that, in his words, "thinking is an adventure" (LH 264). Retracing the aberrant pathways of his philosophy need not lead to the same destination. Although it circles around the same problems, Heidegger's thinking does not come to rest but always tumbles into a new interrogation, where, as Trawny (2019: 2, 9, 31) comments, "[e]very resting point is shaken" and "what seems to be a goal becomes the departure for a new investigation." Heidegger's work reverberates in the present, both vexatious and inspirational, and has been diversely influential in the movement of deconstruction in philosophical circles, for the political resurgence of the New Right in Europe and America, and for the environmental movement that has leant upon his later philosophy of "letting things be" and his critique of modern technology.

When considering existentialism with fresh eyes through the prism of the twenty-first century, we must be careful, as Nietzsche warns, to recognize that existentialist texts can present "snares and nets for careless birds" (HH P1). There is much to ponder, learn, and metabolize in composting the manifold insights of Heidegger, Beauvoir, Sartre, and Nietzsche, as well as Fanon, Marcel, Kierkegaard, and Merleau-Ponty. By bringing to the surface the "inconspicuous furrows in language" (LH 265) deposited by the existentialists and engaging in a productive dialogue with its key concepts, it may be possible for "thinking to come alive again," a type of thinking, as Jacques Derrida (1992: 182–3) said, that is multiple and "for a long time to come, will remain provocative, enigmatic, still to be read." Above other philosophies, existentialism offers fertile ground for new roots and fresh insights into the evolving world around us in the twenty-first century. More than anything else, existentialism focuses our minds on the precarious wonder of the "mystery of being" we all share as partners in the historical now. As well as *realists*, existentialists were also *dreamers* for whom authentic freedom lies in the leap of invention, a spiritual adventure for those with the philosophical courage to question the present and move beyond it.

# 21 QUOTES

CHAPTER ONE

# "God Is Dead! God Remains Dead! And We Have Killed Him!"

## (Nietzsche, *The Joyous Science*) RELIGION

Most of us have heard of Nietzsche's bold claim—"God is dead" (JS 125)—but what exactly did he mean by this and how did he view it overall? Was it with joyous celebration, calm equanimity, or with a foreboding sense of irreplaceable loss?

In this chapter, we will look at how existentialists viewed religion and theology and how they reacted to Nietzsche's startling announcement of the death of God. Following Marcel's criticisms in the 1940s of Sartre's Godless universe in *Being and Nothingness*, existentialism is often schismatically arranged into theistic and atheistic variants, with Kierkegaard, Buber, Marcel, Tillich, and Berdyaev on one side as devout religious believers and Nietzsche, Heidegger, Fanon, Sartre, and Beauvoir on the other as hard-nosed atheists. While broadly accurate, what this division of existentialists into adherents and apostates fails to take account of, as we will see, is the fact that frequently the relation of the existentialist to Christianity or atheism is a highly paradoxical one, a kind of love–hate relationship in which elements of belief and disbelief are intertwined.[1] What appears initially as atheism among existentialists when we dig deeper is more precisely a spiritual yearning for a new, earthly religion that acts as a socio-ethical imaginary to replace nihilism (secular modernity) and transcendentalism (Christianity) in the wake of the death of God. Existentialism's love–hate relationship begins with Kierkegaard who embarked upon the quest for a version of *Christianity beyond Christianity* by radically questioning its rationalist theological assumptions and denouncing the ritualism of the Christian Church.

### LIGHTING THE FUSE

Brought up by a devout and neurotic Lutheran father, religion had to be something intimately felt and intensely experienced for Søren Kierkegaard. "Christianity is suffering" he would later write.[2] His father was the Old Testament law-giver who made young Søren's childhood "an unparalleled torture" (2011: 401). "I acquired such anxiety about Christianity," he later recorded, "and yet |I felt myself strongly drawn to it" (2012: 166). After gaining his doctorate in Theology at the University of Copenhagen, he delivered sermons at the Church of Our Lady in 1847 and practiced delivering his communion discourses for hours on end, refining their rhythm and melody. He contemplated living the comfortable life of a country parson but saw the stifling effects of conformity and institutionalism in the Christian church, a wretched edition of Christianity that had completely departed from the religious orientation of the New Testament. Kierkegaard gave the name of "Christendom" to inauthentic Christianity, a modern delusion that echoes Plato's allegory of the cave. Believers are held captive by the play of shadows, thinking they are Christians but thoughtlessly so by merging the god-relationship with bourgeois values, ignoring the radical spirit of the New Testament and "spiritlessly forgetting that they themselves are being examined" (PJ 634).[3] Kierkegaard was protesting against society becoming God and assuming absolute power over the individual. "Christendom is Satan's invention" (PJ 602), he wrote in 1854, and "[b]eing a Christian in Christendom in plain conformity is as impossible as doing gymnastics in a straitjacket" (PJ 640). Those in Christendom have lost sight of Jesus' suffering and are united in "earthly desires" and "earthly cares," the finite, "the lust for life" (PJ 640).

Kierkegaard views Christianity as a paradox that defies reason and logic. The Christian conception of incarnation is the "Absolute Paradox," "an absurdity to the understanding" (CUP 191), "a breach with all thinking" (CUP 513), for it requires us to believe that the eternal enters the temporal sphere. It is offensive to reason that will "find it impossible to conceive it, could not of itself have discovered it, and when it hears it announced will not be able to understand it" (PF 59). To find God requires the individual to take a *leap of faith* into absurdity, bound up with a passionate personal and focused devotion to that relation:

> The Socratic ignorance which Socrates held fast with the entire passion of his inwardness, was thus an expression for the principle that the eternal truth is related to an existing individual, and that this truth must therefore be a paradox for him as long as he exists. (CUP 180)

"Faith," Kierkegaard proffers, "is as paradoxical as the Paradox" (PF 81). While fiercely critical of Hegel, Kierkegaard was nevertheless influenced by Hegelian thinking, in particular, the *dialectical method*.[4] Humanity paradoxically carries in itself the temporal and eternal along with the finite and the infinite, a contradictory sense of being we cannot fully make sense of or resolve: "A human being is a synthesis of the infinite and finite of the temporal and the eternal, of freedom and necessity" (SD 43). For Kierkegaard, the rationalist attempt to prove God's existence is futile, what counts is personal passion or faith rather than reason or knowledge. Against the ontological proof of God's existence, he argued—"I do not prove . . . an existence, but merely develop the content of a conception" (PF 49). Abstract ideas and impersonal doctrines have no relevance to one's inward passions and inner "subjective truths": "It is subjectivity that Christianity is concerned with, and it is only in subjectivity that its truth exists" (CUP 116).

As Kierkegaard saw it, he was "[t]he Socrates of Christendom,"[5] a Danish gadfly to sting Danish Christians in their complacency and provoke in them a deeper and more authentic relation to God. Attacking its self-serving worldliness, he took "the despairing step of lighting the fuse for established Christianity" (PJ 402) to the point of apostasy. On his deathbed, he refused the last rites to be delivered by a priest but requested a layman instead, such was his disillusion with Christianity as institution.[6] However, though despairing of Christendom's inauthentic turn, he did not lose his faith in God, which remained steadfast. He firmly believed that faith in God's existence lends coherence and purpose to life. He disagreed with Kant's interpretation of Abraham's ethical dilemma on Mount Moriah whether to sacrifice his beloved son, Isaac on the command of God. Where Kant reasoned that God's command was antithetical to moral law and therefore cannot have come from God, Kierkegaard thought that by absorbing God into the ethical sphere he becomes dispensable and will disappear as "an invisible vanishing point, an impotent thought" (FT 59). Without God and cosmic justice, humanity is condemned to a meaningless void:

> if a bottomless, insatiable emptiness lurked beneath everything, what would life be then but despair? If there were no sacred bond that tied humanity together . . . if an eternal oblivion always hungrily lay in wait for its prey and there were no power strong enough to snatch it away—then how empty and hopeless life would be! (FT 12)

## THE ANTICHRIST

Nietzsche never got around to reading Kierkegaard. He wrote to the philosopher Georg Brandes that he intended to address "the psychological problem of Kierkegaard" but feared the Dane was "too full of theology."[7] Like Kierkegaard's, Nietzsche's upbringing was a strict Lutheran one, but he took his questioning of Christianity even further than the Danish philosopher, ending in open revolt and outright rejection. Nietzsche's severance from Christianity took the form of a steady erosion beginning in earnest at school, aged seventeen, when he read the writings of Ralph Waldo Emerson and later, Friedrich Lange's *History of Materialism* which precipitated his "naturalist turn." It was clear that from now on, the Christian religion that he had been steeped in from childhood was just one competing voice among many. The Abrahamic God had lost his primacy. After graduating from school at Pforta, he acceded to his mother's wishes to become a pastor in his father's footsteps but broke off his study of theology at the University of Bonn after a single term and switched to the study of classical philology. This was a symbolic move away from Christianity into the pagan world of the Ancient Greeks, exchanging the study of monotheistic theological texts for the philological analysis of classical ones populated by many gods. In a declaration of his growing dissatisfaction with Christianity, he wrote his sister on 11 June of that year: "If you want to attain peace of mind and happiness, then you should have faith; if you want to be a disciple of truth, then you should probe" (KSB 2.61).

The phrase "God is dead" appears four times in Nietzsche's writing, three occasions in *The Joyous Science* (1882) and once near the beginning of *Thus Spoke Zarathustra* (1883–5). The most cited passage is from JS 125 where God's death is voiced in apocalyptic tones by a madman who enters the marketplace clutching a dimly lit lantern in the full light of day. He wonders whether God's disappearance from a previously theocentric society will catapult humanity, his creator and destroyer, into despair:

> God is dead! God remains dead! And we have killed Him! How shall we, the most murderous of all murderers, ever console ourselves? . . . With what water might we be purified? What lustrations, what sacred games shall we have to invent? Is not the greatness of this deed too great for us? (JS 125)

The death of God elicits a collapse in our whole conception of the world and a deep feeling of disorientation. In *Pensées*, Pascal observed humankind's pilgrim status after the Copernican revolution displaced the Earth from the center of the universe. For Nietzsche, this represents a displacement of God himself that opens up the terror of meaningless, infinite spaces:

> What did we do when we unchained this earth from its sun? Where is it heading? Where are we heading? . . . Is there still an above and below? Are we not straying, as through an infinite nothingness? Do we not feel the breath of empty space? (JS 125)

Nietzsche views the death of God as a world-historical event rather than a metaphysical one. It is not that God was once living and has physically died but that we no longer believe in him or justify our systems of belief by him. With the death of God, all foundations and sources of transcendent values crumble: "what things would have to collapse, now that this belief had been undermined, because they were built upon it, leaned against it and had become intertwined with it; for example, our entire European morality" (JS 343).

The protagonist, apparatus, and setting of JS 125 are symbolic. The madman, an avatar of the Greek philosopher Diogenes of Sinope, represents prophecy, but also incommunicability and social exclusion, for he is not taken seriously by the other people gathered in the marketplace, which is the trading place of ideas where things are allotted a "value." His words appear as insane utterances, as do all improvements in knowledge when they are first presented to old ears not yet ready for the wisdom they impart and the new horizons they herald.[8] On its first appearance in Nietzsche's work (JS 108), the death of God is compared to "a monstrous and unearthly shadow" that will continue influencing the ways we think about the world and will take a long time to disappear: "God is dead: but given the ways of men, perhaps for millennia to come there will be caves in which his shadow will be shown" (JS 108). Secular modernity has found quick replacements for the authority of God—reason, progress, conscience, freedom, the greatest happiness for the greatest number, and the Market—but scientific truth is now the new God. Under the spell of epistemological objectivism, we are still convinced that "truth is divine" and so "it is still a *metaphysical faith* on which our faith in science rests" (JS 344). Although our perspective has changed— "[a]ll experiences shone differently, because a God shone forth from them"—the metaphysical framework of it persists: "We have lent new colours to things; we are constantly painting them anew" (JS 152).

Nietzsche's response to the loss of the guiding hand of God, regardless of the metaphysical shadow it has cast, is cheerful, optimistic, and opportunistic: "we philosophers and 'free spirits' experience the news that 'the old God is dead' as if illuminated by a new dawn . . . our hearts are overflowing with gratitude, astonishment, presentiment and expectation—at last the horizon seems free again, even if it is not bright" (JS 343). He beckons us to replace the passive nihilism of collapse with an *active nihilism of affirmation* in which we reinterpret ourselves in terms of a "pure, newly discovered, newly redeemed nature" (JS 109). This means swapping our divine robes for earthly clothes and "translat[ing] man back into nature . . . [so] that he stands before the *rest* of nature . . . deaf to the siren songs of old metaphysical bird-catchers" (BGE 230). Now that the idea of God is outdated and otiose (BGE 53), what remains is our earthly existence and mortal shroud: "We no longer derive man from 'the spirit' or 'the deity'; we have placed him back among the animals" (A 14). For Nietzsche, humanity has placed so many chains upon itself that it should no longer behave like an animal. Judeo-Christian morality has led to our "de-animalization" (D 106) where the labor of man upon himself through breeding and social custom has turned him into "a tame and civilized animal, a *household pet*" (GM 1.2).

When the motif of the death of God appears at the beginning of *Thus Spoke Zarathustra* as its point of departure, the prophet Zarathustra offers a new tablet of values to divest humanity of the "shadows of God" (Z1 P2). This wisdom is aimed at overcoming the desperate senselessness and abyssal emptiness that follows from God's disappearance, and the gift bestowed is that of the *Ubermensch* (*Superhuman*) and the "heaviest hypothesis" of eternal recurrence. In *Beyond Good and Evil*, Nietzsche offers another alternative to the Christian God in the form of Dionysus "the tempter god and born pied piper of consciences" (BGE 295). Ultimately, the death of God is a painful and traumatic event whose effects linger (JS 108) but one that clears the way for a new ideal where the meaning of the earth will once again appear in the minds of a liberated humanity.

As age crept upon him, Nietzsche became increasingly vituperative toward Christianity. This reached fever pitch in his final works, particularly *The Antichrist: A Curse on Christianity* (1888). He condemned Christianity chiefly for its devaluation of existence and hatred of the body, describing it as "a monstrous mode of valuation" that has produced an "*ascetic planet*," a "nook of disgruntled, arrogant, and offensive creatures filled with a profound disgust at themselves, at the earth, at all life" (GM 3.11). Christianity introduced a new Platonic dualism between Good and Evil into our understanding of the world and "painted the Devil on the world's walls" by bringing sin into the world (WS 78). For all of its philosophical sins, he ranks Christianity as among the most pernicious of all religions: "The Christian idea of God—God as a god of the sick, God as spider, God as spirit—is one of the most corrupt conceptions of God the world has ever seen" (A 18).

Despite his scathing attacks on Christianity, many have read Nietzsche as a religious thinker. In the estimation of Lou Salomé (2001: 24), for example, of all his great intellectual dispositions, "none is bound more profoundly and unremittingly to his whole intellectual being than his religious genius." For some scholars, Nietzsche advances a *post-Christian* rather than an anti-Christian viewpoint, drawing heavily on the Christian notions of radical creativity, apocalypse, and crisis. He tries to save Christianity even as he destroys it, imputing to the *Ubermensch* those qualities that he is no longer willing to see in God. Although he celebrates the materiality of the earth, the real direction of his thought is often the sky and ascent.[9] While Nietzsche's work bears the imprint of Christianity and carries some modifications of it, he looks to *the future* for a source of spirituality or *new religion* to *replace* Christianity rather than *resurrect* it. Although "unconditional honest atheism," he wrote, is "the only air we breathe" (GM 3.27), he viewed atheism (akin to nihilism) as a transitional stage. To abandon belief in a transcendent God is a forward step culturally (D 96), but we must qualify atheism with the commitment to a replacement religiosity—specifically, the Dionysian ideal (BGE 295). For Nietzsche, the fact that the Christian God is such a bad communicator (Z 4.6) has led to skepticism and atheism. Monotheism crushed the concept of humanity underneath an impossible ideal and caused the "premature stagnation" of human development (TI 3.1). Nietzsche disavows founding a religion (EH 4.1, D 542) but proposes a form of piety toward an ideal that satiates the religious instinct without theism (BGE 53). Indeed, holiness is a constant theme he employs to describe a powerful and healthy will to power (Z 1.20). Free spirits, he recommends, should use religion for ethical ends in order to serve the development of humanity (BGE 61).

## GOD ABANDONED?

Like Nietzsche, Sartre was a "theanthropologist," speculating not about God himself and the metaphysical claims of whether God exists or not, but about God in relation to the human and the psychological, ethical, and cultural dimensions of believing or not believing. It's not the metaphysical question of God's existence that bothers Sartre but the psychological and ethical implications of religious thinking—"Even if God existed, it would not change anything" (EH 22).

As a child, Sartre was nursed on Christianity but casually describes in *Words* the genesis of his atheism when aged twelve, he encountered a sudden loss of faith in God while standing on the street waiting for friends:

> One morning, in 1917, at La Rochelle, I was waiting for some companions who . . . were late. Soon I could think of nothing more to distract myself, and I decided to think about the Almighty. He at once tumbled down into the blue sky and vanished without explanation: He does not exist, I said to myself, in polite astonishment, and I thought the matter was settled. (W 155–6)

For the young Sartre, God was "an old flame" (W 65) that flickered inside him for a while and then died. From then on, he devoted his childhood instead to the "religion of letters" of his grandfather, searching for salvation through writing rather than prayer or religious observance. He began to harbor disdain for Christianity when his relatives, split between the traditions of Catholicism and Protestantism, would dispute at the dinner table: "I was the prey of two opposing mystical theologies, but I adapted myself very well to their contradictions" (W 108).

Although influenced by its "theological horizons,"[10] Sartre had little interest in Christianity in philosophical terms or, indeed, as an ethical system of values: "liberty is freedom *without* God" (EM 558). Like Nietzsche, Sartre views God's death as a great opportunity, a golden gift to humankind: "*God's absence* is no longer closure: it is an opening out to the infinite. *God's absence* is greater and more divine than God" (CM 40). He describes God as an old-fashioned concept (EM 776) and a human construct. The idea of God as creator is a myth of inversion for it is God who is dependent on humankind to create Him: "God is a prefabricated image of man, man multiplied by infinity" (FS 439). For Sartre, it is "integral humanity" as a new ethical ideal that can fill God's absence because "I don't need God to love my neighbour" (EM 558).

Despite his optimism, Sartre is fully conscious of the ethical void that still looms as a possibility in humanity's quest to assume the dead God's mission. Existentialists find it disturbing that God no longer exists, for along with his disappearance goes the possibility of finding values in an intelligible heaven (EH 28). Although God no longer speaks to us as before, the need for God lingers: "God is silent, I can't let go of that, everything in me demands God, I cannot forget it" (1947: 154). Just as Nietzsche viewed atheism as potentially a dead negation leading to passive nihilism, Sartre describes it as a "cruel, long-term business" (W 157). He complains that materialistic atheism is hard to sustain as an existential creed. The figure of God furnishes us with a vague sense of destiny without which it is easy to succumb to the nausea of superfluity, of being simply *de trop*: "I don't see myself as so much dust that has appeared in the world, but as a being that was expected, prefigured, called forth" (FS 438). Sartre also notes the link between God and Absolute morality. There are "traces of God" in the moral field insofar as the ideas of Good and Evil persist as moral absolutes, although these are to be conceived non-transcendentally.[11] Even without God, moral activity must be, in some sense, "an absolute in the relative": "I look upon man's morals and moral activity as an absolute in the midst of the relative . . . the absolute as a product of the relative" (FS 438–9). Although we may not believe in God, "there are elements of the idea of God that remain in us and that cause us to see the world with some divine aspects" (FS 438).

Despite his youthful rejection of God, Sartre's autobiography makes clear the affinities between his philosophy and religion. He bids to find an affirmative existentialist philosophy that meets "modern man's enduring religious need" (2010: 235) and overcomes nihilism. His "exultant atheism" is, at the same time, an ambiguous one in which the existence of God is paradoxically both absent and present, engendering a form of secularized religion in which human freedom is tantamount to "becoming a God for oneself."[12] Sartre's atheism was directed at a *particular model* of the Christian deity and should not be construed as an automatic rejection of alternative models of the divine or religious symbolism in general. For Sartre, it is the case that God is dead but not as dead as we might expect.[13] Like Kierkegaard and Nietzsche, he glimpsed the existential power of religious faith:

> God is dead but man has not, for all that, become atheistic. Today, as yesterday, this silence of the transcendent, combined with modern man's enduring religious need, is the great question of the age. (2010: 235)

Of all existentialists, Simone de Beauvoir became the most steadfast atheist. She argued there is "a certain moral and psychological enrichment" in being an atheist (FS 444). To dissolve alienation, it is necessary "first of all not to believe in God." By building up a principled human race without the unity of God we are "at least atheists of an atheism that is expanding and becoming more and more of a reality" (FS 445). But this was certainly not always the case for Beauvoir. In her childhood, she held a passionate faith in God, attending mass three times a week and regularly undertaking religious retreats. She records that "my religious instruction was in fact very thorough." She knew long passages in the Gospel by heart, meditated, and kept a diary to record her "saintly resolutions" (ASD 495). From a young age, she indulged in ascetic religious practices, inventing "mortifications" for herself such as scrubbing herself with a pumice-stone until she bled and lacerating her skin with a necklace—"I longed for apparitions, ecstasies" (MDD 134). Enchanted by her childhood summers in the countryside spent in wonder of "the beauty of the earth and the glory of God," she decided that she would become a Carmelite nun.[14] She became deeply interested in saintly religious mystics, avidly reading the texts of Henri Frederic Amiel, Henri Delacroix, and Jean Baruzi.

As Beauvoir records in her diaries, it was around the age of twelve at the convent school of Cours Désir that her apostasy started to germinate, "a private rebellion within me" in which "I renounced their morality and the God who underwrote it" (ASD 22–3). She noticed, along with her sister Hélène, that it was only the women in her family who ever attended mass and that "men—a superior race—were exempt from God." As culture, politics, business, manners, and customs had nothing to do with religion she "set God apart from life and the world" (MDD 41). Although she was "tempted by Catholicism" as late as 1928, as soon as she "saw the light" about God she made a clean break after which her "incredulity never once wavered." In the end "it was easier for me to think of a world without a creator than of a creator burdened with all the contradictions in the world." Despite feeling that the world had "fallen silent" and experiencing the "terrible significance" of the word "alone" (MDD 137), philosophically she couldn't find a satisfactory answer to the question: "Why the Christian God?" (DPS 284).

In Beauvoir's own testimony, "[t]here is one point upon which my position has not changed . . . it is my atheism" (ASD 495). Although she was disappointed, philosophically speaking, that Merleau-Ponty was not an atheist but sought truth within the confines of Catholicism, she was nonetheless interested in the psychological and special factors that underlie the attitude of practicing Catholics. She judged faith to be "an appurtenance that is given in childhood as part of the middle-class equipment" where often the convert is going through a crisis at the time (ASD 496). In "this Godless place in which I live," faith "allows an evasion of those difficulties which the atheist confronts honestly" (ASD 498). Those who justify their faith often do so with outworn and pitiful philosophical arguments and by conjuring the fables that enchant childhood. For a child, faith amounts to believing in the adults who tell her about God, a dubious compromise that consists "of believing that one believes" (ASD 497). Escaping the clutches of her own childhood piety in her teenage years, Beauvoir came to detest the "self-martyring religion" (MDD 308) of Christianity: "I had had enough of 'Catholic complications', spiritual dead-ends, miraculous make-believes" (MDD 314).

Though staunchly atheist in philosophical terms and distrustful of faith in general, Beauvoir shows some positive interest in the psychological mechanisms of faith in its role in a liberating socio-ecological imaginary, inspired by the religion of the Brazilian *candomblé*, just as Nietzsche was by the cult of Dionysus. Kierkegaard's initial marvel at the edifying and subjectivating power of faith that charged the existentialist momentum was not lost on subsequent atheist-leaning existentialist philosophers who fully appreciated the power of rapturous spirituality as (what Nietzsche called) a "tremendous energy of greatness" (WP 506) that puts us in tune with the existence of the Whole. Passive nihilism in the face of absurdity is an existential choice existentialist philosophers move beyond for, as Beauvoir says, we cannot live as if nothing matters: "I live, even if I judge that life is absurd, like Achilles always catching up with the tortoise despite Zeno" (PC 100). "The fundamental fault of the nihilist," she writes, is that "challenging all given values, he does not find beyond their ruin, the importance of the universal, absolute end which freedom itself is" (EA 82). For Beauvoir herself, being a writer "would guarantee me an immortality which would compensate for the loss of heaven and eternity," allowing her to "re-create myself and justify my existence" (MDD 142).

## A GOD BEYOND GOD

The influence of existentialism on twentieth-century theology is profound. Nietzsche, for instance, has been adopted as a key thinker by a variety of theologians, such as Martin Buber, Karl Barth, Paul Tillich, Thomas Altizer, Gianni Vattimo, and Giorgio Agamben. Following Kierkegaard and his sensitivity to the crisis of faith, they take upon the task of detailing the corruption of Christianity, seeking to cleanse it rather than abandon it.

Buber was attracted by Nietzsche's thinking at an early age, in particular his idea of an affirmative Hebraic religion of self-creativity that was later undermined by later Biblical teachings. His book *I and Thou* exhibits a strong Nietzschean influence in framing a Judaic morality informed by the distinction Nietzsche makes in *On the Genealogy of Morals* between slave morality (based on *ressentiment*, negation, and I-It relations) and master morality (based on an active affirmative morality of I-Thou relations). Barth also engages with Nietzsche's proclamation of God's death as a cultural event where God no longer gives meaning to our existence. This, he argues, opens up the possibility for a new kind of faith, one that frees God from rational proofs and that establishes God as "Wholly Other." This is developed further by Tillich who dismisses God as an object of thought and reconceives divinity as beyond predicates, attributes, and anthropometric projections, a kind of "God beyond God." For Tillich, God is simply a symbol of our "ultimate concern" and Nietzsche demonstrates the utter impossibility of killing God for his "ultimate concern" serves to resurrect God in secular form in the *Übermensch*. Tillich (2001: 174) thus concludes, "Friedrich Nietzsche, the famous atheist and ardent enemy of religion and Christianity, knew more about the power of the idea of God than many faithful Christians."

Following the radical existentialist questioning of Christianity, Tillich holds onto the remnants of an inchoate unknowable God as "ultimate concern" and establishes a position between theism and atheism, one that has been developed by Radical Theology, a kind of "atheism within the spectrum of Christian possibilities."[15] For the Radical Theologian, Thomas Altizer (1966: 104), the death of God is a real cosmological event that unfolds over time. God as a true transcendent supernatural being died when he incarnated in the form of Jesus Christ and self-annihilated: "the death of God does not propel man into an empty darkness, it liberates him from every alien and opposing other and makes possible . . .. the final coming together of God and man." Nietzsche is important in this process of "profanation" because he heralds the "becoming conscious" of the death of God. Altizer understands the death of God as a dialectical process of the "self-negation of Spirit" from theism to atheism out of which a new form of divinity will emerge. He follows Kierkegaard's dialectic but goes beyond the negativity and contradiction which render it incomplete, heralding Nietzsche as a dialectical thinker who surpasses Kierkegaard by affirming a third positive synthesis.[16]

It is clear that existentialist theologizing has lent itself to a diversity of religious thinking, embodying a mosaic of multi-faith perspectives. Marcel and Merleau-Ponty joined the Catholic Church, Jaspers had affinities with a very freewheeling kind of liberal Protestantism, Heidegger was a former Catholic and atheist mystic,[17] Berdyaev a Russian Orthodox, Kierkegaard a Protestant and Buber a Hassidic Jew while Nietzsche, Sartre, and Beauvoir showed a "proud pagan" body beneath their outward armor of atheism that shares affinities with Eastern religions, such as Buddhism, Brahminism, and Taoism. To this extent, existentialism can be seen as a religious Tower of Babel and a pioneer of "Weak Theology," a radical development of theology questioning itself further to embrace a return of faith that is at once both secular and multi-faith.

## THE NEW RELIGION

Rather than as diehard atheists or as closet Christians, it is fairer to say that, though strongly atheistic in terms of philosophical reasoning, Beauvoir, Sartre, and Nietzsche were really neither. Instead, they all openly embraced a form of *imaginative divinity*, a new religion of the earth based on an affective spirituality of existence and becoming, in order to fill the void of ethical nihilism following the death of a defunct Christian God: "Inaccessible to the sacred," Sartre wrote, "I adored magic" (W 77). Broadly speaking, this new divinity displays a deconstructive logic of inversion and displacement, inverting the life-denying metaphysics of Christianity with a "cruel atheism" that ultimately leads to a displaced third orientation that attempts to fill the ethical void "where everything is permissible if God does not exist" (EH 22). This is a life-affirming celebration of existence and freedom expressing the plurality found in the diversity of nature and human individuality. The fact that God became human in the form of Jesus reminds us that we must not seek his bliss in the infinite, but must find his paradise on earth. Nietzsche places Zarathustra's gift of wisdom in continuity with the grace and love of God but revolutionizes this by going beyond the "perfect spiritualization" of love that the saint and Kierkegaard hold for God since that love comes with a consequent great contempt for humankind and its imperfection in the face of the divine ideal. Zarathustra's "horizontal love" abandons all recourse to transcendence and "vertical relations" of hierarchy but offers a form of friendship based on an equal footing, a common belonging and destiny.[18]

Nietzschean religious love represents a "third paradigm" between the "metaphysical paradigm" attributing value to a divine source and the "paradigm of the last man" that assumes that value is purely an individual matter. The "new love" that supplants Christian love and follows from the death of God appears paradoxical and contradictory: "I love the one whose soul is overfull, so that he forgets himself, and all things are in him: thus all things become his going under" (Z P4). This can be read in an ecological sense in which humankind "sacrifices itself to the earth" (Z P4) in the form of a rapturous "religious affirmation of life, life whole and not denied or in part" (WP 1052). Nietzsche describes this as "deification" (WP 534), a sanctifying "ecstatic affirmation of the total character of life" (WP 539) that "replenishes and gilds" life (WP 534), enabling us to grasp the constitutive links between individual and whole (WP 557). In *Thus Spoke Zarathustra*, Nietzsche's prophet embraces the title "Zarathustra, the godless" (Z 4.6), but also declares "I would only believe in a god that knew how to dance" and yearns for a feeling of possession in which "a god dances through me" (Z 1.7). This possession is marked by the power of rapture, a captivation of excitement, intoxication, and transient joy in which one feels the presence of eternal harmony. Through religious pathos and the feeling of rapture, Nietzsche *aestheticizes* religion. Gods become the imaginary or fictive objects of an aesthetic play in which "[t]he wealth of religious feeling, grown to a torrent, breaks out ever again and wants to conquer new realms" (HH 150).

Nietzsche's highly damning condemnations of religion are interlaced with an embrace of his own god, Dionysus, and with a favorable view of religious sentiment. In turn, his main concepts—eternal return, *amor fati*, and the Universal Yes—carry emotional weight and religious force as forms of an ethical imaginary. For Nietzsche, what is divine is that there are many Gods. The death of God heralds the renewal of possibilities of religious experience and the rebirth of the sacred in its many forms. Nietzsche's "new religion" is that of Dionysus (EH P2), a god associated with *joy*, *ecstasy*, *wholeness*, and the *release from care* that is inside the world and changing rather than outside it. The new religion seduces humanity to growth and health in the future transforming itself through a movement to "redeem reality" by immersion in and identification with it (TI 9.10). Religious fervor is identified as a kind of delirium (*folie circulaire*), an alternation of feelings between ecstatic redemption and severe penitence (EH 4.8). It is Dionysus who captures the feeling of ecstatic redemption or rapturous intoxication in which "the spell of individuation is broken, and the way lies open to the Mothers of Being, to the innermost heart of things" (BT 16).

Sartre and Beauvoir also marveled at the power of religious fervor and saw ethical value in a terrestrial religion that envisions a new social order to replace the existing apparatus of oppression and forms of slavish morality. In *Black Orpheus*, Sartre warns that European civilization has developed a purely technological and mechanical relation toward nature that had become lifeless. The white man, consequently, is alienated from nature and remains only on the surface of things, like an engineer, "unaware of life" (BO 38). Taking an exoticized view, Sartre argues that the black man, by contrast, understands nature as a creative power, a kind of Mother Goddess, "an enormous perpetual birth": "the Negro finds the softness of human skin, he rubs himself against the sand's belly, against the sky's loins" (BO 40). This demonstrates a carnal and androgynous connection to nature: "the dynamic feeling of being an erect phallus, and the more deaf, more patient, more feminine one of being a growing plant" (BO 40). Sartre pays homage to black spiritual poetry for its transgressive qualities that challenge the hierarchies of dualistic Christian thinking, using negritude as a means of positing "a secret blackness in white, a secret whiteness in black" (BO 28).

Sartre's observations on the Voodoo religion of Haiti in "Haïti vu par J.-P. Sartre" (a 1949 journalistic piece with Georges Altman published in *Franc-Tireur*) express a great fascination with "*Envoutement vaudou*" ("voodoo bewitchment"). Driven by the rhythm of the voodoo drum, like the one he had imagined as a child (W 79), he marveled at how the religious devotees became entranced in a "religion of possession" centered on the expressive dance of the body. In this form of rapturous spirituality, he recognized the possibility of a completely different cosmology and ontology, "a certain affective attitude toward the world" (BO 36) that forms the imaginary of a terrestrial religion completely different from Christian "Seriousness." These observations present a more "pagan" Sartre[19] for whom humans and nature are not opposed in an irreducible manner. Their separation is not an ontological structure, but only a moment in the historical process of being.

Beauvoir's religious thinking exhibits similar dialectical traits to those of Nietzsche and Sartre, negating the thesis of Christianity with the antithesis of atheism before the synthesis of a "new religion." On her trips to Cuba and Brazil with Sartre, she was enchanted by the religious practices that she witnessed. At carnival time in Havana, she was wowed by "the Negro dancers with magical abandon" (FC 502) and how "they were actually living a moment of their religious life," "transfigured by a mystical joy" (FC 531). In Bahia during their visit to Brazil, they were fascinated by the religious celebrations of the *candomblé*—women dancers in "sumptuous liturgical costumes" with "grave expressions on their faces [that] were signs that they bore a god within them" (FC 530). As she enthusiastically records, "each one intensely absorbed in her own ecstasy yet always in harmony with the movements of the group . . . here, the individual manifestations were kept under control by a collective discipline." Some women were affected very violently by these manifestations "but without once becoming isolated from their companions" (FC 531). What interested Beauvoir most of all was "[h]ow can these trances be explained?" (FC 531) As an answer, she concluded that the cause was not pathological but of a cultural nature when people are torn between two civilizations.

The "Negroes of Bahlia, once slaves, now an exploited class" feel that to preserve their customs and traditions is not sufficient in itself so they also cultivate those techniques which will help them attain a state of ecstasy and so "tear themselves free of the false earthly manifestation in which they have been imprisoned." At the moment when they seem to lose themselves in the dance, "they in fact find their true selves; they are possessed, yes, but by their own truth" (FC 532):

> Even if the *candomblé* does not change men into gods, at least it uses the mediating action of imaginary spirits to restore their humanity to a group of men who have been forced to the status of cattle. (FC 532)

Contrasting the austere Christian religion in Poland as a "reactionary force" obstructing the path to socialism that "still weighs on the peasants as heavily as ever," she heralds the *candomblé* religion of Bahlia and its imaginary of divine possession as a prototype of positive spirituality or new socio-religious consciousness since "it enables a disinherited people to maintain a sense of their own dignity" (FC 656–7).

## EXISTENTIAL GODDING

This existentialist notion of *imaginative divinity*, found in Nietzsche, Beauvoir, and Sartre, perhaps reaches its zenith in Heidegger's thinking which continues the task to think through the death of God and criticize the "last humans" who replace God with hollow substitutes.

Heidegger also understands nihilism as a transitional phase, as the oblivion of Being, awaiting a "turn in Being" in which humans overcome this situation of historical and existential crisis by bridging the separation between heaven and earth. This he describes as a process of *godding* in which we tune in to the frequencies of Being and then project this to create an ethical imaginary that sublimates our historical experience.

Born into a pious family, schooled and trained as a Jesuit seminarian, the "little magician from Messkirch,"[20] took an early interest in Catholic Scholasticism and medieval logic. He began as a Catholic philosopher for whom God was the foundation and guarantor of our cognition of the world. However, reading Schleiermacher and Dilthey convinced him that truths change and a "historicist" or "hermeneutic" approach was required to explain this. In his early *Freiburg Lectures*, Heidegger prepared the way for a "phenomenology of religious consciousness" emphasizing that religion has a way of life of its own, an "entirely originary intentionality," its own "worldliness and valuableness" (GA60: 322). However, it does not bear philosophical scrutiny, since no real religion "allows itself to be captured philosophically" (GA60: 323). Christian philosophy, Heidegger states, is "wooden iron" whereas philosophy must rely on itself "as the free questioning of existence resting purely upon itself."[21] Following the lead of Nietzsche, he strongly criticizes Christian metaphysics: "reinterpreting the Below as the created and the Above as the Creator, and with weapons thus reforged, it set itself against antiquity (as paganism) and distorted it" (GA40: 113).

Like other existentialists, Heidegger never embraced a cold atheism but forever retained a sense of religiosity and continued to draw upon the insights of Christian mystics, such as Meister Eckhart. In 1929, he describes his experience of attending the nocturnal service of an abbey in Beuron as a noumenal event that would "unfold as a seed corn for something essential."[22] As he saw it, the divine is not some region in the beyond but a relation to Being, a transformed reality inside us pertaining to our relation to nature. This is developed in *Contributions to Philosophy* (1936–8) where he introduces a new way of thinking about God that he calls "Godding." "Being is the trembling of Godding" (GA65: 239), Heidegger affirms, in which God is not something confronting *Dasein* but something that proceeds *in it* as a form of ecstatic thinking. In Godding we experience a range of moods—"fright, restrainedness, mildness, jubilation, awe"—that transform us in rare moments and attune us to the mystery of Being (GA65: 21).

Heidegger's 1966 *Spiegel* interview revisits this theme by invoking a form of imaginary divinity as a salvific means against the onslaught of technology, where he declares famously, "only a god can save us." This new divinity he describes as the "Last God," one that is "[w]holly other than the past ones and especially other than the Christian one" (GA65: 403).[23] Christianity was useless for the new inception of Being in Heidegger's eyes since the notion of a "creator God" is complicit with "machination." Akin to Nietzsche before him and the French existentialists after him, Heidegger advanced a form of "disguised theology" (in the words of his former student, Karl Löwith) replete, in his case, with a series of quasi-mystical formulations, such the "Fourfold," "Openness to the Mystery," "naming the unnamable," and "the Holy."[24]

Despite obvious similarities in the New Religion existentialists propose as a socio-ethical imaginary in connecting humanity to a sense of belonging and participation in the cosmos, we should be careful not to overlook differences in the concrete form of the socio-political imaginary they conceive. Where Sartre and Beauvoir view the magical abandon of the dancers of the *candomblé* as a form of political expression that metabolizes injustice, invocating a "Mother Earth" in which we are all brothers and sisters of the earth, Heidegger's new divinity is a political paganism that harks back to an originary halcyon state, a Spartan conception that valorizes myth, struggle, war, obedience, violence, and conquest. Nietzsche's Dionysus lies somewhere between them, a middle ground or historical phase between the pagan matriarchal societies of Demeter and the patriarchal control societies of Apollo.[25] Responding to the death of the Christian God and to its "frightful shadow," existentialist philosophers stared into the abyss of ethical nihilism only to confound it. From Kierkegaard's initial quest to develop a personal understanding of the Christian God beyond the abstract rationalizations of theologians and worldly pretensions of Christendom, existentialism has suggested new possibilities for a concept of God in its wrestling with the ambiguity of the world. Although there are slight variances, some idea of a God beyond God is present in all existentialists from an apophatic sense of a wider totality or mystery in which we participate to a direct celebration and affirmation of our earthly life in the form of a redivination of nature. In the postmodern world of *weak thought* that has followed the collapse of objective values with the death of God, existentialism's God beyond God suggests a new model of religion that incorporates diversity, secularization, mysticism, and religiosity as elements of a life-affirming socio-ethical imaginary.

Bringing religion down to earth, above all, existentialism explores the psychological and sociological consequences of belief in the divine. In his essay "What Is a Free Person?" (1950), Marcel asks "how it is possible for unfreedom to establish itself in the political systems of fascism and Stalinism?." His answer is that secularization has left nothing but the realization and worship of inner-worldly purposes that have become absolute and turned into idols that enslave and diminish, in particular the "idolatry of race and class." "Man can be free, and remain free," he wrote, "only to the extent to which he remains linked to transcendence" (1950: 502). Participation, care, mood, embodiment, and the mystery of Being are all key concepts for existentialists that uphold this transcendent existential connection, whether they are nominally atheists, agnostics, theists, or imaginative deists. In the wake of God's death, existentialism moved toward respiritualizing a cold technocratic world in the form of a social imaginary that grounds a divine ethical relation to others and to nature.

## CHAPTER TWO

# "He Whose Eye Happens to Look Down into the Yawning Abyss Becomes Dizzy"

## (Kierkegaard, *The Concept of Anxiety*) ANXIETY/PSYCHOTHERAPY

*Angst* or anxiety is one of existentialism's lexical exports that has cemented a firm place in everyday vocabulary. It is often repeated we are now living in an "Age of Anxiety," caught in a web of insecurities and pathologies. But what did existentialists mean by the term "Angst" and what did they advocate in the face of it? What is the "dizziness" that Kierkegaard speaks of?

This chapter follows existentialism's development of *The Concept of Anxiety*, beginning with Kierkegaard and Heidegger's idea that it lies deep within individual psychology as an existential response to the reflexive awareness of one's temporal freedom. Sartre and Beauvoir follow this path but concentrate on what they view as inauthentic and authentic responses to this universal experience in the form of "bad faith" or "purifying reflection." Finally, we look at the work of Frantz Fanon, a practicing hospital psychiatrist who developed the existential psychoanalysis of Sartre and Jaspers and the "anti-psychiatry" of François Tosquelles to demonstrate the sociogenic roots of experiences of anxiety and psychological disorders, such as insanity.

## INDIVIDUALIZING ANGST

In *The Concept of Anxiety* (1844), Kierkegaard states "no secret agent knows as cunningly as anxiety how to attack his suspect in his weakest moment or to make alluring the trap in which he will be caught" (CA 115–6). We are always subject to anxiety that is liable to contaminate everyday experience, no more so than for Kierkegaard himself:

> The whole of existence makes me anxious, from the smallest fly to the mysteries of the Incarnation. It's inexplicable, myself most of all. For me, all existence is contaminated . . . Great is my distress, unlimited. (PJ 102)

The Lonely Dane's life was "an exhausting existence" (PJ 213) that made him "in the deepest sense an unhappy individual" (PJ 229). He recorded in his journal he felt so deeply his own "wretchedness as a poor miserable human being" (PJ 487) that "[e]very flower in my heart becomes an ice fern" (PJ 110). Brought up strictly in Christianity, he found himself as a child in "the grip of a congenital melancholy" like "the Christian notion of the thorn in the flesh" (PJ 486) or an arrow of grief buried in his heart. This found its way into his pseudonymous writing:

> There lay between my melancholy and my intimate *Du* a whole world of fantasy. It is this that I have partly emptied out in the pseudonyms . . . that's how in my melancholy I have related to possibility. (PJ 256)

There is not a living person, Kierkegaard writes, who "does not secretly harbour an unrest, an inner strife, a disharmony . . . an anxiety about some possibility in existence or an anxiety about himself" (SD 22). In Kierkegaard's thinking, anxiety is closely linked to temporality and freedom. His pseudonym Vigilius Haufniensis in *The Concept of Anxiety* declares that anxiety stems from the apprehension of one's potentiality and possibilities. Looking into the abyss of possibilities and what-is-not causes a state of dizziness in which one feels in one's bones that a storm is approaching—"the individual trembles like a horse that gasps as it comes to a halt at the place where once it had been frightened" (CA 115). Although this throws the individual into a state of "horror" and "wretchedness" (CA 137), Haufniensis recognizes the positive aspect of anxiety and associates it with greatness in being attuned to one's possibilities, although he suggests that this can be so only with the support of faith in God. He identifies three features of anxiety: (i) it is present in dreaming innocence, a form of instability or presentiment like the awakening of sexuality or Adam and Eve in the Garden of Eden, (ii) it signifies possibility like standing on the edge of a precipice, and (iii) it is part of the human condition due to our ambiguous synthesis as body and soul. Anxiety is not directed to any definite object (like fear is) but is a complex of presentiments that arise from humans reflecting on themselves and represents "freedom's actuality as the possibility of possibility" (CA 42–3). All in all, Kierkegaard assigns a special positive valence to anxiety as "a propaedeutic to faith"—to experience anxiety is to have one's eyes opened to the reality of the human condition and the need for grace.[1]

Heidegger describes Kierkegaard as "[t]he man who has gone furthest in analyzing the concept of anxiety" (BT 492) which he effects by elucidating anxiety's dual aspects of turmoil and freedom. He refers to a "sober anxiety" that is accompanied by "unshakeable joy" (BT 358). It is a disturbing, disclosive mood that alerts an individual to the apprehension of one's mortality and one's existential possibilities in relation to that. Where fear involves a definite "entity-within-the-world," the object of anxiety is "completely indefinite" (BT 231) and turns out to be "Being-in-the-world as such" (BT 230). Anxiety reveals the "utter insignificance" of the everyday world and discloses a feeling of "uncanniness" of "not-being-at home" (BT 231):

> In anxiety what is environmentally ready-to-hand sinks away, and so, in general do entities within-the-world. The "world" can offer nothing more, and neither can the Dasein-with of others. Anxiety thus takes away from Dasein[2] the possibility of understanding itself, as it falls, in terms of the "world" and the way things have been publicly interpreted. (BT 232)

Although anxiety denotes our being-in-the-world, it throws us back on ourselves and our innermost possibilities: "Anxiety brings *Dasein* face to face with its *being-free-for*" (BT 232). In anxiety, "Dasein *is* its world existingly" (BT 416) and understands itself in terms of a possibility to be itself or not itself. As a way of disclosure in which "Dasein brings itself before itself" (BT 226), *angst* is individualizing. Above all, it is the recognition of death that gives Dasein its "moment of vision" and the sense of its possibilities, enabling "the possibility of a disclosure which is quite distinctive" (BT 235). In these rare moments of such "limit-situations," we exist at the peak of our own possibilities. As Rüdiger Safranski (2002: 152–3) comments, in Heidegger's philosophy in *Being and Time*, "[a]nxiety is the shadowy queen among moods." It reveals "the world has nothing more to offer him, nor has the *Dasein*-with of others," a form of peripeteia that drops us out of relations that are settled and sedimented. Heidegger also gives ontological significance to two other moods—boredom and joy—but takes anxiety to be primary: "*From an existential-ontological point of view, the "not-at-home" must be conceived as the more primordial phenomenon*" (BT 234).

## HEIDEGGER'S MINDFULNESS

*Mindfulness* is a key contemporary notion that has roots in Heidegger's thinking. Psychotherapists such as Ludwig Binswanger (1881–1966) and Medard Boss (1903–1990) saw a great deal of merit in Heidegger's philosophy as a therapeutic aid to mental wellbeing and psychological health. For Binswanger, Heidegger "has opened a new horizon of understanding for, and given a new impulse to, the scientific exploration of human existence and its specific modes of being."[3] Key to this is his idea of *Dasein* as a being that seeks intelligibility to itself—a being whose "Being is an *issue* for it" (BT 32).

Implementing Heidegger's existential insights, Binswanger and Boss articulate a form of post-Cartesian psychoanalysis that has three main dimensions—*phenomenological* (focuses on worlds of emotional experience), *hermeneutic* (interpretatively illuminates the structures of meaning that pre-reflectively organize those experiences), and *contextual* (grasps emotional experience as constituted in relational contexts). A key insight of Heidegger's thinking is the analysis of "ground moods"—anxiety, boredom, homesickness, melancholy, and other revelatory moods such as awe, wonder, astonishment—as fundamental affective attunements that *Dasein* makes toward its conditions and possibilities of existing. Post-Cartesian psychoanalysis differs from Freudian psychoanalysis insofar as it replaces the motivational primacy of drives with the primacy of disclosive moods and emotions. By focusing on the context of our "being-with-others" (*Mitsein*) as the fundamental ground of our experience, it also entails a shift from the interior of the isolated Cartesian mind toward a network of co-constitution with outward relational systems.[4] According to Boss, "[Heidegger] saw the possibility that his philosophical insights might not remain stuck in the philosophers' studies, but might benefit many more people, and especially those in need of help." This means establishing an open relationship to the world by sustaining the present without escaping into the future or the past in which things can appear. The manic-depressive, for instance, is too close or too far away from things, unable to stay in equilibrium and swinging between absorption and apathy. Mental ailments and psychological traumas are understood in this way as a "disturbance in existing" in terms of one's affective attunement to the world.[5]

According to Ott (1994: 65, 69), Heidegger first started to show the dark side of a depressive personality in 1911 when his staunch Catholic faith began to crumble in a "spiritual crisis." He suffered an acute mental breakdown in December 1945 following his inquisitional hearing with the de-Nazification Committee for his involvement with National Socialism in the 1930s. In the Spring of 1946 he underwent psychosomatic treatment with Victor Baron von Gebsattel, a physician and psychologist from the Binswanger school of "*Dasein* analysis" inspired by Heidegger's own philosophy. Dr. Gebsattel took him on a hike through the forest in the snow, showed him some "human warmth and friendship," and three weeks later Heidegger "came back a healthy man again."[6] His affective reattunement to the world proved to be a cure for his "disturbance in existing" contextually related to his problematic being-with-others and his social situation. As Safranski (2002: 254, 172) suggests, this "sensitive attunement to the luminosity of the world," a higher attentiveness or "awareness of awareness," is the goal of Heideggerian psychotherapy. It is a practice of *mindfulness* or "momentariness" in which "[t]he moment of vision is nothing other than the look of resolute disclosedness in which the full situation of an action opens itself and keeps itself open."

Heidegger's *mindfulness therapy* recognizes how habitual forms of thinking can trap subjects in negative cycles of behavior that prevents self-formation and growth. Acquiring mindfulness in the Heideggerian sense, means "less philosophy, but more attentiveness in thinking" (LH 265), joining with Zen philosophy in seeking releasement by cultivating somatic practices (breathing, yoga, meditation) and by contemplating paradoxical questions in the place of the futility of metaphysical speculation.[7] Developing existentialist insights into mindfulness as an antidote to anxiety and extending the idea of humans as *bodyminds* provides a pathway to contemporary practices of Sophrology—the study of *consciousness in harmony*—in which mind and body are as seen as intimately connected.

## THE PERILS OF BAD FAITH

In his early work, Sartre develops his existentialist predecessors' *phenomenology of anxiety*. Summarizing their views, he writes, "Kierkegaard, in his description of anguish before sin, characterizes it as anguish in the face of freedom. But Heidegger . . . considers anguish, on the contrary, as the apprehension of nothingness" (BN 66). These are complementary rather than contradictory—Kierkegaard stresses freedom in his view of anxiety, though not omitting finitude, while Heidegger stresses finitude, though not unaware of freedom. Sartre's own account is a subtle dialectic between freedom and nothingness in which he synthesizes these two views. He defines *anguish* as a "fear of oneself" that is "constitutive of pure consciousness" (TE 49). There are, he contends, two escapist ways to flee anguish—by apprehending oneself either "as *an Other*" or "as *a thing*" (BN 84). Anxiety arises because "I mistrust my own reactions" (BN 66), a nothingness penetrates my action—I'm not the self I will be or I am it in the mode of not being it: "It is precisely the consciousness of being one's own future, in the mode of not-being, that we call *anguish*" (BN 70). Coming face to face with anguish, I get the consciousness of my freedom in the affective recognition that there is never a motive *in* my consciousness, but only "*for* my consciousness" (BN 71). This means that I am compelled to decide the meaning of my own being. When the alarm clock rings in the morning, for example, "it is me, and me alone" (BN 77) who confers on the clock its requirement.

In the mode of being conscious of my own being, I come face to face with the nothingness that separates me from the causal temporal sequence between past and future. Sartre's two examples of anguish in *Being and Nothingness* are of the gambler who vows never to gamble again and the hiker who peers over the edge of a precarious mountain path into the chasm below. When the gambler approaches the gaming table, he finds that nothingness secretes itself between himself and his past and suddenly sees his resolutions dissolve (BN 70). The feeling of vertigo felt by the hiker relates to the open possibilities of the future that includes the conduct of "throw[ing] myself into the chasm" (BN 68). In both cases, there is a temporal void, "a nothingness has slid" into the heart of this relation (BN 69) that dissociates me from my past and from my future: "I *am* not the person who I will be" (BN 69–70).

In 1843, Kierkegaard noted in his journal Socrates' remark in the *Cratylus* that "to be deceived by oneself is the worst thing of all, for how could it not be terrible when the deceiver never disappears, even for an instant, but is always ready at hand?" (2008: 169). Beauvoir and Sartre give the name of *bad faith* to this psychological mechanism of self-deception we regularly employ to evade the anxiety of apprehending that one is free and beyond excuse. Together they conceived the idea of bad faith as a concept of dishonesty, a kind of self-delusion they set out to expose "in all its manifestations: semantic quibbling, false recollections, fugues, compensation fantasies, sublimations, and the rest" (PL 128). Beauvoir recounts in *The Prime of Life* how the concept came to her in a sudden moment of clarity when she was thinking of one of her teacher colleagues, Ginette Lumière who seemed "unreal, a sort of mirage": "Thenceforth we applied this term to anyone who feigned convictions or feelings that they did not in fact possess: we had discovered, under another name, the idea of 'playing a part'" (PL 128). Sartre illustrates this in *Being and Nothingness* with the example of a waiter whose "movements are animated and intent, a bit too precise, a bit too quick" (BN 102), and who imitates "the inflexible exactitude of some kind of automaton" (BN 102). His condition, like those of other tradespeople, Sartre observes, "is entirely ceremonial" (BN 103), governed by the social expectations of others. Bad faith, in this instance, means to cancel out one aspect of our ambiguous existence of self and other. When others view me in a certain way and I am "resigned to *being only that*," this is "experienced in the mode of bad faith" (BN 394). In his short story "The Childhood of a Leader," Sartre shows how the budding fascist Lucien falls into inauthenticity when he takes his first maxim to not "look into himself": "The true Lucien . . . had to be found in the eyes of others" (1939: 243).[8] Equally though, Beauvoir states, bad faith resides in the reverse. When I imagine myself to exist as an isolated atom completely unaffected by other people and refuse to leave the "subjective position," this is also a mode of bad faith manifesting itself as egocentricity and as a kind of "paranoia" (ASD 48).

According to Sartre, we have to deal with human reality "as a being that is what it is not, and that is not what it is" (BN 101) for this serves as the condition that makes bad faith conceivable (BN 113). On a basic level, bad faith manifests as an inability to live one's ambiguity authentically, an attempt to downplay or to annul "the twofold property of human beings" (BN 99), who are at once *facticity* and *transcendence*. These two aspects of human reality "are and ought to be capable of a valid coordination," but "bad faith does not want to coordinate them, or resolve them by means of a synthesis" (BN 99). Sartre gives the example of the homosexual who is in denial of his homosexuality against the "champion of sincerity" who urges him to admit to his homosexuality and declare it with unswerving pride. The homosexual is in bad faith by denying his facticity and identifying himself exclusively with his transcendence. He recognizes the facts that would lead an impartial observer to argue his orientation is homosexual but "will refuse with all his might to consider himself a 'paederast'" (BN 108). The champion of sincerity is also in bad faith because he sees the homosexual person as a kind of thing without transcendence, fixing his future destiny with his past actions. Both viewpoints contain some truth but are only partial since they neglect the subtle ambiguous play of *both* facticity *and* transcendence. Avoiding bad faith means being open in recognizing the interplay of both these aspects:

> To the extent to which a set of actions is defined as a paederast's behaviour, and I have performed these actions, I am a paederast. To the extent that human reality escapes any definition in terms of its behaviour, I am not one. (BN 109)

Sartre describes *Being and Nothingness* as "an eidetic of bad faith" insofar as it outlines in detail an inauthentic mode of being in which we desire to "become God," that is, to be our own foundation (*ens causa sui*) and reach the fullness and self-identity of the object while distinguishing ourselves from this to be conscious of it. Hence, bad faith can be conceived as a kind of "frozen reflexivity"—it posits the self as the illusive origin and specious end of consciousness, denying its own spontaneity in the name of identity, conceiving itself as a thing rather than activity.[9] Though a constant adjunct to our lives as an escape from anxiety, bad faith is evanescent, Sartre argues, belonging to psychic structures that are "metastable" (BN 50), subject to sudden changes or transitions, "oscillat[ing] constantly between good faith and cynicism" (BN 91).

In terms of self-deception or lying to oneself, Sartre contrasts his position in *Being and Nothingness* with Freud's theory of the unconscious. On the surface, self-deception seems to present an impossibility—I must know the truth as a deceiver which is hidden from me as the deceived (BN 90). But if I try to lie to myself, such a lie "recedes and collapses before [my] eyes" (BN 90). Freud's solution was to hypothesize a censor to relay messages between the conscious and unconscious in order to re-establish "the duality between the deceiver and the deceived" (BN 91), but this merely reproduces the problem in Sartre's view. Rather than lying to oneself in the form of believing an outright falsehood, bad faith is more a case of playing up one aspect of myself while downplaying another and creating misleading partial truths. This involves exploiting dualities (facticity/transcendence, self/other, future/past, reflective/prereflective) or selective focusing where we apply different standards for different beliefs in handling evidence, fully aware of our good deeds while scarcely noticing those that are not.[10] For Beauvoir and Sartre, bad faith is an indispensable tool for understanding human lives and also an instrument of moral criticism that highlights the ways in which we inauthentically escape anguish and deny our own freedom along with the freedom of others. They offer eudaimonistic arguments for the virtue of authenticity as an antidote to experiences of anxiety, despair, and alienation that diminish the quality and potential flourishing of an individual's life (and their relations with others).[11]

## EXISTENTIAL PSYCHOANALYSIS

Alongside his well-known interest in literary periodicals, Sartre avidly read psychological journals during the 1920s and 1930s.[12] Following Kierkegaard's recommendation that "[p]sychology is what we need and above all a sound knowledge of human life and sympathy for its interests" (PJ 185), from the start psychology was intrinsic to his philosophy. "What I called 'philosophy'," he said, "was purely and simply psychology."[13] From his earliest work on the imagination in the 1930s to his final work on Flaubert in the 1970s, this fascination with consciousness and the human mind never waned. Despite certain criticisms of Freud by Sartre in *Being and Nothingness*, the differences between existentialism and psychoanalysis are often amplified for they share common ground in attempting to define a personal, ethical, and therapeutic approach to studying human nature. The French existentialists preserve the valuable elements in Freud's work, in particular, the emphasis he gives to the body as fundamental in defining experience: "Freudianism's value derives from the fact that the existent is a body," Beauvoir argues, and "the way he experiences himself as a body in the presence of other bodies correctly translates his situation" (SS 69). In *Search for a Method*, Sartre credits psychoanalysis for allowing us "to discover the whole man in the adult; that is, not only his present determinations but the weight of his history" (SM 60).

In *Being and Nothingness*, Sartre suggests that authenticity can be found in "purifying reflection" (BN 279). Whereas impure reflection is contaminated by the desire to make myself an object, purifying reflection is a form of reflexivity that can reveal to us our freedom and image of ourselves as if we were seeing ourselves in a mirror. This is the "simple presence" of the consciousness reflecting to the consciousness reflected on, a kind of "reflective 'reflection-reflecting'" (BN 219). The nothingness that consciousness is cannot be known to pre-reflective consciousness nor grasped as an object by impure reflection but "is accessible only to purifying reflection" (BN 279), allowing us to grasp all the reflective distortions and mystifications, often formed in childhood, that keep us mired in patterns of bad faith. In terms of our emotional life, purifying reflection involves uncovering ulterior motives of various emotions and moral sentiments and their strategic deployment in negotiating the world around us. When asked in 1971 if purifying reflection and therefore authenticity were impossible, Sartre responded, "[y]ou know that I never described this kind of reflection, I said that it could exist, but I only showed examples of accessory reflection. And later I discovered that nonaccessory reflection was no different from the accessory and immediate way of looking at things but was the critical work one can do on oneself during one's entire life, through praxis" (1977a: 121–2). Sartre describes this critical undertaking in regard to oneself guided by a form of "praxis" in which we "turn back upon ourselves" and catch consciousness on the wing without objectifying the ego (BN 222).

Conceiving the self as "a dialectical object," existential psychoanalysis spreads it across the social field. In the first paragraph of *The Transcendence of the Ego*, Sartre states "the Ego is a being in the world, like the Ego of another" (TE 1). This puts into question the epistemological primacy of the first-person consciousness as being of proximal importance. There are times', Beauvoir wrote, "when I find it fascinating to see myself from the outside" (ASD 48). The body as seen from the outside by others is mysterious to the body lived from the inside in my own consciousness: "The self (*moi*) has only a probable objectivity, and anyone saying 'I' only grasps the outer edge of it; an outsider can get a clearer and more accurate picture" (PL 368). There is, Sartre states, a temporal gap, a "circuit of selfness" (BN 159), where consciousness is always chasing itself and must move backward in order to apprehend itself. The intimate consciousness of self is ultimately knowledge of nothingness, of what it is not. The truth of being lies in the objective world. This is why, in Beauvoir's view, "[o]ne of the meanings of paranoia is a refusal to abandon the subjective position: we are all more or less affected by it; we are all more or less blind to our inert presence in the Other's world" (ASD 48).

In Deleuze's (2004: 98) view, the groundbreaking aspect of Sartre's existentialism is the conception of "an impersonal transcendental field, not having the form of a synthetic personal consciousness or a subjective identity." This is what differentiates Sartre's approach from R. D. Laing's despite the deep affinities between them. In *The Divided Self*, Laing (1960: 180) puts larger sociological issues "in parentheses" since they are not of "direct and immediate relevance" to why an individual becomes psychotic. Sartre, by contrast, grants great importance to social structures and institutions and regards the family, for instance, as a certain individual manifestation "of the family structure appropriate to such and such a class under such and such conditions" (SM 61). Equally, for Beauvoir, lived experience is only one side of the coin—the view from within is only comprehensible by grasping the conditions under which those experiences are felt. Self-understanding requires, in Beauvoir's words, not only recreation of "one's knowledge . . . a consciousness," but also to "find the context in which this life took shape insofar as one was unaware of it." It is a question "of starting from the singularity of my life in order to find a generality, that of my era, that of the milieu in which I live" (2011: 291–3), Although existential psychoanalysis broached many themes, such as positive thinking,[14] long before these were discussed in today's self-help books, it does not isolate the individual from their environment and fall back on a (neoliberal) rationality in which one is individually responsible for their psychological wellbeing and a failure if one fails to achieve it.

When Sartre theorizes anxiety in his later work using his adopted *regressive-progressive method* in *The Critique* and *The Family Idiot*, he employs a thorough sociological approach. This means analyzing the interiorization of social codes in the individual before examining the subjective dimension of externalization in the form of action. The problem with previous existentialist accounts was inchoateness in pinning anxiety down. Heidegger ontologizes anxiety and locks it within the individual while recognizing a social aspect but remains vague as to what exactly that is. By describing it abstractly as the normalizing ways of the They, he lacks a proper material, cultural, or socio-economic explanation of the processes of reification which elicit a sense of alienation and collective anxiety. Thus, it can be said that *Being and Time* offers a diagnosis of the mood of anxiety, but no real therapy. Heidegger theorizes the recognition of death as "individualizing," but this recognition was a commonly felt social anxiety after the carnage of the First World War.[15] Thirty or so years later, Beauvoir recognized how the outside impinges on the inside—how anxieties and traumas have a social origin: "the war tore me apart . . . The share of freedom that remained to me was slight . . . Every hour of every day I saw just how much I depended upon events" (ASD 33). In the Cold War phase of the 1950s and 1960s, the collective prospect of life and death was, Sartre attests, the source of "what we feel today in anxiety" (1949: 68–9). In interview with Beauvoir in 1974, he calls for "the only possible radicalization of anti-psychiatry" based on the precept that "illness is capitalism's only possible form of life since alienation, in the Marxist sense, finds its truest expression in mental alienation and the repression that sanctions it" (FS 31).

Sartre's linkage of anxiety, trauma, and mental illness to the processes of the "Objective Spirit" of social reification brings us headlong into the present age of anxiety capitalism. Today, we are bombarded from all directions with a plethora of collective and individual anxiety issues that assail our minds—crime, Artificial Intelligence, cyber-attack, biological viruses, environmental collapse, war, nuclear proliferation, genetic engineering, poverty, and job insecurity, alongside individual anxieties relating to personal image, such as height, weight, baldness, intelligence, ageing, sexual libido, material status, and general popularity. As the Heideggerian psychotherapist, Ludwig Binswanger wrote, describing in one of his patients an extreme case of paranoia about body image that generates hopelessness and leads in the most extreme to suicide:

> Every day she feels herself fatter, which according to her own statement means getting both older and uglier. Here too we find the all-or-nothing principle at work: "If I cannot remain young, beautiful, and thin," we have in her words, "then rather—Nothingness."[16]

## FANON'S PSYCHIATRY OF DISALIENATION

Karl Jaspers and Frantz Fanon were practicing psychiatrists before becoming theorists of philosophy and psychoanalysis. Fanon was heavily influenced by Jaspers' *General Psychopathology*, which combined phenomenological and psychoanalytic approaches, and placed emphasis on meaning rather than facts or behaviors. According to Fanon, "I already knew that there were legends, stories, history, and above all *historicity*, which I had learned about from Jaspers" (BSWM 112). He was drawn to Jaspers' critical phenomenology in his task to make "a constant, solid endeavor to understand man" (BSWM 6), in which the decision to describe implies a critical approach and therefore an urgent surpassing toward some solution.

Complaining that classical psychoanalysis implicitly relies on a universalist model of the psyche and does not consider ethnic differences,[17] Fanon seeks to recalibrate it: "only a psychoanalytic interpretation of the black problem can reveal the affective disorders responsible for this network of complexes" (BSWM xiv). In a racist society, the black person feels anxiety over his embodiment, trapped within a "corporeal schema" in a "Zone of Nonbeing," his subjectivity denied through "being too much body."[18] Fanon points to the inferiority complex felt by many colonized black people to illustrate this. Unlike Freud who roots the *inferiority complex* in childhood traumas, Fanon finds it to be normal for black people which points toward it being culturally formed: "it is cultural, i.e., acquired," a "habit" rather than an "instinct" (BSWM 165). The "historical-racial schema," Fanon writes, is fabricated "out of a thousand details, anecdotes, and stories," supplied "by the Other, by the white man" (BSWM 91). Black children are raised on European culture from storybooks and comics to films where heroes are white and black characters are parodied, secondary or dehumanized. The view of black people as inferior saturates culture with the continual use of darkness and blackness to denote evil and death (BSWM 165–7). But although black people have internalized these norms and come to identify with the white colonizers, the color of their skin marks them out as fundamentally Other: "at the first white gaze, he feels the weight of his melanin" (BSWM 128).

According to Fanon, the inferiority complex results from a deeply ingrained collective unconscious that takes the form of a system of "negrophobia" (BSWM 138) that shapes the behavior and perceptions of each individual. Blacks represent an anxiogenic or phobogenic object for white people. In Fanon's estimation, to overcome the inferiority complex, black people need to experience the performative aspect of their own agency through the articulation of a positive sense of negritude rather than being the pawns of a historical process. In his clinical practice in Algeria, Fanon frequently encountered the "North African Syndrome" in which anxiety and death dominate the minds of those who attempt to live in a society that militates against their humanity since "the first encounter with himself will be a neurotic mode, a pathological mode" (1969: 18).

Fanon initially developed his psychiatric practice as an intern at Saint-Alban in France under François Tosquelles (the founder of *social psychotherapy*) before instituting it at the psychiatric hospital in Blida-Joinville in Algeria. Tosquelles (who also collaborated with Guattari) outlined the two main precepts of institutional or social psychotherapy as (i) never isolate the study of mental illness from its social and institutional context and (ii) always analyze institutions in terms of the real, symbolic and imaginary effects they induce in the individual.[19] From this experience, Fanon further refined his theory of *sociogeny* in which psychological disorders, such as anxiety, trauma and madness, are seen to result from negative social interactions. This led him to develop a humanistic approach to psychiatric medicine and institutional therapy geared toward the aim of creating a thriving community centered around interaction in small groups to discuss mental, occupational, social issues and break the chains of neurosis and psychopathological disorders.[20] Despite executing the odd clinical procedure that may well seem outdated (and even cruel) to modern sensibilities,[21] Fanon humanized the psychiatric wards he was in charge of, removing bars from windows, isolation units, straitjackets and other physical restraints. Although he still pursued a mixed approach, also running clinical trials of new drugs (such as Meprobamate in 1957 to treat patients suffering from acute hypochondria), Fanon's main focus was to encourage the creation of common spaces and the establishment of a "therapeutic community" among patients. He established a neo-society within the hospital that included group therapy, sports teams, recreational outings, afternoon tea conversations, a café and a salon, gardening activities, basket weaving, a theater, a film club, a record-collecting society, as well as a weekly publication *Notre Journal* for the patients and staff. While at Blida-Joinville, Fanon was always innovating and looking for new ways of working with mental illness to resolve anxiety in an "existentialist way."[22] Although a senior administrator called him "madder than the madmen," Fanon's social therapy resulted in significantly reduced conflict within the asylum and violence against carers.

For Fanon, it is essential to tap the lived experience of the colonized rather than impose a universalist model. "Care," "consciousness and love" are the primary task of the therapist who must never operate with an attitude of punishment and turn the institution into "a barracks in which children-boarders tremble before parent-orderlies." Above all, it is necessary to induce the inpatient "to rediscover the meaning of freedom, which is the first milestone on the way to responsibility."[23] Following Tosquelles, Fanon dreamed of going beyond a "neo-society" (which lacks "a creative, innovative dynamic") toward a "geo-psychiatry" where psychiatry is practiced beyond the walls of confinement and unfolds within concrete society itself. In Tosquelles' vision of a "healing collective," the right to vagabondage and the removal of confinement and restrictive space connect to a patient's sense of worth and recognition by the community. To shield patients from the world, Fanon argues, means making a "thingification" of their condition and selves. Creating a sanitized neo-society remains "at the level of magic" where the patient can only "exercise his freedom in the unreal world of fantasy." In the day center the psychiatrist becomes like any other doctor and the practice of psychiatry becomes "an encounter between two freedoms" instead of a "master/slave, prisoner/jailer dialectic."[24] In a similar vein to Richard Wright, an advocate of anti-racist psychiatry who was instrumental in creating the Lafargue Mental Health Clinic in Harlem in 1946, in 1957 Fanon took charge of *Le Centre neuropsychiatrique du jour* at the Charles Nicolle Hospital in Tunis, the first psychiatric Day Clinic in Africa. Working with refugees from Algeria gave him privileged access to the psychologies of young men from rural backgrounds who had suffered family trauma at the hands of French colonial rule—agitation, anxiety, hallucinations, depression, flashbacks, impotence, fits of aggression, guilt, and violent fantasies.

The goal of Fanon's existential psychotherapy is to bring about the organic unity of subject and object—of being-in-the-world as a free consciousness able to materialize its creative possibilities in its relations with others. To this end, in *Anti-Oedipus* Deleuze and Guattari credit Fanon for overthrowing Freud's family romance and tracing instead the political roots of trauma. Fanon also influenced the anti-psychiatry of Franco Basaglia (much admired by Beauvoir and Sartre). Fanon's legacy of disalienation, as Adam Shatz (2025: 381) notes, is the practice of *Clinical Fanonism* that continues in war-torn or deprived places, such as Afghanistan, Syria, and Palestine, treating those anxious souls traumatized by the lived experience of loss, fear, discrimination, and violence.

## THE SANITY OF MADNESS

Madness, perhaps the most extreme of all anxiety-based psychological disorders, is a theme explored extensively by existentialists, paving the way for later thinkers, Derrida, Foucault, Lacan, and Guattari who took the philosophical interest further still. Existentialist philosophers view madness ambiguously as *pharmakon*—both as cure (an escape from the normalizing capture of reason) and disease (a process of fragmentation and breakdown). Kierkegaard is the obvious starting point in existentialism's confrontation with insanity, a living example of his suggestion (quoting Socrates) that "heaven-sent madness" is preferable to any "man-made sanity" (FT 56).

Kierkegaard often recorded in his journals how his melancholia drove him to "the brink of insanity" (PJ 229). On his thirty-sixth birthday on May 5, 1849, he despairs of his "melancholia" and "hypochondriacal evasions" from Regine and his authorship and attributes this to his own hard-wiring: "What makes my life so difficult is that I'm tuned an octave higher than other people are" (2013: 101). Kierkegaard's spirit, as one of his tutors remarked, was "constantly preoccupied with itself," a form of "hyper-reflection" that engaged his "all too inventive brain."[25] Such hyper-reflecting led him dangerously toward discombobulation and inequilibrium: "One thought succeeds another; no sooner have I thought it and am able to write it down than there's a new one—hold it, grasp it—madness—insanity! (PJ 71). This did not go unnoticed to those around him. His brother Peter Christian wrote in his diary in August 1838: "Søren these days is perhaps more than ever before weighed down by brooding, almost more than his health can stand, but it only makes him unhappy, indecisive, and is close to driving him insane."[26] In summer he stayed indoors in his darkened rooms and longed for autumn (his favorite season) as it made him think of the heavens. Existence churned inside him so turbulently "it seems that my feelings, like water, will break the ice with which I have covered myself." On October 2, 1855, he collapsed in the street and was taken to Frederiks Hospital offering the doctor possible explanations for his illness, such as his dark dwelling and the exhausting nature of his intellectual work. The doctors diagnosed his illness as psychical and, soon after, he shuffled off his mortal coil and fulfilled his wish "unceasingly, unceasingly [to] Speak with my Jesus" (PJ 657).[27]

Nietzsche too was prone to fits of insanity. Indeed, there is a certain mystique that surrounds the madness of Nietzsche's final years and some mystery as to what caused it. Was it encephalitis, syphilis, a flight of the untrammeled imagination, a social mask, a performative self-configuration or just the Dionysian terminus of self-dispersal toward which his *Lebensphilosphie* was always bound? Was it a desperate affliction or a saintly gift; a descent into the bowels of despair or an ascent into a rarefied zone? Ironically, in *Twilight of the Idols* Nietzsche roundly condemns the invalid he became: "Society should only have a profound contempt for the man who survives like a vegetable in cowardly dependence on doctors and medicine after he has lost the meaning of his life, the right to live" (TI 9.36). Yet it was only as a "vegetable" and "museum exhibit" of his sister Elisabeth after the onset of insanity in the 1890s that he finally began to achieve the renown he had craved in his earlier, fully sentient years.

On January 3, 1889, Nietzsche left his apartment and caught sight of a carriage driver beating his horse on the Piazza Carlo Alberto in Turin. Weeping, he threw himself around the horse's neck to protect it and collapsed in compassion with the animal. Soon after, he was taken to a psychiatric unit in Jena and diagnosed with "paralysis progressiva." In early 1890, his friend Gast went for long walks with the philosopher whom he suspected did not want to be cured: "it seemed—horrible though this is—as if Nietzsche were merely feigning madness, as if he were glad for it to have ended this way." This echoes Franz Overbeck's impression who, after spending time with Nietzsche, wrote, "I cannot escape the ghastly suspicion . . . that his madness is simulated."[28] Those who visited him during the 1890s tell of his physical degeneration and mute presence but also of "the power of his glance" (Gabriele Reuter) and the "unfathomable exultation" (Rudolf Steiner) of his facial expression. When Horneffer visited Nietzsche in the final months of his life, he described him in beatific terms: "Although his eyes were vacant and his features slack, and although the poor man lay there with crooked limbs, more helpless than a child, a sense of magic radiated from his personality, and his appearance revealed a majesty that I would never experience again with any human being."[29]

Nietzsche's madness was very much a terminal point of Dionysian dispersal that brought "both great terror and joy" (WP 1050). A "*Reverence for madness*" (HH 127) was signaled in his writings as a fault line that became ever more pronounced in his undertaking as "the last disciple of Dionysus" (TI 10.5). In madness, as in dance, Nietzsche affirmed, one has the sense of being possessed by a higher power in order to throw off the yoke of custom. As the *sine qua non* for moral evolution, madness produces innovation and creativity where moral innovators had to feign madness or induce it by means of asceticism (D 14). To project his saintly persona in *Daybreak*, Nietzsche follows the path of the Jewish prophets, the medicine man of the Indians, the Christian saints, the Greenland angekok, and the Brazilian Pajee who created new moral ideals through "ecstasy or mental derangements" (D 14). He foretells that all signs of the *Übermensch* will appear as signs of madness or illness to the human herd: "Where is the madness, with which you should be cleansed? Behold, I teach you the Superman: he is the lightning, he is this madness!" (Z P3). Nietzsche associates madness with far-reaching insights, such as "the madman with the lantern" (JS 125) who casts light on things others don't see and madness as the serum "with which you must be inoculated" (Z P3) to protect against the stifling character of social norms. However, Nietzsche also views madness as manifesting in different forms since social norms carry their own force of madness. He warns us to protect against the insanity of groups who have deviated from health and alignment to the world as will to power (BGE 156). Similarly, he urges us to guard against the "madhouse air" of those whose shepherd is the ascetic priest (GM 3.14) and those whose "bad conscience" leads them to posit a transcendent god as their judge and executioner of their guilt (GM 2.22). Zarathustra also preaches against the madness of pessimism and nihilism conceived as an end state rather than as a transitional phase (Z 2.20).

Like Nietzsche, Fanon recognizes the social dimensions of madness, but without embracing it as an exalted Dionysian state. For Fanon, madness is a pathological condition, the result of social breakdown in which the oppressed and anxious take refuge in their imagination from the reality of their misery. As a clinical physician in France and Algeria, Fanon worked alongside madness day by day. On meeting the anthropologist Alfred Métraux in 1953, they discussed the idea of Voodoo possession, which Fanon argued was always the result of a feeling of guilt, citing the case of an Algerian man who felt responsible for the death of his brothers even though he bore no blame. Theorizing in a similar vein to Beauvoir who viewed the possession rituals of the Brazilian *candomblé* as an attempt "to restore their humanity to a group of men who have been forced to the status of cattle" (FC 532), he saw them as an outlet or release for the internalized violence of the colonial system: "This muscular orgy in which the most acute aggressivity and violence are channelled, transformed and conjured way, is the colonized's relaxation . . . It all has to come out: symbolic killings, figurative cavalcades, imaginary multiple murders." The struggle for liberation leads to the decline of such cults as the violence is channeled into revolutionary energy. "With his back to the wall and a knife to his throat," Fanon attests, the colonized has no real need to tell himself stories or resort to a mythical imaginary (WE 45tm).

In a wider cultural sense, Fanon argues that Western and North African perceptions differ significantly in their understanding of the relation between the mad and their madness. The Western doctors and nurses in psychiatric hospitals viewed the patients as responsible for their actions and punished or censured them accordingly. In traditional North African societies, by contrast, madness was seen to be the result of possession by local spirits, *jinni*. Mental illness was accidental, a contingent condition that had no effect on the true or underlying personality afflicted by possession. Once cured (through pilgrimage, ritual, invocation, or the wearing of magic amulets), the person was invited back into society without suspicion or distrust. Fanon views this approach positively as "a harmonious articulation of beliefs" imbued with a "profoundly holistic spirit that preserves intact the image of the normal man" despite the existence of an illness, which carries "great value" in human terms without venerating insanity or mental illness.[30]

Unlike some poststructuralist evangelists of madness, such as Lacan, Foucault, and Derrida, Fanon never relinquishes the goal of reason, as a weapon of the oppressed against irrational prejudice and cruelty nor does he champion madness as freedom's outer edge and the repository of a counter wisdom. Mental illness, in Fanon's clinical view, is a "pathology of freedom," an alienation from self that impairs one's relations with others and compromises one's possibility for self-determination: "Madness itself does not command respect, patience, indulgence; instead, it is the human being impaired by madness, by the genies; the human being as such."[31] Ultimately, for Fanon, as for other existentialists, "[m]adness is man's means of losing his freedom" that arises when social structures "are opposed to any attempt to place the individual [in a humane place]."[32] The release from mental disintegration and the racial alienation of the colonized requires emancipation from an oppressive social order.

All in all, existentialism has done much to enlarge our understanding of anxiety and psychological wellbeing by linking it centrally to human freedom. Ontologically, Kierkegaard, Heidegger, and Sartre show how *angst* is an affective recognition both of our finitude and freedom, "a disclosure which is *quite distinctive*" (BT 235) that acts as a propadeutic to realizing our innermost possibilities and achieving authenticity. The canonical existentialist works of Beauvoir, Sartre, and Fanon are rich in insights with regard to the internalization of social meanings and one's embodied experience in the world, showing how experiences of anxiety, depression, and trauma are deeply imbued with social meanings. Unlike traditional psychiatric practice that has "the inveterate tendency to depersonalize or reify persons" (Laing 1960: 23), existentialism views humans as *creatures of becoming* in a dialectical chain composed of multiple dynamic organizations that are socially, materially, psychologically, and temporally realized in relation to the past, present, and future possibilities.

Along with Beauvoir and Fanon, Sartre developed a more dialectical view in which many traumas and anxieties are *sociogenic* resulting from the reificatory norms of capitalism that alienate individuals from themselves, from others, and from their own praxis. This dialectical view shows how anxiety results from the closure and the *impossibility* of realizing freedom in the social sphere as well as from the apprehension of its possibility in the psychological realm. To combat these pervasive effects, existentialism proposes the therapeutic practice of *intellectual conscience* (Nietzsche), *mindfulness* (Heidegger), and *purifying reflection* (Sartre) that reaches its culmination in Fanon's *psychiatry of disalienation*. But, in the end, although therapeutic practice can vastly alleviate anxiety and disalienate the sufferer, even the most sociogenically motivated of all existentialists—Fanon—expresses doubt (harking back to Kierkegaard) as to whether we can ever fully escape angst's cunning ways that creep upon us in vulnerable moments:

> we are for ever pursued by our actions. Their ordering, their circumstances and their motivation may perfectly well come to be profoundly modified *a posteriori*. This is merely one of the snares that history and its various influences sets for us. But can we escape becoming dizzy? And who can affirm that vertigo does not haunt the whole of existence? (WE 203)

CHAPTER THREE

# "Remain True to the Earth"

## (Nietzsche, *Thus Spoke Zarathustra*) ECOLOGY

Earth's ecology dominates the concerns of the twenty-first century shaped by the catastrophic narratives of environmental collapse in the Age of the Anthropocene. In this chapter, we look at what existentialism can offer our contemporary ecological consciousness. Against certain misconceptions of existentialism as being anthropocentric and anti-nature, the greater truth, as we will see, is that in their quest to "remain true to the earth" (Z 1.22.2), existentialist thinkers bestow a set of valuable ecosophical tools to make sense of our present environmental predicament. From Nietzsche's idea of "assimilation," Heidegger's notion of "letting things be," Merleau-Ponty's "Flesh of the World," and Sartre's concept of "hodological space," existentialist philosophers show how we are symbiotically connected to our environment which acts as a medium of circulation where "man is mediated by things to the extent that things are mediated by man" (CDR 82).

Existentialism takes much of its philosophical and historical lineage from Romanticism, railing against the rationalism of Enlightenment thinking and emphasizing human feeling, emotion, and attunement to the beauty of the natural world. In *Sonnets to Orpheus*, Rainer Maria Rilke, the German poet who along with Novalis and Hölderlin was an inspiration to Heidegger, poetizes the continuous intimate exchange between self and world where emotion colors our perception of things that nature and environment impress upon our senses. Against the processes of mechanization and disenchantment, Rilke encourages an *ecstatic* relationship to nature that we can achieve through works of art and the use of creative imagination that celebrate its sensuous glory, dynamic power, and infinite rapture.

Although, like Plato in Raphael's painting of *The School of Athens*, Kierkegaard was often looking up to the heavens instead of down at the earth, he was far from immune to nature's rugged power and beauty. In 1835, he records in his journal the pleasure he felt walking in the Danish woods and hills near his favorite spot at Gilbjerget, surveying all below him and intoning the song of the sea's "deep but calm solemnity" and the vespers songs of the birds (PJ 26). Nature impressed upon him "how great and yet how insignificant I am. Those two great forces, pride and humility, amicably combined" (PJ 27). It is in the midst of nature, he intones, where a person "free from life's often suffocating air, breathes more freely":

> here the soul opens willingly to every noble impression. Here a human being steps forth as nature's master, but he also feels that in nature something higher is manifested, something he must bow down before. He feels a need to surrender to this power that rules it all (PJ 28)

Marcel joins this chorus of praise and awe, celebrating nature as dense and brimming with otherness, an "overflowing richness of reality" whose mystery lies beyond rational explanation. In *Man against Mass Society*, he calls for a holistic relation to nature in contrast to the technological reduction of the lifeworld that kills our sense of wonder in the world. Rather than isolation from the non-human, existential authenticity should foster harmony with our own natural element and with the rest of nature. As humans, Marcel argues, we should consider life as a "gift" and "care" about our world in which nature's objects should be "sacred," "holy," "special," or "consecrated," miraculated objects that enchant and plenish our existence.[1]

## NIETZSCHE'S NATURE

In Nietzsche's writings we find a pious and joyful veneration for nature found in few, if any, other philosophies. Nietzsche's thinking is a precursor of an ecological consciousness in Western philosophy that questions humanity's environmental impact in an Anthropocene age: "hubris is today our entire position on nature, our violation of nature with the help of machines and the ever so thoughtless ingenuity of technicians and engineers."[2] Nietzsche had a deep love for nature and its transformative, generative powers. As a youngster, he felt happiness and companionship when out hiking in the countryside on school field trips singing patriotic songs and playing humorous games. Later in life, he walked in the mountains near Nice for seven or eight hours at a time and likened his solitary treks in the mountains to Zarathustra's ascent, a wandering exile looking down from the summit. Influenced strongly by Ralph Waldo Emerson whose essay "History" in praise of "spiritual nomadism" he copied into his notebooks during his adolescence, he was fascinated by the intimate connection between self and environment and how one's habitat can warp or shape desires and mood.

Nature is absolutely central in Nietzsche's work. His concept of the *free spirit*, so important to his middle works, was inspired by the coast of Sorrento which he observed from his rented room watching the rushing of the waves and fathomless sea "with its rippling snake-skin and beast-of-prey beauty" (HH 49). According to Nietzsche, our relation to the environment is one of *incorporation* and *assimilation*, a constant transfer of energies and forces between things. In determining who we are, "nutrition, place, climate," he argues, "are inconceivably more important than everything one has taken to be important so far" (EH 2.10). On August 6, 1881, he experienced his transformative moment of *eternal return* in front of a pyramid-shaped boulder on his way to the mountain lake at Silvaplana–Surlej, a region he described as "the sweetest corner of the earth." This was a moment that marked his decisive step to his "naturalization" as he called it. His years of wandering and traveling among nature were a process of healing of body and mind.

Nietzsche's paean to nature in *Thus Spoke Zarathustra* is centered upon Zarathustra's injunction to "[r]emain faithful to the earth" (Z 1.22.3) and is his attempt to develop a new philosophy in which the earth and ecology are central. As Zarathustra marvels, nature not only provides food for nourishment, but does so in an aesthetic way, with beautiful and beckoning colors, tastes, and aromas. However, human despoliation of the earth has caused it to suffer through exploitation and pollution: "The earth has a skin; and this skin has diseases. One of these diseases for example is called 'human being'" (Z 2.18). Zarathustra is nevertheless optimistic—though much of the earth is ravaged and polluted, it still retains tremendous possibilities for growth and renewal as "the heart of the earth is of gold" (Z 2.19). In his more optimistic moments, he imagines the earth as a vast health resort and gigantic tree of life (WS 188–9) but voices apprehension for the "*Menschen-Erde*" (human earth) that can manifest itself as a hell or a garden.

An important metaphor in Nietzsche's ecology is the *garden*. Convalescing from his "abysmal thought" of eternal return, Zarathustra is cheered by his animals' news that the world is awaiting him as a garden (Z 3.13). In Nietzsche's vision of earth's transformation, gardens are sites of becoming that offer aesthetic and multisensory stimulation, earthly experiments that are responsive to variations in their surrounding environment and which offer a diversity of possibilities. Gardens are not just empty spaces but distinctive places like heterotopias with pervasive affective qualities that can nurture or block creativity. They represent the perfect metaphor for human inventiveness and creativity, an experiment and conversation with nature in the form of a nature-culture hybrid. Advising the "good Europeans," "free spirits," and "philosophers of the future," Nietzsche sounds an ecological plea: "please don't forget the garden, the garden with the golden trellises!" (BGE 25). In Shapiro's (2016: 136) view, Nietzsche's idea of the *earth as garden* is his attempt to sketch "a geoaesthetics and geopolitics of the Anthropocene." He offers an earth-centered reversal of biblical themes, from the innocence of the Garden to the terror of the Apocalypse and Antichrist in which his correlation of garden-happiness with sensuality reverses the biblical garden story where Eve and Adam feel shame in the discovery of their nakedness. He pictures the garden as a perfect nature-culture continuum, subscribing not fully to Emersonian wilderness but favoring the flourishing of style "within a *half wild* environment" (KSW 9.256). Nietzsche's *Übermensch* who "speaks from the heart of the earth" (Z 2.18) and the free spirits whom he urges to take on the task of the management of the whole earth (HH 25), herald a new direction in philosophical cosmology that makes the relationship between humans and the earth the central concern of our twenty-first-century self-understanding.

Nietzsche's new direction Henk Manschot (2021: 75) terms "terrasophy," a philosophical viewpoint that takes the earth "as not an object but a partner" and recognizes the will to power as a universal and abundant creative force in nature and in things. This transforms our relationship to Gaia from one of a furious and vengeful goddess to the face of a caring mother. Deleuze and Guattari (1994: 102) describe his thinking as "geophilosophy," an approach that avoids statism, emphasizing a plurality of forms of human habitation, including nomadic and other non-state groupings within fields of the unconstrained movement of bodies and thought. An ecological reading of Nietzsche's philosophy dispels the view (promulgated by Heidegger) that his will to power involves the domination of the earth by humans. Instead, it recognizes Nietzsche's view of the will to power as a *universal creative force in nature*. It traces his relational ontology of *assimilating and incorporating forces* and follows his numerous injunctions to remain true to the earth, establishing the world as an Epicurean garden of free air that offers solitude, creativity, and play.

## HEIDEGGER'S *GELASSENHEIT*

Heidegger always felt ill at ease in cities and metropolitan centers and is mythically associated with his rustic log cabin at Todtnauberg where he would often retreat to mindfully philosophize and lead the daily life of a traditional Saxon peasant, gathering herbs and firewood and communing with nature as he wandered through the ancient woods. Here, he reveled in "the bracing air of the mountains" and savored a rhythm of life which "appears to the mind as something pure, simple and immense."[3] When philosophizing about nature, Nietzsche was the thinker closest to him through various meditations on his thought or the attempt to distance himself from him. Although he (questionably) classifies Nietzsche as "the name for an age: the epoch of the development and installation of the mastery of the human over the earth" (GA50: 84),[4] his own thinking follows many of the same contours as Nietzsche's "terrasophizing."

Heidegger's so-called Turn in the 1930s was an attempt to distance himself from what he saw as the metaphysical anthropocentrism of *Being and Time* where he placed humanity as the guardians and ciphers of Being (BT 269). For Heidegger, *world* and *earth* are "essentially different and yet never separated . . . The opposition of world and earth is a conflict" (GA5: 34) via which the truth of being arises in a way that is both revealing and concealing. Nature is much more than the objects of scientific inquiry, it is rather an "upsurging presence" (GA9: 190) in which things present themselves of their own accord: "*physis* is indeed *poiêsis* in the highest sense" (QCT 10). Technology can only conquer nature as "standing reserve" because modern science already projects nature mathematically as object, as "a coherence of forces calculable in advance" (QCT 21). Indeed, once nature is conceived neither as Aristotelian teleology nor divine Christian purpose, it becomes material for "the organized global conquest of the earth" (GA6.2: 358), a new conception that "sets upon . . . unlocks and exposes" (QCT 15) nature in order to stockpile it as "standing-reserve" (QCT 17). This logic of domination "drives out every other possibility of revealing" (QCT 27) and has precipitated the abandonment of being, manifested in the anxiety of "not being-at-home" which he attests "has never been greater than today" (GA65: 139).

In his thinking after the Turn, Heidegger emphasizes "the power of the earth" as a home (GA39: 88). The earth is "the building-bearer, nourishing with its fruits, tending water and rock, plant and animal"[5] and it is incumbent on us to set the earth free in its own essence by letting things be and blossom. In *Origin of the Work of Art*, he distinguishes between world (the plenum of human concerns) and earth (which does not yield entirely to human attempts to understand it). An authentic relation to Being requires us to dwell on the earth poetically with an awareness of our sheltering relation with Being itself. This is achieved through *Gelassenheit*—letting things be without attempting to control or exploit them. Heidegger emphasizes this further in *The Question Concerning Technology*, a treatise of environmentalism that urges a revelatory poetic stewardship of the earth in terms of authentic living communities. For Heidegger, humans are the beings that inquire about their own being and so have a special relationship to Being although Being maintains its particular elusiveness that we cannot grasp as a direct object of thought. It grounds all possible knowledge but cannot itself be known directly.

In "letting beings be," we reveal two types of concealment, one that is inessential (faulty philosophical understanding practiced by modern science) and one that is irreducibly essential (the partial and incomplete manner of grasping things phenomenologically). Once we forget and ignore this mystery of concealment, the world is filled out by calculation and instrumentality and we feel homeless as Being as a whole is forgotten (GA9: 337). In Lee Braver's (2016: 254) words, *Gelassenheit* represents for Heidegger "the spark, the halo of a small, fragile light in which reality comes to know itself through us," a form of releasement that dwells with and on our experience, a careful attending to the way things show themselves to us like the way one cares for and nurtures a plant. Through appreciation of this cosmic gift, we attain a form of releasement as when we are captivated and enraptured by a work of art. Heidegger ends *The Question Concerning Technology* with Hölderlin's words: "where danger is, there grows the saving power also." This urges us to find a new way of revealing nature (as a "blossoming-forth of things") by cultivating attunement and dwelling poetically upon the earth (QCT 24).

Despite the ontological parochialism and Eurocentrism of Heidegger's conception (for which Derrida and Deleuze in particular heavily criticized him), much of his thinking around "lettings things be" has strong parallels with Eastern philosophy, opening up a clear path toward "the inevitable dialogue with the East Asian world" and enabling the development of radical "planetary thinking" (GA9: 424). As Bret Davis (2016: 467) argues, *Gelassenheit* has resonances with the Daoist and Zen idea of non-doing. This involves the idea of the radical "step back" into the nothingness that was one's original state and a close attentiveness to the influence of the environment and affect. In the1966 *Spiegel* interview, Heidegger suggests that by attuning ourselves to the blossoming of the earth and connecting ourselves to ancient traditions of thinking we can "enable the human being to have a free relationship to the technical world" (GA16: 677) and create a clearing in which we can once again understand Being's cosmic gift.

## SARTRE'S NAUSEA

In her diaries and interviews, Simone de Beauvoir often contrasts her own love of nature with Sartre's dislike of it. Where Sartre "detests the country," she writes winsomely about "a red cliff, an apple tree in bloom, a meadow . . . an endless hedge of plane trees, or the golden sands of acacia leaves in the fall." "I think that trees, stones, skies, the colours and sounds of the countryside," she marvels, "will never lose their capacity to touch me" (FC 303). But, for Sartre, a man "allergic to chlorophyll" and exhausted by green pasturage (PL 13), the efflorescence and rugged power of the natural world did not occasion any great joy: "More than the pure air of the mountain peaks or the open sea, he enjoys an atmosphere full of tobacco smoke and warmed by human breath." Beauvoir compares his attitude to nature with Roquentin's nauseous aversion to sensing the "brute existence" of a chestnut tree in the park:

> Roquentin's crisis reaches its paroxysm in a public park, and nowhere does the presence of things show itself with more indiscretion than in the heart of nature. Sartre detests the country, with its proliferation of plants and swarms of insects. At most, he tolerates the level sea, the smooth desert sands, or the mineral coldness of mountain peaks, but he is really happy only in cities, at the heart of a universe constructed and populated with fabricated objects (2004: 230)

In contrast to Beauvoir's judgment, there are a growing number of scholars who discern an implicit ecological logic in Sartre's writings, especially the *Critique*.[6] When we scan the range of his works, we find a *multivalent* formulation of nature—as threat, as Feminized Other, as escape and cradle of retreat, as rapture—and not just a negative uniform view. Indeed, as Ally argues (2017, 2020), Sartre's work contains a (submerged) ecological perspective from which it is possible to articulate the broad contours of "a new socioecological imaginary." Although Sartre is guilty at times, as Ally (2017: 323, 26, 385) recognizes, of a "fourfold flaw"—"reflexive anthropocentrism," "heuristic exceptionalism," "categorical exclusivism," and "naive instrumentalism"—we should be careful not to dismiss Sartre's ecological credentials by overlooking the subtlety of his vision. These flaws ebb and flow throughout his writings (and sometimes even within the same passage!) but are not essential to the structure of his wider ontological thinking. Generally, Sartre's account of nature balances on a thin, ambiguous line, a "line without thickness" (CDR2: 329), of keeping the human and non-human heuristically apart while insisting that they are ontologically entwined. This functions as a "lived contradiction" in his schematic philosophy that his dialectical approach illuminates. As Ally (2017: 506, 353) suggests, Sartre can be viewed in this light as a thinker who stands on the cusp of the "Holocene-Anthropocene transit" between a waxing Earth and a waning world. His designation of the Earth as "the Elsewhere of Elsewheres," as absolute otherness, (CDR 323–4) signifies the tragic underside of late-Holocene thinking since, as he recognizes counter to this in *Saint Genet*, the environment is all around us: "We rapidly cart away the dead, we stealthily recover waste, every day we mask, in the name of cleaning up, the destruction of the day before. We conceal the pillaging of the planet" (SG 24).

Exploring Sartre's work, we can discover, in Ally's (2017: 364, 392) words, an "*ecology of intelligibility*," "a vital community of logics," and "an inferential ecosystem of sorts" peppered with emergent ecological sensibilities and earthly sensitivities that can illuminate our present Anthropocene predicament.[7] In the

*Critique*, for instance, where he describes the "destructive apparatus" of the Chinese peasant and the practice of deforestation (CDR 162), Sartre demonstrates how worked-over matter takes on an alien presence, resisting us through passive action and confronting us as a counter-finality that can have disastrous consequences. Matter is conceived in these terms as an actant within a human/non-human assemblage and far from the passive unity of the inert *en-soi* that scholars hastily take to be his overriding viewpoint. He recognizes our Anthropocene collective fragility, both in terms of our self-induced suicide through ecological ruin and atomic annihilation (CDR2: 306) but also in the face of planetary contingencies, such as "some sidereal catastrophe" (CDR2: 310) or some "cosmic cataclysm" (CDR2: 321) that might "exterminate our species" (CDR2: 326). Often, Sartre follows Nietzsche in adopting a Dionysian view of nature alluding to its manifold secrets and a forgotten sense of its abundance and beauty: "man is everywhere crisscrossed by Nature. He himself is a natural being, to the extent that Nature is magic" (NE 352). In *Words*, he associates closeness to nature with a pre-reflective wisdom: "truth flows from the mouths of babes and sucklings. Still close to Nature, they are cousins of the wind and the sea: their stammerings offer broad and vague teachings to him who can hear them" (W 28–9). He repeats this magical conception of nature in *Black Orpheus* as a creative power, a kind of Mother Goddess, "an enormous perpetual birth" (BO 40). In the final phase of his thinking, he re-imagines this celebratory pagan conception, formulating the concept of the "mother-matrix" that he hoped to develop into a philosophy of "Mother Earth" (HN 90).[8]

Curiously then, despite Beauvoir's *ad hominem* observations about Sartre's pervasive nausea of the natural world, it is in Sartre's theoretical work more than in her own that we find, as Mary Edwards (2023: 73) states, "the kind of ecological awareness that is associated with the term 'Anthropocene' today" in which nature is construed as having been irrevocably touched by culture within a symbiotic nature-culture continuum.[9] Although Sartre's ecosophy blossoms in the *Critiques*, the shoots of this were already growing in his early philosophy. In *Being and Nothingness*, for instance, Sartre describes "the real space of the world" as "hodological space" (BN 415). Hodological space denotes the dynamic relation between agent and environment where the subject generates a constantly fluctuating "field of force" in the course of interacting.[10] As Sartre explains, "around the other, an entire space is grouped, and this space is made with my *space*; it is a regrouping, at which I am present, and which escapes me, of all the objects that populate my universe" (BN 350). Space is thus not striated with strict divisions and boundaries but an open smooth space in which forces converge and coalesce, causing ontological dislocations in individuals through a state of transfer: "Originally, space is a qualitative and magnetic field" (NE 361). In his rich phenomenological descriptions, Sartre describes a reality in which *en-soi* and *pour-soi* share "a synthesis of depth" (BN 757) or "fusion of ends": "the for-itself's absorption by the in-itself, [is] like ink by blotting paper" (BN 790). He describes how emotions "feed" or are "nurtured" on objects as objects take on affective textures or moods; evocative qualities appear at the heart of objects in such a way that the affected subject and the affective objective are bound in an indissoluble synthesis (IM 139).

In Sartre's novel *Nausea*, Roquentin experiences a melding of the organic, inorganic, and human in his encounters, in which "things behave like living organisms, seething, growing, threatening him by their mere presence."[11] He is mired in phenomenology, experiencing a rich affective exchange with the outside world that gets inside consciousness and the body "penetrating me all over, through the eyes, through the nose, through the mouth" (N 181). Objects and bodies are far from dead lifeless matter but are alive with their own intentionalities, qualities, and dynamic uprisings, "every now and then objects start existing in your hand" (N 176). Experiencing the chestnut tree,[12] Roquentin is not an active agent but the passive recipient of sensation: "The chestnut tree pressed itself against my eyes . . . The soft sound of the water in the Masqueret Fountain flowed into my ears and made a nest there, filling them with sighs" (N 183). Objects carry their own agency—"A tree is scratching the earth under my feet with a black nail" (N 181)—and place Roquentin under their influence: "I was inside; the black stump *did not pass*, it stayed there, in my eyes, just as a lump of food sticks in a windpipe" (N 188–9). Things themselves are the carriers of sensation (N 226) and the body itself has its own motility irrespective of consciousness: "My body turns very gently towards the east, wobbles slightly and starts walking" (N 227). Roquentin feels himself to be continuous with nature (though he finds it repugnant) for "[his] body is co-extensive with the world, spread right through things" (BN 428), sharing a common existence of contingency in the same space and time: "*Superfluous*: that was the only connexion I could establish between those trees, those gates, those pebbles . . . And I—weak, languid, obscene, digesting, tossing about dismal thoughts—*I too was superfluous*" (N 184). His fate, he concludes toward the end of the novel, is to "[e]xist slowly, gently, like these trees, like a puddle of water, like the red seat in the tram" (N 223).

Existentialism has proved to be hugely revelatory in framing contemporary theory, providing the philosophical foundation for several strands in posthumanist thinking, such as *philosophical posthumanism*, *vibrant materialism*, *object-oriented ontology*, and *eco-phenomenology* that follow the existentialists in emphasizing the view of the radical interconnection of the human, non-human, and other-than-human. The "connective tissue" (BN 755) between objects and subjects in Sartre's ontology shares a close bond with posthumanist eco-aesthetics. Gernot Böhme (1995: 119), for instance, elaborates a form of biosemiotics where things in the environment are in communication with each other, a form of "being-in-communication" in which beings "tincture" the environment in which they are perceived.[13] Central to posthumanist thinking is the concept of *autopoiesis* to explain the ability of a system/organism to creatively maintain and reproduce itself.[14] This concept was elaborated by the Santiago School of Francisco Varela and Humberto Maturana, who credit Sartre's dialectical investigation in the *Critique* as their prime inspiration for it, citing a footnote where Sartre suggests:

> It is possible that a deeper knowledge of its object, through its contradictions, will force biology to consider the organism in its totality, that is to way, dialectically, and to consider all biological facts in their relation of interiority. (CDR 34n16)

For Sartre, it is matter that connects us to all other beings, but matter is not something passive, fixed, and inert to be shaped by some external force (CDR 163). Rather, it is a process of "materialization" which is dynamic, shifting, entangled, diffractional, and performative, always, as Deleuze and Guattari (1987: 451) describe it, "matter in movement, in flux, in variation, matter as a conveyor of singularities and traits of expression." Indeed, Sartre's analysis of *practico-inertia* and *counter-finality* in the *Critique* gives us a vivid illustration of how, in Jane Bennett's (2017: 447) words, "non-human things and forces actively shape the bodies they encounter, including the humans."

The *return of the object* in philosophy is associated with the High Priest of French postmodernism, Jean Baudrillard, who argued that we must proceed with an examination of the object in opposition to phenomenological and existentialist views of the subject. Ironically though, he cites Sartre's description in *Nausea* of Roquentin's raw experience of the sheer brute contingency of the chestnut tree as the inspiration for the trajectory of his theorizing.[15] Indeed, *Being and Nothingness* is *overpopulated* with phenomenological explorations of objects to the point where, as Eleanor Kaufman (2024: 671–2) comments, "were we not taught to read Sartre as a preeminent humanist existentialist philosopher, we might consider him perhaps the first of the object-oriented ontologists, someone thinking concertedly about the being of objects long before this came into fashion."

## MERLEAU-PONTY'S ECOPHENOMENOLOGY

The work of Sartre's friend and existentialist colleague, Maurice Merleau-Ponty, is paradigmatic for many ecophenomenologists and is often viewed as a philosophical bridge between existentialist phenomenology and French poststructuralism. His *ecophenomenology* is grounded in the vision of a dynamic composite interconnected self, enmeshed in the "Flesh of the World" (VI 127)—a view of the human self as free and responsible, but thoroughly entangled with others and its environment.

Like Heidegger and Sartre, Merleau-Ponty was immersed early on in the phenomenology of Husserl. This interest grew in 1939 when he visited the Husserl Archives in Louvain and read parts of Husserl's last unfinished manuscript, *Crisis*, a work in which the German philosopher moves away from his earlier idealism, replacing the abstract notion of the "Transcendental Ego" with that of the intersubjective "lifeworld." In his early work, Merleau-Ponty also builds upon Marcel's notion of *incarnation*, viewing the subject and world as a "unified gestalt" in which the world is a possibility for the body and the body is experienced as a potentiality for action in the world. In "man," however, Being ceases to fully coincide with itself as he is able to differentiate himself from it—humans transcend Being and are transcended by it: "I am not, therefore, in Hegel's phrase, 'a hole in being', but a hollow, a fold, which has been made and which can be unmade" (PP 215). Our "operative intentionality" embeds the human body in the world not as Husserlian or Cartesian epistemological spectators but as actional subjects motivated by practical interests: "Consciousness is in the first place not a matter of 'I think that', but of 'I can'" (PP 137).

Merleau-Ponty develops a philosophy of our embeddedness in "Primordial Being" intent "upon finding a primitive contact with the world, and endowing that contact with a philosophical status" (PP vii). Subject and object are not two opposed domains to be somehow united; they are both aspects of the same flesh: "the flesh seeing itself, turned upon itself, overlapping itself, folded upon itself, reversible" (PP 111). To return to things themselves as Husserl beckoned, is to return to "that world which precedes knowledge, of which knowledge always *speaks*, and in relation to which every scientific schematization is an abstract and derivative sign-language" (PP viii). The task of philosophy is thus a paradoxical one of saying the unsayable and can only proceed indirectly, allusively or metaphorically. The method of understanding the bodily human subject in the world is *dialectical*, Merleau-Ponty argues, which is to be understood as "the tending of an existence toward another existence which denies it, and yet without which it is not sustained" (PP 167–8). For Merleau-Ponty, perception is always *participatory*—the body is "possessed" by the things perceived in a profound intimacy of the ceaseless dance between the carnal subject and its world.[16] As a carnal subject, I live the world in the form of a mutual interaction, a reciprocal encroachment, an intercourse "a coition, so to speak, of my body with things" (PP 322): "the sensible takes possession of my ear or my gaze, and I surrender a part of my body, even my whole body, to this particular manner of vibrating and filling space" (PP 212). We do not encounter a lifeless world of inert matter, "our gaze, prompted by the experience of our own body, discover[s] in all other 'objects' the miracle of expression" (PP 197). Nature is thus, for Merleau-Ponty, an interconnected organic network or a biospheric web of interrelations, "an intertwined and actively intertwining lattice of mutually dependent phenomena, both sensorial and sentient," as David Abram (1997: 85) describes it, of which "our own sensing bodies are a part."

In *The Visible and Invisible* (his final book interrupted by his death in 1961), Merleau-Ponty expresses the *consanguinity* of the human animal and its world, switching emphasis from the human body to a collective materiality, a common Flesh that signifies our flesh and "the flesh of the world" (VI 127). The human body is now conceived just as one variant of "carnal being," a "prototype of Being," a unity and mysterious harmony of what touches and is touched, what sees and what is visible (VI 136, 133). We are intertwined with the flesh of the world, Merleau-Ponty contends, existing in a kind of reversibility with other beings and things:

> between my body looked at and my body looking, my body touched and my body touching, there is an overlapping or encroachment so that we must say that the things pass into us as well as we into things. (VI 123)

Perceptibility is *diacritical*, a doubling up of seen/being-seen, uttering/being-heard, a "relation of reciprocity in which neither of the relata is intelligible apart from the other" (VI 264). In contrast to what has can be perceived as the *linguistic idealism* of some poststructuralist thinking, for Merleau-Ponty language is *gestural*. Communicative meaning is always affective, rooted in the sensual dimension of carnal experience and the body's capacity to resonate with its world, inseparable from the sound, the shape, and the rhythm of the words: "Language is a life, is our life and the life of the things" (VI 125). It is related to the complexity of our earthly matrix, "the very voice of the trees, the waves, and the forests" (VI 155). Within our gestural patterns of speech, our bodies are orientated meaningfully toward objects: "the words, vowels and phonemes are so many ways of 'singing' the world" (PP 187).

Merleau-Ponty outlines the concept of the *chiasm* in *The Visible and Invisible* that he likens to a crisscross of the various sense modalities that continually conjoin into a single vision—a point of reciprocal participation in perception between our flesh and the encompassing flesh of the world. Each organism lives in a chiasmic embrace with the surrounding world that forms a matrix for its existence and its practical possibilities. In this erotic chiasmic embrace, surface is not a boundary but rather a membrane or point of access: "through this crisscrossing within it of the touching and the tangible, its own movements incorporate themselves into the universe they interrogate" (VI 133). As vectors of force and affectation, all objects in Merleau-Ponty's relational universe, as in Sartre's hodological space, incorporate themselves and are assimilated into others: "The landscape thinks itself in me, and I am its consciousness" (SNS 17).

## THE EXISTENTIALIST GARDEN

Existentialism provides a rich seam of ecological insights indispensable for a holistic understanding of our Anthropocene situation. Like a Zen Garden, the existentialist garden of the Earth is a place of mindfulness and atmospherics where the vicarious transfer of energies between things thrown together by Being takes place in a carnal dance within assemblages from which composite singularities enter and exit. From Rilke to Merleau-Ponty and all those existentialists between them, we are left with reverence for the mystery of Being and the all-encompassing matrix of existence that is the natural world. From Nietzsche's ideas of *assimilation* and the *earth as a garden*, to Heidegger's concepts of *physis* and *Gelassenheit*, Sartre's ideas of *hodological space*, the *psychoanalysis of things* and the *practico-inert*, and Merleau-Ponty's vision of the *Flesh of the World* and the *chiasm*, existentialism urges us to "remain true to the earth" through the theorizing of a dynamic conception of nature that expresses the depth of human biophilia and the evolutionary hard-wiring of a close connection to the earth. This stands refreshingly in opposition to the "earth alienation" and "earth sickness" that afflicts humanity and planet Earth in the twenty-first century.

Existentialists were early detectives and chroniclers of the collapsarian Anthropocene, an age of mass extinction, toxic poisoning, nuclear waste and radiation, petrocapitalism, and extractive colonialism that all unfold in asymmetrical power relations within a destructive, exploitative system. Nietzsche's plea for "the breath of a free, playful air" (EH 1.8) and Sartre's warning of the "pillaging of the planet" (SG 24) have been lost in an environment of "toxic embodiment" where human and non-human bodies are immersed in "transcorporeal" interactions with toxic assemblages like carcinogens, asthmagens, neurotoxins, mutagens and endocrine disruptors which flow and accumulate in exposed natural and urban environments.[17] Yet, on the horizon of collapse, the existentialists offer us some hope and guidance with the heuristic tools their philosophy has crafted to heal the skin of the earth as Zarathustra wished. This means imagining ourselves as *planetary existents* rather than global agents, a mode of identification where we pay attention to the deep history of the Earth, to the networks of assemblages, and to the myriads of singularities of which humanity is just one actant among others.

Above all, existentialism teaches us the lessons of *interconnectedness*, *entanglement*, *trans-substantiation*, and *chiasmic embrace* where there runs a line of incorporation between beings, a process of double-capture where bodies are reciprocally affected as they interact. As Nietzsche told us nearly one hundred and fifty years ago, humanity, "a courageous and richly endowed animal" has become "the most imperiled, the most chronically and profoundly sick of all sick animals" (OGM 3: 13) detached from nature and the natural within it. But this nausea or earth-sickness within "bursts from him with such violence that it at once becomes a new fetter":

> The No he says to life brings to light, as if by magic, an abundance of tender Yeses; even when he *wounds* himself, this master of destruction, of self-destruction—the very wound itself afterward compels him *to live*. (OGM 3: 13)

Staying loyal to the earth and showing a sensitivity to the vicarious causation that connects all material beings, existentialism teaches us a vibrant ecology of environmentalism, a "bestowing love" (Z 1.22.2) of care in "letting beings blossom" that suggests a positive pathway for change in the present Anthropocene Age.

CHAPTER FOUR

# "One Is Not Born, but Rather Becomes, Woman"

## (Beauvoir, *The Second Sex*) GENDER

Traditionally, gender was not a topic Western philosophy had taken much interest in other than to assume an androcentric viewpoint in which man was lionized as a rational being (*animale rationale*) and woman denigrated as a creature swayed by emotion and irrational moods. Kierkegaard, it must be said, subscribes to this traditional view of gender essentialism. In the mid-1830s, his journalistic debut in Copenhagen's Flying Post—"Another Defence of Woman's Great Abilities"—was a sardonic dismissal of female emancipation. He records in his journals of the 1840s, woman is "more sensual than man" and although religion and philosophy may see them as identical, "it is not so foolish as therefore to forget the truth of the difference, in an aesthetic and ethical light" (PJ 185). In his spat with the *Corsair*, he accuses the editors of acting "[o]nly as the woman, the weaker sex," urging them to "be a man, hold your peace" since "it is womanish to keep running after someone with expressions of spurned love just to abuse him" (PJ 219). Dismissing woman's ability to reason and show erudition, he comments how "[t]he woman is the body, she has no head, no thought worth pursuing" (PJ 253). In more recent times, Fanon has been denounced as a misogynist (for suggesting that white women fantasize about being raped by a black man) and criticized for being the absent father and typical male he accused his own father of having been.[1]

Along with John Stuart Mill (*On the Subjection of Women*, 1869), Nietzsche was one of the first philosophers to properly scrutinize gender relations and to directly consider woman's identity. In so doing, he proceeded to *deconstruct* gender and trace the relative interplay of biological, social, and psychological factors that make women and men who they are. In the twentieth century, the French existentialists continued this examination and it was "The High Priestess of Existentialism,"[2] Simone de Beauvoir, who put gender truly under the philosophical microscope with her 1940s classic *The Second Sex*, described by Lorraine Hansberry (1995: 129) in the 1960s as perhaps "the most important work of this century." With gender wars ablaze in contemporary culture, we ask in this chapter: what can Beauvoir's seminal existentialist text and other existentialists teach us today?

## *THE SECOND SEX*

Simone de Beauvoir is the emblematic intellectual woman and the quintessential feminist voice of the twentieth century. Her book *The Second Sex* published in 1949 and written to dispel the "volumes of idiocies" (SS 3) that had previously been published about gender is "the feminist Bible" for those wishing to comprehend the plight and situation for women down the centuries.[3] More cordially received in the United States than in her native France, the book sold copious amounts and became "a trumpet call to women's liberation" which, as Elizabeth Lawson (1954) described, despite some shortcomings, was a "magnificent contribution" due to its "freshness, originality, and continuous revelations and delights." Hansberry later echoed this view, cherishing *The Second Sex* as a "girlfriend" she would call on again and again, a shaft of light and a testament to her own suffering in the struggle for self-understanding and liberation.[4] As Beauvoir's records, *The Second Sex* is a text that has "troubled people's minds" and has been seriously "misread and misunderstood" (FC 191), but it is one of her greatest achievements that still holds relevance decades after it was written:

> When all is said and done, it is possibly the book that had brought me the greatest satisfaction of all those I have written . . . If I am asked what I think of it today, I have no hesitation in replying: "I'm all for it." (FC 191)

Retrospectively, Beauvoir describes how, in writing *The Second Sex,* she undertook to recount systemically, from childhood to old age, how differences between men and women were created. She examined "the possibilities this world offers women, those it denies them, their limits, their good and bad luck, their evasions and their achievements" (FC 196). Following its publication, the book, the like of which had "never been written before,"[5] generated a wave of protests and was seen as downright scandalous. She was publicly insulted and accused of attacking the "French male" by, as she put it, "some very active members of the First Sex," accusing her of being "unsatisfied, frigid, priapic, nymphomaniac, lesbian, a hundred times aborted" and even offering to cure her of her frigidity and "to temper [her] labial appetites" (FC 197). François Mauriac labeled *The Second Sex* as "extremely pornographic," writing (with some irony) to a contributor at *Les Temps Modernes*—"Your employer's vagina has no secrets from me" (FC 197). In America, the mainstream reception was less acerbic, but mainly condescending, *New Yorker* magazine describing the author of *The Second Sex* not as a serious, authentic philosopher but as "the prettiest Existentialist you ever saw."[6]

When thinking about writing a book about women, Beauvoir asked herself the initial question: "What has it meant to me to be a woman?" (FC 195). First, she had to describe the condition of women in general, starting with the myths that men have forged about her "through all their cosmologies, religions, superstitions, ideologies and literature." This took her on a "journey into history" where woman was revealed as "a by-product of the economic evolution of the masculine world" (FC 103). Once she began to delve deeply into the question of her gender, Beauvoir realized just how much being a woman had affected her life and how all women must take part in the mysterious reality known as femininity (SS 3). Femininity, she discovered, is neither a natural nor an innate entity, but rather "a condition brought about by society, on the basis of certain physiological characteristics" (PL 367). The first three chapters of *The Second Sex* criticize those who ascribe women's inferior position in society to fixed biological characteristics, innate psychological dispositions, or the necessity of economic history. According to Beauvoir, psychoanalysis is correct in concentrating on the body as "a lived reality" (SS 49) but is mistaken in refusing "the idea of choice and its corollary, the notion of value" (SS 56). Although a woman is connected intimately to her body, such that bodily functions may appear as a fixed destiny, "she is not the slave to her nerves and hormones" (SS 730) for she is not "a fixed reality, but a becoming" and her body "is not a *thing*, it is a situation" (SS 46). Thus, "[o]ne is not born, but rather becomes, woman" (SS 293). A woman's body creates a situation for her but how she lives her gender is the product of her exposure to social and cultural norms, how she internalizes them, and then re-externalizes them in the form of choices and actions: "In truth, society invests me from the day of my birth; it is the bosom of society, and in my own intimate relationship with it, that I decide who I am to be" (PL 435).

## IMMANENCE AND TRANSCENDENCE

*The Second Sex* was very much a continuation of Beauvoir's earlier work in *The Ethics of Ambiguity* (1947) structured around the explanatory couplet of *transcendence* (conscious activity, active disclosure of the world, a going-beyond, involvement with others) and *immanence* (materiality, passivity, confinement to the present). In Beauvoir's view, woman is "denied transcendence" (SS 677) and "wallows in immanence" (SS 653). Her sense of autonomy is felt as a contradiction, giving rise to frustration and resentment. The world does not appear to the woman as a set of tools halfway between her will and her goals, as Heidegger defines it: "on the contrary, it is a stubborn, indomitable resistance; it is dominated by fate and run through with mysterious caprices" (SS 654). Historically, women have been consigned to childbirth and the rearing of children, which were not freely chosen projects: "to give birth and to breast-feed are not *activities*, but natural functions; they do not involve a project" (SS 75). Through her body, woman is "more closely subjugated to the species" (SS 63) as she spends significant time and energy fulfilling natural functions. There is a biological differentiation that forms the basis for the social construction of gender inequality. Confined to the home and regime of undervalued repetitive tasks, woman has few means of expressing her transcendence since she is tied down in immanence, submitting to biological fate and social expectation: "her wings are cut and then she is blamed for not knowing how to fly" (SS 660).

By contrast, in production and warfare men are not locked into immanence since they undertake actions that transcend his animal condition and allow him to impose on things "the form that fits his project" (SS 86). A sense of powerlessness is engendered in women through being denied education and opportunities open to men and being consigned to repetitive tasks. The demands of facticity come to dictate their expectations and behavior, leaving no space for projects of transcendence, autonomy, and play. Women experience a degradation "of freedom into facticity" (SS 17) where they are "enclosed in immanence" (SS 665). Viewed from without as an object, some women fall into narcissism, romantic love, and extreme religiosity in order "to achieve transcendence through immanence," but according to Beauvoir, we can only truly achieve transcendence through the validation of our projects by others:

> It is the existence of other men that wrests each man from his immanence and enables him to accomplish the truth of his being, to accomplish himself as transcendence, as flight towards the object, as a project. (SS 163)

Some scholars sense a contradiction in Beauvoir's account in which women are presented as *ontologically free* but *situationally unfree* since many women voluntarily renounce their freedom in the form of bad faith for fear of social ostracism. The world is structured into such a way that lures them to their oppression in a way that is "nearly irresistible" (SS 770). It is perplexing, say her critics, how she accuses women of bad faith and in the next breath releases them from the responsibility of this choice by recognizing the social limitations on individual freedom, arguing that women have been forced into immanence and otherness, and that traditions imprison, determine, and limit them. Moreover, she "plummets even further down the slippery slope of determinism," according to Skye Cleary (2015: 130), when she attributes a greater weight to female biological destiny than the male.[7]

These criticisms highlight the *lived ambiguity* of woman's experience in Beauvoir's account. Although biology is an important factor in understanding gender, we can only clarify biological data "by examining them in light of ontological economic, social, and psychological contexts" (SS 48). She makes it clear that woman's character is not dictated "by her hormones or predestined in her brain's compartments: they are suggested in negative form by her situation" (SS 653). For Beauvoir, freedom always remains *situational* and bound up in the dynamic dialectic of transcendence, and transcended. The feminine is a synthesis of "economic, social and historical conditioning" (SS 653), but at the same time, the ontological transcendence of women remains in the way that they interpret and live out this synthesis: "No biological, psychical or economic destiny defines the figure that the human female takes on in society" (SS 293).

Women are in Beauvoir's mind, "[h]alf victim, half accomplice" (SS 287). The only way to understand this is by tracing the strands of this lived ambiguity, rather than stating in binaristic terms we are *absolutely free* or *absolutely determined*. In truly understanding Beauvoir, we should embrace the ambiguity and ask what these ambiguities enable in the acting out of gendered identities. "To discover woman," she argues, "we will not reject certain contributions of biology, psychoanalysis, or historical materialism: but we will consider that the body, sexual life, and technology exist concretely for man only insofar as he grasps them from the overall perspective of existence" (SS 68). Biology alone, or indeed any single axis explanation, cannot provide an answer to the question that concerns the book: "why is woman the *Other*?" (SS 48). But, according to Beauvoir, since she is beguiled by the "eternal feminine myth," "[t]he man who sets the woman up as *Other* will thus find in her a deep complicity" (SS 10). This marks a difference with other oppressed groups since "blacks endure their lot in revolt—no privilege compensates for its severity—while for the woman her complicity is invited" (SS 180). Women don't seek eliminativism. A woman "could not even dream of exterminating males" insofar as "a cleavage of society by sex is not possible" (SS 9). Although neither is a minority group, unlike proletarians, women don't say "we" and posit themselves as subjects (SS 8).

How one translates Beauvoir's epigrammatic "*On ne nait pas femme: on le devient*" depends mainly on whether you take her as a social constructionist *tout court* or as an existential phenomenologist.[8] Parshley's early translation that omits the indefinite article ("one is not born, but becomes woman") inclines us toward the former position whereas Borde and Malovny-Chevallier's later translation (" . . . a woman") implies agency, singularity and a more existentialist reading, and it is this dilemma that most sharply divides Beauvoir scholars. In Hanberry's (1995: 135–6, 139) view, Beauvoir inclines *too much* toward social constructionism in certain parts of *The Second Sex*, particularly where she dismisses women's fashion as complicity (SS 177) and takes woman's complicity to be more entrenched than for other groups (SS 180). What this overlooks is women's agency whether in the self-expression of fashion, which is "another measure of freedom not to be discredited" or the transformational capabilities of individuals and the acts of resistance against sexism's structuring oppressions. In *The Second Sex*, Beauvoir acknowledges the rebelliousness of "the Jew," "the Negro," and "the proletariat" while emphasizing the complicity of the woman. What she misses, according to Hansberry (1995: 139), is that "[w]oman like the Negro, the Jew, like colonial peoples, even in ignorance, is *incapable of accepting the role* with harmony." Her inferior role is not welcomed or complicitly accepted since it is "imposed on her by force."

While some complain that Beauvoir attributes too much immanence to women and too much transcendence to men, it is a mistake to view *The Second Sex* as a text of social constructionism for it remains an existentialist text that rejects fatalism. After all, it ends on a prophetic and messianic note when Beauvoir announces "[t]he free woman is being born" (SS 767). As inspiration for writing *The Second Sex*, Beauvoir came to realize that "there are deep analogies between the situations of women and blacks" (SS 12). After reading Gunnar Myrdal's *An American Dilemma* (1944) and Alva Myrdal's observations in "A Parallel to the Negro Problem," she became fully aware of the structuring oppression of blacks that was forced on them by conditions created by the ruling class—material inequality, cultural exclusion, stereotypes and fixed expectations, inferiority/superiority complexes. Equally however, in expressing the psychological situation of women, Beauvoir was strongly influenced by the phenomenological approach of Richard Wright that understands racism in terms of the *lived experience* of black people and W.E.B. Du Bois' *double consciousness* (the "strange experience" of perceiving oneself in the eyes of others as an undesirable or dangerous object) (SS 311).

## THE SOCIAL OTHER

The *Social Other*, a concept Beauvoir develops in *The Second Sex* to explain women's historical oppression, is one of existentialism's most valuable legacies to contemporary social theory. For Beauvoir, "Otherness" is the "original category" and alterity a "fundamental category" of human thought (SS 6). Examples she provides of others are: "For the native of a country inhabitants of other countries are viewed as 'foreigners'; Jews are the 'others' for anti-Semites, blacks for racist Americans, indigenous people for colonists, proletarians for the propertied classes" (SS 6). The woman stereotype of the "eternal feminine" (SS 4) has analogues in the stereotypes of "the black soul" and "the Jewish character" (SS 12): "whether it is race, caste, class, or sex reduced to an inferior condition, the justification process is the same" (SS 12). Historically and culturally, woman "is the Other" to the "Absolute" of the male subject, depicted as emotional, irrational, amoral, devious, vain, weak, passive, and helpless. These may sometimes describe real features but are manifestations of woman's immanence and social conditioning and not part of her "essence" (SS 17). The female has been associated in culture varyingly with nature, artifice, sexuality, purity, life, death, danger, and nurturing, but these are always in opposition to the dominant values and definitions assumed by men, which are those valorized in wider society: "This is the fundamental characteristic of woman: she is the Other at the heart of a whole whose two components are necessary to each other" (SS 9). Beauvoir analyzes how women internalize the notion of themselves as the Other—she discovers inferiority as a given essence "that imperiously modifies her consciousness of herself" (SS 312). With limited choice and the force of social pressure, women become complicit in a patriarchal society for "[r]efusing to be the Other, refusing complicity with man, would mean renouncing all the advantages an alliance with the superior caste confers on them" (SS 10).

Beauvoir's pioneering concept of the *Social Other* has been pivotal in the postmodernist quest for understanding social differentiation and revealing the discourses that sustain regimes of otherization. Luce Irigaray, for instance, develops Beauvoir's social other showing how the figure of woman has been repeatedly inscribed as the disavowed other configured as lack, excess, resource, or threat and made the object for a male subject. Taking the form of creative appropriation, proliferation, and re-signification of gendered identities rather than the affirmation of one's true self, Irigaray (1985: 355) argues for the promotion of the "Other of the Other," a space of articulation where women can define and enact their own identities. In this space, the Other/Same binary model established by patriarchal logic is replaced by "the generativity of co-constituting rhythms that shape self and other together."[9] Exploring gender, race, class and age in a theory that points toward intersectionality, Beauvoir shows how female is the Other of intimate space in the same way racialized people are the Other of geographical space, proletarians are the Other of the workspace and public space, and the old are the Other in time.[10] Despite some lacunae,[11] *The Second Sex* remains an indispensable text in its elucidation of the *Social Other* as a key tool in understanding oppression and alienation in contemporary society.

## THE SITUATION OF WOMEN (AND MEN) TODAY

Where do Beauvoir's insights sit in the contemporary world after many years of anti-discrimination and equal opportunities legislation? During her lifetime, Beauvoir witnessed great changes for women in society as they gained the same rights as men to suffrage, education, employment, divorce, and contraception.

In 1972, she published an article in *Le Nouvel Observateur* "Response to Some Women and a Man" in which she addressed criticisms that she had devalued motherhood in *The Second Sex*. She declared that motherhood can be chosen deliberately and that she was "aware of the joy that children can bring when they are wanted." She didn't want to impose her own way of life on all women since she was "actively fighting for their freedom: freedom to choose motherhood, contraception, or abortion." Women can love monogamously and maternally depending on their situation, but the myths and importance afforded to motherhood are suspect and can be damaging to both women and children.[12]

Despite some obvious improvements for women, "[w]hen I wrote *The Second Sex*," Beauvoir later judges, "my belief in the coming victory of women was premature" (ASD 498). In a lecture "The Situation of Women Today" given in Japan in 1966, she declares that feminism is "far from being outdated" and showed great concern for "antifeminist regression" that she sensed was gaining momentum. Seven years later, in a 1973 interview with Alice Schwarzer, she observes:

> Men have obviously changed. I think that the emancipation of women has actually made them more hostile towards women than they were; they have become more aggressive, more pushy, more sarcastic and more offensive, than they were in my time.[13]

Fast-forward fifty years to the present time and these sentiments still have currency. The Internet has become a global sounding board for such hostility and promotes a "vicious circle" (SS 771) of enmity between the sexes. Many social media echo chambers and pornography sites reinforce gender division and stereotyping through misogynistic portrayals of women and the brutalizing of the sexual act. Beauvoir sensed these developments as historical possibilities and was acutely aware of the complexities of gender politics in terms of the objectifying gaze of capitalist society.

Contrary to the contemporary drift toward gender enmity, Beauvoir's goal is unequivocally one of coalition building between the sexes: "The fact is that neither men nor women are satisfied with each other today . . . [but] no physiological destiny imposes eternal hostility on the Male and Female as such" (SS 769). Despite proclaiming "loud and clear, 'I am a feminist'"[14] and breaking many taboos in *The Second Sex* around female sexuality, such as lesbianism, she was acutely aware of some of the pitfalls in achieving progressive social change for both sexes. Although Beauvoir remained "warily silent" about her attractions and encounters with other women, she maintained "[w]omen should not let themselves be conditioned exclusively to male desire any more."[15] Lesbianism, she wrote, "is one way among others for women to solve the problems posed by her condition in general and by her erotic situation in particular" (SS 448). Between women, love can be contemplative and reciprocal: "caresses are meant less to appropriate the other than recreate oneself slowly through her" (SS 441). However, she was also conscious that female homosexuality could sometimes be used inexpediently as a "political weapon" by imposing "sexual dogmas" and fabricating unnecessary division between genders:

> Is it true that any sexual relationship between a man and a woman is oppressive? Couldn't one work toward, not refusing this relationship, but making it so that

> it isn't oppressive? The claim that all coitus is rape shocks me. I do not believe this. When they say all coitus is rape, they are taking up masculine myths again. That would mean that the man's sexual organ is a sword, a weapon. The issue is inventing new sexual relations that are not oppressive.[16]

In understanding political lesbianism "[w]e have to investigate why they're separatists," she states, through "an attempt to rediscover their identity as women."[17] As for herself, however, "I am absolutely against all this since it means falling once more into the masculine trap of wishing to close ourselves in our differences. I do not believe we should deny these differences; neither do I believe that we should despise or ignore them." Ultimately, she concludes, "it comes down to playing a man's game to say that the woman is essentially different than the man. There exists a biological difference, but this difference is not the foundation for the sociological difference."[18] What women seek, according to Beauvoir, is not a superficial emancipation but the "decolonization of women" (ASD 484). Refusing all masculine patterns is wrongheaded: "Just as the proletariat makes its own use of the heritage of the past, so women must take over the tools forged by men and use them for their own interests." What is called for is "a revision, not a repudiation, of knowledge" (ASD 494–5). Male/female relationships cannot be adequately understood on a *dyadic* or *interpersonal* basis since relations are always embedded in and delimited by larger collective ensembles:

> men do not define themselves first as individuals; men and women have never challenged each other in individual fights; the couple is an original *Mitsein*; and it is always a fixed or transitory element of a wider collectivity. (SS 47)

In Beauvoir's view, "[o]ne can be close to a man and be a feminist."[19] In fact, women's liberation ultimately goes hand in hand with the liberation of men as both sexes are conditioned by restrictive normative social codes: "'You are not born a male; you become one'. For masculinity is not given at the beginning, either" (ASD 484). By drifting in the universal, Beauvoir encourages men's phenomenologies and narratives alongside those of women to negotiate gender relations in contemporary capitalism. Men also face women returning discrimination as a reverse discourse in the form of anti-masculine feminism in a society where their traditional stable edifices of meaning and worth as bread-winners are heavily jeopardized. The prevalence of male suicide suggests strongly that living up to masculine norms in contemporary times can be unbearable or deeply problematic for many men. Men too are objectified for commercial gain in capitalist culture, creating a "vicious circle" where "each sex is victim both of the other and of itself" (SS 771). Beauvoir warns of the pervasive dangers and dysmorphic anxieties of commercial objectification in which "[p]arts of our bodies are displayed on the city streets for the glory of this profit-driven society." This is different to erotic literature (such as her own) since "instead of being *offered* to [individual] freedoms," bodies "are *imposed* upon all eyes that are subjected to them, willingly or not."[20] This is an extension, in her eyes, of the "abstract severity" of the objectifying gaze and its role as a narcissistic mirror in reflecting one's desired image of oneself. This contrasts with the authentic look that is not inhuman but confirms the living subjectivity of the Other, a living body in the presence of two living eyes. Beauvoir's ultimate vision is that of gender equality and authentic love where male and female are reciprocal, conscious, and free, committed to each other's projects and to each other as sexual subjects.

Despite her vast influence on feminist thinking, Beauvoir has not always been well received by second-wave or third-wave feminists. Her chapter on biology in *The Second Sex* is controversial for some feminists as she is accused of devaluing woman's body and describing women's experience of it in negative terms, referring to "the subordination of the organism to the reproductive function" as "imperious" for women (SS 44). Also, is it the case that Beauvoir underestimates the degree of freedom, praxis and creativity involved in domestic activities and the rearing of children, aspects of women's lived experience that are hardly mentioned at all? One may also point to the lack of Beauvoir's ethnographic range in describing women's experiences to the extent that it may appear, as Sheila Rowbotham (2011: xv–xvi) comments, that Beauvoir herself, a white middle-class Frenchwoman, is "the buried case study." In retrospect, Beauvoir reflected that her Hegelian framework in *The Second Sex* based on the categories of male-subject and female-object was too idealistic and could have been more materialistic (as in Sartre's *Critique of Dialectical Reason* which emphasized the categories of need and scarcity) (FC 192). "I have avoided confining myself to feminism," she stated, for women's emancipation depends also "on the future of labour in the world" (ASD 491).[21]

## EXISTENTIALISM, GENDER, AND ANDROGYNY

Although Beauvoir is ambiguous about her gender identity—"the manner in which I am and am not of my sex"—she endeavors to meld the feminine and masculine within her into a *creative synthesis*: "I want to remain a woman, still more masculine by her brain, more feminine by her sensibility."[22] When younger, she states, "I flattered myself that I combined 'a woman's heart and a man's brain'" (MDD 296). She is critical in this respect of those who, through bad faith, associate exclusively with reason *or* passion, such as when women forsake their intelligence and transcendent qualities to become "a thing of flesh" (SS 686). She celebrates the day to come when "the child [will] feel an androgynous world around her and not [just] a masculine world" (SS 778), when she is able to express the presence of both sexes within her, thereby destabilizing the fixed and firm binary oppositions of male/female. Although there are places in *The Second Sex* where Beauvoir argues for gender binarism—"The division of the sexes is a biological given, not a moment in human history" (SS 9)—she also suggests that "the very meaning of *division* of the species into two sexes is not clear" (SS 21) and, while at present "humanity is split into two categories of individuals," in the future "perhaps they are destined to disappear" (SS 4).

Nietzsche and Sartre are two other existentialists who tackle the question of gender and approach the theme of *androgyny* in their thinking. Nietzsche's ambivalence toward women is common knowledge. The philosopher whose Zarathustra advocates taking the whip to women (Z 1.18) was at the same time always gentle, polite and respectful to them. After his death, his philosophy was heralded by

German feminists, such as Lily Braun, for its defense of the individual in the face of the pressures of conformism and its "urge towards *Persönlichkeit*, the revaluation of values, the affirmation of life, the will to power." Braun found in Nietzsche "an instinct towards ennoblement" and a "religion of joy" that rejects ascetic morality "saying 'yes' to life, proclaiming a Dionysian dithyramb to woman's future."[23] In more recent times, Sarah Kofman is a philosopher who has grappled directly with Nietzsche's claim to be "the first psychologist of the eternal-feminine" (EH 3.5), presenting his work as a mixture of both positive and negative interpretations. For Kofman (1998: 44–6, 197), there is no essentialist idea of woman in Nietzsche. Instead, what we find are "Nietzsche's many heterogeneous texts on woman" in which some women are given a higher value as more life-affirmative than some men. His first nihilistic image of woman is associated with the Greek goddess Circe as a goddess of seduction, magic, and trickery who in Homer's *Odyssey* attempts to fatally entrap Odysseus and his men. By contrast, in the preface to the second edition of *The Joyous Science* (1887), Nietzsche uses the Greek female demon Baubo (the "female Dionysus"), as a symbol for "truth" as she is subversively associated with female fertility, fecundity, perspectivism and creation.

In Nietzsche's thinking, we can see a sublimating dialectic of the feminine and masculine at play. Arguably, he valorizes the feminine over the masculine but seeks like a "noble individual" to lessen "the deadly hatred between the sexes" (EH 3.5) and elide binary divisions. Nietzsche theorizes gender as *performative*. Women take up their previous articulations and failures and then enact new ones, putting on masks even when they appear to be revealing something about themselves (JS 361). The feminine art of seduction can lead astray in a negative way, like Christianity or Circe (A 44, Z 4.15), but is also positive attracting by "another ideal" (JS 382) rather than compelling or forcing (BGE 295). Dionysus is venerated as the experimenting or tempting god who *integrates* masculine and feminine principles (EH 3.6).[24] What is most important about these two drives is their interaction and reciprocity—the feminine without the masculine is simply "weak" (JS 24) while the masculine without the feminine is simply "strong" (BGE 241). Neither, on its own, is healthy or productive (TI 9.38). Zarathustra is symbolic of his "feminine-masculine" dynamic. He is accompanied at all times by the eagle (as the masculine Greek) and the snake (as the feminine Judaic) (BT 9). Indeed, *Thus Spoke Zarathustra*, the work Nietzsche valued the most of all his writings, is very much a "feminine-masculine" composite, an amalgam of poetry and philosophy that combines both his "feminine hand" and his masculine "writerly voice."[25] Thus, Nietzsche's polysemous writings on gender can be viewed productively as a deconstructive maneuver for overcoming binarisms. This leads toward an economy of the *androgynous* or ("feminine-masculine") that pluralizes rather than binarizes sexuality and gender. Significantly, Nietzsche himself, a synthesis of effeminacy and machismo, titled the fourth book of *The Joyous Science* "Sanctus Janarius," paying homage to the martyred saint known in Naples as San Gennaro for his striking feminine characteristics, soft beauty, and period bleeding. Considered both man and woman, he is the patron saint of androgyny, a perfect synthesis of the masculine and feminine.

Like Nietzsche, Sartre was brought up fatherless and lived for periods of his adult life with his mother, Anne-Marie. In interview with Beauvoir in the 1970s, he recalls the early ingrained sexism that was part of his environment and became part of him: "The domination came from my childhood. My grandfather dominated my grandmother. My stepfather dominated my mother . . . And I retained that as a kind of abstract structure . . . establishing itself as a type, a pattern" (FS 300). The violence and bullying he suffered as a schoolboy at La Rochelle made him take that violence into himself and implement "a physically confrontational masculinity" as one "who can endure hard blows" (1995: 175). Alongside learning how to box, his masculine sense of self was built around his heroic project of writing: "For a long while I treated my pen as a sword" (W 157). Although friendship with other males (Mahieu, Nizan, Aron, Merleau-Ponty, Camus, Cau) was an abiding feature of his life, these were built on philosophical allegiances rather than any kind of shared intimacy, and when these alliances split, the friendship ended in adversarialism. As he later confessed, "I can't imagine tenderness in my relation with men" (1995: 277). Continuing the filial intimacy young Jean-Paul felt from a young age with Anne-Marie, close female relationships dominated his life.

Although Sartre introduced the theme of gender into his philosophy, he never ventured headlong into the area of feminist thinking as such.[26] His early work in *Being and Nothingness* attracted some feminist criticism, particularly his discussion of viscosity and "the obscenity of the feminine sex" (BN 794) towards the end of the book. As Guillermine de Lacoste (1999: 292) argues however, his later work, as well as his work in his *Notebooks for an Ethics* in the late 1940s, belongs to an economy that aims at gender-free distinctions (active and passive/masculine and feminine). To avoid essentialism, Sartre's thinking contains the ideal of bisexuality or "the presence of both sexes" within each of us, two economies within a single person. In *Hope Now*, Sartre reconfigures the notion of *fraternity* as no longer "fraternity-terror" as he had done in the *Critique*, but as a "feeling" for a notion of "open" fraternity that extends beyond closed groups to include all of humanity. He articulates a new ideal of non-violence and fraternity based on the birth from a common Mother (HN 87) or "mother-matrix." He tells Lévy that woman has "the womb that gives life, the breasts that nourish and the back that carries," establishing a relationship where "the motivations for an act come from the affective realm" (HN 89).[27] In an interview in 1965, he aligns himself openly with a feminine economy of thinking: "But when the day comes, of course, the special qualities of [sensitivity] for which I prefer the company of women will be due purely to chance . . . They'll cease to be a feminine prerogative."[28] Ten years later, he tells Beauvoir that there was a sort of woman inside him (1976a: 116). In his final years, he fulfills the project articulated in *Notebooks for an Ethics* of "getting rid of one's ego," reaffirming and reinforcing the notions of reciprocal giving and tenderness (1977b: 81).

Enacting the "dialectical development" of "the feminine and masculine poles of the world" (BN 779), on a personal level Sartre follows Nietzsche and Beauvoir in identifying himself as *androgynous*. Referring to Flaubert's "androgynous nature," he states, "I'm certainly androgynous myself, which is not a flaw" (1979b: 37). In another interview, he attributes sensitivity and subjectivity to women and rationality and objectivity to men but states that there are some "men-women" (*hommes-femmes*) who have more subjectivity, a point of androgyny with which he himself identifies: "I was to have the sex of angels, indeterminate but feminine around the edges."[29] He views himself as "*homme-femme*"—"although I'm still male, I'm only very faintly so" (FS 285)—and declares his attraction for androgyny in men, that is, those who have not split their masculine and feminine sides. Summing up his view of gender identity, Sartre advocates a passage beyond traditional binary conceptions of gender, presaging the postmodern turn toward gender multiplicity, androgyny, and fluidity: "male and female is a somewhat primitive sexuality—generally speaking, there are things over and above that. In itself, that's a matter of some importance" (FS 285).

Existentialism was the first philosophical school to properly deconstruct the notion of gender, and there is much our thinking can learn from its androgynous economy. Beauvoir's central insight that "[o]ne is not born, but rather becomes, woman" (SS 293) and, equally, "[y]ou are not born a male; you become one" (ASD 484) manifests the intimate dialectic between freedom and necessity and the complex interplay between the "three ecologies" of *body*, *society*, and *self* that makes us who we are. *The Second Sex* remains an authoritative, fecund, and trailblazing text for feminism and gender studies despite its problematic and myopic aspects that, as Kathryn Belle (2024) highlights, caused Beauvoir to sabotage some of her better insights she should have traveled further with.

In *Beauvoir in Time*, Meryl Altman (2020: 5–6) urges us to revisit Beauvoir's work in contemporary times since she has been particularly ill-served, in both France and the United States, by feminist theorists "who while continuing to appropriate her insights, also used her as a kind of transference fetish—idealized icon and/or punching bag—rather than responding to what she actually wrote." Above all, Beauvoir provided a philosophical idiom, a set of terms and concepts that open up a way for a developed intersectional account of gender identity showing how existentialism "is still 'good to think with' *now*." In a 1976 interview with John Gerassi, Beauvoir acknowledges the limits of *The Second Sex* and suggests if it were repeated, it should be a "collective effort" with different women speaking from diverse situations and backgrounds and rooted in practice rather than theory:

> What is really needed is that a whole group of women, from all sorts of countries, assemble their lived experiences, and that we derive from such experiences the patterns facing women everywhere, What's more, such information should be amassed from all classes.[30]

Sporadically, Beauvoir does show an awareness of the different intersectional factors in one's identity and choices, when for instance, she addresses women's lack of solidarity with other groups—"As bourgeois women, they are in solidarity with bourgeois men and not with women proletarians; as white women, they are in solidarity with white men and not with black women" (SS 8)—as well as their conservatism—"If she belongs to the privileged elite that profits from the given social order, she wants it unshakable" (SS 641). By extending Beauvoir's insights into intersectionality, it is possible to concretize her coalitional approach further and engage in what Maria Lugones calls a "complex communication" that recognizes all marginalizations and is attuned to difference, multiplicity, and belonging.[31]

Beauvoir's influence as a philosopher continues to grow. In France, there has been a renewed interest in her work. In a 2003 conference, the philosopher Julia Kristeva gave Beauvoir more credit (for advancing feminism by conceiving gender as *performative*) than she had previously in her 1979 essay "Women's Time" (when she accused Beauvoir of valorizing masculinist norms). What weds Beauvoir's work to the present, above all, is her *interdisciplinary* approach, combining phenomenology, sociology, biology, history, anthropology, and economics into an overarching existentialist narrative. She provides an interlocking account of the subject as an ambiguous, mutually shifting balance of the three ecologies of a *body-social-self* continuum that rejects one-axis approaches (SS 67). Judith Butler's postmodern idea of gender identity as *performative* has borrowed heavily from Beauvoir's existentialist account of the self not as "a fixed reality, but a becoming" (SS 45).

Beauvoir's existentialist legacy lives on like a parturient force in the contemporary mind. The posthumanist movement of xenofeminism, for example, described as "an intersectional universal" assembled from the needs of "every human, cutting across race, ability, economic standing, and geographical position" takes existentialist inspiration in building bridges between all of us who together share, suffer and co-experience the historical and chronological now.[32] As Rachel Jones (2024: 335) comments, recent feminist philosophy is significantly "indebted to and in generative tension with Beauvoir's approach." Coming "after Beauvoir" is both a chronological and a substantive issue as feminists variously seek to "continue, contest or shift away from her philosophical and ethical approach." Although she is sometimes accused of being downbeat at the prospect of liberating women (and men) in the future due to the "mystifications" of the feminine condition and the stubborn intransigence of patriarchy, she does embed a silver lining in *The Second Sex* and in interviews later in her life. Freedom can always break the circle and "create new situations" (SS 780), and although downtrodden, women's lack of power has resulted in many positive qualities such as "patience, sympathy, irony," which, she adds, men should strive to acquire.[33] Toward the end of the text she advises that women "must refuse the limits of their situation and seek to open paths to the future" (SS 664) that will make possible "new carnal and affective relations of which we cannot conceive" (SS 781). Only a lack of imagination can impoverish the future: "tomorrow's humankind will live the future in its flesh and in its freedom" (SS 781). In a prophetic voice that echoes through the years, she announces "[t]he free woman is being born" (SS 767). Hence, describing Beauvoir, Judith Wilson heralds her as quintessentially "Other"—a thinker "who stole patriarchal fire to blaze liberatory trails" and whose radical impact remains the benchmark for critical social theory.[34]

CHAPTER FIVE

# "Racism, Hatred, Resentment . . . Alone Cannot Nurture a War of Liberation"

## (Fanon, *The Damned of the Earth*) RACE

Above all other philosophical schools and *isms*, existentialism put the issue of race on the philosophical map. Following the naturalist turn of the late nineteenth century in Europe, Nietzsche was one of the first philosophers to grapple directly with the question of race and began a long existentialist dialogue that would culminate a century or so later in Frantz Fanon's benchmark text, *The Damned of the Earth* that remains authoritative today in the study of Critical Race Theory, more than sixty years since it was written. As we will see in the course of this chapter, when we scan ideas of race in existentialist thinking from Nietzsche through Heidegger and then to the French existentialists, we get a variant picture and see the full spectrum from the worst kind of deep-rooted racism to the most defiant and stentorian anti-racism.

## EXISTENTIALISM AND ANTI-SEMITISM

As Robert Bernasconi (2023: 248) judges, in terms of race/ism, Nietzsche is very much a "transitional figure." His rejection of anti-Semitism and advocacy of racial mixing demonstrate a progressive edge to his thinking, but his promotion of a racialized biopolitics was grist to the mill for the later Nazi ideologues. Scrutinizing the three modalities of history (monumental, antiquarian, and critical) in terms of their use for life, he showed a commitment to racialized breeding and combined it with a celebration of certain forms of human extinction, thereby showing how easily the theme of evolutionism could turn into a justification for eugenics and genocide. In doing so, he conjoined philosophical speculation with naturalist science as part of the burgeoning discourses of race in the mid to late nineteenth century influenced by Lamarck, Darwin, and Galton.

In the Germany of Nietzsche's time, anti-Semitism was rife. Nietzsche's one-time mentor and inspiration Richard Wagner was not alone when, in "The Jews in Music" (1850), he vilified Judaism as "the evil conscience of modern civilization." Nietzsche however was a dissenting voice against anti-Semitism and lambasts Wagner for promoting it, criticizing anti-Semites as "speculators in idealism . . . who today roll their eyes in a Christian-Aryan-bourgeois manner and exhaust one's patience by trying to rouse up all the horned-beast elements in the people by a brazen abuse of the cheapest of all agitator's tricks, moral attitudinizing" (OGM 3: 27).

Nietzsche's views of Judaism are in the main mixed with admiration and disapproval. Above all, he associates Judaeo-Christian morality with the revolt of slave-morality and the victory of *ressentiment*: "the Jews, that priestly people, who in opposing their enemies and conquerors were ultimately satisfied with nothing less than a radical revaluation of their enemies' values, that is to say an act of *spiritual revenge*" (OGM 12: 7). Although he complains that the stock-exchange Jews were "perhaps the most repulsive invention of the whole human species," he thought Jewish people would be "just as usable and desirable an ingredient" of a new mixed European race as "the remains of any other nation." He describes Jews as a spirited "quality race" (WP 864), who rank well above the Germans in terms of "an unequalled popular-moral genius" (OGM 1: 16). Commending them for "their energy and higher intelligence, their capital of spirit and will," Nietzsche thanks the Jews "to whom we owe the noblest human being (Christ), the purest philosopher (Spinoza), the mightiest book, and the most effective moral code in the world" (HH 475). Rallying against the overt anti-Semitism of his times, Nietzsche calls upon his readers to "(a)ssociate with no man who takes part in the mendacious race-swindle."[1]

Nietzsche conceives race in terms of *inheritance*, although he more generally views this as social rather than genetic. Specific traits can be realized through breeding and social practices (OGM 2: 7). Although he advocates miscegenation, he warns that when races mix that have long been separated, the resulting hybrids are indecisive and lack a sense of balance. As a philosopher of the future, his wish is to create or breed a race rather than preserve one in order to produce a "stronger" type, the *Übermensch*. He declares in no uncertain terms that this will entail "[t]he annihilation of the decaying races" (WP 862). Above all, Nietzsche's discussions of racialized breeding brought into focus the biopolitics of the state and the colonization of race through techniques of biopower, a form of racism modeled on war, economics, science, and political control.

Heidegger interprets Nietzsche as a metaphysical thinker and not a biologist, following him in condemning all those who participate "in the fake race-swindle" (GA90: 254). However, Heidegger's promotion of anti-Semitic racialized thinking within his philosophy of historical Being (*Seinsgeschichte*) is existentialism's bleakest legacy and ethical *cul-de-sac*. The deep-rooted anti-Semitic sentiments he (and his wife Elfride) expressed in private, as well as the many anti-Semitic actions he undertook while Rector at Freiburg University from 1933–4, are well documented. As early as the 1920s, Heidegger proclaims himself as a "spiritual anti-Semite" opposed to Germany's escalating Jewish "infestation."[2]

The publication of Heidegger's *Black Notebooks* in 2014 has given even greater bite to his fiercest critics, such as Richard Wolin, who regard his philosophy and politics as twin bedfellows where "his anti-Jewish enmity forms the basis of this philosophical diagnostics." For Wolin (1990: 83), Heidegger's anti-Semitism is no "judgemental myopia," "accidental miscue," or "philosophically inconsequential *lapsus*" despite his own exculpatory remarks or the attempt of some neo-Heideggerians to place a *cordon sanitaire* between his philosophy and his life. Developing the categories of

*Being and Time*, Heidegger presents race as an existential prism of experience or "mood" that conditions Dasein's relations with others as an embodied being: "What we call 'race' is related to the bodily" (GA38: 65). As "[m]ood makes manifest 'how one is' . . . and brings Being to its 'there'" (BT 173), *Existenz* is fundamentally and inevitably racial. The emphasis on race increases after 1932 and Heidegger's turn can be seen in this respect as a "racial *Kehre*"[3] that replaces the parochialism of "ownmost potentiality-for-Being" with the collective orientation of the national community or *Volksgemeinschaft*. [4] *Black Notebooks* II–VII document Heidegger's switch from "existential ontology" to the "history of Being," a move from "sterile" first philosophy to "metapolitics," that is, the "metaphysics of German Dasein," a redemptory mission or salvific role to German Dasein as an onto-historical elect.

Heidegger's *Volkish* theory of the singularity of "western-Germanic historical Dasein" is predicated on the notion of German exceptionalism: "*only someone who is German is capable of poetically articulating Being in an originary way*" (GA94: 27). In his *Heraclitus Lectures* (1942), he develops the imperialist vision of Germany as "master of *Mitteleuropa*" since the Germans and they alone can save the West for its history: "The planet is in flames. The essence of man is out of joint, only from the Germans can there come a world-historical reflection—if, that is, they find and preserve 'Germanness'."[5] Appealing to the "primordial laws of our Germanic tribal heritage" (GA36/7: 89), he invokes the idiolect of "racial hygiene": "The breeding of ever-higher thought-forms is of greater importance than the mere communication of knowledge" (GA94: 124). These "thought-forms" can be traced back to the pre-Socratic Greeks, in particular, Heraclitus, who stands as a symbol of the "primordial power of western-germanic Dasein."[6]

According to Heidegger, in Kantianism and liberalism, "the essence of man is dissolved into a free-floating consciousness . . . and a universally logical 'world reason,'" thus diverting attention "from man *in his historical rootedness*, his folkish tradition, and his origins in *soil* and *blood*." As a result, "man becomes a servant of an indifferent world culture" (GA16: 132). The rootlessness of contemporary life is the basis of an escalating disintegration where attempts at renewal and innovation will remain hopeless unless we succeed in returning "to the nurturing powers of our native soil" (GA16: 55). This Heidegger refers to as "*Heimat*," a homeland where I am born and grow old: "A *Heimat* is something I have on the basis of my birth . . . A *Heimat* expresses itself in *rootedness-in-soil* and *being bound to the earth*."[7] Rootedness has ontological significance for Heidegger, wherein the capacity for ontological insight is racially encoded. Rootless peoples (e.g., "World-Jewry") are viewed as ontologically deficient, incapable of grasping and articulating Being (GA96: 46). In *Nature, History and State* (1934), Heidegger considers the Jews as an "anti-race" (*Gegen-Rasse*) that lacks the authenticity of "rootedness-in-soil":

> The nature of our *German* space is revealed in a distinctly different manner to a Slavic *Volk* than it is to us. *In the case of Semitic nomads, it will perhaps never be revealed at all.*[8]

As the primary carrier of an empty rationality and calculability, Jewishness represents chaos and mechanism, at once disorganizing and sterilizing (GA96: 67). Heidegger accuses the Jews of being hidden string-pullers, conspiratorially impossible to "pin down" and thus "ungraspable" (GA96: 262). Ultimately, as rootless, Jews do not *have a world* (Heidegger's ontological criterion for being human) and are therefore more like plants or stones than they are humans. In his 1949 Bremen Lectures on "Technology," Heidegger accuses the Jews of dying an irresolute inauthentic death: "Hundreds of thousands die en masse. Do they die? They perish" (GA79: 56). His "*Technik*-critique" is bound up with his anti-Semitism in a form where the Jews bear responsibility for their own "self-annihilation": "One of the stealthiest forms of Gigantism, and perhaps the most ancient, is the fast-paced *cleverness of calculation, huckstering, and intermingling* whereby [world] Jewry's *worldlessness* is established" (GA95: 97). Displacing moral agency from the National Socialist state, he insinuates in *Letter on Humanism* (1947) that "reason," "subjectivity," and "metaphysics" are ultimately responsible for the Final Solution. Practicing a kind of Holocaust inversion,[9] he attributes responsibility to the Jews for their own "self-annihilation" thereby distorting, relativizing, or flipping the roles of perpetrator and victim: "When the essentially 'Jewish' in the metaphysical sense struggles against what is Jewish, the zenith of self-annihilation has been achieved" (GA97: 20). In Heidegger's Volkish account, the Jewish apparatus of modern "technics" turned against the Jews themselves.

As was clearly evident in his 1966 *Spiegel* interview ("Only a God can Save Us"), Heidegger never revokes the view that "*National Socialism moved in the right direction*" or shows any *prise de conscience* concerning the atrocities of Nazism. Contrasting his own view with "vulgar National Socialism," he maintains that the National Socialist Revolution was "the work of men who seek to realize *a new spiritual order*" (GA16: 151).[10] For Heidegger racial thinking (*Rassengedanke*), in which each Volk possesses unalterable racial character, is not just purely a biological question but a spiritual mission of regeneration. *Ethnos* rather than *demos* is the primary carrier of historicity and the driving force of Heidegger's History of Being. His analysis, as Eric Nelson (2016: 488–90) comments, is "beholden to ethnocentrism," centered on a Greco-Germanic axis that marginalizes and minimizes multiplicity and perspective. He failed to confront his own personal complicity in the 1930s, never disavowed its political or normative aims and showed continuing resistance to the denazification campaign working against him. He exhibited no care or concern for injustice or the obliteration of human rights and considered democracy to be a greater form of fascism. Exhibiting "fundamental thoughtlessness" and "banal indifference" to suffering, when he laments the loss of life, it is only German lives that concern him. This "inability to think" within his later History of Being is almost welcomed by Heidegger himself as he extinguishes philosophy altogether, replacing it with the "metapolitics" of "deed" and "struggle" after his racial turn in the 1930s: "Today, we must finally put an end to philosophizing, since *Volk* and race are no longer adequate to it. Its power shrivels and is degraded to the point of impotence" (GA94: 66).

Fearful of "democratic invention," and of "a public space where freedom could appear" (Arendt),[11] Heidegger's racial thinking catapults his philosophy into contradiction. Although he inveighed against "the reduction of the intellect to technics," this did not prevent him, as Emmanuel Levinas (1974: 170) comments, "from supporting a brutal regime more inhuman than the machine age he criticized." Also, despite being highly critical of "Plato's Doctrine of Truth" in the 1930s, he was strongly enamored of the "draconian-authoritarian features of Plato's Spartan-influenced political doctrine," a concept of the "Total State" in which there will be enacted a comprehensive capture of the individual. In his excoriation of "inferior races," such as Slavs, Africans, and, especially, Jews, he praises "[e]xtermination . . . [as] that which assures [Germany] against the prospect of defeat" (GA50: 70). With its romanticized images of a pastoral *Heimat* and "rootedness-in-soil," the "steely romanticism" of Heidegger's philosophy (and Nazi ideology) may have started off green but, through the prism of ethnocentric racial thinking, as Wolin (2022: 118, 82) comments, it "soon became bloody red."

It was in Post-Occupation Paris in the 1940s that a *critique of racism* found a genuine home in existentialism. Sartre's critical analysis of anti-Jewish ideology in *Anti-Semite and Jew* (1946) lies in stark opposition to Heidegger's ethnocentric History of Being. By understanding racism, Sartre's hope was to eradicate it completely and create a society free of oppression, whereas Heidegger's racial thinking was designed to reinforce hierarchy, justify German supremacy, and usher in the Total State of the Teutonic nation. In this book, Sartre employs his existential concepts of *the gaze* and *bad faith* to understand anti-Semitism in the minds of its victims as well as its perpetrators. Famously, near the beginning of the book, he states: "If the Jew did not exist, the anti-Semite would have to invent him" (ASJ 8). Sartre rejects the idea that there is some fixed essence shared by Jewish people, a nature fixed by ethnicity (ASJ 25–6). But he also rejects "the democrat" who denies any significant difference between ethnic groups (ASJ 55). This is also a means "to suppress the Jew" (ASJ 144). Whereas the first view obliterates the person and makes the person "all Jew," the second dissolves the Jew and makes them "all person" (ASJ 57). But, Sartre argues, we must accept that it is the whole Jewish person "with his character, his customs, his tastes, his religion if he has one, his name" (ASJ 147) and not just some abstract version of humanity. "Man always the same in all times and all places" (ASJ 55), does not exist—"there are Jews, Protestants, Catholics, there are Frenchmen, Englishmen, Germans; there are whites, blacks, yellows" (ASJ 144–5).

According to Sartre, the Jewish person can respond to their situation either inauthentically or authentically. In inauthenticity they attempt to deal with their situation "by running away from it" (ASJ 92) by accepting that there are such things as ethnic essences, even if the features of which are different to those ascribed by the oppressor. In order to counter the idea that "Jews are dishonest by nature," for example, the Jew might assert the opposite—that Jews are innately honest. Authenticity, by contrast, means avoiding bad faith and fixed ethnic essences by recognizing that the authentic individual "is what he makes himself, that is all that can be said" (ASJ 137). The authentic Jew must embrace their situation and take pride in humiliation by asserting their Jewishness as a set of cultural traits they have freely chosen. There are authentic individuals, Sartre adds, but these are rare for "[t]here is no doubt that authenticity demands much courage and more than courage" (ASJ 90).

In later years, the perceived hebreophilia of Sartre and Beauvoir became the source of some controversy. Quite possibly, the coterie of Jewish friends, partners (Claude Lanzmann), adopted children (Arlette Elkaïm Sartre, Sylvie le Bon), and intellectual collaborators (Benny Lévy) they were surrounded by may have influenced their judgment on the question of Zionism, Israel's sovereignty, and Jewish messianism. One must also remember the lasting psychological scars of the 1930s and 1940s, a time when, as Beauvoir wrote, "[t]here were tens of thousands of Jews wandering over the face of the globe in order to escape the torture chamber or the concentration camp" (PL 358). They have both been accused of expressing pro-Israeli sentiment and thereby turning a blind eye to Palestinian suffering. Josie Fanon, Frantz's wife, for instance, wrote to the publisher Maspero requesting that Sartre's preface be omitted from all future editions of *The Damned of the Earth* "because of the pro-Zionist and pro-imperialist position taken by its author with respect to Zionist aggression against Arab peoples." More specifically, he had publicly defended Israel's actions in the Six-Day War of June 1967 and signed a petition that had described Israel as being under threat from its Arab neighbors and denying it was part of "the imperialist camp."[12] In *All Said and Done*, Beauvoir recognizes how her support for Israel as an independent state ostracizes her from many on the Left but does not view Israel as colonialist or as a "bridgehead for imperialism" (ASD 436). However, she does urge it to return the territories it has occupied and to stop all aggression (ASD 437).

Clearly, from the outset Sartre and Beauvoir were pulled both ways by the Israel-Palestine conflict and tried to maintain a balanced, considered view. On several occasions, they both signed petitions for peace and non-aggression between Israel and Arab countries. Torn between his intimate circle of Jewish friends and the friendships he had cultivated with many Arabs during the Algerian War, Sartre announced in December 1965 that they would publish an issue of *Les Temps Modernes* presenting both sides of the Israel-Palestine argument. After visiting kibbutzim and talking to Arabs in Israel in 1967, his mood changed as he voiced doubts about the right to the sovereignty of an Israeli state when weighed against the interests of the million Palestinian inhabitants that had been expelled from the territory. Increasingly, Sartre came to question whether Israeli sovereignty was compatible, in the concrete form it had assumed, with the freedom, rights, and self-determination of the Palestinian people. In 1976 he received an honorary degree from the University of Jerusalem and in his acceptance speech he said he wanted to promote a productive dialogue between Israel and Palestine: "I have been Israel's friend for a long time . . . but I am also concerned with the Palestinian people, who have suffered a great deal." He spoke of his travels in Egypt and said he would gladly accept a similar honor from the University of Cairo if offered to him (FS 97). As Beauvoir reports, he felt strong sympathy for the Palestinians and concern for the direction of the Israeli state: "I never met a single Arab who felt satisfied with his life in Israel. I never met a single Arab who said that at the present moment he had the same rights an Israeli citizen" (ASD 422). In 1972, following the murder of Israeli athletes at the Munich Olympics, he did not condemn the Palestinians involved: "a state of war exists between the Palestinians. In this war the Palestinians' only weapon is terrorism" (2003: 7). Since

"Israel would reject all concessions" this was their only option even if this did not advance their cause tactically. What is urgently needed, Sartre said, is a negotiated settlement and an agreement upon the limits of violence: "we must now, right away, solve the Palestinian problem and this problem has become everyone's" (2003: 7).

*Anti-Semite and Jew* was existentialism's first foray into understanding and condemning racism, developing critical tools Sartre would sharpen in the years that followed 1946. Even after the Liberation and during the Occupation, he had seen the humiliation and fear of Jewish people in France. The main thrust of his arguments in the book was against anti-Semitism rather than being pro-Jewish. Taking inspiration from Richard Wright's idea that "there is no Negro problem in the United States, there is only a White problem" (ASJ 152), he presents racial prejudice as an irrational passion in the mind of the anti-Semite who "makes the Jew" in order to objectify, Otherize and ultimately subordinate him. Moreover, he viewed racism as pervading every facet of the individual anti-Semite, forming a "syncretic totality" that frames their view of the world (ASJ 10). Over time, Sartre appreciated that Jewish identity is not something that is entirely fabricated by the anti-Semite, but also has been sedimented over thousands of years of Hebraic teaching, Yiddish texts, and Jewish messianic culture. The Jewish person is not an empty shell once we strip away the external characteristics assigned by the anti-Semite. The cultural identity of the Jew is grounded in the situation that is common to Jewish people who must formulate their projects in the light of it.[13] He admitted in later years that his book was well intended but superficial: "I wrote without any documentation, without reading one Jewish book. . . I wrote what I thought."[14] For Sartre, anti-Semitism "is a total choice that a man in a situation makes of himself and of the meaning of the universe" (ASJ 148). Therefore, to battle anti-semitism we must change the situation that produces the perspective that chooses it: "Thus we do not attack freedom, but bring it about that freedom decides on other bases, and in terms of other structures" (AS 148). In *Anti-Semite and Jew*, Sartre recognizes that he had started at the level of the individual but that only a transformation of society could eradicate anti-Semitism: "it could not exist in a classless society" (ASJ 149). But at this stage he lacked the full conceptual resources to take this enquiry further.

## RECIPROCAL INFLUENCES

There is a reciprocal curve of influence between certain strains of Afro-American thought and French existentialism. In 1903 the American sociologist, writer, and political activist W.E.B Du Bois formulated the idea of a "double consciousness" in *The Souls of Black Folk*, highlighting the way in which it is impossible to have a unified or singular identity under conditions of oppression. Bound by facticity and received social meanings but also a self that freely determines itself through projected meanings, black consciousness is haunted by "a sense of always looking at one's self through the eyes of others, of measuring one's soul by the tape of a world that looks on in amused contempt and pity."[15] In *The Comet* (1920), Du Bois explores absurdity through the filter of racial segregation and oppression. A bank employee Jim is sent to an underground vault to retrieve some papers and survives the impact of a comet spewing poisonous gas colliding with Earth. He appears for a while to be the sole survivor of the catastrophe and for the first time enjoys everyday activities, like entering a restaurant on Fifth Avenue previously forbidden for black people. After briefly enjoying his freedom and forming a liberating relationship with a white survivor, other survivors steadily emerge and soon racial segregation is re-established. Du Bois' story suggests that not even an Apocalypse or some great catastrophe can cleanse human society of racial discrimination altogether. Another black American writer Ralph Ellison brings existentialist concerns together with the inspiration of jazz in *The Invisible Man* (1952). The novel follows the protagonist who falls down a manhole during a riot, which is then covered over by police officers. He lives underground in a forgotten basement section of a building and ponders the invisibility of black people in a racially oppressive society. Finally, he realizes that he must enter back into society, assume a communal sensibility, and a responsibility for the essential unity of human experience as a whole by transcending racial division.

Alongside entries in her autobiographies, Beauvoir's view of America is summarized in two pieces, "An Existentialist Looks at Americans" (which appeared in the *New York Times* magazine in May 1947) and *America Day by Day* (1948), a travelogue documenting her four-month stay in America in 1947. In tune with Heidegger's sentiments in his 1946 essay "What Are Poets For?" that America was importing into Europe "empty indifferent things, sham things, dummies of life" (1971: 113), Beauvoir was struck by the crass commercialism she saw everywhere:

> The fact is that the word "abstraction" constantly comes to mind when I try to define my vision of America . . . With quality lacking, the only measure that remains with which to estimate the work and achievement of man is a quantitative one—money (PW 311)

On the other side, there was much to excite her about America's vibrancy and its counter-culture, which she experienced first-hand when she visited Nelson Algren. Impressed by the service of Reverend Adam Clayton Powell Sr. at the Abyssinian Baptist Church in New York, she describes it as "less of a religious gathering than a political meeting" (1952: 50) which led her to become interested in the plight of black people in America and their way of expressing it through art and culture. She dedicated *America Day by Day* to Richard and Ellen Wright with whom she became good friends on her visits to the United States. In 1940 she read Wright for the first time and, in its inaugural issue, *Les Temps Modernes* published one of his stories "Fire and Cloud" which Sartre held up as a model of "engaged literature." Wright's novel *Native Sun* and autobiography *Black Boy* gave Beauvoir a literary model for describing alterity and the effects of inequality on self-identity as she explored in *The Second Sex*. Inspired by Dostoevsky, Kierkegaard, and Heidegger, Wright employed existentialist themes of freedom, anxiety, loneliness, and dread in "The Man Who Lived Underground" (1942). He introduced her to the book *American Dilemma: The Negro Problem and Modern Democracy* (1944), written by Gunnar Myrdal, a Swedish sociologist, that had a profound influence on her thinking. The Wrights brought to life for Beauvoir the stark, grim realities of racial segregation and prejudice:

> From the cradle to the grave, working, eating, loving, walking, dancing, praying, he can never forget that he is black, and that makes him conscious every minute of the whole white world from which the word "black" takes its meaning. Whatever he does, a negro remains in "bondage." (1952: 50)

Reading Myrdal's book and conversing with the Wrights about the racialized dimensions of American society made her "begin again to think about the book I began about women's situation." In order to properly explore society's gendered dimensions, she ventured, "I should like to write a book as important as this big one."[16]

Sartre was also friends with the Wrights, and he flags a clear influence on his thinking in *Anti-Semite and Jew*: "Richard Wright, the Negro writer, said recently: 'There is no Negro problem in the United States, there is only a white problem'. In the same way we must say that anti-Semitism is not a Jewish problem; it is our problem" (ASJ 152). In *Notebooks for an Ethics*, he also references Myrdal's *An American Dilemma* as an influence on his thinking in his analysis of oppression, racism, and slavery. In his childhood and youth, Sartre held a romanticized image of American freedom and adventure that he fed with the novels of Dos Passos and Hemingway alongside American film, music and culture which he wrote about in his essay "I Discovered Jazz in America" (published in *The Saturday Review* in November 1947). Politically speaking, however, he was well aware of its capitalist and racist underbelly. In 1946 he broached the question of racism in America in a series of articles denouncing the Jim Crow Laws and, in *The Respectful Prostitute*, a controversial play deemed at the time as "anti-American" in which a black man is framed for a crime he did not commit in order to exonerate a young abusive but well connected white man. Lizzie, the central character knows "the Negro" is innocent but, compromised as she is by her own profession as a prostitute, is bribed by a senator and his son to lie and condemn the innocent black man to death. The play grimly illustrates the brutal racism of white society and the hopeless plight of the black person, themes that he developed in greater philosophical detail in his 1949 essay *Black Orpheus*.

## *BLACK ORPHEUS*

*Black Orpheus* was Sartre's response to a request to write a Preface to an anthology of poetry by Black Francophone writers edited by Léopold Sédar Senghor who was a major figure within the *Négritude* movement in 1940s France. Instead of a brief introduction, Sartre composed a major interpretative essay, privileging the dialectical account and brand of universalism of Aimé Césaire over the backward-looking perspective of Senghor by calling upon Blacks to sacrifice their negritude in favor of the realization of the human in a raceless society. The essay's title alludes to Orpheus, the lyrical musician and poet of Greek mythology, who descends to the Underworld to rescue his love, Eurydice. Turning around to look back as he is leaving, he loses her and is torn apart by the followers of Dionysus, the God of wine and frenzy.

Sartre compares this to the descent of the negritude poets into blackness where critical reflection or reason becomes the black person's downfall.

Oppressed in body and soul, Sartre argues, black people are alienated "in the midst of the cold buildings of the white culture and the white techniques" (BO 19). To remove the chains of oppression, they are forced to return to African culture, a "redescent into the burning Hell of the black soul" (BO 21). Although the "Negro, like the white worker, is a victim of the capitalistic structure of our society" (BO 14), his situation is different. Where the proletarian looks outwards to the objective conditions of his situation, "exactly the opposite of a redescent into one's self" (BO 13), a black person retreats into subjectivity and poetry, placing him "upon the terrain of Reflection, where he wishes to rediscover in himself certain objective traits growing out of African civilizations, or hopes to find the black Essence in the wells of his soul" (BO 17). For Sartre, the beliefs of a given society are captured in "the untranslatable locutions of its language" (BO 22). Because they have no common language, the black poets of the African diaspora have to appropriate the adopted language of the white colonizer in order to express their thoughts: "to incite the oppressed to unite they must have recourse to the words of the oppressor . . . It is in this language, pale like the flesh of the chicken, pale and cold as our gods . . . they communicate" (BO 22–3). However, their use of the French language is deconstructive, enacting "the holocaust of words" and the "auto-destruction of the language" (BO 25) and subverting the language that consecrates the priority of white over black (BO 27). Negritude thus functions as "a sort of poetic psycho-analysis" (BO 58) in which the black man must overcome the facticity of blackness: "it is at the bottom of his heart that he finds race and it is his heart which he must tear" (BO 63).

Using a dialectical method, Sartre conceives negritude as a "dialectic law of successive transformations" that empowers the black man to coincide with himself in his negritude (BO 31), a "moment of separation or of negativity" (BO 15) or "anti-racist racism" that paves the way for the abolition of racial and ultimately class differences (BO 59). Although the poets of negritude are returning their "steady and corrosive gaze" on the white man who "has enjoyed for three thousand years the privilege of seeing without being seen" (BO 10,7), they must celebrate but ultimately disavow their color. Negritude must surpass itself as it appears as the weak stage of a dialectical progression. In order to achieve the universal, the specific must annul itself. Black people must paradoxically renounce what they have achieved in the same way that "the white worker also takes conscience of his class to deny it, since he wishes the advent of a society without class" (BO 62): "At a blow the subjective, existential, ethnic notion of negritude 'passes' as Hegel would say, into the objective, positive, exact notion of the *proletariat*" (BO 59).

## *BLACK SKIN, WHITE MASKS*

It was Francis Jeanson, Fanon's editor at Editions de Seuil (also the editorial director at *Les Temps Modernes*) who suggested the title of Fanon's groundbreaking book. Jeanson described *Black Skin, White Masks* as a hymn to concrete freedom in which

Fanon is speaking "for all his real brothers and all his living sisters—just as he is speaking for all those who, because they fail to recognize them and challenge their membership of the human race, therefore fail to recognize themselves and exclude themselves from the human race." The book, in Jeanson's view, is a masterpiece in diagnosing the inhumanity of an alienated, mystificatory, and pathological society.[17] It is composed as a kind of *bricolage*, assembling what is ready to hand, including the phenomenology of Sartre, Jaspers, and Merleau-Ponty, the cultural discourse of negritude, literature, and the discourse of psychiatry in which he was trained (generously sprinkled with psychoanalytic theory). Regularly shifting language from medical discourse to poetry, richly biographical but not a pure autobiography, the book is "fissiparous" (BSWM 1), a split consciousness like the experience of the black person that its pages describe.[18]

*Black Skin, White Masks* (1952) explores the divided consciousness and the lived experience of the colonized black person. Fanon is critical of Sartre's *Black Orpheus* for renouncing existentialism by ignoring the lived experience of those oppressed and viewing negritude as a transitional stage of "strategic essentialism"[19] in the passage to a universal state of emancipation: "Consciousness committed to experience knows nothing, has to know nothing, of the essence and determination of its being" (BSWM 113). Although Fanon warns against enthusiasm and the illusion of an "unthinking position," he complains "Jean-Paul Sartre has destroyed black enthusiasm" since "I did not create a meaning for myself; the meaning was already there, waiting" (BSWM 113). Positing negritude as an inevitable stage in the unfolding of historical development diminishes it by classifying it as an immature phase on the way to a more advanced position Sartre himself occupies in order to recognize this development (BSWM 114). Commenting on Aimé Césaire in Chapter Six, Fanon states "we can understand why Sartre sees in the black poet's Marxist stand the logical end to negritude" (BSWM 174). But by collapsing the subjective into the objective in *Black Orpheus*, Sartre's dialectic is not properly dialectical as it does not consider posed contradictions in terms of lived reality that can lead to new directions and possibilities emerging.

Ultimately, for Fanon, Sartre was right about negritude—"by naming me [he] shattered my last illusion" (BSWM 116). He helped to establish a more positive and richer image of Black culture and Fanon agrees that negritude cannot liberate the colonized simply by positing a counter-image.[20] But Sartre forgets that the black man suffers in his body quite differently from the white man: "at the first white gaze, he feels the weight of his melanin" (BSWM 128). He cannot simply return the objectifying look of the white man because "the white man is not only 'the Other,' but also the master, whether real or imaginary" (BSWM 117n24). This gives the black man a deep feeling of inferiority, of being guilty of a profound sin without knowing what the sin is (BSWM 118). The crushing moment of realization for Fanon was being seen as a threatening "*nègre*" by a child on a train in Lyon—"*Maman*, look at the negro. I'm scared! Scared! Scared!"—that caused him to cast an objective gaze over himself and discover his ethnic features with a feeling of being "deafened by cannibalism, backwardness, fetishism, racial stigmas, slave traders" (BSWM 91–2). This is the "lived experience"[21] of a black person in white society, the experience of being objectified by the gaze of the Other under the weight of "an epidermal racial schema" (BSWM 92): "I came into this world anxious to uncover the meaning of things, my soul desirous to be at the origin of the world, and here I am an object among other objects" (BSWM 89). The image of the body is always present on the edge of consciousness, an image constructed by "blue eyes" that "burns me to a cinder" (BSWM 94). In one of a series of lectures he gave at the University of Lyon between 1959 and 1960, Fanon likens the white gaze to the effects of the surveillance of workers in the factory and how they give rise to neuroses suffered by shopworkers and telephonists who undergo a "conditioned reflex" when observed judgmentally by another person.[22]

For Fanon, there is no more unity to black identity other than its social construction: "The black man is not. No more than the white man" (BSWM 206). He criticizes psychoanalysis for its failure to adequately trace this influence in the formation of identity. Although claiming in Chapter Two that both Freud and Adler "help us to understand the black man's notion of the world" (BSWM 43), in Chapters Six and Seven he exposes the incongruity between the psychoanalytic schema and the reality of the black people. For Fanon, "[i]f there is a flaw, it lies not in the 'soul' of the individual, but in his environment" (BSWM 188). Where Freud locates trauma as repressed in the unconscious, for the black man, trauma is felt in everyday situations, "he lives his drama" (BSWM 129). A normal black child will become abnormal at the slightest contact with the white world when she sees the stereotypical representation of blacks (as genital and evil) in the popular imagination (BSWM 122). Fanon thus replaces the collective unconscious in Jung (Jung confused "instincts" and "habits" that are culturally acquired) with the mechanism of "cultural imposition" (BSWM 167). For Fanon, as for Sartre, we must never lose sight of the economic and social in the formation of identities since we cannot understand the psychology of the individual without considering the social environment: "The inferiority can be ascribed to a double process: First, economic. Then, internalization or rather epidermalization of this inferiority" (BSWM x–xi).

According to Fanon, the struggle against racism cannot remain on the level of language alone for "to speak is to appropriate its world and culture" (BSWM 17). In speaking the language of the White, the black person assumes a position of inferiority, a semiotic compromise. The Antillean who forsakes creole to speak formal French is donning a white mask (BSWM 22). Thus the creolization of the French language doesn't hold the same revolutionary potential as it had held for Senghor and for Sartre in *Black* Orpheus. To address the black person in pidgin is to demean him "tying him to an image, to snare him" as "the eternal victim of his own essence" (BSWM 18). In Fanon's view, "Creole seems destined sooner or later to become a relic of the past" once the disinherited classes have access to public education (BSWM 11). The strategy of negritude is ultimately doomed to failure as it operates within the logic of binary classification controlled by whites. Fanon argues that the dissolution of racialized black and white identities will ultimately liberate everyone. "Through the particular" we must "reach for the universal" and define ourselves in terms of our common humanity. In the end section, "By Way of Conclusion" Fanon celebrates a Sartrean freedom of autonomy, reciprocity, and transcendence:

> Superiority? Inferiority? Why not quite simply try to touch the other, feel the other, discover each other? Was my freedom not given to me to build the world of the *You*? (BSWM 206tm)

But before embarking on a "positive voice," he states, freedom "needs to make an effort at disalienation" because "man is always congested, drowned in contingency" (BSWM 206). To reach authenticity, social change is required rather than just a radical conversion in the minds of black and white people. This, Fanon concludes, can only be achieved through a long process of struggle and "permanent tension" (BSWM 206).

## THE PROGRESSIVE-REGRESSIVE METHOD

Fanon experienced visceral revulsion at all forms of racism for dehumanizing the individual: "Anti-Semitism cuts me to the quick; I get upset. A frightful rage makes me anaemic; they are denying me the right to be a man" (BSWM 69). Although, in his view, "[c]ertain pages of *Anti-Semite and Jew* are some of the finest we have ever read" (BSWM 158) in terms of understanding racism, the gaze of the anti-Semite is a direct one in this book, whereas in Sartre's later work it is mediated by society's material and economic infrastructure. This overturns the dominant idea of racism as located in the sentiments of the individual. Rather, it is "a *praxis* illuminated by a theory ('biological', 'social', or empirical racism, it does not matter which) aiming to keep the masses in a state of molecular aggregation and to use every possible means to increase the 'sub-humanity' of the natives" (CDR 721). Racism is not so much inside the head but "outside, in the world, among others" in the system of social relations and institutions. Sartre's conclusion in *Anti-Semite and Jew* that the battle to defeat anti-Semitism is to change the situation and perspective of the alienating gaze was insufficient since true transformation will only occur with a "restructuring of the world" (BSWM 63) and a structural account of racism. As Fanon diagnosed it, racism is located in the collective unconscious (BSWM 72). The real source of conflict lies not in individuals but in "social structure" (BSWM 80).

Fanon's overall position is "profoundly existentialist," making use of Sartre's *existential-dialectical method* as "the only concrete approach to reality" (SM 21).[23] He states in the Introduction to *Black Skin, White Masks* the fourth and fifth chapters are on "a fundamentally different level" to the rest of the book, which is "regressive" (BSWM xiii). The term "regressive analysis" was borrowed from Sartre[24] who employed it to describe the reflexive process that leads back to "the original relationship that the for-itself chooses with its facticity and with the world" (BN 598). It moves from the present to the past, but must be supplemented with an understanding that moves in the other direction of the future "through a synthetic progression" where "we come back down to the envisaged act and we grasp the integration within the total figure" (BN 600–2). As Fanon informs the reader, "[t]he future must be a construction supported by man in the present," signaling a path from inauthentic relations to authentic ones (BSWM xiii). On the progressive pole, Fanon rejects the idea that a person's past completely determines their future for "I can also revise my past, prize it, or condemn it, depending on what I choose" (BSWM 202). He also rejects the idea of a fixed human nature: "In the world I am heading for, I am endlessly creating myself" (BSWM 204). "It is through self-consciousness," that is, an awareness of the structures of human existence and the renunciation of race "that man can create the ideal conditions of existence for a human world" (BSWM 206). Developing the rich resources of the French existentialists' account of the lived body as a component of one's facticity into an analysis of the experience of the racialized body, Fanon theorizes race not as a mere brute fact but as an "unrealizable," never given and in constant renegotiation.

Sartre updated his understanding of racism in a speech in 1956 (subsequently published as "Colonialism is a System") in which it is no longer the gaze but the rigors of the system that fabricates identities, constructing the indigenous and the colonizers through the system of functions and interests it imposes on them. In this system "the purest of intentions, if conceived within this infernal circle, is corrupted at once" (2001: 31). European workers and public officials are partly exempted by Sartre as at the same time innocent victims and beneficiaries of the system (2001: 32n).[25] This is developed further in the *Critique* where Sartre attempts to reconcile "system" or "structure" with praxis within an overarching comprehension of dialectical reason where the process of practico-inertia or sedimentation "transforms human praxis into *antipraxis*, that is to say, into a *praxis without an author*" (CDR 166).

According to Sartre, colonialism is a "practico-inert system" (CDR 720) in which "the activity of others . . . is sustained and diverted by inorganic inertia" (CDR 556). In the "pitiless reciprocity" of the colonial system, the colonizer must dehumanize himself in the process by extinguishing those aspects in himself that are viewed as characterizing the sub-human colonized—"they must harden, give themselves an opaque consistency and impermeability of stone" (2001: 52–3). Colonialism is the common interest of the colonists, not a conspiracy as such but a shared set of interests (economic) held by all colonists (CDR 300n). Racism need not be owned or proclaimed but takes root in the acquiescence to others and to social forces, a morally corrupting material system rather than a system of false ideas. It is, as Sartre defines it, "a passive constitution in things before being an ideology" (CDR 739), such as when ethnicity and property prices form a kind of "serial unity" in alterity. In relations of "serial alterity" all colonialists act as is expected of them, issuing beatings for discipline, for example, "because this is *what one does*" (CDR 731n). Race, like class, is "the crystallized practice of previous generations," a social matrix of intelligibility, the "petrification of action" in the form of the practico-inert (CDR 171). What is needed is a critical appraisal of what appears in lived experience since racism is not simply about what is thought or felt about those of another race but about material power structures that produce racist and unequal relations.

As Bernasconi (2023: 179, 189) recommends, we should not read "Lived Experience," Chapter Five of *Black Skin, White Masks*, in isolation from the rest of the book for it highlights lived experience at the expense of the individual's social and economic context and so goes against the grain of the book's wider argument. The book has a dialectical structure and so one must always be aware of the point in the overall structure before reaching conclusions. Although Fanon describes Sartre's *Anti-Semite and Jew* as containing passages of great wisdom and agrees that, as it is the anti-Semite who makes the Jew, "*it is the racist who creates the inferiorized*" (BSWM 73), in this book Sartre did not properly expose the social structure of society that sustains this experience. Chapter Six, "The Negro and Psychopathology," examines the "unreflected" mechanisms (BSWM 167–8) that lie behind the experiences of individuals described in Chapter Five. For Fanon, genuine disalienation can only take place in a materialist sense: "We shall see that another solution is possible. It implies restructuring the world" (BSWM 63). Thus, Fanon's conclusion to Chapter Five "I began to weep" (BSWM 119), gives a false impression of where his dialectical argument ended up. The book concludes with a final prayer: "O my body, always make me a man who questions!" (BSWM 206). Because it is bodily experience that locks black people into their bodies through "cultural crystallization," it is through an alternative bodily experience that a break becomes possible: "Yet, with all my being, I refuse to accept this amputation. I feel my soul as vast as the world, truly a soul as deep as the deepest of rivers; my chest has the power to expand to infinity" (BSWM 119). To be willing to be its own nothingness and accept death in the struggle for the creation of a better world enables an authentic grasp of the reality (BSWM 202). Critical reflection arises when the unreflected imposition of a culture is brought to consciousness, enabling one to break the vicious circle and restore to the other, through mediation and recognition, their human reality. What emerges is the need for combined action on the individual and the group:

> As a psychoanalyst I must help my patient to "*consciousnessize*" his unconscious . . . but also to act along the lines of a change in social structure. (BSWM 80)

## ANTI-RACIST RACISM

As Beauvoir describes it, Fanon's *The Damned of the Earth*[26] is "an extreme, total, incendiary, but at the same time complex and subtle manifesto" (FC 606) for which Sartre wrote an equally, if not more, inflammatory Preface. It has served as "a Bible" to numerous anti-colonial movements and should be understood in conjunction with Sartre's *Critique* that Fanon read with enthusiasm. When he asked Sartre to write the Preface through a third-party, he asked that Sartre be told "each time I sit down at my desk, I think of him."[27] As Beauvoir later recalled, on meeting her, Fanon talked volubly about Sartre whose philosophy had influenced him and spoke passionately about the *Critique*, especially the analyses about terror and brotherhood (FC 597).

Despite his earlier criticisms of *Black Orpheus*, Fanon ultimately endorses Sartre's idea of "anti-racist racism." In *Damned of the Earth*, Fanon's point remains the same as before in *Black Skin, White Masks* but his tone hardens. Organizing around race can combat racism for the oppressed to move from seriality to solidarity, but it is *violence* rather than just action that is now "the royal mediation." Equating existential neuroses with objective conditions, Fanon adopts Sartre's idea of *dialectical reason* in which "[c]oncrete thought must be born from praxis and must turn back upon it in order to clarify it" (SM 22). Through the project of liberation "the colonized subject discovers reality and transforms it" (WE 21). Praxis enlightens the agent (WE 44), revealing both the means and the end and it is through praxis rather than lived experience that the agent achieves liberation in the form of "a new politics which in no way resembles the old" (WE 95). In Fanon's development of Hegel's Master-Slave dialectic, colonialism "is naked violence and only gives in when confronted with greater violence" (WE 23). This is not at a call to slaughter but a redemptive drama of Hegelian recognition in which the violence of the colonizer has reduced the colonized to a state of "non-molecular being" and the colonized must make themselves human again.

Fanon's assessment of race, colonialism, and neo-colonialism is consistently grounded in the economic. He identifies "a look of envy" in the consciousness of the colonized (WE 5) and conceives racism as a form of exploitation. He adopts Sartre's earlier controversial phrase "anti-racist racism" (BO 118) as intolerance of intolerance rather than the promotion of a racial ideal or unit in a strategic bid to go beyond it: "Racism, hatred, resentment, and 'the legitimate desire for revenge' alone cannot nurture a war of liberation" (WE 89). Involvement in the struggle is essential, and it must have a direction: "people must know where they are going and why" (WE 135). What Fanon and Sartre expose are both the attractions and problems of universalism and the need for intersectional linkage to fully understand racism. They share the ultimate goal of universalism but are wary of it being used as a guise for imperialism. Fanon argues that a *universal theory* is highly problematic because the experience of all black people is not the same across all situations and depends also on class and gender. The experiences of a medical doctor from Martinique are much different than those of children working in the sugar fields of Guadeloupe (BSWM 198–9). The mistaken idea of a fraternity of all blacks proceeds from fantasy making black people all the same everywhere and at all times. In this way, myths of negritude can bolster rather than challenge the process of colonialism, inhibiting cultural blending and cross-fertilization that can significantly improve race relations as in post-revolutionary Cuba, for example.[28] Neither black nor white can realize their full humanity when both are locked into the racial system of identity and exploitation, and in dismantling this system, White liberation may well come about through the actions of blacks. To become "fully human" is possible for either group: "Disalienation will be for those Whites and Blacks who have refused to let themselves be locked in the substantialized 'tower of the past'" (BSWM 201).

For Fanon, critique of the present implies a solution (BSWM 63). His goal to provide "a mirror with a progressive infrastructure where the black man can find the path to disalienation" (BSWM 161) is ultimately a scheme of mutual recognition: "but let us remember that our purpose is to make possible a healthy encounter between Black and White" (BSWM 80). He formulates his language of "non-being, of authenticity, and of upsurge" in dialogue with Sartre but develops it further. Because of the inferiority complex, authenticity is possible for blacks only with a restructuring of society. The answer lies in positive action "[t]o induce man to be *actional*" (BSWM 197) in order to risk his life and find his freedom by transforming the structures of society. The struggle to achieve authentic humanity is hence both a yes and a no:

> Yes to life. Yes to love. Yes to generosity. But man is also a *negation*. No to man's contempt. No to the indignity of man. To the exploitation of man. To the massacre of what is most human in man: freedom. (BSWM 197)

## CRITICAL PHILOSOPHY OF RACE

Inspired by existentialism, the critical philosophy of race (CPR) is a growing field of enquiry that analyzes how racism has emerged historically within the power structures of capitalism/colonialism. In order to understand racism in its myriad forces, CPR combines the lived experience of racism with a knowledge of history demonstrating the entanglement of nature and culture in which race is not an originary phenomenon but constructed through social practice. This means collapsing the nature/culture dichotomy in pursuit of the existential concrete advocated by Merleau-Ponty: "the distinction between the two planes (natural and cultural) is abstract: everything is cultural in us . . . and everything is natural in us" (VI 306–7). But to say that race is artificial is not to say that it is arbitrary since racial identities are sedimented into one's conceptual horizon. They are the product of material forces and relations of reciprocal antagonism but not recognized as such and are experienced as facticity.[29]

Fanon's analysis of the lived experience of Black identity has left its mark on academic thinking and has been inspirational for biographical accounts of the experience of racism as the *Racialized Other*, whether Black, Asian, Irish, Latin American, or Native Indian. But this only goes so far for the existentialist since what is needed is a deeper understanding of the operation and mechanisms of structural racism. Psychoanalysis, for instance, can only disintoxicate violence by addressing the inferiority complex on an individual level rather than in terms of Fanon's sense of "cultural imposition." As Beauvoir laments, for instance, it was hoped that African decolonization would add "a new colour to the rainbow" and fresh life to civilization, but neo-colonialism allied to capitalism ensued in Africa. Oppressive material structures stayed in place, and therefore social oppressions continued (ASD 448). She accused Fanon in this light of ignoring the importance of gender alongside race and class and for being "profoundly mistaken" when he foretold that the Algerian women would escape from male oppression because of the part they had played in the war (ASD 443).

What the existentialist account highlights are both the continuities and discontinuities of race/class/gender. Its methodology alerts us not only to the generalized social regimes of Otherizing that target oppressed groups but also the asymmetries that pertain between different forms of oppression. Fanon shows, for instance, how the black man represents an anxiogenic or "phobogenic" object for the white man (BSWM 129). This makes the black man experience the dissonance of his body and longs for anonymity where he can "slip into corners" (BSWM 96) without being dissected by blue eyes. His facticity is betrayed through the pigmentation of his skin and trapped in a corporeal schema, whereas the Jew "can even forget his Jewishness, hide it or hide it from himself" (BSWM 159). Although the black man can overcome the social determinants of class, he is incapable of escaping his race. The gaze of the whites sends him into a "suffocating reification," fixed by the gaze of the other "in the same way in which you fix a preparation with a dye" (BSWM 89). There are times when the Black is "locked in his body" (BSWM 200). In this way, Fanon warns of the error of equating anti-Semitism with negrophobia (BSWM 160). Like Sartre's Jew, the Negro is "overdetermined from without" (ASJ 95) through a system of cultural imposition (BSWM 169), but negrophobia is more extreme advocating specific physical brutalities, such as castration for blacks (BSWM 140). When he is talking about the colonized, Fanon writes, "the colonizer's language is a zoological one" and what was so shocking when "not so long ago, Nazism turned the whole of Europe into a veritable colony," was that Hitler unforgivingly humiliated the white man.[30]

## AFROFUTURISM, EX-COLONIALISM, INTERSECTIONALITY, AND RACIALIZING ASSEMBLAGES

Several strands of contemporary race theory have absorbed and developed existentialist approaches. Afrofuturism, for instance, is inspired by jazz-fusion (Sun Ra, George Clinton) and the black fiction of Richard Wright, operating at the interface of performance, aesthetics, history, culture, and politics. Afrofuturists follow existentialism in emphasizing the role of the imagination in "imagining the impossible, imagining a better place, a different world." Within an Afrofuturist non-linear and fluid imaginary, it is possible to reconceptualize alternative self-representations, aesthetic markers that serve as new potentialities of subjective understanding. Blackness is an abstraction that has no essential grounding but is, in Fanonian terms, a historical enunciation conceptualized and continually reconstructed in the process of making and doing. In this context, technology has a double historical relation as a tool of subjection but offers a future means of deliverance through self-discovery.[31]

Following on from Sartre's and Fanon's critique of neo-colonialism as a system of extractive colonialism disguised as free exchange between sovereign states, Zakiyyah Jackson (2020) offers a theory of "ex-colonialism" that he describes as a movement of discontinuity that provides "a framework for disrupting and healing the ongoing social traumas inflicted through settler-colonization" and establishes a collaborative pathway for a more hopeful politics of interaction. Sharing many features with existentialist critique, ex-colonialism advocates a way out of contemporary systems of racialized oppression and environmental destruction by emphasizing "the complex interdependence of nature-cultures," and formulating an "ethics of relational sovereignty" based on the concepts of interconnected subjectivity, ontological generosity and shared empowerment. It combines the perspectives of "more-than-human" and ontological plenitude of Indigenous thinking with the affective subjectivity of existentialism, defining political action as "not an end state but a perpetual task" responding to forms of cultural imposition, macropolitical oppression, and micropolitical regimes of subjectivation.[32]

Existentialism's (quasi-) intersectional methodology anticipates postmodern theories of intersectionality, such as Kimberlé Crenshaw's (1991), that subvert hegemonic configurations of race, class, and gender, as well as other discursive formations of difference. While Crenshaw's is a humanist theory with a specific focus on oppression and identity, others have turned to *assemblage theory* to explain racism as a series of racist events, acts, and situations in order to explain the complex relation between agency and structure as in Sartre's and Fanon's existential-dialectical method. In *Habeas Viscus* (2014), Alexander Weheliye develops the idea of "racializing assemblages" that accounts for the ways in which socio-political relations of violence mark the flesh and develop ontologies of humanity into "full humans, not-quite-humans and non-humans" to render certain bodies as exceptional and others as "disposable." Drawing on Fanon's theory of *sociogeny* and bodily objectification in the anchoring of difference, Weheliye analyzes the ways that bodies are politically disciplined within a "hieroglyphics of the flesh" that designates a hierarchy within bodies.[33]

The originality of Beauvoir and Sartre as philosophers confronting racism and as "curator[s] recasting negritude"[34] together with Fanon's development of existentialist, phenomenologist, and psychoanalytic theory, have been central to the emergence of critical race theory which is rooted in experience, directed toward the concrete, and committed to "healthy encounter[s]" (BSWM 80) between freedoms. Their struggle against racism and to understand (neo-) colonialism has helped significantly to forge new tools of comprehension—the *Social Other*, *sociogeny*, the *practico-inert*, *cultural imposition*, *sedimentation*—that, alongside more recent theories of ex-colonialism, provide "a transformative critique" yielding significant potential for posthuman racial liberation.[35] Expressed through the "relational difference" of intersectionality, these are tools that can be utilized elsewhere for articulating the lived experience of other Otherized groups within a framework of coalitionist theory and practice.[36] As Fanon expressed, every racism is an assault on the idea of a shared humanity and existentialism, in its most deconstructionist moments, is not just a repudiation of racism, but of the category of race itself.

CHAPTER SIX

# "Without Music, Life Would Be a Mistake"

## (Nietzsche, *Twilight of the Idols*) MUSIC/ART

Existentialists regularly philosophize about art's primal power as a salvific balm for the absurdity and suffering of life. "Truth is ugly," Nietzsche writes, and "[w]e possess *art* lest we *perish from the truth*" (WP 435). Following Schopenhauer, the philosophical inspiration of his early years, Nietzsche assigns special metaphysical significance to art to counter "the terrible wisdom of Silenus" (BT 4) that tells you it is better not to have been born. The Greeks understood that it is primarily through tragic art that we can create meaning and find purpose in an objectively meaningless world:

> We are to recognise that all that comes into being must be ready for a sorrowful end; we are forced to look into the terrors of the individual existence—yet we are not to become rigid with fear: a metaphysical comfort tears us momentarily from the bustle of the changing figures. (BT 17)

Hence, "it is only as an *aesthetic phenomenon* that existence and the world are eternally *justified*" (BT 5). When faced with suffering, loss, mortality, and finitude, "*art* approaches as a saving sorceress, expert at healing" (BT 7). For the early Nietzsche, as a form of "magical enchantment," art dispenses a "magical power of blessing" (BT 9) and "magic transformation" within a Dionysian experience that expresses nature "in its rapture" (BT 8).

Existentialist thinkers all display an interest in art, infusing their writings with literary iterations, fictional prose and poetry. Despite his warnings against the "aesthetic stage," Kierkegaard nevertheless included many studies of literary and artistic works in his texts. Art opens us up to the Other, Marcel argues. It is not self-centered or "self-hypnotic" but reveals our "deep rootedness in being" in which we communicate with others. Creativity as "situated transcendence" need not consist solely in the production of art-objects, but manifests itself also through love, communication, friendship, generosity, attentive listening, and the curation of shared experiences.[1] In "What Can Literature Do?," Beauvoir praises the existential merit of literary fiction since it reveals how the world may appear in the perspectives of others. Art promotes freedom and maintains our relation to possibility, enabling us to understand and reveal the world in new ways as a generative exercise in becoming. For Camus and Sartre, art must be *committed* and in service of the downtrodden, acting as a kind of mirror in which society sees itself as seen. In this way, as Nietzsche says, the artist performs a kind of "dancing in chains" (WS 140), interpreting, deconstructing, utilizing, and transforming inherited cultural and linguistic schemes: "every mature art has a host of conventions as its basis—insofar as it is a language. Çonvention is the condition of great art, *not* an obstacle" (WP 809). Although it disrupts and alters familiarity, creative language is not antithetical to common meanings. True or great art reveals and discloses the truth of the world (Heidegger, Jaspers), attuning us to a knowledge of things that surpasses everyday language.

In this chapter, we examine the existentialist love affair with art, beginning with Nietzsche's division between decadent and authentic art and Heidegger's idea of "art without the artist" before moving on to consider music's special rapport as the quintessential art form that existentialist philosophers place above all others.

## DECADENT ART AND AUTHENTIC ART

Despite existentialism's lionization of art, we must be careful in assigning a blanket aestheticism since existentialists are also cynical of the notion of *art for art's sake* (*art pour l'art*) and criticize decadent art. This cynicism begins with Kierkegaard in *Either/Or* where he offers a choice between the aesthetic and ethical lifestyles posited as two opposing, exclusive and exhausting alternatives. The aesthetic is whimsical, uncommitted, hedonistic, subordinated to interest, and empty while the ethical is abstract, universalistic, and formal, devoid of subjective nuance and personality. According to Kierkegaard, there are three dimensions to the aesthetic lifestyle: dreaming, desiring, and seeking. Just like childhood, it is full of exciting possibilities and adventures, personified by Mozart's Don Giovanni who is a prisoner to his natural urges, insatiably moving from one pleasure and gratification to the next with no regard for others. Music is the perfect medium of Don Giovanni's expression—immediate, energetic, sensual, and arousing (EO 69, 111). Condemned as a moral villain, he is prone to boredom, imbroglio, and misfortune. Ultimately, the aesthetic realm is presented by Kierkegaard as the inferior of three lifestyles, trumped by the ethical realm (with its duties and responsibilities to others) and, above all, by the religious realm (with faith and commitment to a higher order).

Nietzsche's view of art runs in parallel with the evolution of his thinking. His early work champions the idea of *art as salvation*, viewing the "Dionysian wisdom" of music as the highest and most profound of all artistic expression that articulates the "gospel of universal harmony," not as religion or morality but as purely aesthetic (BT 22). True art is both token and salvation of a unified culture, employs myths that unify a people (BT 23), and creates tragedy as a means for glimpsing and resolving psychological and metaphysical realities. After his turn away from Schopenhauer and Wagner toward naturalism in his middle period, he places art and science in a different order of priority (D 433), viewing art as a dangerous narcotic (HH 108), as "degenerate" (HH 158) or as a form of deception involving the positing of metaphysical illusions or falsehoods (HH 220). In turn, he is somewhat more circumspect about noumenal pronouncements ("as though the innermost abyss of things were speaking imperceptibly" (BT 21)), dismissing the idea that music could ever be objective (HH 10). It is not a "direct language of feeling," but merely "empty noise" into which we project memories, associations, and physical responses (HH 216).

From *The Joyous Science* onward, however, his perspective is more nuanced and pivots on a distinction between true art and degraded art. He returns enthusiastically to his former ideal of art as a means to a new ideal, urging us to live as a work of art (JS 78) and to pursue an "art of life" (A 56) as a tool for combating asceticism (GM 3.5). Zarathustra associates artistic creation with *procreation* and *pregnancy* (Z 2.2) and is in awe of music's special powers, beckoning us to "Sing! Speak no more!" (Z 3.16.7). He contrasts music's revelatory disclosure of Dionysian insight as a superior discourse to the regime of words and concepts that obscure the reality of things in everyday language: "Speech is a beautiful foolery; with it man dances over all things" (Z 3.13.2). Art is necessary to decalcify sedimented ways by revealing things in a new light. As truths are illusions which we have forgotten are illusions and seem to a people to be fixed, canonical, and binding, we need to create new names and new values for new things to emerge and therefore for reality to change: "It is only as creators that we can destroy" (JS 58). Central to Nietzsche's distinction between *true* and *degraded* art is the role of the body. His philosophy emphasizes the importance of rhythm that imposes form upon the real establishing order in terms of measurable space and time through a form of compelling (JS 84). He links music and thought in general with the metaphor of dancing—thinking is "being able to dance with the feet, with concepts, with words" (TI 8.7). In his physiological conception of art, rapture is the basic aesthetic state (TI 9.8). All art "exercises the power of suggestion over the muscles and senses, which in the artistic temperament are originally active" (WP 809). Music is the means by which "the passions enjoy themselves" (BGE 106) and making music "is another way of making children" (WP 800).

As Vanessa Lemm (2021: 84–5) warns, we must be careful not to foist upon Nietzsche a simple voluntarist notion of art. Nietzsche never authorizes the presumption that the *Übermensch* will take the place of God as an *alter deus*. Reading Nietzsche as overly focused on the heroic task of gaining mastery over shaping life ignores the way he conceives the an-archic character of creativity as a process or event open to chaos and contingency. Rather than being trapped within a metaphysics of subjectivity that views art solely as the expression of a creative will, Nietzsche posits the artistic event as a complex dialectic between freedom and resistance, the singular and universal, the human and inhuman, potential and potential not-to. Creativity is not disembodied but rooted in animal life and the non-human dimensions of life, not an attribute of the self but the life of an individual as a function of a creative activity. For Nietzsche, the death of God leads to a naturalistic conception of creativity inspired by Greek and Renaissance art that provides insight in how to deactivate the "work-artist-operation machine" without falling into the "anthropological machine."[2] All that remains is "nothing but the animal in the philosopher" and it is in this animality that we can rediscover the link between nature and creativity (JS 109). Nietzsche harks back to the Greeks to a naturalism that affirms life and the creativity of nature and that views the artistic process as a complex dialectic between artist and time. Great deeds are events that cannot be traced back to an individual act or cause but entangled "historically and physiologically" in an assemblage or constellation (TI 10.44).[3]

For Nietzsche, art is a name for a dimension of *physis*: "Art itself wells up in man as a force of nature and disposes of him, whether he wills it or not" (WP 798). Even creative thought is the work of the body and its ancient wisdom: "when they are asked to question how they performed their master stroke and from what sphere the creative thought came to them . . . hardly do they dare to say, 'It came out of me, it was my hand that threw the dice'" (WP 659). Nietzsche's "*physiology of aesthetics*," a quest to uncouple creativity from subjectivity which, he complained, "is practically untouched and unexplored so far" (OGM 3: 8), was taken up with zeal and explored in depth by Heidegger.

## ART WITHOUT THE ARTIST

In his later work, Heidegger eschews the notion of "subjective spirit" as a basis for great art: "It is precisely in great art . . . that the artist remains inconsequential as compared with the work, almost like a passageway that destroys itself in the creative process for the work to emerge" (PLT 40). Rather than a voluntarist origin, Dasein is more a passive midwife of Being, solicitously attuning itself to the call of Being as a kind of passageway or conduit. He erases all traces of his earlier philosophical voluntarism in *Being and Time* of "resolve" and "authentic potentiality-for-being" with poets, artists, and philosophers as "the great creators," redefining the vocation of humanity as the "shepherd of Being."

Like Nietzsche, Heidegger views nature as creativity without a creator: "*physis* is indeed *poiesis* in the highest sense" (QCT 10). He describes art as "a bringing forth of beings" that is possible only "in the midst of the being that surges forward, growing of its own accord, *physis*" (GA5: 48). Art is world-disclosing, and it is the way that the world is made manifest in new ways through a form of *unconcealment* that constitutes the work's truth. By way of example, Heidegger analyzes Van Gogh's painting of a pair of peasant shoes that effects "the opening up of that which the material, the pair of peasant shoes is in truth." This entity, he states, "steps out into the unhiddenness of its being" so that there is a "happening of truth" in the painting (GA5: 21). For art to be authentic, it must participate in the encounter between beings and Being: "Art is truth setting itself to work" (PLT 39). The virtue of art is its "founding function" in relation to the historical life of a *Volk*. From the viewpoint of Heidegger's "*intractable antimodernism*,"[4] modern art is destructive because it lacks both a relation to Being as well as to the life of a historical people: "The attitude of the litterateur and esthete is merely a late consequence and variation of the spirit falsified into intelligence" (IM 47). Against cosmopolitanism and the notion of art for art's sake,[5] Heidegger asks "does not the flourishing of any genuine work depend upon its roots in a native soil?" (DT 47).

In *Poetry, Language, Thought*, Heidegger presents the Greek temple as displaying the world-creating, history-founding vocation of art, establishing the spatial co-ordinates in which human interaction unfolds: "The temple, in its standing there, first gives to things their look and to men their outlook on themselves." Acting as a prism for the ordering and experiencing of human life, it

> fits together and gathers around itself the unity of those paths and relations in which birth and death, disaster and blessing, victory and disgrace, endurance and decline acquire the shape of destiny for human being (PLT 42)

He connects this to a critique of modernity in which impoverishment of spaces and environmental alienation has become widespread. Alongside architecture, Heidegger hails poetry as a disclosive artwork that can become epic and articulate the destiny of a *Volk*. Poetry is the "*voice of the Volk*" that establishes its historicity and is "the self-disclosing . . . of the simple and essential decisions in the destiny of a historical people," an expanse in which "a Volk first returns to itself for the fulfilment of its destiny" (EB 48, 42). In Heidegger's view, Friedrich Hölderlin is the archetypal poet of German destiny, "the voice of a Volk" like Homer was the bard of the Greeks, an "authentic repetition" of the Greek beginning.[6] Developing Nietzsche's view of art as a complex dialectic between freedom and necessity, Heidegger argues art is not to be understood as expressing the feeling of the artist, but as an event brings Being into the light of truth. The rapture that art brings, both in its creation and experiencing, is not an "inner feeling" but "a mode of the embodying, attuned stance toward beings as a whole" (1987: 1.105). The artist and her work are co-substantial, but it is ultimately Being through which art is expressed that precedes both:

> As necessarily as the artist is the origin of the work in a different way than the work is the origin of the artist, so it is equally certain that, in a still different way, art is the origin of both work and artist. (GA5: 1)

Reconceiving art by questioning its voluntarist assumptions, the philosopher Giorgio Agamben has drawn upon Nietzsche and Heidegger. Citing Nietzsche's notes, he develops the idea of the work of art without the artist: "The work of art, where it appears without an artist, e.g., as body, as organism . . . To what extent the artist is only a preliminary stage. The world as a work of art that gives birth to itself" (1999: 93). It was in the Renaissance, Agamben (2019: 7, 21) argues, where "art has withdrawn from the sphere of activities that have their *energia* outside themselves" and now resides "in the mind of the artist." The Renaissance secularized the idea of divine creation and crowned the artist as the supreme operator of the "artistic machine," thereby devaluing the work of art itself as contingent or secondary. But in Agamben's conception of art that follows Nietzsche's and Heidegger's, in the act of creation the impersonal "precedes and oversteps the individual subject."

In *The Birth of Tragedy: Out of the Spirit of Music*, Nietzsche praises "the Heracleian power of music" (BT 10) in connecting the individual to the primal energies of nature. As the highest expression of his ethics of play and pre-reflective freedom, it is the material *energeia* of music above all other arts that overflows the individuals who compose or perform it.

## MUSIC'S SPECIAL RAPPORT

Beauvoir appreciated many forms of art and aesthetic objects, such as hermetic poems, surrealist films, abstract art, illuminated manuscripts, ancient tapestries, and African masks (PL 40), but "it has been through music," she recounted, "that art has mingled familiarly with my everyday life" (FC 499) with a kind of "obsessional intensity" (PL 422). Contemplating a bright morning sky while listening to music was the thing that would bring her an instant feeling of fleeting happiness (FS 423) and take her "to another universe, ruled by necessity and composed by a substance, sound" (FC 246). By her estimation, she played the piano "very, very badly" (FS 220) but music still held great importance in her life and occupied a large part of her time (PL 423). She usually avoided concerts, loathing "their pompous solemnity" (ASD 219) and preferred to wait for the recording of the works that interested her.

Soon after the end of the war, Beauvoir bought a phonograph and assembled "a little record library" with Sartre's help—Schoenberg, Berg and Webern, Vivaldi, Franck, Debussy, Ravel, Stravinsky, Bartok—and with Boris Vian's help—Charlie Parker, Duke Ellington, Dizzy Gillespie. Although canned music at that time was "a long way from being as fresh as the real thing" (FC 246), she soon acquired a collector's zeal for vinyl, feeling elation "at the sight of these silent yet sound-laden discs." "I love looking at my multi-coloured record sleeves," she enthused, "austere or gay, concealing such tumults and harmonies beneath their glossy surfaces" (PL 499). After giving away her phonograph and not attending any concerts for a long time, she reconnected with music in 1958 by purchasing a hi-fi, spending a whole winter listening to Webern whose music was "as dense as a sculpture by Giacometti," as well as the avant-garde composers such as Stockhausen, Xenakis, Penderecki, Ligeti, Boulez, Nono, and Henze. "[E]very kind of music interested me," she marveled (FC 498). She was particularly fond of Boulez's music and recounts a conversation they had in which the French composer explained to an interested Beauvoir how classical music is recorded in the modern era, in small fragments then spliced together to remove mistakes and strive for perfectability (FC 591). Listening attentively, she wanted "both to be intoxicated by music and to understand it intellectually" (PL 422).

Fanon's favorite type of music was the music of his childhood, the beguine music of Alexandre Stellio (clarinettist and leader of a Creole orchestra), a syncopated dance music with strains of New Orleans jazz that was very popular in France before 1939. He was more interested in jazz than classical music but this was as much for its sociological significance as a form of Black music and culture in a racist White society than for its aesthetic value. In 1959, he analyzed the reactions of white jazz fans to new styles such as Bebop which reflected a new worldview and hope for the black community. For white fans, according to Fanon, this was a bastardization and betrayal since jazz had to be "the broken and despairing nostalgia of an old negro trapped between five whiskies, the curse upon him and the racist hatred of whites."[7] To some extent, Fanon offers a view of music similar to that of Kierkegaard in *Either/Or* where it is depicted as a kind of entertainment for the masses that mollifies the suffering of the oppressed. Kierkegaard uses the analogy of the tyrant Phalaris who imprisoned his victims in a brazen ox and tortured them over a steady fire. Their screams could not reach the tyrant's ears to strike terror into his heart but reached them sounding like ravishing music (PJ 603). Fanon examines the rituals of cultural performance where the dominated group is displaced out of the lived reality of cultural life and experiences a living death in the form of a "zombification of culture." Fixing blacks as people of the past, the Blues is the "slave's lament" presented for the admiration of oppressors that can only be maintained by the specific malediction of racial suffering: "There is no blues without oppression and racism."[8] As Lewis Gordon (2015: 88) notes, Fanon's view of the Blues as a kind of sedative administered by the oppressors offers an "asymmetrical reading" that is at odds with other Black writers, such as Ralph Ellison for whom the Blues is about dealing with one's personal suffering in an absurd and unjust world:

> The blues is an impulse to keep the painful details and episodes of a brutal experience alive in one's aching consciousness, to finger its jagged grain, and to transcend it, not by the consolation of philosophy but by squeezing from it a near-tragic, near-comic lyricism. As a form, the blues is an autobiographical chronicle of personal catastrophe expressed lyrically.[9]

Blues is to this extent a form of non-delusional happiness, a realization rather than diversion, "the beauty of moonshine versus sunshine," where life is not something to escape but to confront. Full of repetitions and revealing new layers of meaning reflecting the cyclicity of life, the Blues provides a catharsis and return to a point of origin.[10] In *The Damned of the Earth*, Fanon tempers his skepticism more in keeping with his personal habits in which he often sang West Indian beguines, played guitar, and danced to the popular Black music of his time. Revising his earlier view in which he saw the Blues as purely a performance or entertainment medium, he extols the creativity and defiance of Bebop which transcends the fetishizations of whites where the black musician "will blow his trumpet to his heart's content and his husky voice will ring out loud and clear."[11]

## THE PIANO: SARTRE, NIETZSCHE, AND MARCEL

Beyond the lure of philosophy, Sartre, Nietzsche, and Marcel were seduced by music's siren call and wanted deep down in their hearts to become professional musicians. Sartre's early writings explore art's redemptive qualities. In his story *Er the Armenian*, Apollo exclaims, "[a]n ethics, what foolishness! But guard the desire to create a work of art." *Nausea* is often viewed as both a symptom and antidote of the faith in art as an aesthetic cure for an ontological sickness in which Roquentin can cleanse himself of "the sin of existing" and "look back on his life without repugnance" (N 251–2). This ambivalence toward art is repeated in *Existentialism is a Humanism* where Sartre defends existentialism against the charge of aestheticism or *l'art pour l'art* (which he also criticizes in *What Is Literature?* and *The Family Idiot*). However, he draws a strong parallel between ethical invention and the creation of works of art as they both originate in the imagination. Sartre had an interest in many of the arts. Alongside his interest in literature and drama, as early as 1924 he had written "Apologie pour le cinéma" in which he describes the beauty of the union of image and motion in art form: "The film is the poem of modern life" (EJ 392). He also applauds cinema's anti-elitist spirit and its advocacy of moral values that are often implicit but easily discernible. The Fine Arts also captured his imagination. He had a lifelong interest in painting and sculpture, writing essays on studies of Titian, Tintoretto, Mason, Giacometti, and Calder and commented in a letter to Beauvoir that he was thinking of developing a system of aesthetics based on cinematic art and a theory about the function of image in the arts. Despite the variety of his interests, however, *music* was his prime love and childhood choice:

> I resolved to dispense with speech and live through music. . . Taken in huge doses, the music would at last begin to work. Like a voodoo drum, the piano would impose its rhythm on me. The *Fantaisie Impromptu* would oust my soul, dwell in me, endow me with an unknown past, a brilliant, deadly future. I was possessed; the devil had seized me and shaken me like a plum tree. (W 79)

"I was born in the midst of music" Sartre recounted in the 1970s. His grandfather and mother were very musical, and Anne-Marie would often play long and difficult pieces by Chopin and Schumann in the afternoons (FS 219). Her playing of Chopin's *Funeral March* moistened his eyes with tears while her renditions of Chopin's *Ballades* would be the soundtrack to inspire him to act out his adventures as a child (W 78–9). Sartre started piano lessons at around the age of ten and practiced pieces by Chopin, Franck, Bach, Beethoven, and Schubert (FS 220). In Chopin, he shared a favorite composer with Nietzsche. He would play the Polish composer assiduously, again and again, and "steep myself in the passionate melancholy" (W 80). While at the ENS he gave piano lessons and, by all accounts, had a fine baritone voice and an extensive repertoire, including *Old Man River* and all the current jazz hits (MDD 335). During the years of his greatest political interventionism in the late 1960s, he still maintained an almost daily regime of playing the piano. He rarely risked writing his own music down, but he did compose a sonata in the style of Debussy that he described as a simple private exercise.[12] Surprisingly, apart from a preface to René Liebowitz's *The Artist and His Conscience*, Sartre wrote very little on the subject of music. In an interview with *Obliques-Arts*, he expresses his preference for classical music over the avant-garde, for an art of sounds over an art of noise. He was not opposed to new creative forms (like serial music and aleatoric music) but wondered where the beauty lies in such art forms: "I no longer know what this new beauty is; do they even care about it any more?"[13] When asked by Beauvoir "how does it come about that in spite of loving, understanding and living in music you've never really been tempted to write about it?," he answered that music is a unique phenomenon and "has a language of its own" (FS 222) that does not translate well into the conventional language of words and rational analysis.

Like Beauvoir, Sartre was steeped in classical music but, inspired by Miles Davis and Charlie Parker, it is in jazz that his deepest musical desires lay. The young Sartre dreamt of being a jazz singer, and jazz, "the music of the future" as he once described it, is the musical genre that best represents "freedom-as-praxis" for him. Although this is most fully expressed in his later philosophy of intersubjectivity in the *Critique* and *Hope Now*, it appears also in his early work such as *Nausea* and *Being and Nothingness*. In the former, jazz functions first, to espouse Sartre's opposition to the distinction between high and vernacular art and, second, as an exotic Other to represent *la mentalité primitive* in an increasingly industrialized and depersonalized modern world.[14] In *Being and Nothingness*, he describes *rhythm* as a unifying bond that facilitates fusion between individuals:

> the rhythm that I generate comes into being jointly with me and laterally, as a collective rhythm; it is my rhythm to the extent that it is their rhythm, and vice versa. That is precisely the basis of the experience of the we-subject: in the end, it is our rhythm (BN 559)

Even more besotted by music than Sartre was Nietzsche, whose relation to it was visceral. In a letter to his friend Erwin Rohde following a Wagner concert in Mannheim in 1871, he declared, "[e]verything that . . . cannot be understood in relation to music engenders . . . downright aversion and disgust in me" (KSB 3.257). His approximately seventy works (*lieder*, symphonies, choral works, piano pieces) were not a mere hobby divorced from his philosophical writings but lie at the very heart of his thinking. Music is absolutely central to his Dionysian philosophy. Rhythm and tempo are key features of his writing (he often referred to his books in terms of musical scores) and denote a certain style connected to the cycles of life and the flux of feelings (EH Z3), sometimes slow and cautious (D P5) and sometimes quick and lively (BGE 213). Indeed, "the whole of *Zarathustra*," he suggests, "may be reckoned as music" (EH 10.1).

Nietzsche began his study of the piano aged nine and soon developed a passion for Bach, Haydn, and Mozart. In 1857 he began to compose music, encouraged by his mother who passed on her skill and arranged for piano lessons. Aged seventeen, at Pforta he started to experiment in his musical tastes, leaving Beethoven and Haydn to one side for the music of Schumann. He embarked on an intense spree of composition and in 1874 wrote a piano piece (for four hands) *Hymn to Friendship* that he adapted to Lou Salomé's poem *Prayer for Life* in 1882, an intimate expression of their love (that they could play together without Paul Rée sitting between them). His childhood friend Paul Deussen described how, when taken by a guide in Cologne to a brothel (instead of his request for a restaurant), Nietzsche confessed to him in a letter that he was "speechless" when surrounded "by a half dozen apparitions in tinsel," whereupon he went instinctively to the piano and struck several chords before hurrying outside. In 1877 he listed a hierarchy of things according to the pleasure they afforded with musical improvisation at the pinnacle followed by Wagnerian music and then lust.

Losing himself in activity, Nietzsche would play piano for hours on end, experiencing a sustained form of rapture in which "[e]very fibre and nerve of my being is tingling" (KSB 2.332). He had strong aspirations to become a professional composer that was mortally deflated when in 1872 he sent his *Manfred Meditation* to Hans von Bülow who was far from impressed, stating that "you display a frenzied imagination" and "persistently defy every rule of tonal connection."[15] As Nietzsche retells it in *Ecce Homo*—"I composed a counter-overture for *Manfred* of which

Hans von Bülow said that he had never seen anything like it on paper, and he called it rape of Euterpe." (EH 3.4). Unlike Schumann's delicacy, Nietzsche's playing was akin to his writing—powerful, brutal, sweeping, and polyphonic, letting the piano resonate sonorously.

Although he was infatuated for a period by Wagner and Bizet, Chopin was Nietzsche's firm companion, a composer he never denied his passion for. He listened to Chopin's *Barcarole* over and over again, associating it with his love for Italy and Mediterranean culture. He connected his own Polish origins to Chopin's "princely nobility," imagining himself as a brother to the composer. One of his youthful compositions, a Mazurka, reproduces many elements of Chopin's *Mazurka op.7, no.1.*[16] Wagner was at first the great redeemer who embodied the Romantic aspect of Schopenhauerian "great art," but Nietzsche eventually tired of him and, as his estimation of Wagner deteriorated, he reached the point where he had nothing but deep contempt for Wagnerian theater. Expecting an art of cultural regeneration, on visiting Bayreuth in 1876, he found instead an extortionate, soulless circus with Wagner in the middle as the great showman and egomaniac:

> It was not just that the complete indifference and illusion of the Wagnerian "ideal" was palpably evident to me at that time . . . the pitiful assemblage of patrons and little patronesses . . . The entire idle dregs of Europe coming together, and every prince racing in and out of Wagner's house as though it were more of a sporting event. (KSW 14.492)

The final straw for Nietzsche was Wagner's *Parsifal*, a work that expressed anti-Semitic sentiment and projected Christian ideals (EH 2.5–6).

Like all potent drugs, music can be abused and Nietzsche eventually came to the conclusion that this was Wagner's crime. With "the great charlatanry of Richard Wagner" (WP 825), music has been deprived "of its world-transfiguring, affirmative character, that is décadence music and no longer the flute of Dionysus" (EH 3WC1). Wagner's obsession with unending melody, Nietzsche opines, induces the effect of "walking out into the sea where one loses one's foothold and surrenders to the water and the waves." His music marks the "wildness" and "decay" of rhythm that lacks all proportion, causing a different sort of motion of "swimming, hovering . . . but no longer a walk or a dancc" where the foot "gets cross" and hankers for "rhythm, dance-measure, and the regular beat of the march." Primarily, Nietzsche's objections to Wagner's music are physiological ones: "I can no longer breathe freely when this music begins to operate on me; my foot immediately becomes indignant at it and rebels" (JS 368). The "nauseating sexuality" of Wagner's music epitomizes decadence and kept him "dangerously tied up" but now "no one has been more pleased to be rid of it."[17] In Wagner, Nietzsche glimpsed his own decadence and eventually revolted against it.

Gabriel Marcel's love of music is every bit as evangelical as Nietzsche's. "[M]usic has not only played a great role," he writes, "it has been one of the original components of my very being" (MP 42). Like the German philosopher, Marcel sees his philosophy as so dependent on music that it "commands the entire development of my thought" (EB 50). He compares his work to a country like Greece:

> The continental part is my philosophical writing . . . the islands are my plays . . . And the element which unites the continent and the islands in my work is music. Music is truly the deepest level. In a certain way the priority belongs to music.[18]

In 1959 Marcel complained philosophy hadn't paid enough attention to music and reiterated Schopenhauer's view that music is the expression of a deeper underlying cosmic will. As a music critic, he published over a hundred pieces on music and as a proficient pianist he composed thirty pieces for piano in the style of Ravel and Debussy, some written for poems by Baudelaire, Valéry, Rilke, and Hölderlin.[19] He felt the same power of incantation in music as he found in certain landscapes. Walking in the forests in Sweden as a boy, he discovered "a natural symphony of water, stones, pines and birches" (MP 44) which attracted him to Grieg and Schumann and especially Debussy whom he praised for being "penetrated by the mysterious power of nature" (MP 142). For Marcel's father, music became a surrogate religion, but for Gabriel, immersion in music was a kind of response to a call, an openness to being in which one takes a certain possession of oneself (MP 125). It was music that had set him on the path of religious conversion and faith and at age forty he joined the Catholic Church. To his mind, love of music and the Arts "implies a passionate interest in individual beings and an irresistible attraction toward reality in its inexhaustible mystery" (EB 21). It is music, and music almost exclusively, "which has been for me an unshakable testimony of a deeper reality in which it seemed to me that everything fragmentary and unfulfilled on the sensory level would find fulfilment" (EB 31). He connects this love to key concepts to illuminate the human situation—*ontological weight*, *feeling*, *participation*, *inter-subjectivity*, *hope*, and *creative fidelity*.

For Marcel, the "light of Being" is not discovered through intellectual reflection but involves concrete dwelling and participation in the "mystery of Being." Sound is an encroachment that binds me into a living presence and participation with the world of which feeling is the index and manifestation. This we experience as "ontological exigency," a natural demand to participate and feel belonging in a totality. In Marcel's view, music works against "first reflection," a broken world where mind is separated from body, people are broken off from each other and humankind is severed from the divine (MP 66). "Secondary reflection" by contrast involves a recollection of our self-scattered across various functions, a kind of "inward grip" or mode of attunement that Marcel felt most of all when extemporizing on the piano. Music evokes in us "a pure erotic" (MP 120), a sense of childlike wonder and enchantment. It articulates the totality of Being in a participative mode open to all humankind, providing a sense of plenitude and assuring a communion in confrontation with the musical object (EB 26). The greatest musical works, Marcel surmises, seem "to invoke directly a certain communion" (EB 26): "Through a phrase from Brahms . . . I have suddenly come to see that there is a universality which is not of the conceptual order . . . But how hard it is to understand" (BH 136). There is "authentic spirituality" or "musical mysticism" (MP 94) found in the best works of Bach, Mozart, Beethoven, Schumann, Brahms, Wagner, and Fauré who are "conjurors" (MP 112). It is in this universality that the individual "finds its substance and takes flight" (MP 105). According to Marcel, the way diachronic and synchronic sounds succeed and accompany one another only to disappear over time expresses "the tragic tension implicit in the struggle against time" (MP 118). Harmonic relations have affective effects that are "magical," "incantatory," "marvelous," "enchanted," or "haunted" operating in the zone where the soul is the animating principle that dwells in the body. They evoke a "fairy space," something we don't intellectually recognize but feel emotionally: "If it is not charm and magic, music is nothing but mathematics or scholasticism" (MP 128). This feeling is the index of our participation in the "wonder of Being" akin to Nietzsche's Dionysian experience, something sub-rational and incarnate, of being enfolded in the concrete totality where near and far, past, present, and future pass into one another.

When improvising on the piano, Marcel recounts, "a barrier was broken through and I then had the feeling of gaining entrance into myself and at the same time of evolving, with an ease that astonished me, inside an unknown world in which the possibilities of discovery were seemingly inexhaustible" (MP 51). For Marcel, Nietzsche, and Sartre—a veritable musical trio of existentialists—the piano represented a necessity in their life, an active retreat that enabled the singular affirmation of a self who cannot be summarized into abstraction. Improvising Chopin, Schumann, and Debussy transported them to worlds without power, taking them out of the general linearity of time and loosening their engagement with their own situation, offering a privileged time for subjectification within the creative activity of play. For Sartre, playing the piano signified the harmonious fusion of *pour-soi* and *en-soi*, a body of desire and glory without want, remainder or approximation, involving the fluttering and subtle movement of temporalities where the artist becomes one with his body.[20]

Music, as Roland Barthes remarks, facilitates "the freedom to be delirious,"[21] a form of pre-reflective praxis that is not a psychotic delirium but one which allows one to follow one's unchartered paths. In Nietzsche's case, the piano became his last means of communication and subjectification as he wandered ever further down the path of mute insanity in his final years. After being committed to a psychiatric clinic in Jena, he voiced words rarely but still "spoke" music volubly every day, improvising and performing on the upright piano in the cafeteria. On visiting him in 1890, his friend Peter Gast was astounded by the contrast between the fluency of his piano playing and the scarcity of his words: "Not one wrong note! Interweaving tones of Tristan-like sensitivity . . . Beethoven-like profundity and jubilant songs rising above it. Then again reveries and dreams."[22]

## MUSIC THERAPY

Art, Nietzsche esteems, "approaches as a saving sorceress, an expert in healing" (BT 7). When Sartre poses the question of art's salvation in *Nausea*, it is through music and, more specifically, a jazz song. The overwhelming sweetish sickness of Roquentin's nausea abates when he hears a record *Some of These Days* playing in a café. It begins with a piano intro, which segues into the singer's warm voice. For the next few minutes, all is well with Roquentin's world for he is "*in* the music" (N 38).

Each note in the melody leads to the next with a necessity that bestows purpose on his existence. For once, everything is poised and smooth. His movements flow with ease and grace as if he were dancing, until the song ends and everything goes to pieces again. The sound of the saxophone and the musical progression of the notes momentarily quell the nausea he feels and sublimate his disenchantment. The necessity Roquentin feels is not an ontological necessity, however, but a phenomenological one of constructing fixity for transient forms that is temporally felt and which dissipates once the record ends.

Existentialism, above all other philosophies, grasps the primordial status of music as a *via regia* into the heart of Being. Furthermore, it underscores music's redemptive and therapeutic power, its function physiologically and psychologically, to contribute to the flourishing of the humans (and other living beings) who create and participate in it. Alongside its practical everyday use, Nietzsche and Marcel recognize the cosmological significance of art and music, encompassing the wisdom of the ancients, such as Pythagoras' Music of the Spheres, and previsaging contemporary scientific theories, such as String Theory or Enactive Cognitive Science by configuring nature as *poiesis* or as "art without an artist." Beyond its ontological features, existentialists also grasp music's *social* properties as both communication and participation. Music, as Marcel observes, is "guided by a feeling of participation that gives a sense of cohesion and plenitude in principle shareable by any well-disposed human being" and gives us access to the heart of a foreign culture (MP 105) by transcending the boundaries of that culture to a universal intersubjectivity: "Music appears as the sensuous, and at the same time supra-sensuous, expression of that inter-subjectivity which opens philosophic reflection to the discovery of the concrete thou and us" (EB 50). Although he didn't write much on the subject, Fanon offers a sociological perspective and, like Nietzsche and Sartre before him, explores music's political ramifications as both freedom-in-praxis and cultural opium.

Time is still catching up with the innovations of existentialist philosophy. As a psychiatrist at Blida-Joinville in the 1950s, Fanon worked with a local musician Abderhamane Aziz in an attempt to provide *music therapy* for his patients when he heard the ululations of local Algerian women and experienced the joy they brought to musical evenings held in the hospital. He saw at first hand the psychological and physiological benefits of music and the positive therapeutic forms of sociability it engenders.[23] With his "*physiology of aesthetics*" (OGM 3.8), Nietzsche explores music's materiality and its profound effect on the ecology and health of the body. Contemporary practitioners in music therapy are tasting the fruits of the seeds sown by existentialist philosophy. At the piano, Nietzsche, Sartre, and Marcel were not just journeying into their imagination but primarily grounding and developing their body's motility comprised of muscular reflexes, somatic memory, manual dexterity, neural pathways, and chemical balances. If playing, experiencing, and participating in music is a key ingredient in the arrest of Alzheimer's disease and mental decline, there can be no more an apposite or poignant image than Nietzsche flourishing on the piano with "sensitivity" and "Beethoven-like profundity" in the Sanitarium at Jena communing with the mystery of Being as words and other means of expression failed him.

CHAPTER SEVEN

# "To Life, to the Here-and-Now Reality"

## (Beauvoir, *The Prime of Life*) REASON/EMOTION

This chapter analyzes existentialist epistemology, the way that existentialists theorize the world around us, and more specifically, the role of reason and emotion in acquiring knowledge. Often recounted is the story of how Sartre first realized the significance of the "phenomenological method" when Raymond Aron pointed out to him that he could philosophize about everyday objects, such as the cocktail glass on the table in front of him, by "returning to the things themselves." Rather than escaping into fictive transcendent realms or "the illusion of backworlds" (BN 2), existentialism stays grounded in the here-and-now, on our embodied existence in the world of objects, other people, and material forces. In a struggle against rationalist metaphysics, Kierkegaard was the first to decry abstract thought and telescope the living, *existing* person within the thought:

> because abstract thought is *sub specie aeterni*, it ignores the concrete and the temporal, the existential process, the predicament of the existing individual arising from his being a synthesis of the temporal and eternal situated in existence. (CUP 267)

Abstract thought is undialectical and ignores paradox, according to Kierkegaard, which is different from plain contradiction—"Paradox unites the contradictories" not by resolving them in a rational structure, but through individual resolution, the "happy passion. . . call[ed] 'faith'" (PF 47). All subsequent existentialist thinkers, as we will see, follow the Danish philosopher's revolt against rationalism, and from it, develop their own reconstruction of the role reason plays in their formulation of *new empiricism*.

### NIETZSCHE'S INSTINCTS

Nietzsche is a fierce critic of rationalism, a professed Dionysian and Epicurean, who invokes the sanctity of the senses as the conscious and unconscious sources of our knowledge. In Nietzsche's inversion of Platonism, the empirical, changing world is authentically real, whereas the world of Ideas is a mirage, an illusory fictive realm designed to denigrate the material world and render the masses governable by the arcane and elite few who are able to access objective transcendent truths. Platonism obscured the wisdom of the Pre-Socratics (especially Heraclitus) and disassociated knowledge from empirical life. Socrates was "an instrument of Greek disintegration . . . a typical décadent" who made existence inferior to ideas: "'Rationality' *against* instinct. 'Rationality' at any price as a dangerous force that undermines life" (EH 5.1).

Nietzsche's empiricism or "Sensism"[1] in which "[i]deas are worse seductresses than our senses" (JS 372tm), is grounded in the "wisdom of the body" and its complex sensorial apparatus: "It is not the senses that deceive. Our nose, of which, as far as I know, no philosopher has ever spoken with due respect, is as yet the most delicate scientific instrument in existence: it is capable of registering vibrations where even the spectroscope fails" (WP 461n162). He offers *a non-ocularcentric* epistemological perspective, in which *all* the senses play their part in interpreting and gaining knowledge of the world: "For as long as one is experiencing something, one must give oneself up to the experience and close one's eyes: that is to say, not be an observer of it while still in the midst of it" (WS 297). All that we know is dependent upon our perspective on the world, which is determined by the precise functioning and configuration of our senses:

> My eye, whether it be keen or weak, can only see a certain distance, and it is within this space that I live and move . . . We are like spiders in our own webs, and, whatever we may catch in them, it will only be something that our web is capable of catching. (D 117)

In place of standard epistemology, Nietzsche advances "a perspective theory of affects" (WP 462). Thoughts, he argues, are the sign of the play and struggle of instinctive drives, "the shadows of our feelings—always darker, emptier, and simpler" (JS 179). He believed early on that consciousness was a surface conditioned by the unconscious or instincts lying beneath it, and by 1889 had gone a long way to rejecting psychology altogether in favor of physiology. Our behavior, he argues, results from "[c]ompetition between affects and the dominion of one of the affects over the intellect" (WP 613). Describing human virtues as "physiological *conditions* . . . refined *passions* and enhanced states" (WP 255), he proposes that our "most sacred convictions" and our supreme values are "judgments of the muscles" (WP 314). Valuing the pre-reflective, instinctual operations of the body, Nietzsche dethrones reason and the importance of the rationalizing mind, asking, "[h]ow did reason come into the world?"—and answering "[a]s is only proper, in an irrational manner, by accident" (D 123). Reason itself is blind to its own shortcomings: "It is an illusion that something is *known* when we possess a mathematical formula for an event: it is only designated, described; nothing more!" (WP 628).

By apotheosizing reason, philosophers have hitherto followed Plato in denouncing the body and the senses, but Nietzsche warns, "[f]ear of the senses, of the desires, of the passions, when it goes so far as to counsel against them, is already a symptom of weakness" (WP 778). Self-cultivation and flourishing involve "domination of the passions, not their weakening or extirpation!" and knowing "how to press these magnificent monsters into service" (WP 933). Indeed, the most spiritual among us must feel the stimulus and the charm of sensuous things: "The strength and power of the senses—this is the essential thing in a well-constituted and complete man" (WP 1045). Ultimately, he concludes, it is the body that leads the mind and passion that guides reason: "[t]he will to overcome an emotion is only the will of another emotion or of several others" (BGE 117). More than anything, it is a mistake to polarize and completely separate reason and emotion, for in degrading passion, or indeed in rejecting reason altogether, we act "as if every passion did not possess its quantum of reason" (WP 387).

## HEIDEGGER'S IRRATIONAL MOODS

Following Nietzsche, Heidegger places *mood* center stage and relegates reason and intellect to secondary importance. His existential phenomenology delineates how we never encounter the world neutrally but how it is revealed to us through mood as a form of receptivity or modulation that precedes reflection: "mood is a primordial kind of Being for *Dasein . . . prior to* all cognition" (BT 175). Feelings and emotions, such as anxiety and joy, "are not just an appendix of psychological events" but are "bodily conditions" (GA18: 197–8) and Dasein's "primary way of orienting itself, of clarifying its being in the world" (GA18: 262). They are revelatory insofar as they disclose to us our participation in Being and enable us to attune to the riches of direct experience and the environment around us. Heidegger attacks overemphasis on epistemology and knowledge in philosophy that reinforces the subject-object dualism. Our primary concern is *affective* and *practical*, theoretical knowledge is always secondary: "Objects never reveal themselves individually and such as they are but only . . . as part of a 'totality of equipment'" (BT 97).

In his work of the 1940s, Heidegger exalts poetry and myth above philosophical analysis and theoretical knowledge—*Mythos* over *Logos*. His hope was that by "*destabilizing the grammatical representations of language*," we could bring to an end the dominion of "logic" (GA36/7: 104) and overcome subject/object dualism. He follows Kierkegaard in setting fire to reason and embracing its other side: "Theoretically, I myself come from the experience . . . which people now do not know what to make of and for which the comfortable name of the irrational has not been invented" (GA56/7: 117). As Heidegger seeks refuge in the recrudescence of myth and openness to mystery, he forsakes reason *in toto*, declaring in a 1953 lecture: "Thinking begins only when we have come to know that reason, glorified for centuries, is the most stiff-necked adversary of thought."[2] Logic and reason stand as barriers to authentic thinking about Being: "At bottom, this magic word 'validity' is a *tangle of confusion, perplexity, and dogmatism*" (GA21: 79).

Echoing criticisms of Heidegger by the Frankfurt School (including Adorno, Habermas, and Marcuse), Wolin (2022: 90–7) accuses him of promulgating a "poeticizing gnosis," some kind of "nature-oriented superstition" or "primordial thinking" that glorifies ontological fatalism, submissiveness, and heteronomy. Instead of casting the subject or reason in a new light, Heidegger just abandons them. But, as Adorno avers, reason remains an indispensable source of negation and critique. It should be reworked and not buried for, recognizing that reason has been historically constituted and overdetermined, we "must strive, by way of the concept, to transcend the concept."[3] Heidegger's "forgetting of reason" (*Logosvergessenheit*) and his aversion to inherited philosophical positions, according to Wolin (2022: 364, 90), became so extreme that, ultimately, he deprived himself of the conceptual and discursive tools necessary to render his doctrines intelligible and coherent. "Authentic thinking," exempts itself from philosophy's requirements, exemplified by his polemic dismissal of "Enlightenment" in *What is Called Thinking?* (1954) as a standpoint that "darkens the essential heritage of thinking" (GA8: 214). Heidegger's task of thinking is increasingly tied to an escalating rhetorical and linguistic obscurantism to compensate for phenomenological concreteness, taking us beyond reason and representation: "if man wishes to find himself once again in 'proximity' to Being, he must, first and foremost, learn how to *exist in the Nameless*" (GA9: 319). "Making itself intelligible," he stated, "is suicide for philosophy" (GA65: 435). For Wolin, Heidegger's retreat into "the Nameless" in his quest to overcome metaphysics inaugurated the "post-truth era" where proposition or evidential basis is replaced by "unconcealment," lending itself to a *de facto* credo of would-be tyrants and despots. His critique of propositional truth in "The Origin of the Work of Art"—"Truth is in its nature untruth"—flounders in its inability to distinguish between truth and error, as with the notion of "conscience" in *Being and Time*, which was left criterionless and non-falsifiable.[4] Ultimately, Heidegger leaves truth at the mercy of poets, philosophers, and state-makers, leaving no possibility that it might emerge from an open exchange of ideas, or a *sensus communis*, arguing in *An Introduction to Metaphysics*: "*Truth is not for every man, but only for the strong*" (GA40: 142).

Although the French existentialists are very much in line with Heidegger's de-rationalized conception of truth, they do not wish for reason's total oblivion, still retaining in some form a conception of truth that stands in relation to reason. While they follow previous existentialists in treading the path of the irrational, they stop short of the thickets at the very end of that path upon which Heidegger's (and Kierkegaard's) thinking became entangled. Deconstructing reason, like Nietzsche, they endeavour to reconstruct it.

## THE FRENCH EXISTENTIALISTS: BERGSONIANS IN THE MAKING

Nietzsche, Bergson, and Husserl are the main luminaries that alight Sartre's early work, culminating in *Being and Nothingness* in 1943. As early as the 1920s, he rejects a dry conceptualism with the appeal to "feelings" and "affect," following very much a Nietzschean line. As Beauvoir recounts,

> he went to unheard-of extremes in his total rejection of universals. To him general laws and concepts and all abstractions were nothing but hot air . . . He, on the other hand, wanted to grapple with this living reality, and despised any analysis which limited its dissecting to corpses. He envisaged a worldwide system of intelligence centred upon the concrete. (PL 31)

One of Sartre's earliest and most stubbornly held beliefs was "the autonomy of the irrational mind" (PL 182), viewing habit, along with Merleau-Ponty, as the product of a pre-reflective mind or self that inhabits the body. Inspired in the 1930s by Husserl's rallying call to return "to things themselves," there were three main aspects of phenomenology that fascinated him—(i) the massive, seductive, but also frightening presence of things; (ii) its sensitivity to the inner riches and depths of consciousness, the world of the *pour-soi*; (iii) the attempt to resolve the inner tension and duality of consciousness and world. Sartre's own phenomenology is a form of empiricism that, unlike Husserl's *Cartesian Meditations*, eschews scientific rationalization and seeks intuitive knowledge.

Alongside German influences, it was perhaps the French philosopher, Henri Bergson, who exerted the greatest influence on the early thinking of the French existentialists, and it is possible to see Marcel, Sartre, Beauvoir, and Merleau-Ponty very much as "Bergsonians in the making."[5] From early on, French existentialism picked up the baton from Bergsonism, a concrete philosophy, as Merleau-Ponty said, that enabled "a contact with things" (S 183). Marcel greatly admired Bergson, dedicating his first major work of philosophy, the *Metaphysical Journal* (1927) to the philosopher of lived experience and opponent of abstract systems, "whose thought and words took a sure and lasting hold of me."[6] In *Time and Free Will* (1889) and *Matter and Memory* (1896), Bergson makes a distinction between our conceptual knowledge of the external world and consciousness as known from within. Intellect and scientific knowledge proceed by analysis and classification, viewing the world as composed of discrete, isolatable units externally related to each other. In *Creative Evolution* (1907), he analyzes the creative freedom of the cosmos that finds its self-awareness in the experience of human freedom. Reason serves life in the sense of survival as the adaptation of the living creature to the given conditions of its existence, but it is *intuition* that brings us closer to the secret of life.

Inspired by Bergson's *Time and Free Will*, which she read aged eighteen, Beauvoir underwent "a great intellectual rapture" seeing in his philosophy "palpable reality" instead of "logical constructions" (2006: 66). "I didn't want to speak with that abstract voice," she recalls, and vows to "become a kind of female Bergson" (MDD 208). Reading Bergson motivated her to write "the novel of the inner life" (PW 264) linking philosophy together with fiction. She chose to write novels because literature gives us "imaginary experiences that are as complete and disturbing as lived experiences" (PW 270). Later, she drew upon Bergson's ideas of individuation and speciation in *Creative Evolution* to explain the greater difficulties for women in achieving individuation than for men. Similarly, Sartre read Bergson in his final year at school that propelled him toward a philosophy of the concrete. He was particularly influenced by Bergson's notion of duration in *Time and Free Will* as a prototype for his pre-reflective consciousness and his idea of the human being as a flight toward the future. But whereas Beauvoir leaned more heavily toward Bergson's intuitionism and toward ineffability, Sartre expressed a more rationalistic desire to explain the world. As she recounted: "I reflected that words have to murder reality before they can hold it captive, and that the most important aspect of reality—its here-and-now presence—always eludes them" (PL 40). Where Sartre said we must "grasp the meaning of phenomena and pin them down in words," she thought that "reality extends beyond anything that can be said about it; that instead of reducing it to symbols capable of verbal expression, we should face it as it is—full of ambiguities, baffling, and impenetrable" (PL 144).

## THE NEW EMPIRICISM

The history of modern philosophy can be seen as a perpetual tug-of-war between *rationalism* and *empiricism*, between the mind and the senses. To some extent, existentialism represents a continuation of the synthesizing project of Kant, but where Kant wanders ultimately toward rationalism, existentialists move in the other direction, toward a *renewed empiricism*. Existentialist philosophers develop the radical empiricism of Kierkegaard and Nietzsche with an interest in the concrete data of immediate experience rather than in theoretical constructions. Describing things phenomenologically as they are given to the experiencing and affective subject, for existentialists, reality cannot be squeezed into an abstract *a priori* system. By dissolving individuality into the totality of the Historical Spirit, "Hegelianism," Marcel writes, "inspired me with a profound mistrust" (PE 78). In the phenomenological ontology of Heidegger (in *Being and Time*) and Sartre (in *Being and Nothingness*), we find a general descriptive anthropology, describing the richness of immediate experience and the pervasive structures or moods that underlie it.

Epistemologically, the "new empiricism" or "higher empiricism"[7] of the existentialists avoids pan-objectivism (which reduces everything to an object) and pan-subjectivism (which reduces everything to some subjective state), especially the former as it denies the reality of the existing concrete subject. This differs significantly from Cartesian subjectivism and previous forms of empiricism, such as Russell's phenomenalism, in which external persons and things are only known through indirect inferences from privileged internal data contained in the mind. It is also opposed to theories of mechanical materialism that dissolve agency altogether in the causal chain of external forces. For existentialists, the mind does not create its objects but apprehends them by a *relational* act. It is still the thing that appears however I determine it. John Wild (1962: 138) succinctly describes the existentialist position:

> I find myself not in two worlds, but in one. The ultimate horizon is not just spatial, but spatio-temporal in character. External events, internal feelings and acts, the theoretical objects of science, so far as these are verified, are all in one moving world horizon. I can think of myself alone. But this is a sheer abstraction. Being-in-the-world belongs to my very existence. No world, no subjective existence . . . Internal data have no special epistemological privilege . . . Nor do I have to infer the existence of other "minds" from any more certain data. Being-with-others belongs to my own existence. I cannot be aware of the latter without being aware of the former. To feel alone is a privative mode of feeling-with, which is the more primitive phenomenon. Awareness is not being in a mind container; it is being towards something - a relation.

For Merleau-Ponty, perception is not entirely passively received (as in traditional empiricism) or actively constituted (as in intellectualism) but is *sui generis*, a real phenomenon reducible to neither: "In perception . . . I live the unity of the subject and the intersensory unity of the thing, and do not conceive them after the fashion of analytical reflection and science" (PP 238–9). There is a kind of anonymity in perception, which means that my perceptions are never completely "mine" but are enmeshed in an intersubjective dimension that he describes as "the One." In sensation I experience "a modality of general existence . . . which runs through me without my being its author" (PP 216). In *The Visible and the Invisible*, he shifts his emphasis, exercising a Heideggerian move. Where *Phenomenology of Perception* is centrally concerned with human existence, the focus of his final work is Being at large, conceived as much vaster than human existence and where the human is but one "variant" of "carnal being" (VI 136). Akin to Heidegger's "authentic thinking" about the "Nameless" (GA9: 319), philosophy for Merleau-Ponty is no longer the interrogation of human existence but the disclosure of mysterious Being as it *is*, not filtered through our human concepts and intellectualizations. Thus, we must proceed allusively, metaphorically, and indirectly without distorting Being by trying to capture it: "If one wishes to maintain its spirit it is perhaps necessary not even to name it. The sort of being to which it refers, and which we have been trying to indicate, is in fact not susceptible of being designated positively" (VI 92). Most of all, we must appreciate that the "hyper-dialectic" at play within the concept of Being precedes all dualisms upon which previous philosophy has relied:

> nature and men and history are all understood not as substances definable by a principle attribute, but as movements without a locatable discontinuity, where the other is always implied. No separation of matter-idea, object-subject, nature-man, in itself-for itself, but one single Being where negativity works. (1975: 168)

In a move to escape Cartesianism and yet secure the reality of Kierkegaard's "existing individual" (CUP 267), Merleau-Ponty and Sartre both offer a *modified cogito* in which philosophy is the reflective attempt to understand our pre-reflective embodied engagement with the world. In *Phenomenology of Perception*, Merleau-Ponty associates existentialism with a "new cogito" not based on Cartesian transparency but "the blind act by which I take up my destiny as a thinking nature and follow it out . . . [thus] introducing another philosophy, which does not take us out *of time*" (PP 374). This he describes as a "glimpse of myself," a "tacit awareness" and "inarticulate grasp" that precedes knowledge and speech (PP 404). Dismissing the "view from above" (VI 69), he posits the pre-reflective cogito as an immanent modification of lived experience. Establishing a "living link" between the I and world, and exploring preferentially the zones of experience "in which being and consciousness coincide" (PP 492), Merleau-Ponty proposes a form of embodied philosophizing or "true reflection" (PP 452) that recognizes its own contingency and dependence on the pre-reflective givenness of the world prior to Cartesian separation and mechanistic determination, "a creative operation which itself participates in the facticity of that [unreflective] experience" from which philosophy springs (PP 61–3). Philosophy provides us with an indissoluble bond between our openness to a world that remains resolutely other and our reflective return to ourselves, an intertwining of immanence and freedom. Hence "true philosophy" involves "leaving oneself" and "retiring into oneself" (VI 49, 199), a "double movement of perspectivism" (centrifugal and centripetal). In *Being and Nothingness*, Sartre adapts the same strategy, retaining an amended, non-Cartesian conception of the (pre-reflective) cogito in which "any conscious existence exists as the consciousness of existing" (BN 12). Against the idea of "objective truth," he argues that no detached or spectatorial truth is conceivable that doesn't involve the standpoint of the agent: "The point of view of pure knowledge is contradictory: the only point of view is that of *committed* knowledge" (BN 415).[8]

The existentialist bid to reformulate a new cogito in which we can "catch a glimpse" of our pre-reflective awareness was a continuation of Marcel's recognition that my own existence is an "existential indubitable" (MB 88): "I exist means not I *think*, not even I *live*, but I *experience*" (EPC 29). For Marcel, philosophical inquiry must always return to the "irreducible self" in the "here" and "now" of immediate existence and experience. This is a form of "exclamatory awareness" or "existential certitude" without which all abstract philosophy is moribund (MB 125). We must pass beyond mere "primary reflection," a kind of self-distorting reflection, like science, that is built into our language and brackets its own subjective perspective, to "secondary reflection" that dismantles existing structures of thought and entrenched preconceptions. When inquiring about being and existence, the ontological status of the questioner is "of highest importance" (BH 71). The task for philosophy is one of *evocation* rather than ordering or analysis, to undertake the precarious and paradoxical task of elucidating the inexpressible, and through art, indirectly express existential truths. Above all, the mystery and exigency of Being is revealed in our concrete relations with others as much as by reflexive means.

Existentialism's "new empiricism" operates at a synthesizing level "beyond that of traditional empiricism" (TW 229), Marcel argues, since it involves a creative relation to the world rather than the passive reception of sense-data: "the error of empiricism consists only in ignoring the part of invention and even of creative initiative involved in any genuine experience."[9] Standing against dualism, it maintains all experience is embodied: "the idea of a pure thought anterior—even in a rational sense—to all experience is certainly a pseudo-idea; it is the product of a schematic and illusory reflection" (MJ 75). There is no sense in saying "I am other than my body" (EPC 34), but, Marcel avers, this also means that "I am also my habitual surroundings" and that "I am my past" (MJ 259). In abstracting myself from given circumstance, from the empirical self, from the situation in which I find myself, "I run the risk of escaping into a real never-never or no-man's land—into what strictly must be called a *nowhere*" (MB 133).

For existentialists, there are many forms of feeling or thought intermediate between the purely physical stage and the stage of conscious intellectual operations. The new empiricism they develop establishes an open, pluralistic image of thought that avoids the mistake of rigorously dividing sapience from sentience and consigning everything that is not purely rational and abstract into the category of causal deterministic mechanisms. Nietzsche's "sensism," for instance, goes beyond standard ocularcentric/

spectator conceptions of "knowledge" to a more synaesthetic conception of "comprehension" based on the model of *affective transfer* and the *wisdom of the senses.*[10] Building on Nietzsche's critique of "the backworlds illusion" (BN 2), Sartre takes the "monism of the phenomenon" (BN 1) as the guiding methodological and substantive principle of his phenomenology. In his later *progressive-regressive method* in the *Critique*, his task is to draw philosophical significance from concrete descriptions of experience whereby lived experience is shown to bear and to be borne by social and historical structures and personal-intentional singularities. Just as in his earlier phenomenological work, "[w]hat do we see?" (CDR2: 23) is the essential starting point to his later philosophical investigations.

## THE REASON OF EMOTION

Striving to grasp the mystery of Being, Romanticism was a major influence on existentialism but shorn of its metaphysical baggage. Escaping a world of dry rationalism, existentialists find the world as a mysterious, contingent, and unpredictable realm. In the (magico-realist) novels of Kafka, Sartre, and Beauvoir, the world is never entirely stable as people and objects are capricious, subject to mood changes and sudden transformations. In Sartre's philosophy, moods/emotions are analyzed as ontologically revelatory, but also ploys to cover up a more fundamental truth, functioning in many instances as *magical mystifications* for our behaviour. Magic and reality are coextensive—there is no real without the irreal and *vice versa*. Consciousness in the world is always "pregnant with the imaginary," "a surpassing of the real" (IM 186). Emotion is purposive in Sartre's view, and is about transforming the world. In *Sketch for a Theory of the Emotions*, he complains that psychologists studying emotion "try to confront their subject as the physicist confronts his" (STE 1), working from the essential principle "that their enquiries should begin first of all from facts" (STE 2). This commits the error of treating consciousness as a physical thing, falling prey to the *bewitchment of the ego* and thus losing the experiential quality, magical nature, and phenomenological dynamic of emotion. Sartre is aware of the need to explain emotional behaviour as involving *both* a genuine belief in the projected quality and an awareness of its falsity. This permits an escape route from the captivity and magical hold of the emotions only through rare moments of "pure reflection" where the subject apprehends her feelings as involving some form of self-deception.

The aim of this purifying reflection is to discern whether our captivating emotions are life-enhancing or life-stultifying, whether they diminish or enhance freedom. Sartre's development of emotion as "a different way of eluding a difficulty, a particular way of escape, a special trick" (STE 25) overlaps with Nietzsche who shows how passions are not just physiological disturbances but also a form of emotional intelligence and an element of strategic agency. For Nietzsche, emotions often mask their true nature and beneath their surface lurks the purposive force of ulterior ones. Pity is really an expression of egoism and fear (HH 103), magnanimity is cloaked egoism and revenge (JS 49), neighborly love is a way to avoid self-reflection rather than a concern for others (Z 1), generosity is motivated by a desire to rule over others

(Z 3), humility is "timid baseness" (GM 1.14), a means to gain moral superiority, and erotic love is a form of possessive greed (JS 14). Hence, for the existentialist, every passion harbors a purpose and its own "quantum of reason" (WP 387).

## REASON REREASONED

Epitomized in the title of William Barrett's popular 1958 book *Irrational Man: A Study in Existential Philosophy*, existentialism is labeled with encouraging irrationalism, particularly in the work of Kierkegaard and Heidegger. Existentialism's valorization of emotion and its strictures against abstract reason may seem to conflict with the philosopher's obligation to reason as a lover of wisdom free from whim or *parti pris*. This presents the danger not just of the irrational, but of the anti-rational, that can as easily assume the forms of inhuman cruelty or ethical suspension, such as Abraham's sacrifice of Isaac or National Socialism in 1930s Germany.

Unexpurgated irrationalism, however, is not typical of existentialism. Reason cannot simply be dissolved but is needed to get beyond reason, requiring *both* the principle of reason *and* what is beyond the principle of reason. Existentialists beckon us to look at different *forms of reason* other than abstract reason alone, to develop a "logic of persons" and a "logic of collectivities" in addition to our "logic of things."[11] Looking beyond his one-time friend, Heidegger, Karl Jaspers is more appreciative of rational thought and suspicious of irrationalism, thinking it foolish to reject or condemn reason altogether. Although reality goes beyond reason, there is no great divorce or unbridgeable gap between them, for there is some correspondence between reality and our concepts as both are incorporated within the "encompassing." For Jaspers, the philosopher's path may well traverse with that of mystics and poets, but his path is also one of rational discourse and reflection, which may be called scientific in the broader sense of being evidential: "Unless an idea is subjected to the coldly dispassionate test of scientific inquiry, it is rapidly consumed in the fire of emotions and passions, or else it withers into a dry and narrow fanaticism" (1951: 159).

While championing instinct, pre-reflexivity, and mood, Nietzsche and the French existentialists critique reason in its abstract logical analytic form. However, they seek to reconfigure or resurrect it in "historical," "dialectical" form. The existentialist rejection of rationalism is not a rejection of reason *per se*. Rather, it consists in re-evaluating the role of reason and in grounding it in the body and the senses. Very systematically, Nietzsche's work proceeds to critically examine and reject received philosophical opinions on metaphysics, morality, religion, art, and politics, leaving him as a "free spirit" untainted by dogma. This critical reflexivity waxes in his middle writings where he poses as an Enlightenment thinker who is more enlightened than Kant. Imploring "[t]his Enlightenment we must now carry further forward" (D 197), he portrays himself along with other free thinkers as "children of the Enlightenment" (HH I 55). By rejecting the German attitude toward morality which is one of obedience, and which finds its heightened form in Kant's categorical imperative (D 207), and seeking to become the master of himself (D 206) by grounding reason in the body, Nietzsche endeavors to place the Enlightenment on firmer ground. Similarly, Sartre presents *dialectical reason* in the *Critique* as an alternative form of comprehension that recognizes collectivities and "thinks in terms of solidarity" (CDR 468) to the bourgeois model of Analytic Reason that separates everything into distinct parts, assumes the objectivity of the spectator, and encourages social atomism (CDR 297). Dialectical reason is the "living logic of action" (CDR 38) indistinguishable from "the relations which each person has with everyone through inorganic materiality" (CDR 36). It is a process more than a philosophical method and can only be recognized as it reveals itself in being. The task, he asserts, is descriptive and phenomenological; it "must be recognized *where it is there to be seen*" (CDR 34).

As a general orientation, existentialists deconstruct the reason /emotion dichotomy and dissolve the traditional opposition between them. "Reason without heart and heart without reason," according to Marcel, "are equally inauthentic."[12] Existentialists follow Nietzsche's call for a "new Enlightenment" that would reevaluate reason as a positive, practical human force, but one that does not extirpate emotion. In confronting modes of oppression, for instance, Sartre castigates the anti-Semite for his imperviousness to reason by living in a state of passionate hatred toward a particular ethnic group (ASJ 20). In *Black Skin, White Masks*, Fanon finds himself caught in a performative contradiction—at the same time as he decries reason and constructs a critique of the collapse of reason into Western White rationality, he attempts to reason with the reader and fight against the irrationality of racism.[13] He laments the fact that in the phobic atmosphere of White society, "affect has a priority that defies all rational thinking" (BSWM 133). Remaining true to life and what Beauvoir calls "the here-and-now reality" (PL 145), existentialism moves us beyond simple dichotomies of reason and emotion toward a *new empiricism* and greater comprehension that examines the ways in which they intermingle. Existentialism's *dialectical reason* radicalizes the Enlightenment project at the same time as it puts great store by the revelations and mystifications of the senses and passions, demonstrating, as Kierkegaard says, "[h]ow far imagination is at work in logical thought, how far the will, how far the conclusion is still a decision" (PJ 177).

CHAPTER EIGHT

# "Now I Bid You Lose Me and Find Yourselves"

## (Nietzsche, *Thus Spoke Zarathustra*) POLITICS

Undoubtedly, existentialism's involvement with the politics of its day was significant, eventful, and sometimes reproachable. Politically, existentialism is a prism that reflects the full spectral range of colors from the brown-shirted ultra-fascism of Heidegger and Carl Schmitt, to the deep green of ecopolitics, through to the red *ultra-gauchisme* of Sartre and Beauvoir with various Liberal and Socialist hues in between. All of these colours are woven together, to some extent, or other in Nietzsche's multicolour protean political thinking. In this chapter, we look at how the range of ideologies that Nietzsche bequeathes is taken in different directions by the existentialists who follow him in their quest to develop and articulate an existentialist *politics of authenticity*.

## NIETZSCHE, A MELTING POT OF IDEOLOGIES

Nietzsche is complicated to read politically as his work, taken as a whole, is a melting pot of ideologies. As a political "monster thinker," he has been appropriated by all factions and stripes, variously heralded in Germany in the years around his death as the "social philosopher of socialism" (Lindau), the "social philosopher of capitalism" (Mehring) and the "prophet of a new age of anarchism" (Landauer).[1] Subsequently, he was lauded as "a great fighter" by Adolf Hitler and became synonymous with Nazi ideology to the extent that, as Alfred Baeumler remarked, "if today we shout 'Heil Hitler' . . . at the same time we are also hailing Nietzsche."[2] Although there are some constants that run through his political thinking—in particular, the necessity of the *individualistic principle*—the kind of political Nietzsche you get very much depends on which period of his thinking you focus on.

Raised in a conservative and religious household, when he came of age politically in the 1860s, Nietzsche's views were staunchly royalist, displaying a deep respect for the grand heroes of history and the great nation. Once the war was underway with Austria in 1866, he supported the Prussian military machine, serving two stints in the army (as a soldier and medical orderly). In the 1870s, his Bismarckianism expressed itself as an aloof disdain toward party politics, demanding a cultural rebirth inspired by Greek culture, the music of Wagner and the pessimism of Schopenhauer. Developing Schopenhauer's aristocratism and calling for tragic greatness in culture as the aspiration of the political state, he argues that some political theories, such as socialism, are unduly sentimental and fail to recognize that each culture must accept the necessity of slavery (BT 18) in order for great art to prosper. He celebrated Schopenhauer initially as the philosopher of a regenerated Germany who became a cultural figurehead for his generation as Hegel had been for his in the 1830s. Although he later rejected his mentor, Nietzsche was attracted to his anti-orthodoxy, his aestheticism and his rousing call to follow our consciences, resist absorption into the masses, and "[b]e your self!" (UM 3.127). Unlike "we moderns" who glorify "the dignity of man" and "the dignity of labour," the Greeks understood that a life devoted to toil made it impossible to become an artist. The need for art rests upon a terrible basis:

> In order that there may be a broad, deep, and fruitful soil for the development of art, the enormous majority must, in the service of a minority, be slavishly subjected to life's struggle, to a greater degree than their own wants necessitate (G.S 6)

Nietzsche's essay "The Greek State" denounces the "drone-like individuals" of the modern masses where culture and state are reduced to the furtherance of the wishes of egoistic individuals, propelling the "deviation of the state tendency into a money-tendency" (G.S 7, 15). Modern humans are no longer political animals in the Greek sense, for we are unwilling to organize ourselves as "material for society." He advocates war in order to reinstate the collective purpose and body of the state: "although it comes along like the night, war is nevertheless Apollo, the true divinity for consecrating and purifying the state" (G.S 15).

In the early 1880s, Nietzsche's political views underwent a decisive transformation, propelling him to a more progressive and liberal perspective. He became an earnest critic of modern German politics, viewing the Bismarckian state as a philistine enforcer of racist, nationalist, and statist policies. This mirrors his split with Wagner who turned from libertarian revolutionary to the favorite of the king of Bavaria and a reconciled supporter of the Reich. His break with Wagner is equally a break with the political idealism and cultural romanticism of his youth. In this middle period, a milder Nietzsche emerges, one who believes that democratic politics can promote and further culture. What is needed to cure social ills, Nietzsche now suggests, "is a gradual transformation of mind: the sense of justice must grow greater in everyone and the instinct for violence weaker" (HH 452). He declares that "the democratization of Europe is irresistible" (WS 275) and foresees a future "democracy as something yet to come" (WS 293), which will overcome polarities of wealth and power and render obsolete the dangerous ideologies of nationalism and socialism. He suggests an enlightened labor policy that will guarantee workers' protection against injustice and exploitation and secure the contentment of body and soul (WS 286). A strong pan-Europeanism and hope for a new European humanity is proposed as a healthy alternative to nationalism:

> the separation of nations through the production of *national* hostilities . . . is in its essence a forcibly imposed state of siege and self-defence inflicted on the many by the few and requires cunning, force and falsehood to maintain a front of respectability. It is not the interests of the many (the peoples), as is no doubt claimed, but above all the interests of certain princely dynasties and of certain classes of business and society, that impel to this nationalism. (HH 475)

In thinking about how to guard against oligarchical concentrations of power, Nietzsche suggests democratic politics as a site of pluralism that incorporates resistance to, and emancipation from, tyrannical forces. He displays a newfound sensitivity to the worker and the oppressed, complaining how in modern society, "man is in ruins and scattered over a battlefield." Zarathustra laments the death of peoples unified "by tablets of the good" and the birth of "the new idol," the state (Z 1.11).

Nietzsche's middle writings unquestionably present a pluralistic, democratic vision in which *agonism* is posited as an alternative to the idea of equality as a basis for democracy, emphasizing difference above sameness. His perspectivism lends itself to an ethic that subverts normalization and allows space for difference to be, undermining traditional and aristocratic justifications that invoke timeless truths and historical necessity. In *Human, All Too Human*, for instance, he defends the right of the masses to determine their own existence and government:

> if the purpose of all politic really is to make life endurable for as many as possible, then these as-many-as-possible are entitled to determine what they understand by an endurable life; if they trust to their intellect also to discover the right means of attaining this goal, what good is there in doubting it? (HH 438)

Nietzsche defines democracy as the form of political organization that "wants to create and guarantee as much independence as possible: independence of opinion, of mode of life and of employment" (WS 293). He speaks of a *new form of democracy* "as of something yet to come," characterized by the independence of opinion and new modes of life and employment: "That which now calls itself democracy differs from older forms of government solely in that it drives with new horses: the streets are still the same old streets, and the wheels are likewise the same old wheels" (WS 293). He praises democracy as a provisional instrument for overcoming militarized nationalism (WS 275) and for breaking up rigid class hierarchies and liberating individual ambition (JS 348). The "new democracy" is one that will allow "a plurality of norms," honor "the right of individuals" and avoid the "doctrine that there is only one type of man, and only one standard appropriate to him" (JS 143).

As the 1880s progressed, Nietzsche's politics flipped again, reverting back toward the aristocratism of his early period. He now increasingly links democracy with tyranny in the form of popular sovereignty, the promotion of uniformity, and the elimination of qualitative diversity. In the texts of his middle period, he criticizes the archaic nature of hierarchical social structures and traditional feelings of subordination but reverses direction in his mature aristocratic politics. He replaces the idea of social and moral change taking place through a process of liberal recommendation with a process of aristocratic legislation, promoting "Machiavellianism" (WP 304) which, in his middle period, he associates with the despotism of socialism and clearly rejects because of its reliance on force, obedience and deception. In *Beyond Good and Evil*, Nietzsche asserts that every enhancement of the human type is the work of a society based on an order of rank and differences of value between humans. Society "needs slavery in some sense" as "scaffolding" (BGE 258) for some individuals to achieve "the highest value," and "deepest significance." High culture requires "*instinct for rank*" (BGE 263), a pyramid structure for the elevation of its highest specimens:

> The essential characteristic of a good and healthy aristocracy is that . . . it therefore accepts with good conscience the sacrifice of untold human beings who, *for its sake*, must be reduced and lowered to incomplete human beings, to slaves, to instruments. (BGE 258)

In *The Joyous Science*, Nietzsche talks of the "children of the future" who are neither liberals working for progress nor socialists who dream of equal rights and the abolition of slavery, but "conquerors" who love danger and war and who realize that every enhancement of the human requires a new kind of enslavement (JS 377). He justifies aristocratic rule by drawing on the notion of will to power that seeks to enhance its power, grow and become predominant: "Exploitation does not pertain to a corrupt, or imperfect, or primitive society: it pertains to the *essence* of the living thing as a fundamental organic function; it is a consequence of the intrinsic will to power, which is precisely the will of life" (BGE 259). The exploitation of one group, or individual by another, he asserts, is "the *primordial fact* of all history" (BGE 259).

Nietzsche's affinity with Nazism can be extracted from his Machiavellianism, his advocacy of elitism, struggle, suffering, and cruelty to achieve political ends, as well as his criticisms of compassion and pity. It was the popularity of his writings in Germany during the First World War that allowed the Nazis to exploit him as an ideological ally during the interwar period. Nietzsche gave the Nazis intellectual credence and substance, helped along by his literary executrix and sister, Elisabeth, who presented him as a philosopher of German imperialism and militarism, even inviting Hitler to visit the Nietzsche Archive and, on one occasion, presenting him with her brother's walking stick. Philosophers, such as Baeumler and Rosenberg, were enlisted by the Nazis with the task of propagating Nietzsche's philosophy. In Baeumler's 1931 *Nietzsche as Philosopher and Politician*, Nietzsche is the philosopher of the Nordic race and his attacks on the German people were directed toward those non-Germanic elements, such as Christians and Jews. Other works, such as Härtle's *Nietzsche and National Socialism* and Oehler's *Nietzsche and the Future of Germany*, reinforced this militaristic message of Nietzsche as the true philosopher of National Socialism. Fired by Nietzsche's ideology of war, it is rumored that German soldiers went to war in 1914 with a copy of *Thus Spoke Zarathustra* in their kitbags (though Oscar Levy casts some doubt on this).[3]

But it is a curious twist of fate that Nietzsche should become a "Proto-Nazi" and "a great fighter" for the National Socialist cause. The *Alldeutsche Verband*, the leading nationalist organization in Germany despised Nietzsche, and this was largely the case where strongly *völkisch*, or nationalistic values prevailed. Some nationalists rejected Nietzsche's notion of "the blond beast," thinking "beast" to be too base and unworthy for the German spirit.[4] The Nazi ideologue Ernst Krieck warned against the adoption of Nietzsche: "All in all, Nietzsche was an opponent of socialism, an opponent of nationalism, and an opponent of the idea of race. If one overlooks these three intellectual trends he might perhaps have made an outstanding Nazi." Arthur Drews echoed these sentiments, describing Nietzsche as "enemy of everything German," "an out-and-out individualist," and "a good European" who assigned to the Jews "a key role in the fusion of all nations."[5] On the Left, the dissemination of Nietzsche's work after his mental collapse in 1889 was quickly taken up by socialists, anarchists and feminists who were inspired by his quest for individual self-realization and creative personality, highlighting his atheism and anti-nationalism that alienated him from German conservatism. Progressives see in Nietzsche the "unmasking trope," his ironic stance to the modern world and his genealogical deconstruction of power, providing the material for the development of a new progressive politics, a "radicalized liberalism," or "liberalism with teeth."[6]

These multicolored interweaving strands (of elitism and libertarianism) in Nietzsche's political thinking were stretched, manipulated and rewoven in different ways by subsequent existentialists.

## HEIDEGGER'S NATIONALIST CONSERVATISM

Despite his attacks on conformism and "bovine nationalism" (WP 748), Nietzsche was a vital resource for the Conservative Revolution of the 1920s / 1930s in Germany, which was the breeding ground for Heidegger's early political allegiances. Heidegger's early philosophy in *Being and Time* is "unabashedly conservative," emphasizing historicity and the insignificance of the individual while praising individual resolution. His idea of authenticity is described by some critics as a "Lutheran-existential" conceptualization, a "new pseudo-radicalism," a "sort of escapism," a "sham-freedom" in which our resolution is not going against the crowd but of giving it our personal assent.[7]

Heidegger rejects Descartes' cogito because of its aversion to history, arguing that it provides philosophy with a "false origin," a ground that is no ground in the rootless "I think." Heidegger's remedy for the problem of dissociated subjectivity was replacing the self-reflection of consciousness and the rational norms that derive from it with the power of rooted tradition based on the notion of a mythical primordial experience (articulated in his treatment of "authentic historicity," "Tradition" and "Repetition" in Division II of his *magnum opus*): "In communication and struggle, the power of destiny becomes free. Dasein's fateful destiny in and with its 'Generation' constitutes the authentic occurrence of Dasein" (BT 452). In *Introduction to Metaphysics* (1935), he pays homage to the "inner truth and greatness of National Socialism" and advances an ontological justification of Nazi Germany as "the most metaphysical of nations." His enthusiastic employment of the *Führerprinzip* prompts his summons that "the Might of the Führer becomes fused with Being and the soul of the *Volk*" (HJ 77). Freedom, he argues, cannot be found in licentiousness that avoids commitment, but is bound to the furtherance of German destiny: "Freedom is not '*freedom from*' Obligation, Order, and Law. Freedom is '*freedom for*': for a decisive commitment to our collective spiritual deployment on behalf of German destiny" (GA16: 96).

Rejecting the rationalism of the Enlightenment, Heidegger draws upon Nietzsche's exaltation of myth in *The Birth of Tragedy* as a powerful strategy to bring about cultural wholeness. In the Davos event of 1929, Heidegger famously disputed with Ernst Cassirer. Cassirer questioned Heidegger's "metaphysics of myth" highlighting the regressive tendencies endemic to political myth that undermine the capacity of language for critique, or demystification. In riposte, Heidegger attacked the abstract Enlightenment notions of *freedom and reason* and rejected the separation of *Mythos* and *Logos* that previously had existed in a primordial unity before Plato. He argues that myth "names Being in its primordial looking-into and shining-forth"[8] and posits an ontological kinship between Germans and Greeks, who are the *only* authentic historical peoples and are ethnically related (GA38: 153). Heidegger appropriates the aristocratic, elitist, and militaristic aspects of Nietzsche's variegated political thinking. Developing Nietzsche's reflections on state builders in *On the Genealogy of Morals* as "violent ones," he links the authentic historicity of a Volk with its capacity for self-assertion. This ontological-historical "right" is bound up with the "right to conquest" and those who lack this are "unhistorical." In *Nature, History, State,* Heidegger offers a philosophical justification for the "Law of Expanding Spaces" and Nazi policy of *Lebensraum* by asserting the Volk's willingness and power to strike out and expand: "We can only genuinely speak of state when, in addition to rootedness-in-soil, the will to extend its reach, to interaction, also becomes a factor."[9]

In combating European nihilism, there are no half-measures and active nihilism must actively intervene. Heidegger bangs the drum of military nationalism, arguing only a maximum of brutality and destruction can clear away the detritus of Western civilization on the brink of collapse: "Everything must be exposed to complete and total devastation" (GA96: 195). In an address on "the German University" in 1934, he celebrates the war experience and the "spirit of the front" as crucial elements of Germany's path to National Socialism: "The *Frontgeist* is the knowing will to a new *Gemeinschaft*" (GA16: 300). *The Black Notebooks* confirm that Heidegger supported National Socialism not despite its barbaric methods but because of them: "National Socialism [as] a barbaric principle . . . Therein lies its essence and capacity for greatness" (GA94: 194). As Rector of Freiburg University, one of Heidegger's first steps was to introduce military service as a statutory part of the curriculum: "a fierce battle must be waged in the National Socialist spirit." That spirit, he asserts, "must not be stifled by humanizing, Christian ideals that suppress its imperatives" but act as a pedagogical force that educates the nation's elite and a site for new leaders based on the powers that "Hitler is making into a reality." He supported numerous measures to hasten the militarization of university life, integrating sport and socialization camps in order to foster a rigorous ethic of "work discipline" and "service" to National Socialism and to bring about the total capture of the whole person.[10] Authentic work, he argues, is linked to a *volkisch*-fate that is purposive beyond the narrowly instrumental of modernity and is bound "into the one great will of the State." His Rectorial Address of 1933 states emphatically: "The individual by himself counts for nothing. The fate of our Volk in its State counts for everything . . . It is not working for the State that the danger lies: the danger lies in indifference and opposition."[11] Extolling the "ecstacies of work," Heidegger advocates the "nationalization" of *Arbeit* as a main ingredient of National Socialism's "total transformation of German Dasein." Work benefits afflictions of spirit since it teaches severity and proximity to the soil but it is also a form of "unveiling or world-disclosure" giving rise to a basic mood that enables Dasein to merge with the "rapture of things."[12] Militarizing his existential ontology in *On the Essence of Truth* (1933–4), he views *Arbeit* as a manifestation of "Dasein's becoming essential . . . in its practical encounter with the essence of things." It instils "the essence of State as a form that permanently structures and compels self-responsibly acting Dasein." The essence of work is concerned with the empowerment of Dasein, a modality of Being-in-the-world that licenses a certain primordial violence toward "beings," or "things" (GA36/37: 86).

Heidegger's political philosophy is unapologetically elitist, a theory of educational dictatorship in which the nihilism of the indigent present can only be overcome by a select cadre of poets, thinkers, and statesmen, "the great creators." The mysteries of Being are accessible to only a privileged few: "The true is not for every man but only for the strong" (IM 133). The great creators are warriors in the "primordial struggle" for Being that ground a historical destiny for a nation (IM 62). Heidegger admires the Ancient Polis for its primacy of "rank and domination." His conception of the pan-Germanic repetition of the Ancient Polis is tied to the *Führerprinzip*, the notion of "leader-creators" in a "Total State" (IM 133). The work of the state establishes a "clearing," or a "lighting" by which the unconcealment of beings can take place: "Another way in which truth occurs is the act that founds a political state" (PLT 62). The "creators" are "violent men" who stand above and beyond the law and smash the encrusted powers of convention. For Heidegger, the poet belongs to the pantheon of "demigods" whose mission it is to mediate between the spheres of "gods and men" as a kind of "*Dichter-Führer*." In his aestheticized political state, the work of art illustrates the play between "Earth" and "World" revealing the dynamic of unconcealment and concealment as the ontological condition for truth (qua "*Alethia*," or "unveiling"). But he links this to rootedness and German exceptionalism: "Unconcealment does not transpire somewhere in and of itself or as a property of things. Being happens as the history of human beings, as the history of a Volk" (GA34: 145).

*Domination*, *power*, *will*, *destiny*, *rank*, and *war* are the key elements of Heidegger's ultra-conservative and illiberal political vision,[13] a politics based squarely on hierarchy and ethnography. Just as Kierkegaard had been a "snide observer" of the 1848 revolutions in Europe as another undesirable "manifestation of the Public,"[14] Heidegger rejects socialism and Marxism as a thoughtless outgrowth of Judaeo-Christian egalitarianism (GA65: 54). He describes the influence of Russia and America as "*the demonic* (in the sense of *destructive evil*)" leading to "the boundless etcetera of Indifference and Always-the-sameness . . the domination of ... the indifferent Mass, [combined with] an active onslaught that destroys all Rank and every world-creating impulse of Spirit," blocking Germany's prospects for "another Beginning" and "*new spiritual energies unfolding historically from out of the middle*" (GA40: 49). Lamenting the incursion of foreign influences on German Dasein, Heidegger's *Heimatdiskurs* emphasizes nearness and regional belonging linked to a concept of cultural homogeneity that facilitates otherness and exclusion: "*Foreign being distorts and disrupts our specific essence. Why is it that the Germans are so susceptible to being seduced by that which is foreign?*" (GA97: 47). Heidegger's scorn for democracy is pronounced and he believes it should be his responsibility to lead the leader in the manner of a contemporary philosopher-king. He shares Jacob Buckhardt's view that democracy was the cause of the downfall of the Ancient Greek Polis. In *What is Called Thinking* (1954), he praises Nietzsche's condemnation of democracy as a "*degenerate form of the state*," stating that there is no essential difference between communism, fascism and world democracy as they all equally express the "universal domination of the will to power." Decrying the "democratized disintegration" of contemporary institutions (in a section omitted from the first section of his Nietzsche Lectures), he warns "Europe always seeks to cling to 'democracy,'" failing to recognize that the latter will be 'its historical death'" (GA43: 193).

Along with Carl Schmitt, Heidegger has been hugely influential for the ideas of the European New Right, usurping the revolutionary impulses of the Left for the ideology of New Rightism with the notions of *rootedness*, *native soil*, *ethnic belonging*, and *resolute decisionism*. Schmitt's political existentialism mixes together Heidegger's "potentiality-for-Being-a-whole" and Kierkegaard's "teleological suspension of the ethical" to develop the idea of the Total State. His most influential work *Political Theology* (1922) advances the decisionistic theory of sovereignty in which emergency powers should be freed of constitutional restraints. Its opening sentence states famously with true Machiavellian bravado: "Sovereign is he who decides on the state of exception." This is akin to Heidegger's moment of resolve or limit–situation in *Being and Time*, an event when "Dasein glimpses transcendence, and is thereby transformed from possible to real Existence." In the passage to the authoritarian state, Schmitt calls for a plebiscitarian democracy that is only a "pseudo-democracy" since it detaches democracy from its supporting liberal institutions that safeguard civil liberties. Like Heidegger's aversion to "foreign being" (GA97: 47) and contemporary New Right opposition to multiculturalism, he premises the idea of the Total State on the notion of national homogeneity that requires, if necessary, "*elimination, or eradication of heterogeneity.*"[15] Schmitt welcomes technology as an "active metaphysic" that promises the "unbounded power and domination of man over nature, even over human physics" and significantly opens up prospects for the realization of the Total State: "Technology is no longer a neutral basis . . . and every strong politics will make use of it . . . Its ultimate meaning will be revealed when it is known what type of politics is strong enough to master the new technology, and what are the real friend/enemy groupings that arise on this new basis." Glorifying war and struggle as a form of "existential meaning" and supporting the notion of the *Führerprinzip*, Schmitt welcomes the possibility that the total mobilization of the state will extend to all spheres of life, including the "intellectual and moral formation of the citizens."[16]

After WWII, Heidegger was subject to the denazification process of the new German state for his collaboration with National Socialism and was on the defensive. He claimed that his lectures on Nietzsche between 1936 and 1940 constituted a form of spiritual resistance to National Socialism (GA16: 402) rather than a justification of it, and that actual Nazism was just another form of modern subjectivity (GA5: 92–3) and "the will to will." He later referred to the years 1933–4 as his "great blunder" (*grosse Dummheit*) in which his reading of the National Awakening of 1933 in terms of the Nietzschean doctrines of the will to power, self-overcoming and the *Übermensch* led him to support National Socialism as the "saving power" for western humanity—a case, he laments, of Nietzsche leading him astray.[17]

In his postwar philosophy, Heidegger rebalances the relation between Being and Dasein against the voluntarist dimension of *Being and Time* and embarks on an anti-humanist trajectory toward, "destiny," "releasement," and "letting things be." In the 1966 *Spiegel* interview, he dismisses the capacity for human action, freedom, or reason to shape the course of history: "philosophy will not be able to effect any immediate change in the current state of the world. This is true not only of philosophy but of all purely human reflection and endeavor. Only a god can save us." By presenting Being as an omnipotent primal force, or unmoved mover, Heidegger effectively destroys freedom and, say his critics, engages in an act of self-exculpation, a strategy of denial for his great blunder of 1933. Extirpating the last vestiges of a "philosophy of subjectivity" from his thinking—"[t]he advent of beings lies in the Destiny of Being" (LH 234)—he succeeds' only by endowing Being with the characteristics of an all-powerful meta-subject instead of attempting to reintegrate *Dasein* into a series of intersubjectively-oriented goals and achievements. For Jaspers, Heidegger's philosophy of heteronomy in which our projects are determined by the "destining of being" is "essentially unfree, dictatorial, and incapable of communication" since it dissolves the conceptual space in which freedom can be expressed and exercised.[18] He describes Heidegger in this light as "a kind of sorcerer" who leads people astray "away from reality."[19]

To his critics, Heidegger's ontologizing is a case of historical conceptual subterfuge in which he explains away the excesses of National Socialism. His diagnostic view succumbs to a self-defeating "pseudo-concreteness" since it remains aloof to proper historical and empirical analyses (e.g., his treatment of *Arbeit*) while resting content with abstract flights of speculation. With his emphasis on Being, fate, authority, obedience and the Total State, Heidegger offers a practical-political solution of disengagement and disenfranchisement that, in Wolin's (1990: 151) words, "consists in the perlocutionary effect of a diffuse readiness to obey in relation to an auratic but indeterminate authority."

## MERLEAU-PONTY'S NEW LIBERALISM

Existentialism's relationship to Marxism is complex to say the least, ranging from cold rejection (Kierkegaard, Nietzsche, Heidegger, and Marcel) to provisional warm embrace (Sartre, Beauvoir, Merleau-Ponty, and Fanon). Merleau-Ponty was initially attracted by Marxism's political potential for it is Marxism that holds the key to the dialectic as a way beyond "the discordant functioning of human intersubjectivity" (PP 97) in the modern era. He criticizes liberalism as a form of idealism that attempts to understand the world in terms of ideas and values alone. It denies the dialectic where values and the "factual situation" are born and produced together (AD 5). The German Occupation showed just how dependent individual freedom is on social conditions and how hollow it can be in conditions of repression. Liberty is "a false ensign . . . as soon as it becomes only an idea and we begin to defend liberty instead of free men" (HT xxiv). In *Humanism and Terror*, he charges liberalism with playing the role of a hypocritical defender of ruling-class interests placing abstract liberal freedom above "concrete liberty" (HT xxv) or "practical freedom" (HT xxiv) and ignoring the mediation of structure and institutions on human interaction.

Merleau-Ponty attempts to "existentialize" historical materialism/Marxism by expressing it in "another language" that describes the human creation of the social world in "ways of existing and coexisting" (PP 171). Class, for instance, is not an impersonal fact or an objective determination, but a mode of existing:

> What makes me a proletarian is not the economic system or society considered as systems of impersonal forces, but these institutions as I carry them within me and experience them. (PP 443)

For Merleau-Ponty, Marx does not just replace Hegel's Idea with matter but also *intersubjectivity* as the vehicle of world history: "It is man involved in a certain way of appropriating nature in which the mode of his relationship with others takes shape; it is concrete human intersubjectivity" (SNS 129). Because we are *in* the world, "we are condemned to meaning, and we cannot do or say anything without its acquiring a name in history" (PP xix).

By 1950, Merleau-Ponty was having grave doubts about Marxism-in-practice. He changed his mind about the experiment of communism in the Soviet Union, judging its method of collective production to have become an excuse for oppression and the justification for a "cruelly hierarchical society" (S 265). The subjective has been subordinated to the objective by degrading and subjecting human relations to the objective demand of economic development. With the divorce between the Party leadership and the will and consciousness of the working-class came the permanent institutionalization of violence: "Nothing allows us to say precisely: here Marxist politics end and there the counter-revolution begins" (HT 91). The dialectic is truncated and the possibilities for humanism become lost as terror and inequality are institutionalized in the name of the Revolution. With growing scepticism, Merleau-Ponty wonders whether the violence of the Soviet Union is "the infantile disorder of a new history, or merely an episode in an unchanging history?" (HT 98). At the end of the 1940s, he adopts a policy of "critical support"; and "wait and see Marxism,"[20] and despite all his reservations, he maintains his faith in Marxism as the only political theory where there is a "sense of a mutual relation between men [and] any rationality in history" (HT 153).

The Korean War of 1950 demonstrated the extent of Soviet acts of imperialist aggression and abruptly ended Merleau-Ponty's "critical support" for Russia, signalling in his mind the impossibility of a return to a humanist Marxism.[21] His retreat from Marxism is expressed in *Adventures of the Dialectic* (1955), a book consisting of "several small works" (AD 3) that demonstrate the collapse of the Marxist dialectic into objectivism (Lenin, Lukacs, and Trotsky) or subjectivism (Sartre). Its purpose is to show his rejection of Marxism and to herald a movement toward a "new," or "radical" liberalism that he associates with pluralistic thinking, advocating parliamentarianism as a minimal guarantee of oppositional thinking. He judges capitalism to be different than it was of old out of which "another politics than its own can pass" (AD 227) and, in a series of articles for *L'Express in* 1952, he expresses support for the Keynesian policies of Pierre Mendès-France.

To his critics, Merleau-Ponty's volte-face is a contradiction of his earlier account of the dialectical theory of the young Marx in which he was critical of attempts to conflate Marxism and Bolshevism. In *Adventures of the Dialectic*, he treats them as synonymous and disregards those forms of Marxism not based on vanguardism. In stark contrast, his existentialist colleagues, Beauvoir, and Sartre, take a very different path, opposing "a centralizing, abstract socialism" but asserting the value of "another socialism, decentralizing and concrete" (FS 13).

## THE ANARCHO-SOCIALISM OF BEAUVOIR AND SARTRE

The spring of 1939 was a watershed moment for Beauvoir and Sartre when they renounced their "individualistic, anti-humanist way of life" and "learned the value of solidarity" (PL 359). Beauvoir recounts how "[o]ur love of freedom, our opposition to the established order of things, our individualism, and our respect for the working-classes—all these brought us close to the anarchist position" (PL 42). In the 1950s and 1960s, they felt horror over French colonialist policy, and as Beauvoir laments, a sense of national shame and aversion:

> What I find physically intolerable is being forced to be an accomplice of drumbeaters, incendiaries, torturers, and mass murderers; it's my country all this is happening to, and I used to love it; and without chauvinism or jingoism, it's pretty difficult to be against one's own country. Even the countryside, the sky over Paris, the Eiffel Tower, are poisoned for me. (FC 420)[22]

Their anarchism was, in Beauvoir's words, as "deep-eyed and aggressive as that of the old libertarians," and stirred them to withstand any encroachment by society on their private affairs: "We were against institutionalism, which seemed incompatible with freedom." The idea of "permanent revolution" suited their "anarchist tendencies" far better than that of constructing a socialist regime inside one single country (PL 76, 135). What they truly wanted was a *libertarian form of socialism*: "one that seeks justice without restraining liberty, one that imposes responsibilities on individuals but without abolishing individual freedom" (SS 68). "Socialism," according to Beauvoir, "represents a greater freedom; an economic freedom in the first place and then a cultural freedom, a freedom of action, experienced every day, a freedom in the great choices" (FS 398). Categorizing her lifelong political valency as "a left-wing individualism" (FS 381, 399), she envisages a form of socialist alliance (in contradistinction to the state socialism of the USSR) where people are not conditioned by a society but shape themselves according to their own options.

In a 1975 interview, Sartre identifies himself as an anarchist throughout his entire life: "I have never accepted any power over me, and I have always thought that anarchy, which is to say a society without powers, must be brought about" (1975). Of course, his Marxist phase is well documented (as a fellow-traveller with the French Communist Party (PCF) in the 1950s), but this was a label he rejected in his later years. Whereas in 1957 he declares that Marxism is the "unsurpassable philosophy of our time" (SM 31), describing it as "simultaneously a totalization of knowledge, a method, a regulative Idea, an offensive weapon, and a community of language" (SM 6), in a 1975 interview with Michel Rybalka, he answered unequivocally "no" to the question of whether he was still a Marxist. In other interviews, he continues to distance himself from Marxism and associate his thinking instead with anarchism: "I was always more of an anarchist than a Marxist . . . [My] anarchism . . . was really an expression of freedom, the freedom I described earlier, the freedom of a writer."[23] "I was an anarchist without knowing it when I wrote *Nausea*," he affirmed, and "I have always thought that anarchy—which is to say, a society without powers—must be brought about" (1977a: 389). For Sartre, anarchism is the only political philosophy that is consistent with freedom, the highest existentialist value of all:

> I have always loathed hierarchies and in some of the present-day antihierarchical conceptions I see a sense of freedom. There cannot be any hierarchy with regard to freedom. There is nothing above freedom. I therefore decide for myself and no one can force my decisions. (FS 353)

Sartre's alliances with the Communists (France 1952–6, Soviet Union 1954–6, Algerian rebels 1955–62, Castro's Cuba 1960–1 and Maoist New Left groups 1970–3) were not ideological partnerships but rather cases of tactical cooperation. He was faithful to his own principles, in particular his four bugbears of *militarism*, *colonialism*, *racism*, and *bourgeois morality*. He was an early supporter of Russian dissidents against Stalinism (by 1963 *Les Temps Modernes* had already published three of Solzhenitsyn's novels). After 1968, Sartre and Beauvoir became "the godparents" of the political movements of individual freedom based around gender, ethnicity and sexual orientation, articulating a politics that is, according to Ronald Aronson (1995: 34), "feminist, pro-gay liberation, anti-racist and ecological."

Like other existentialists, Sartre shows a deep concern for individual freedom, autonomy, and subjectivity, and fears the totalistic, state-centric varieties of socialism. Marxism is not a creed for him but a heuristic tool in his thinking and a springboard toward a more explicit anarchist position. His anarchism values freedom above all else and is wary of all social groups, appealing directly to the power of artistic self-development and individual authenticity in and against a social world of conformity. He conceives society not as an organic whole but as a complex collection of separate individuals and assemblages, a "detotalized totality." This, in Storm Heter's (2020: 532) view, makes Sartre a "syndicalist," or "democratic Anarcho-Socialist,"[24] both fearful and in awe of the transformative power of group being, placing him at a distance from individualists (such as Stirner) and collectivists (such as Hegel). Like the social anarchists, he imagines a socialist alternative to the capitalist state, but he values collectivity as a process of freely configuring groups that enable the widest expression of individualities as opposed to degraded serial forms of social existence that inhibit it.

All in all, Sartre views the state as a totalized monolith. He discards the liberal idea that democratic states express a social contract among equals since citizens obey the law not by choice but as a result of mystification and violence. The state is not a neutral arbitrator that mediates the interests of smaller groups, or communities but operates through ruses or "traps" (especially voting) where the ruling class creates the spectacle of a collective will. Society is not a genuine group but an atomized mass forming the "container" and "battlefield" for competing groups: "Thus it would be wrong to see the State *either* as the concrete reality of society (as Hegel apparently wished, or believed), *or* as a pure, epiphenomenal abstraction" (CDR 639). For Sartre, the state can never be regarded as "the product or expression of the totality of social individuals" (CDR 636) since it is characterized by seriality and other-directedness: "the relation of the State to concrete society can never, even in the best of circumstances, transcend other-direction" (CDR 654). In the 1970s, Sartre wrote two essays, "Election: A Trap for Fools" and "Justice and the State," in which he appeals to the ideal of non-oppression to reject both thick and thin justifications of the state: "State Justice was created precisely in order to perpetuate exploitation" (1977a: 175). Political representation, he avers, is but "a falsification of the popular will" (1977a: 176), a type of blackmail that creates inert gatherings of people who "cannot resist the State" (CDR 636). Sartre illustrates this through the experience of the secret ballot and its other-directedness: "No one can see you, you have only yourself to look to; you are going to be completely isolated when you make your decision" (1977a: 200). For Sartre,

> Universal suffrage is an institution and therefore a collective which atomizes or serializes individual men. It addresses the abstract entities within them—the citizens, who are defined by a set of political rights and duties, or in other words by the relation to the state and its institutions. (1977a: 202)

Although he concludes in *Being and Nothingness*, "[o]ntology itself is unable to formulate moral prescriptions," it does allow us, he adds, "to glimpse what an ethics that took up its responsibilities by confronting a *human reality in situation* might be" (BN 809). In looking to a future beyond the state, Sartre's anarchist syndicalism, exemplified by his prototype of the *fusing group* in the *Critique*, is an expression of his ontology of emergent interactionism, offered as a sublimation of multiplicity and unity, self, and other. He describes his vision of a *flourishing humanity* as an individual adventure in the dimension of the universal shot through with open possibilities:

> But my destiny is me coming to myself as an image. What is more, humanity is an individual adventure that takes place in the dimension of the universal. The individual coming to himself in terms of the features of the universal, this is humanity's destiny (NE 422)

Key to this are the notions of *intersubjectivity* and *reciprocity*: "we can conceive of an absolute conversion to intersubjectivity. This conversion is *ethical*. It presupposes a political and social conjuncture (suppression of classes and the State) as its necessary condition, but this suppression is not sufficient by itself" (NE 407). Building and forging a flourishing humanity, we pass from the particular to the universal, thereby transcending the old society and the old History. In a classless society where there is no oppression that "breaks apart intersubjective solidarity" (NE 427), my Ego will "lose itself in the absolute dimension of freedom" (NE 418). Flourishing humanity will not be marked by division and hierarchy but by integration and love, a new phase of existence which we must work for based on the model of the festival:

> it is a break with the spirit of seriousness, expenditure, nihilation, passage to the *festival*. Indeed, the festival is liberation from the spirit of seriousness, the end of economies, the overthrowing of hierarchy, and the absorption of the Other by the Same, of the objective by intersubjectivity, of order by disorder. (NE 374)

In interviews in the 1970s, Sartre conceives democracy not merely as a type of government but as a *form of life* where fraternity forms the bond of relationships between people in society: "our goal is to arrive at a genuinely constituent body in which each person would be a human being and collectives would be equally human" (HN 67). In Sartre's final ethics, the future "is a pure future beyond the system" that has "to be created—not by building a system (not even a *socialist system*) but by destroying every system" (2008: 251). This would be a witnessing of "what Malraux, in *Days of Hope*, called the Apocalypse, that is to say, the dissolution of the series into a group-in-fusion. And this group, though still unstructured, that is to say, entirely *amorphous*, is characterized by being the direct opposite of alterity" (SG 357). Fired by the imagination and realized through praxis, humanity is an evolving notion designating a power of political transformation and invention: "The essential moment therefore is that of creation, that is, the moment of the imaginary, of invention" (NE 464).

## THE STATELESS STATE

According to John Macquarrie (1973: 188–89, 76), if existentialism points to any political creed, it would be "to the absence of government, to anarchy." For any concrete philosophy, the corporate personality of the state is an abstraction, a fiction that must not be valued above the real personalities of citizens. Existentialism brings to light the ambiguous dynamic between privacy and community, shunning atomized individualism but also excoriating mass uniformity. To square the circle of individual and group, it delivers us to the paradox that "true community allows for true diversity." To this end, as Macquarrie states (1973: 90), we should not dismiss existentialism as a romantic aberration of political theory but rather "a prophetic voice, seeking to enhance the sense of the humanity of man and to guard it against further erosion."

Although his writings pervade a strongly anarchistic ethos of forsaking leaders and finding yourself (Z 1.22.3), many of Nietzsche's direct comments on "the *species anarchistica*" (GM 3.26) are openly critical. He charges anarchism with pretending to be different to other ideologies like democracy, equality, or socialism, but is really of the same kind as it is founded on *ressentiment* and reaction (GM 2.11), expressing a desire for pity and the herd (BGE 202). Anarchists can be individuals of great power but this often manifests itself in self-denial and simple destruction (D 184). The anarchism Nietzsche has primarily in mind when denunciating it is nineteenth-century Russian anarchism. Anarchists like Kropotkin were deluded in believing that there could be a quick and painless transition to a world of mutual cooperation. Revolutionary anarchists (such as Bakunin who was Wagner's ally in 1848) were nihilists whose violence and terrorism were fuelled by a raging *ressentiment*. Their activities would only encourage the state to intensify its own violence and declare states of exception.

Despite negative comments of this kind, Nietzsche was popular with the Anarchist movement in Germany after his death as the "prophet of a new age" for his critique of the state, as well as his craving for "union with the earth" and his defense of plurality, experimentation and *Persönlichkeit*.[25] His middle writings are replete with a dark image of the modern state and call for a new form of democracy yet to come (WS 293) to replace it where the individual is no longer "a perfect instrument" (WP 757) of state control. Rejecting contractarian narratives, he makes no bones about the fact the state was formed through blood and conquest and not consensus:

> blond beasts, a conqueror and master race which, organized for war and with the ability to organize, unhesitatingly lays its terrible claws upon a populace perhaps tremendously superior in numbers but still formless and nomad . . . He who can command, he who is by nature 'master'," he who is violent in act and bearing—what has he to do with contracts! (GM 2.17)

According to Nietzsche, the oldest state appeared as "a fearful tyranny, as an oppressive and remorseless machine, and went on working until this raw material of people and semi-animals was at last not only thoroughly kneaded and pliant but also *formed*" (GM 2.17). The state's existence is predicated on a form of organized immorality: "*internally*: as police, penal law, classes, commerce, family; *externally*: as will to power, to war, to conquest, to revenge" (WP 717).

Nietzsche's middle writings pose the question of the state's legitimacy by critiquing its nationalist ideological noise, its aversion to nomadism and its reactive security hysteria. The state uses exaggerated emergencies to beguile the public with "investigations, undertakings, reorganizations" (HH 448). In the face of democratic forces, rulers "cling with their teeth to their dignity as warlords: for this they require wars, that is to say states of exception in which that slow constitutional pressure of the forces of democracy lets up" (WS 281). The state is incompatible with great culture as education becomes corrupted, turning citizens into state functionaries and wasting the talent of exceptional individuals:

> Culture and the state—one should not deceive oneself about this—are antagonists . . . All great ages of culture are ages of political decline: what is great culturally has always been unpolitical, even *antipolitical*. (TI 8.4)

Most importantly for Nietzsche, the state is bound up with political theology: "The belief in a divine order of political affairs, in a *mysterium* in the existence of the state, has a religious origin: if religion disappears the state will inevitably lose its old veil of Isis and no longer awaken awe" (HH 472). He briefly entertains an alternative vision of a reformed state that employs religion as a mythical instrument and is founded on a meritocracy, but without the buttress of a political theology, "a later generation will also see the state to become meaningless in certain stretches of the earth" (HH 472). Over time, he imagines the state will dissolve and some other organizing power will emerge just as the state superseded previous forms of association, such as the clan, family, or *polis*.

Nietzsche brings his critique of the state to a crescendo in *Thus Spoke Zarathustra*, viewing it as the enforcer of a slow euthanasia for its people: "State I call it where all are poison drinkers, the good and the base; state, where all can lose themselves, the good and the base; state, where the slow suicide of all is called—'life'" (Z 1.11). From his rented room in Sorrento, he could see two islands from his window—the Blessed Isle (the island of Ischia, bathed in the light of the sun) and next to it the Fire Hound Isle (the volcano Vesuvius, full of smoke, lava, noxious emissions and explosive violence). Zarathustra declares that Fire Hound Isle symbolizes the state:

> Like you yourself the state is a hypocrite hound; like you it likes to speak with smoke and bellowing—to make believe, like you, that it speaks from the belly of things. For it wants absolutely to be the most important animal on earth, this state; and people believe it, too. (Z 2.18)

The "hypocrite hound" is the engine of an "Infernal Racket" that signals the violent changes it forces through, although these are not a change of values but ones of expediency (Z 2.18). A "horse of death jingling with the trappings of divine honours" (Z 1.11), the state is full of "superfluous people" who desire power and the lever of power over others, a place where often "filth sits upon the throne—and often the throne upon filth, too" (Z 1.11). As "the coldest of all cold monsters" (Z 1.11), the state enacts its violence through the scarlet judges who cruelly enjoy sending the criminal to his death (Z 1.6).

Zarathustra is, in many ways, the anarchist *par excellence*: "Where the state *ends*, look, look, brothers! Can't you see it, the rainbow, and the bridges of the overman?" (Z 1.11). He urges us to "[l]eave the idolatry of the superfluous" and "[l]eave the smoke of human sacrifices" (Z 1.11). He seeks out friends to share joy and agonistic tension with but finds they have become followers instead of believing in themselves: "Now I bid you lose me and find yourselves; and only when you have denied me, I will return to you" (Z 1.22.3). He seeks equals, creators, harvesters, and celebrants: "Companions the creator seeks and not corpses, not herds, or believers either. Fellow creators the creator seeks, those who inscribe new values on new tablets" (Z P9). Against the scarlet judges of the state, Zarathustra has the vision of an anarchistic community of self-policing autonomous individuals: "Can you give yourself your own evil and your own good and hang your own will over yourself as a law? Can you be your own judge and avenger of your law?" (Z 1.17).

Someday, Nietzsche hopes,"we will no longer have the heart for the logical sin that lies concealed in anger and punishment, whether practiced individually, or socially" (WS 183). Lives should be lived from the inside, for an individual is entitled "to determine what they understand by a tolerable life" (HH 438). This is in opposition to the (socialist) state which "outdoes everything in the past" and aims at the "destruction of the individual" by reducing her to an "*organ of the community*" (HH 473). True justice originates between parties of approximately equal power where there is no clearly recognizable superiority of force: "Justice is thus requital and exchange under the presupposition of an approximately equal power position" (HH 92). Against the warmongering of the state, he champions the values of peace and cooperation, describing the wisdom of neighbouring chieftains who came to the recognition "how each could even assist and rescue the other in times of need instead of exploiting and augmenting this need of his neighbour as heretofore" (WS 190). As a general principle, Nietzsche warns us to consent to "*As Little State as Possible!*" (D 179).

Inspired by existentialism, especially Nietzsche's "spiritual nomadism" (D 452) and Sartre's *fusing group*, postmodernists, such as Deleuze (1992, 1988), propose an alternative logic of collectivization, a collaborative alliance that sets a new agenda for posthuman politics as a "destituent logic" to the "constituent logic" of control societies. Such an alliance heralds a "new politics" of nomadic thought that decodifies the state without recodifying it by pursuing "a logic of coessential positivities and coexistent affirmations." Melding together Nietzsche's anarchistic and ecological perspectives, Deleuze and Guattari (1994: 102) advocate *geophilosophy*, an approach that avoids teleology and statism, emphasizing a plurality of forms of human habitation, including nomadic and other non-state groupings, in which seas, deserts, caves and mountainous terrains all become forms of smooth space, fields of unconstrained movement of bodies and thought.[26] The posthumanist destituent logic of the *stateless state* engenders a radical form of democratic alliance, a kind of "democratic confederalism," or "democracy without the state" similar in concept to Nietzsche's "new democracy" and to Sartre's "decentralizing and concrete socialism" (FS 13).[27]

## FANON'S HUMANIST NATION STATE

Fanon holds the view that we should not preordain what the state can become since its possibilities are manifold and can only be realized through willed action. He is not vehemently anti-Statist in the same vein as Sartre, or Nietzsche and supports *rebuilding* rather than *demolishing* the state apparatus. Historical conditions evolve, reality is contingent, and concerted action has to be worked through to see what will emerge in a radical democracy when sovereignty is in the hands of the people. He envisages a new kind of state to be possible, one no longer premised on repression and exploitation but one that substantiates culture and materializes freedom. In 1959 at the Second Congress of Black Writers and Artists in Rome, Fanon lectured on the importance of the *nation state* as a political and cultural unit without which cultures degenerate and eventually perish. In *The Damned of the Earth*, he writes: "The nation is not only the condition of culture, its fruitfulness, its continuous renewal, and its deepening. It is also a necessity" (WE 197). Against the general consensus of the Congress, he argued for a strategic alliance of federal nation states in the place of a supranational pan-African political body. Following decolonization and independence, it is necessary to reestablish "the sovereignty of the nation" and create a new national reality, a "nation born of the concerted action of the people," as a willed nation not defined by ethnicity, or religious creed.[28] Modelling his ideas on Sartre's account of the fusing group in the *Critique*, Fanon envisages an emerging Algerian nation where "the racial and racist level is transcended."[29]

Unlike Sartre's anarchist route, however, Fanon seeks salvation for humanity on the path of the composite nation "to embrace the nation as a whole, to embody the constantly dialectical truth of the nation, and to will here and now the triumph of man in his totality" (WE 141). "To politicize the masses," Fanon writes, "is to make the nation in its totality a reality for every citizen" (WE 140). Although nation was the decisive category in Fanon's affirmative thinking, race (despite being "an obscure ideological formation concealing an economic reality"), would still play an important role—"it is clear that what divides this world is first and foremost what species, what race one belongs to" (WE 5). However, Fanon concludes, "[t]his historical obligation to racialize their claims, to emphasize an African culture rather than a national culture leads the African intellectuals into a dead end" (WE 152). In Fanon's view, nationalism is an unavoidable rite of passage, "a necessary but far from sufficient condition for liberation, perhaps even a sort of temporary illness that must be gone through." It is always possible for nationalism to become sclerotic and obstructive to freedom when "the sun of independence" results in "another form of dependence," decorated with "a national anthem, a flag, frontiers, and nationalist fervour."[30]

Fanon preaches welfare nationalism based on a secular, multiracial, multicultural "national consciousness" in which everyone had a participatory measure in the general will. This pluralist, democratic national consciousness, he argues, is radically different to previous nationalisms since it will "shake the worm-eaten foundations of the edifice" (BSWM xi) that it inherits. Ultimately, a new humanistic culture is dependent on "national liberation and the renaissance of the state" in which equality is the key principle. A progressive nationalism is an active exercise of self-reflection that leads us to the realization of our fundamental connection and therefore "[n]ational consciousness, which is not nationalism, is the only thing that will give us an international dimension" (WE 199). "For Europe, for ourselves, and for humanity," Fanon urges in the closing words of *The Damned of the Earth*, "we must turn over a new leaf, we must work out new concepts, and try to set afoot a new man" (WE 255).

By twisting and stretching Nietzsche's political insights, and, as Michel Foucault (2001: 53–4) prescribed, "making them groan and protest," existentialism yields radically divergent conceptions of the state from Heidegger's Total State based on the *Führerprinzip*, to the Stateless State of Sartre's syndicalism predicated on the spontaneous and co-operative coming together of free emergent groups and individuals, to the reconstructed Humanistic State advocated by Fanon. It reflects the many colors that have illuminated existentialism's iridescent political spectrum lighting up the knot of tensions and contradictions present in Nietzsche's catholic political vision. Above all, inspired by Nietzsche's middle writings and his promise of "a democracy yet to come" (WS 293), French existentialism urges people to lose their political crutches, abandon leaders and "find themselves" (Z 1.22.3) through forms of collective action that express and guarantee their precious individual freedoms.

## CHAPTER NINE

# "Language Is the House of Being. In Its Home Man Dwells"

## (Heidegger, *Letter on Humanism*) LANGUAGE/WRITING

Language, more than anything, defines *Homo Sapiens* and explains our evolutionary rise from marginal mammalian hunter-gatherers to "Masters of the Earth." Without the ability to relay information, communicate abstract ideas, record our thoughts, express emotion through words and song, create histories, and invent mythical worlds, we would not be recognizable as the exceptional hominid animals that we are. In common with other philosophical schools, such as Logical Positivism (1920s) and Structuralism (1960s), existentialism makes language a special concern and places it at the epicenter of thought but denies that thought and reality coincide in some kind of exact correspondence. Existentialists are concerned not with language's logical structure, or grammatical syntax but with its existential significance in disclosing Being and communicating socially. Like Wittgenstein of the *Philosophical Investigations*, existentialists view language as *constitutive*. It is not the clothing but the body of my thought, Merleau-Ponty argues, and forms the limit of my world: "Thought is no "internal" thing, and does not exist independently of the world and of words" (PP 182). For Heidegger, language is an *existentiale*, a basic possibility of being belonging to Dasein that is central to human life: "Living, for the human being, means speaking" (GA18: 21). It is the primary mode of being-in-the-world by which we are able to comprehend the things around us: "The fundamental mode of being in which the human being is in its world is in speaking with it, about it, of it" (GA18: 18). Like the later Wittgenstein, existentialists offer some guidance for the proper, or rightful use of language since not only can language reveal but also conceal and bewitch.

This chapter examines the central importance existentialists give to language as a dwelling in which our experiences are formed and its role in both illuminating and obfuscating consciousness. Starting with Heidegger's *word mysticism* and moving on to Sartre's *sacrilizing of language*, we end with a discussion of what writing meant to existentialists and how they advise reading their various texts.

## CONSTITUTION, TRUTH AND BEWITCHMENT

Heidegger's views on language are mainly expressed in *Being and Time* (1927), *The Origin of the Work of Art* (1935), and *Remembrance* (1943). In *Being and Time*, language is understood primarily as a phenomenological tool that helps us to be in-the-world and make sense of it, since in order to use things I must have a "context of signification" for which words provide a script (BT 150). Language is grounded in pre-established significations as the common product of previous speakers and is inadequate to express my own authentic existence. The "call of conscience" that beckons Dasein to its "ownmost possibility" is wordless, a keeping-silent which is "indefinite," and outside the worldly articulations of discourse and understanding (BT 273).

For the later Heidegger, language is the vehicle of articulation through which we become intelligently aware of Being, a dwelling in which we belong rather than a cage that imprisons us. As the "house of being," we did not invent language and could not have done since, before speaking, we must be addressed by Being. Although in *Being and Time*, he dismisses a "word-mysticism" (BT 262), he moves towards one in his later writings, showing his fascination with the etymology and primordial meaning of words where he believes Being manifests itself through them. His "phenomenology of words as clues" maintains that if language is the domain and gift of Being, then there occurs in it some revelation of the character of Being, although we can only talk about the mystery of Being obliquely and symbolically. Here, Heidegger follows Jaspers who also explores the relation of language to the ultimate mystery of Being. This is revealed not literally but in "ciphers" that evoke transcendence but cannot conceptualize or objectify it. Writing of "that striking paradox of a language to end language," Jaspers travels towards mysticism where, influenced by the Asian and European mystics, such as Meister Eckhart who also impressed Heidegger, he finds "a marvellous power in these attempts to pass not only beyond all ciphers, to reach the unthinkable, unspeakable ground that bears us and encompasses all encompassing."[1] In *Poetry, Language, Thought*, poetry is the royal way of expressing and revealing the multidimensionality of Being: "The nature of art is poetry; the nature of poetry, in turn, is the founding of truth" (PLT 72). Beyond this, art, and poetry play a crucial role in the process of "state-founding." In "Holderlin and the Essence of Poetry" (1930), he declares: "Language is the *Ur*-poetry through which a *Volk* poeticizes Being . . . By virtue of great poetry, a *Volk* enters into *history*" (GA40: 180). As a consequence, he lambasts the linguistic "degeneracy" of *Weltsprache*, or a "cosmopolitan language" as "*out of joint*," and he champions local dialect. Language that is authentic "*is always a particular language that is innately derived from what is Volk-related and tribal . . . It is always the language of a Heimat . . . Language is language as mother tongue*" (GA13: 156).

Heidegger's treatment of language offers a somewhat ambiguous view of individuality and sociality. His initial view in *Being and Time* attests to the belonging-together of the human species and the publicness of words away from which true authenticity can be found in the wordless "Call" that summons individuals to realize their innermost possibilities. Idle talk does not really communicate, or disclose reality in its fullness but reiterates cliché and simplification, preventing a creative encounter with things themselves by leveling down. His later view translates authentic individuality into the entity of the Volkish state, and language itself becomes just one of Being's historical manifestations in its "destining." Anticipating later poststructuralist theories, Heidegger presents humanity as the pawn or effect of language that acts as "the house of the truth of Being": "Language brings about and produces man, and so thought, man would be one promise of language" (GA12: 12). In its essence, language is not the utterance of an organism but the clearing-concealing advent of Being itself:

> Man acts as though he were the shaper and master of language, while in fact language remains the master of man . . . For strictly, it is language that speaks. Man first speaks when, and only when, he responds to language by listening to its appeal. (PLT 215–6)

The later thinking of Heidegger is guilty of reifying language and succumbs to the urge to make language into "a quasi-divinity," an autonomous realm of Being that "uses," or "positions" humanity for its own articulation.[2] Although the task of philosophy as outlined in *Being and Time* "is to preserve the *force of the most elemental words* in which Dasein expresses itself, and to keep the common understanding from levelling them off to that unintelligibility which functions in the end as a source of pseudo-problems' (BT 262), many see in Heidegger's philosophy a performative contradiction in his injunction to "avoid uninhibited word-mysticism" (BT 262). Seeking to dissolve the leveling of language that bewitches our understanding of the world and to find a new poetic tongue for expressing the mysteries of Being, critics divide as to whether he provides us with a set of neologisms and new metaphors that come from nowhere like "lightning bolts which blaze new trails," or whether "Heidegger-Speak" is really "Heidegger-Cackling," a bewildering profusion of fuzzwords designed to impress rather than to inform or clarify.[3]

## LANGUAGE, SELF AND OTHER

Throughout his writings, Nietzsche heeds the heaviness of our social conditioning and the way that social and historical forces produce and also delimit the individual. His early work presents the individual as a cipher and singularization of the collective (a Universal Singular) bound by an objective spirit that ushers in a horizon of myths and common understandings (BT 23). The past has layered structures within us, deposited through constituted meaning and memory: "the human carries around the memory of all previous generations" (PTAG 35) unaware that she is voicing "[t]he spiritual activity of millennia laid down in language" (PTAG 31). Central to the "reality of the Other" is language since consciousness, according to Nietzsche, develops only under "the pressure of the need for communication" (JS 354). The subject derives from the outside born out of intersubjective practices and forged out of collective demands rather than emanating from inside as in Descartes' cogito. The constituent power of the imagination that lies at the heart of the conscious self is, first, and foremost, an *intersubjective* thing, a social and historical act of singularity expressed *within* and *through* language:

> Consciousness is actually nothing but a network of connections between man and man . . . The man who devises signs is at the same time the man who is always more acutely self-conscious; it is only as a social animal that man has learnt to become conscious of himself. (JS 354)

The French existentialists also viewed language as constitutive of thought, an intersubjective medium through which we can express our singularity and freedom. According to Merleau-Ponty, through language I transport myself into the other's perspective and become vulnerable to them: "Speaking and listening . . . presuppose the capacity to allow oneself to be pulled down and rebuilt again by the other person" (PW 17). Language embodies reversibility of perspective, an openness to the other that also expresses differences in our singularity, a "dwelling" (S 232) in which we do not coincide with ourselves since we can frame new meanings and subvert existing ones. This creates a shared world, or common meeting place of unanticipated possibilities in which we can articulate our experiences and encounter the other in surprise and encroachment, trespassing (PW 133) and mutual transformation (PW 142).

Rather than imposing the universal on the particular, language is a spontaneity that gives new meanings to a constituted world. We must not let the search for shared meaning obscure the strangeness and singularity of the Other and "iron out the I and the Thou in an experience shared by a plurality, thus introducing the impersonal into the heart of subjectivity and eliminating the individuality of perspectives" (PP 355–6). In order to preserve the active speaking subject, Merleau-Ponty calls into question "the very conception of language as pure object" (SNS 87). Linguistic structure is not an autonomous entity of which individual speakers are passive recipients and automatic transmitters since these structures can "burst apart" as people and groups also shape language creatively (S 124). Expression does not disappear as the individual "tak[es] up a position in the world of his meanings" (PP 193).

At the same time, language outstrips the speaker. Speech is "an originating realm" (PP 174) where the meaning of what we say extends beyond the initial intention of our words to create an infinite array of significations. Subjectivity is inseparable from language-in-use at the moment of execution but the subject dissolves in the articulation of itself as it becomes a mere property of a symbolic system. Evangelizing language, Merleau-Ponty advocates a "new humanism" severed from its metaphysical anchors that resides in the transformative power of speech and dialogue where we can express a desire for a possible imagined future and articulate the ways in which we can make it concretely real (S 241):

> man is the being who . . . represents himself to himself, sees himself, imagines himself, and gives himself rigorous or fanciful symbols of himself, it is quite clear that in return every change in our representation of man translates a change in man himself. (S 225)

Sartre's early work defines language as "being-for-other from the outset" (BN 493) that extends to "all expressive phenomena" (BN 494), including gestures, body language, mannerisms and dress. He prefigures Merleau-Ponty's claim that language presents a third genus of being, arguing that my being-for-others is language and begins to elaborate on how language influences values and conditions subjectivity that he develops in much more detail in his later work. In *Being and Nothingness*, Sartre maintains while the language I speak does not emanate from me, it "cannot constitute an external limit of freedom" (BN 519). Nevertheless, he theorizes the self as a *dialectical object*, a synthesis of subjective apprehension and external objectification.[4] We learn about ourselves through language as objects for the other's gaze as "a source of fascination and of horror" (BN 362). Language is a kind of "third eye" that enables us to see "into our neighbour's heart" (WL 12). Since it forms part of the raw material out of which we collectively create meaning in the world, structuring our lived experience and knowledge, "nothing precedes language" (FI 38). Meaning is only communicable through language for it is the acquisition of language that delivers us from the "profound and solitary reality" of our first years (SM 63), catapulting us into a shared world where every object is replete with meanings and where we are never "really alone" because our "thoughts are communicable" (SG 590).

Through the concepts of "Objective Spirit" and "practico-inert," Sartre acknowledges the crucial role of language in constituting subjectivity. The beliefs of a given society, he states, are captured in "the untranslatable locutions of its language" (BO 22). After 1945, he stresses our situatedness in language, which he describes as the "objectification of a class, the reflection of conflicts, latent, or declared, and the particular manifestation of alienation" (SM 113). In *Saint Genet*, language is said to become Genet's "most inward reality and the most rigorous expression of his exile" (SG 276), while in *What Is Literature?*, writing is seen as the essential medium for the expression of freedom in communication with others. By the time of Sartre's later period, self and language are irrevocably interwoven: "significations come from man and from his project, but they are inscribed everywhere in things and in the order of things" (SM 156). *Search for a Method* reiterates Sartre's linguistic encoding of the self, showing the ways in which language and culture "are not inside the individual like stamps registered by his nervous system. It is the individual who is inside culture and inside language" (SM 113). "Man is for himself and for others," he affirms, "a *signifying* being . . . a creator of *signs*" (SM 152). He develops this deconstructive impetus further still in the *Critique* writing openly of language comprising "acts without an author" (CDR 152) and "constructions without a constructor" (CDR 754). Sartre presages poststructuralist accounts in recognizing that "structure produces behaviour," but warns that we should not pass over the reverse side of the dialectic in silence: "Man can only 'be spoken' to the extent that he speaks" (FI 2). Although like Heidegger, Sartre's later thinking highlights the constitutive powers of inherited linguistic schema, he does not reify language into a quasi-divinity but instead provides a mediated dialectical understanding that enmeshes structure *and* agency.

## SACRALIZING LANGUAGE

The Spanish proto-existentialist Miguel de Unamuno was one of the first to appropriate the novel form to express existential truths. He viewed philosophy and poetry as twin sisters, understanding language as creative more than descriptive. Novelists such as Fyodor Dostoevsky and Franz Kafka foreshadowed many existentialist themes taken up by Kierkegaard, Beauvoir, Sartre and Camus, such as the death of God and alienation (*Notes from the Underground*), thrownness and absurdity (*The Trial*), and ontological lostness and bewilderment (*The Castle*). In her 1946 essay *Littérature et métaphysique*, Beauvoir displaces the traditional boundaries between philosophy and literature, placing them in a reciprocal position where one functions as a type of excess, or *supplement* (both addition and replacement) to the other. The true novel is metaphysical insofar as it explores the historical and temporal dimension of lived human experience, something the philosophical text can only convey abstractly. For Beauvoir, the literary text remains opaque and ambiguous, irreducible to its exhaustion by reason, exploring the space in-between that reflects a view of reality as dense, multi-layered, and mystifying, requiring choices and interpretations of a situation whose meaning emerges rather than is given:

> Existence—others have said it and I have already repeated it more than once myself—cannot be reduced to ideas, it cannot be stated in words: it can only be evoked through the medium of an imaginary object; to achieve this, one must recapture the surge of the backwash, and the contradictions of life itself. (FC 332)

Beauvoir's views on literature are most fully expressed in her contribution to a 1964 symposium "What Can Literature Do?" and her lecture "My experience as a writer." Literature communicates to us, she explains, because the world is not a fixed totality but rather a "detotalized totality" (1965: 76). We live in a common world but with our own singular perspective on it formed through experience, class, social condition, situation and our chosen projects. We can thus communicate with each other but there is nonetheless still something about our singularity that is incommunicable and opaque to others: "I am the only subject for myself who says 'I'," and it's the same for everyone" (1965: 78). Literature gives us otherwise barred access to another's consciousness, or singular voice: "Literature is—if it is authentic literature—a means of going beyond separation by affirming it. It affirms it because when I read a book, a book which is important for me, someone speaks to me; the author is part of her book" (1965: 79). By identifying with the author, their world becomes temporarily mine: "I abdicate my 'I' in favor of that person who is speaking; and yet I remain myself" (1965: 82).

Beauvoir wrote literature so that "each of the sounds that I could draw from myself had a chance to awaken echoes in a great many other hearts" (FC 276). The writer attempts to set up communication with others by means of the uniqueness of his personal experience and yet "the words born from his pen escape him. The reader is more fortunate; he is an active partner and yet the book showers unexpected wealth upon him" (ASD 130, 155). Beauvoir wallows in the resplendent magic of words to express and convey emotion: "There are days so beautiful that you want to shine like the sun, I mean to splash bright words over all the world; there are hours so black that no other hope is left but the cry that you would like to vent" (FC 666). "The metamorphosis of the human grub into a speaking individual," she exclaims, "has something amazing about it" (ASD 22). Words bestow a "transcendent power" on those who read and write them:

> Words without doubt, universal, eternal, presence of all in each, are the only transcendent power I recognize and am affected by; they vibrate in my mouth, and with them I can communicate with humanity. They wrench tears, night, death itself from the moment, from contingency, and then transfigure them. (FC 666)

Essentially, writing is creation: "each page, each sentence, makes a fresh demand on the powers of invention and requires an unprecedented choice. Creation is adventure, it is youth and liberty." This has a liberating and transformative effect on the writer who "escape[s] his own petrifaction at the moments when he is writing" (FC 671). She doesn't discriminate against any kind of writing—"No particular kind of writing is on the face of it privileged; none is condemned" (ASD 130)—including poetry which "I hardly read at all" yet is "a very special means of communication" (ASD 189). Although her works might grant her a posthumous presence in the world of others, communication in the present is the key motivation of her literary praxis: "A writer's works may live on and on, and I wanted to share a perennity in which I should myself be embodied, but above all I wanted my contemporaries to hear and understand me" (ASD 38–9).

Like Beauvoir, Sartre was struck by the "transcendent power" of words. Devouring the toxic "ancient bile of Flaubert" when young led him, he confesses, to confuse "literature with prayer," and make a "human sacrifice" of it, furnishing him with a neurotic attitude towards writing (W 113). His understanding of literary survival (expressed in *Words*) "was obviously a kind of transfer from the Christian religion" (FS 171). Shifting the presence of sacrality into the realm of literature, Sartre felt in his vocation as a writer he was "receiving Holy Orders" (W 250). He was first and foremost a writer before he was a philosopher but philosophy was integral to his writing: "A writer had to be a philosopher. As soon as I knew what philosophy was it seemed to me natural to insist upon that in a writer" (FS 139). As Beauvoir recounts, Sartre was "inexhaustible" in his writing, forever composing "a whole series of ballads, counting-out rhymes, epigrams, madrigals, thumbnail fables, and occasional poems of every description" (PL 18). He was seized by the "unknown magic" of language in which words are grouped together and then all of a sudden disclose the world and imbue it with a heightened meaning (FS 140). He held belief in a magical idea of literature where "[t]he book belonged to the imaginary, but beyond the book there was truth" (FS 216). In contrast to the contingency of real life in which "people moved about, they were ordinary" (FS 141), a book has a definite duration that constitutes "the work's necessity," tying author and reader into a complex relationship of time and seducing the reader not dishonestly but through the apprehension and search for veracity—"seduction by the truth" (FS 211). Sartre follows Heidegger in assigning language and words a special role in revealing reality. Above all else, he equates the creation of words with liberty: I've always looked upon [writing] as one of the forms of freedom" (FS 167). The function of literature is the appeal of the author to the freedom of the reader by revealing "a world to be impregnated always with more freedom" (WL 47). The committed writer knows that words are action, and that "to reveal is to change and that one can reveal only by planning to change" (WL 14). Writing is a creative act of freedom that aims at a total renewal of the world.

In *What is Literature?*, Sartre distinguishes between prose and poetry. In prose language serves as an instrument which points to something external to it and is therefore capable of revealing its meanings, but poetry is concerned with language as an end in itself and is therefore not concerned with communicating the world and does not qualify as "committed literature." Sartre excludes poetry from his conception of literature as it lacks specific referents since it surrenders words to ambiguity by eliding specific meanings. Poets and painters can present a dilapidated building but only writers can describe it and make it seem like "a symbol of social injustice and provoke your indignation" (WL 4). By 1960, however, Sartre changes his view and describes the poet Mallarmé as fully engaged: "his commitment seems to me as total as possible: social as much as poetic" (1972: 14). He comes to appreciate the Heideggerian perspective that poetry can be a spur to action in disclosing the world anew. For Heidegger, it is poetry that annihilates the dichotomy between subject and object that has insinuated itself into the grammar of Western thinking creating bewitchment and concealment. Poetry has the special capacity to render clear the "undiscoverable" of the earth, revealing a mystery without touching, invading, or controlling it. Through the power of poetry "we can move out of our everydayness," and never return to it as we left it (GA39: 22). Moreover, it creates and establishes a collective bond and identity. Poets are "state–creators" who articulate and find a common home for a fundamental mood: "Poets have mostly arisen at the beginning, or at the end of a world period. With song the nations step out of the heaven of their childhood into active life, into the land of Culture" (GA39: 20).

## WRITING AND READING

Existentialists were constantly pushing the envelope with their innovations in spreading philosophical ideas beyond the secluded ivory towers of academia, weaving together the personal and political as they explored alternative forms in their *literary phenomenology*, writing journals, plays, novels, newspaper articles, and making films, alongside the traditional philosophical treatise. Kierkegaard and Nietzsche explore different formats and styles of writing, writing in pseudonyms, autobiographies, aphorisms, diaries and poetry. Marcel, alongside his dramatic works, eschews a systematic philosophical method in favor of a "neo-Socratic" method of questioning and dialogue. Heidegger evangelizes poetry in the place of philosophy as an ideal mode of communicating and revealing Being. His diverse texts—lecture courses, articles, meditations, correspondences, dialogues and poems—all contribute to the "scripturality" of his philosophy and bear testament, as he described it, to the "now rare handicraft of writing" (GA9: 174).

With the act of writing comes the task of reading. It is often asked how we should read the works of the existentialists when they are expressed in literary, pseudonymic, or aphoristic form. There is uncertainty, for instance, about when Kierkegaard is being ironic in his texts or how much the views of the "indirect communication" expressed through his pseudonymous authors represent his own, written as they are in the form of diaries, fragments and postscripts.[5] Fanon's texts are written in the tradition of West Indian narrative storytelling, as spoken-word performances (to his wife Josie and his secretary Marie-Jeanne Manuellan) in which he voices his thoughts aloud as they take shape in the presence of the other. Heidegger's later texts are infused with poetry while the philosophical discourse of *Being and Time* proceeds in a "*non-argumentative and evocative fashion*," persuading the reader not with traditional forms of argumentation but through rhetorical strategies and the employment of neologisms whose conceptual self-evidence is merely assumed.[6] Beauvoir and Sartre wrote novels and plays in which they "set great store by nuances and ambiguities" (FC 332) that often test, or contradict the views which they express elsewhere. Nietzsche, the trained philologist, is ironically the hardest of all to pin down. Which mask of his do we take as his true face—Zarathustra, the Free Spirit, the Antichrist, Dionysus, the Nietzsche of his notes, or that of his published work only? Deliberately, he implores us *not* to understand him and thereby domesticate his thinking. His aphorisms require exegesis in order to decipher them and a higher level of engagement to be understood (GM P8). They enable him to purposely approach deep problems like cold baths: "one gets in quickly, one gets out quickly" (JS 381). They are necessarily incomplete (HH 207) and serve as tests for the reader (Z 1.7), lending them an interactive quality. The use of aphorisms, along with the use of paradox, wordplay, metaphor, and masks, invites evaluation and interpretation through its very form and constitution. One has no choice but to interpret and evaluate what Nietzsche actually means. Utilizing the gnomic form in his *War Diaries* and *Notebooks from Youth*, Sartre observes how "this free and fragmented form isn't subject to prior ideas, you write each thing according to the moment and only take stock when you want to" (1983: 14).

Nietzsche's aphoristic style, as Christine Daigle (2021: 34, 37) points out, is particularly advantageous for his endeavors, but the fact that he also uses other styles, such as poetry, essay writing, and even gospel-like song in *Zarathustra*, indicates the need for a style that is multiple in order to describe life and its dynamic play of forces. The Nietzschean method allows us to "go back to things themselves," as they appear in their non-systematic and non-linear way, and it does so by offering multiple perspectives on things. The aphoristic style Nietzsche adopts is indicative of how he conceives of human experience—not as a rationalistic, systematically organized, continuous, linear narrative, but rather as a collection of perspectives gained through a plentitude of experiences. The aphorism does not aim to unveil the truth about a specific reality or experience, but instead it aims at disclosing a possible truth, one truth among many others. It is from the effectiveness of the incomplete that the beholder is driven to work to form a more lucid picture (HH 178).

Although Nietzsche commends the play of perspectives, he warns us: "Above all, do not mistake me for someone else" (EH P1). He has firm expectations of his readers who must acknowledge the temporal quality of "the art of reading" (GM P8). It is essential, he advises, to slowly digest his texts:

> read slowly, deeply, looking cautiously before and aft, with reservations, with doors left open, with delicate eyes and figures . . . My patient friends, this book desires for itself only perfect readers and philologists: learn to read me well! (D P5)

Philology, the interpretation of texts, is to be understood as "the art of reading well"—to be able to read off a fact "without falsifying it by interpretation, without losing caution, patience, subtlety in the desire for understanding" (A 52).

Sartre's philological ideas of good reading are mixed, often balancing on a tightrope of humanist and anti-humanist equivocation. While stating in an interview, for instance, that "the life of people who write is projected in the writing in one way, or another" (1979b: 29), he maintains elsewhere that "the text towers above its author" (WL 34). He acknowledges that reading is always subject to many interpretations: "I know that other readers appropriate the idea at the same moment [as I do] who surpass the same material toward nearly the same, but *sensibly different* meanings" (IF3 52). What one reads is "enriched in my eyes by a thousand interpretations that escape me" (IF3 52). In Sartrean reading, we can recognize the notion that meaning always lies elsewhere to be decided at a later date: "the thought [read], in the instant I make it mine, remains definitively other, an other's thought that commands me to resuscitate it" (IF3 51). For Sartre, although words take on a life of their own when "language presents itself, in effect, as an autonomous system" (1966: 88) and where "structures express, or constitute intentions that determine me without being mine" (1977a: 10.97), nonetheless they still bear "the trace of man" (1966: 88) as they are taken up and used by speaking subjects. "[W]riters are alive before being dead" (WL 23), Sartre states, and we must be aware that the author silently communicates the metaphysical dimensions of their own lived experience and imparts his own style of living, or peculiar *flavor*. This is condensed in the text and can "be reconstituted by the end of a long acquaintance or biographical study" (FI2 8). The subject is always entangled within her own works, "projected in the writing in one way or another" (1979b: 29), or as Kierkegaard says, as "a sort of emanation in the text" (PJ 99). This view—"[t]he man is to be found in his book" (FS 15)—is never fully relinquished by Sartre, and one expressed poignantly in *Words* as he considers his own posterity through writing:

> Other consciousnesses have taken charge of me. They read *me* and I leap to their eyes; they talk about *me* and I am on everyone's lips, a universal and singular language; I have made myself a prospective interest for millions of glances. For anyone who knows how to like me, I am his most intimate disquiet: but if he wants to touch me, I draw aside and vanish: I exist nowhere but I *am*, at last! I am everywhere: a parasite on humanity, by my good deeds I prey on it and force it endlessly to revive my absence. (W 122)

Existentialism brings to life with critical scrutiny the central importance of language in understanding human reality—"Living, for the human being, means speaking" (GA18). It teaches us how language illuminates and constitutes the world around us. Sacralizing language, existentialist philosophers (Sartre, Jaspers, Marcel) uncover the force of words as a "transcendent power," or cipher through which the mystery of Being is glimpsed, as a dwelling place that we inhabit with others (Heidegger, Merleau-Ponty, Nietzsche) but also, as Beauvoir conceives, as a kind of "black magic" with "sinister effects" (MDD 18) that can bewitch our very thoughts and cloud our heads in metaphysical fog. Above all, as Fanon articulates, language, expressed most poignantly through writing, is a house of communication in which we live our lives alongside real, or imagined others:

> Writing is certainly the most beautiful discovery since it allows man to remember, to present things that have happened in order and above all to communicate with others, even when they are absent. (2015: 263)

CHAPTER TEN

# "In All Areas of Existence, Man Will Be Encircled Ever More Tightly by the Forces of Technology"

## (Heidegger, *Discourse on Thinking*) TECHNOLOGY/SCIENCE

Existentialists are not known for their technophilia. Indeed, in *The Prime of Life*, Beauvoir summarizes their techno-skepticism in no uncertain terms: "we despised science and technology" (PL 42). Her comments are indicative of the general mood of existentialist literature that paints a drab picture of life in the soulless environs and technology-saturated spaces of modern mass society. Fyodor Dostoevsky's *Notes from the Underground* (1864) is the narrative of the underground man who confesses to being a "sick man" alienated from a superficial, materialist and abstract society. His alienation is overwhelming and he falls into despair, unable to requite the love offered to him by Liza, a young prostitute. Rainer Maria Rilke's only novel *The Notebooks of Malte Laurids Brigge* (1910) echoes Dostoevsky in bemoaning the alienation, noise and friction of modern urban society. Franz Kafka's *The Trial* (1925) reveals modern life at its most impersonal, bureaucratic, senseless and coldly brutal as the protagonist Josef K. is arraigned and eventually shot for a crime the nature of which is never revealed to him by the faceless authorities which control and orchestrate his fate.

Existentialist philosophers largely follow suit with their literary forbears. In *Being and Having* and *Homo Viator*, Marcel scrutinizes the modern world as a broken world in which, through petty materialistic relationships and a narrow concern for technology, humans have lost appreciation of the natural world, other people and culture. His philosophical project is to recover our fallen position, a path of realignment to reinvoke a sense of respect and sacredness to the mystery of being. Heidegger offers a similar diagnosis and possible cure. Inspired by Rilke's pure phenomenology of the objects of modern life, along with Kierkegaard's decisionism and his antipathy for the Crowd, his 1927 *Being and Time* delineates the public world of the They, a type of mass existence governed by instrumentality, inauthenticity and idle talk where everyone is "Other than himself," and whose point of exit is through resoluteness, and the siren call of conscience. Since its publication, Heidegger's seminal essay *A Question Concerning Technology* (1954) has become the go-to reference for a philosophical understanding of technology, both in terms of what it *is* and what it *means* for the future of humanity's earthly existence.

As Dominic Smith (2024: 236) observes, however, Heidegger's account has tended to overshadow others, such as that of Kierkegaard, Ortega y Gasset, or Sartre, who differ from Heidegger's fatalistic approach and offer a more mediated, empirical reading of technology and its multivalent effects. Although Heidegger's "tool analysis" in *Being and Time* was very influential, his later philosophy of *enframing* has been eclipsed by more concrete approaches that are less abstract. "Heidegger," according to Smith, is now shorthand for a "classical" philosophy of technology as a "totalizing force" that abstracts from concreteness and particular artefacts and which has obscured other existentialist approaches which are heterogeneous. In this chapter, we begin with Kierkegaard's analysis as an early observer of modern technology through his critique of abstraction and trace how subsequent existentialists developed his insights into their own diagnosis of modern technocratic society.

## EARLY OBSERVERS

As offspring of the nineteenth century, Kierkegaard and Nietzsche were witness to the birth of many modern technological advances. The invention of electromagnets (1825), the microphone (1827), typewriter (1829), postage stamp (1837), machine gun (1862), telephone (1876), lightbulb (1878), cash register (1884), automobile (1885), and gramophone (1887), to name only a handful, were all technological items that would have a huge bearing on the landscape of modern life. In Kierkegaard's mind, however, it was the invention of the advanced printing press in 1801, twelve years before his birth, which affected him the most. Despite the fact that such technology would spread his ideas around the globe,[1] he judges the press to be a great menace to society and a key technological condition for the "monstrous non-entity" of "the Public" (1978: 90). In his journals he records the daily press is "a dreadful evil" antithetical to Christianity that is governed by envy, abstraction and anonymity. It is a "human fantasy" that "exercises enormous power" over individuals, "an abstract attempt to constitutionalize a lack of conscience as a principle of the state and humanity" (PJ 502). According to Kierkegaard, mass public opinion spread through the press "works as a colossal abstraction, the generation," which "is designed to make personality impossible" (PJ 570). It is mass disseminated public opinion that drives the crippling phenomenon of *leveling*, a technologically mediated process that imperils authentic subjectivity, or selfhood. In this process

> no particular individual can take the lead in levelling for then he would, after all, become the commander and escape this levelling. Particular individuals may contribute to levelling, each in his own little group, but levelling is an abstract power and is abstraction's victory over individuals (1978: 84)

The overall result of the pursuit of "advancement by way of the numerical" that governs the abstractions of mass society is that "the entire race is degraded" (PJ 573). With an alarmist catastrophizing tone, Kierkegaard adjudges individuals have become less and less significant in the face of the abstract mass and that "THE DEMORALIZATION OF THE HUMAN RACE advances at an increasing pace" (PJ 634).

Nietzsche voices similar concerns about mass technological society. On discovering Dostoevsky's *Notes from Underground* in a bookshop, he felt extraordinary joy and the immediate instinct of kinship for the Russian writer. He too perceives the "dwarfing of man" (WP 890) in commercial society, "turning humanity into *sand*!" (D 174) by grating off the rough edges of life in a collective drive toward timidity and uniformity. The capitalist work ethic is self-destructive, Nietzsche complains, and work is a mere mechanical activity, resulting in "absolute regularity, punctilious and unthinking obedience, a mode of life fixed once and for all, fully occupied time, a certain permission, indeed training for 'impersonality', for self-forgetfulness" (GM 3.18). This is a process of collective loss in which "man is diminished" (WP 866). Modern workers are perhaps, even though this is "slavery in a higher sense" (A 54), worse off in some ways than slaves (HH 457) since factory work robs the worker of his artisanal craft and obliterates individuality (D 173). Moreover, industriousness and technology infect all aspects of life in modern capitalism from science and art (UM 1.8), religion (BGE 58) and relations between women and men (BGE 239). In full agreement with Kierkegaard, Nietzsche identifies "parliamentary government and the press" as the main architects of the leveling process "because these are the means by which the herd animal becomes master" (WP 753).

While technology was first viewed in the late nineteenth century as an organ-extension of humanity, the machinery of war in the First World War and the rapid industrialization of the West brought technology to the critical perspective of Ortega Y Gasset, Marcel, Berdayev, Spengler, Cassirer, and Jünger who gave it a strong existential twist. In his 1940 essay "Man the Technician," Ortega argues we have no choice "whether to live in nature, or to take advantage of . . . supernature" (1962: 152). Ortega conceives of the individual as a kind of "shipwreck," and the situation as the ocean dominated by technologies as vectors of culture, economy, and social mores. Cast adrift, humanity "may easily lose sight of technology and of the conditions—the moral conditions, for example—under which it is produced and return to the primitive attitude of taking it for the gift of nature which is simply there."[2] Like Marx's account of commodity fetishism, Ortega's "supernature" identifies oscillating forms of enchantment and disenchantment that mystify the social and material relations that comprise it. However, although we quickly succumb to technology's allure and find ourselves dependent upon its material infrastructure, there is always a hidden feeling of uncanniness, or "unhomeliness" to this artificial environment.[3]

In *Man against Mass Society* (1951), Marcel echoes Kierkegaard's lament of technological modernity that has led to the development of greater conformity, "a kind of lowest common denominator of well-being" (MAMS 86). The popular demand for equality leads to leveling down, and feelings of resentment. Wallowing anxiously in "an atmosphere of latent fanaticism" where disaster threatens (MAMS 151–2), "mass men" become prey to false prophets and dangerous demagogues. In this soulless technological environment, life is being less and less felt "as a gift to be handed on, and more and more felt as a kind of incomprehensible calamity" (MAMS 94). When we are taken with "having," we enter into relations where possessions begin to possess us and a man becomes "the prisoner of his techniques" (MAMS 83). There is a "secret bond" between "the physical destruction wrought by the atomic bomb and the spiritual destruction wrought by techniques of human degradation" (MAMS 14). Nazi labour camps, state genocide, and systemic extermination are a logical consequence of bureaucratic programmes of depersonalization that view humans "on the model of the machine" (MAMS 179). Hence, if a person's output falls below his maintenance, "he should be sent to the scrap heap like a worn-out car" (MAMS 182).

According to Marcel, politically organized resistance is futile and alienating: "There can be no question here of my attempting to define anything resembling a political line of action. What we have to do with is rather an inner attitude" (MAMS 244). He warns against involvement in the political sphere[4] beyond the personal sphere for "it is not the business of the philosopher, or the sage to take charge of a technocratic world; he could only do so by making himself a slave" (MAMS 271). In this vein, he criticizes Bertrand Russell for his involvement beyond "the spiritual domain" (TW 31) in protesting against nuclear armament. For Marcel, we must maintain faith and hope against the dehumanizing onslaught of the technocratic world that is empty and hollow. In the spirit of abstraction we face a metaphysical crisis of values that can only be overcome through "grace," and "God's "light":

> there is probably no more dangerous an illusion than that of imagining that some readjustments of social or institutional conditions could suffice in itself to appease a contemporary sense of disquiet which arises, in fact, from the very depth of man's being (MAMS 37)

Marcel and other existentialist philosophers witnessed first hand the horrors of the Second World War. The creation and deployment of the atomic bomb in a nuclear arms race marked a new phase for a technological and spiritual evolution of humankind. Allied with the discovery of the genome and new untold possibilities of biogenetic design, now humanity was able to forge its own destiny with the power of an ancient demiurge through *techne* to create and obliterate life. At stake in an "Age of Total Technological Mobilization" is humanity's precarious and jeopardized existence, a topic Heidegger first addresses head-on through the concept of *enframing* in his landmark work *The Question Concerning Technology* (1954).

## HEIDEGGER'S ENFRAMING

When in the 1950s Heidegger mentions the "encounter between global technology and modern man," he may well, as Thomas Sheehan (2015: 273) notes, have been reflecting on his own life. His romanticized vision of the bucolic simplicity of rural life in south-west Germany was threatened by the looming spectre of technology.

He witnessed the horrors and devastation that technology caused in the First World War, but he was even more anxious about what he thought lay behind it—a ceaseless will to dominate the world by refashioning it according to human design. In modernity's rush to rationalize and control all things, what was quickly disappearing from the horizon was Heidegger's abiding concern—the mystery of existence which lies prior to and deeper than reason, science, and technology as the final source of all meaning. The "age of consummate meaninglessness" into which technological frenzy has delivered us is a world away from the "original manner" of living in the world for the Ancient Greeks for whom:

> The existent is that which sprouts and opens itself up, that which, as being present, comes upon man as he is present . . . The existent does not become existent as a result of man first looking upon it, let alone in the sense of imagining . . . Instead it is man who is looked upon by the existent, by that which opens itself up to that which is present and assembled around him. (1950: 88)

Where modern man is a prisoner of his projects and so loses sense of the mystery of the world, the Ancient Greek inhabits an open space in which "each thing—a tree, a mountain, a house, the cry of a bird—loses all indifference and commonplaceness" (IM 20).

In Heidegger's diagnosis of catastrophic modernity, "the entire globe is shifting out of joint" (GA9: 242). Employing Nietzsche's phrase—"the desert grows, the wasteland spreads"—he depicts the "age of the world picture" (WCT 29) as a "spiritual decline," and "darkening of the world" that involves all things sinking to the same depths, "the boundless etcetera of the indifferent, the ever-the-same," and "the rootless organization of the average man" (GA40: 40). The hopeless frenzy of unchained technology is the frightful shadow left by the death of God under which humanity imperils itself. Reflecting a deep disdain for mass society and culture, Heidegger's writings attack many facets of modernity—radio and film (GA79: 77), big cities (GA16: 521), modern literature and art (GA16: 670), along with American tourists (GA75: 221) and tourism in general (GA15: 389). Lamenting the squalid tale of technology and uprootedness, he judges that "[r]adio and every sort of organization" have destroyed "the inner growth, i.e., the constant regrowth, into the tradition of the village and thereby destroy[ed] the village itself" (GA94: 364). Even National Socialism became an obstacle to the retrieval of Being for Heidegger due to its "machinational victories of machination—gigantic forms of the consummation of modernity" (GA96: 127) that no longer marked it as "the second inception" but as the very consummation of modernity. In the push for technological supremacy,

> [t]he spiritual strength of the West fails, its structure crumbles, this moribund semblance of a culture caves in upon itself and drags all powers into confusion, suffocating them in madness. (GA16: 117)

Heidegger's key concept to explain the demise of the West is "the instrumentalization and misinterpretation of spirit" (GA40: 40) in the form of *enframing* (*Gestellung*). This denotes "the world of exploitation,"[5] a particular dispensation that treats nature in terms of its exploitability-for-consumption. In a world of extractable resources, the being of things is now their ability to be turned into products for use and enjoyment. Through enframing, technology instrumentalizes nature so that it appears in some quantifiable manner, remaining determinable as a system of information. After challenging nature, technology orders it so it becomes available for use and exploitation. According to Heidegger, technology is not just simply "applied science" but "modern natural science is grounded in the development of the essence of modern technology."[6] Heidegger strips away science's sham-objectivity because science is not disinterested but is bound up with the enframing of the world as an instrumental complex to be controlled and manipulated. It represents a metaphysical world-picture engaged in a form of unconcealment that defines the totality of modes in which Being is apprehended by the Cartesian subject. In this metaphysical framework, beings are comprehended as objects for humanity as "master of the earth" instead of "letting things be" in the simplicity of their Being. We thus never grasp the essence of things—their being—since our metaphysical predisposition is to see only what we project onto them. Things become a "standing reserve," devoid of meaning and significance, as part of a vast "ordering process" set in motion by the economy. Even "the farthermost corner of the globe has been conquered by technology and opened to economic exploitation" (GA40: 40). The forester in the wood, for example, "is today commanded by profit-making in the lumber industry, whether he knows it, or not." He is made subordinate to the orderability of cellulose, which is used for newspapers in the pages of which "a set configuration of opinion becomes available on demand" (QCT 18).

As an "unconditional objectification of everything present" (EP 86), modernity is the result of a logic of self-assertion in overdrive. In the total devastation left in its wake, humanity—the labouring animal—is left "to the giddy whirl of its products so that it may tear itself to pieces and annihilate itself in empty nothingness" (EP 87). Enframing the world, technology has seized nature and reorganized it within an instrumental complex (such as parks, holiday resorts, and golf courses). The river Rhine of Hölderlin's eponymous poem remains in the landscape not otherwise than "as an object on call for inspection by a tour group ordered there by the vacation industry" (QCT 16). Nowhere is immune. Even the ocean floor, outer space, and subterranean regions are subject to the organizing unity of humanity. In the consummation of metaphysics, humans themselves have become "standing reserve," like the production of corpses in the gas chambers (GA79: 27). With some prescience, Heidegger predicts that the human will become material for its own production: "some days factories will be built for the artificial breeding of human material, based on present-day chemical research" (GA7: 93). The overall picture he paints is one of relentless accretion. Technology is an avalanche set in motion by humanity gaining mass until it finally smothers and asphyxiates its maker:

> [T]echnological advance will move faster and faster and *can never be stopped*. In all areas of existence, man will be encircled ever more tightly by the forces of technology. These forces, which everywhere and every minute claim, enchain, and drag along, press and impose upon man under the form of some technological contrivance or other—these forces, since man has not made them, *have moved long since beyond his will and have outgrown his capacity for decision*. (DT 51)

Many scholars accuse Heidegger of fatalism. In Wolin's view (1990: 163–6), Heidegger dismisses all attempts to understand technology in anthropological terms and stresses the inability of humanity as a collective subject to control the technological apparatus. At the same time as he demonizes technology, he resigns humanity passively to its pathologies, hoping for an eventual shift in the winds of Being. His theory effectively reinforces the logic of technological domination it sets out to oppose (by ontologizing it as the modern human condition) and thus closes off the space of social agency needed to combat it. This reveals the "pseudo-concreteness" of his philosophy and the betrayal of its original promise as a phenomenology of existential concretion. Heidegger disqualifies *praxis*, assumes *techne* to be all-dominant and advocates *poesis* in the form of "poetic transcendence" as the only option: "The only possibility available to us is that by thinking and poetizing we prepare a readiness for the appearance of a god" (OG 57). Rather than reconstructing reason, delineating its boundaries and showing how practical reason (discrimination of ends) has been subjected to a hegemonic instrumental rationality, Heidegger attributes this to the "will to will," and decouples the development of technology from human practical reason, positing it as an inevitable force. As Michael Zimmerman (2007: 313) remarks, "far from constituting a proto-Green alternative to the technological disclosure of beings, Heidegger's thought may affirm the inevitability of humanity's domination of nature."

In *Making Sense of Heidegger* (2015), Sheehan asks us to continue to read Heidegger as a phenomenologist throughout his oeuvre even if his history of Being takes an eschatological path away from that purpose. Heidegger does offer a scintilla of hope and praxis in escaping technology's "giddy whirl" (EP 87) and "hopeless frenzy" (GA40: 40). Although there is little Heidegger offers as a prescription for "overcoming" technology, or even an exhortation about how to act, there are glimpses of resistance and possibilities of liberation. He states in the *Zollikon Seminars*, for instance:

> "Cells" of resistance will be formed everywhere against technology's unchecked power. They will keep reflection alive inconspicuously and will prepare the turnaround for which people will clamor when the general desolation becomes unbearable. From all corners of the world, I now hear voices calling for such a reflection and for ways to find it—voices that are renouncing the easily attainable effects of the power of *technik*.[7]

In *Being and Time*, Heidegger insists that "[h]igher than actuality stands possibility" (BT 63) and though we can speculate on the future, "[t]he question of existence never gets straightened out except through existing itself" (BT 33). We do ultimately have a choice as to how we face nature—whether we let it emerge on its own, "bringing forth" its qualities (*Aletheia*) and "let it be," or whether we challenge it to come out and instrumentalize it (*Gestell*). To illustrate this difference in orientation, Heidegger gives the example of a bridge (that respects the river as it arches over it linking the two river banks) in contrast to a hydroelectric power plant (that turns the river into an inventory where the river is "built into the power plant") (QCT 16). "The essence of ex-sistence," Heidegger avers, "consists in safeguarding and preserving the openness of the appropriated clearing—that is, of the last god—in things" (GA65: 35). He invokes the Greek *techne* in its double legacy as *both* technology and art. Quoting Hölderlin's maxim—"where danger grows, so grows the saving power"—he holds out the hope that *techne* as a form of unconcealing can liberate itself from itself as a "bringing forth of the true into the beautiful."[8] A new growing awareness will initiate a change in the world's present condition leading to "an altogether different age of the world" in which "'the god of gods' perhaps appears" (GA5: 326). Only when the danger "first comes expressly to light as the danger that it is, will this turn—from the forgottenness of appropriation to the protection of its essence—properly occur" (GA79: 71). This "god of the gods," that is, the finite, mortal, hidden, and inexplicable clearing in which we are thrown open to the "truth" of Being, alone can save us.

Heidegger's groundbreaking text *The Question Concerning Technology* provides us with many valuable insights into the enframing logic of modernity. His ethos of releasement, of *letting things be* and unconcealing them artistically as they bring forth their qualities, represents a liberating model in our relations with the natural world in the Age of the Anthropocene. He shows us a rationality beyond enframing that involves new ways of seeing, hearing, feeling, and touching things, a new sensibility that opens up pathways for freedom from enslavement to the technological apparatus. What is lacking in Heidegger's account, as Sheehan (2015), Wolin (1990, 2022), Rorty (1991), Trawny (2019) and a whole host of others agree, is a coherent sense of collectivity, or democratic consensus in becoming, in Rorty's words, "the mistress rather than the servant" of technology. What he offers instead, as Sheehan (2015: 268) describes it, is "an interiorized resistance, a philosophical quietism" in which we maintain a certain distance from "techno-think and techno-do" as we tune into our nature as guardians of Being. When you align this with Heidegger's own political ethos of "militant nationalism" that glorifies "struggle," and "war" (in direct contradiction to his idea of "releasement"), his narrative of technology takes on, as Zimmerman (2007: 319) comments, the character of an "incipient ecofascism," or "religious tribalism" clothed in "conservative, anti-urban proto-Green politics."[9]

While suggesting possible pathways toward releasement from technology's frenzied grip, ultimately Heidegger's analysis of technology lacks nuance, or differentiation. As Harman comments: "technology is [for Heidegger] a gloomy drama in which every invention merely strips the mystery from the world and turns all things into a manipulable stockpile of present-at-hand slag . . . The problem with his analyses is not their pessimism, but their monotony."[10] Heidegger's homogenizing gaze misses the complexity of modern technology, whether in the form of the machines, the mindset, or the world of meaning, whose essence he claims to reveal. The empirical examples he provides are few and quite thin, and they are usually set against his idyll of pre-modern rural Germany. Mechanized agriculture is contrasted with peasants working their fields. A hydroelectric plant in the middle of the Rhine is set over against a wooden bridge crossing the river. The present-day timber industry is compared to a woodsman (one's "grandfather") who trudges through the Black Forest (GA7: 15, GA16: 28, GA16: 9, GA18: 7).[11] In so doing, he comes close to offering a phenomenology of the contemporary life-world and concrete historical analysis similar to the Marxist notion of *reification*, but generally relapses into the mystification of neo-ontology. Heidegger's analysis of the vast phenomenon of global technology would have made more sense, as Sheehan (2015: 284–8) argues, had he ditched his "jeremiad against modernity au large" with a rich phenomenology of the "lived sensorium" in the technological age embedded in economic, social, political, and cultural contexts that cannot be captured in thinned-out anecdotal descriptions. He doesn't ask, for example: what are the specific contexts, the historical "worlds" that are operative in the new relations of contemporary *technik*? While in his early years, Heidegger states "[w]e cannot separate metaphysics from positive research" (GA29/30: 279), he ignores that principle when it comes to his later "history of Being."

Just as Heidegger had done, Sartre took a "historical turn" in his later thinking but where Heidegger bypasses "positive research" (GA29/30: 279), in the *Critique of Dialectical Reason*, Sartre provides an embedded concrete account of the processes of abstraction and reification of global capitalism to explain what he calls the "practico-inertia" of modern technological society.

## SARTRE'S PRACTICO-INERTIA

Sartre and Beauvoir's appraisal of technology-mad America was very much like Heidegger's. The United States, Beauvoir opines, had been transformed for the worse:

> This country, once so passionate about individualism . . . had itself become a nation of sheep; repressing originality, both in itself and in others, rejecting criticism, measuring value by success, it left open no road to freedom except that of anarchic revolt; this explains its youth, their refuge in drug-taking and their imbecile outbreaks of violence. (FC 385)

According to Beauvoir, the technological age is an "age of *other-conditioning*" driven by a logic of control: "In the technocratic world that the West is attempting to impose on us, the only things that count are tools and organization, the means of attaining other means with no end ever in sight" (FC 654). "All those mechanical discoveries which so astounded the journalists," she said, left her and Sartre "completely cold," and "[i]t did not seem to us that emancipation would be helped by progress in technology" (PL 133).

In *Being and Nothingness*, Sartre touches upon the technological world without really exploring it in any great depth. In line with Heidegger's *Being and Time*, he views our primary mode of being-in-the-world as practical: "My surroundings are the implement-things that surround me" (BN 657). However, he does not think that instrumentality is our *only* means of relating to the world, even if it is our first. Describing it as a "categorial classification" (BN 60), he adopts an open-ended, phenomenological approach that describes the structure of instrumentality without assuming it to be the *sole* orientation we can adopt toward the natural world. Indeed, he takes calculative thinking to have the hallmark of "seriousness," a mode of being that he pejoratively contrasts with play (BN 753–4) and aesthetic contemplation (IM 193). The *Critique* develops Sartre's account of social relations and the world of "worked matter." Driven by material need, instrumentalization is grounded as a real dimension of the relational nature of our lived experience: "Every praxis, whatever else it may be, is first an instrumentalization of material reality" (CDR 161). Through praxis, the individual is in turn worked upon by the matter that he shapes: "objectification (or man working upon matter) and objectivity (or totalized matter working upon man)" (CDR 284). The dialectical circularity of praxis and matter gives rise to contingent social arrangements that, once fixed, serve to circumscribe the very freedom from which they originate. Sartre explains this with the concept of the *practico-inert* which, as Frederic Jameson (1991: xxiii) states, is a "new concept and a new and durable philosophical term . . . a more precise way of designating objects which are not mere things and agencies which are not exactly people either." The practico-inert represents the accretions and the sedimentations of past action in the form of a network of meanings and demands to be interiorized by totalizing individuals and groups, referring to the role of human action in constituting an inert social reality that in turn comes to dominate further action. Sartre describes this process in the following way:

> in dissolving the inherited practico-inert, the sovereign and, through him, the society, interiorize the social structures it conditioned; and the transcendence of this interiorization, that is, its practical re-exteriorization, has as its outcome, in a slightly different context, the constitution of another practico-inert that reconditions men, into personal structures and finally praxis itself. (CDR 2:288)

For Sartre, the practico-inert is the sedimentation of past praxes, "simply the activity of others in so far as it is sustained and diverted by inorganic inertia" (CDR 556). It forms the "objective spirit," which acts as "the medium for the circulation of significations" (CDR 776) and exerts its force as a shifting and dynamic "quasi-totality" that conditions modes of subjectivity and intersubjectivity (CDR 324). Social life is composed of three different "modalities of action" that combine free praxis with practico-inertia—individual ("constituting") praxis, common ("constituted") praxis, and praxis-process (unites praxis with otherwise "necessary" social relations). Sartre demonstrates how impersonal practices populate the social field as "full of acts without an author" (SM 163–4) but are, at the same time, dependent upon human praxis for their continuation. In the form of the practico-inert, worked matter emerges as a shifting and transformative quasi-totality that surrounds and conditions us (CDR 324). In his example of the disastrous effects of deforestation in China, Sartre describes how the farmer experiences a form of "practical destiny" constituted by the "magical field of counterfinality" (CDR 224). The material field, synthesized by "the serial infinity of human acts" (CDR 219), becomes "a strange and living being" (CDR 169). Matter is a "magical field" (CDR 224), full of "vampire objects" (CDR 169) that soak up the lifeblood of praxis:

> All of us spend our lives engraving our maleficent image into things, and this image fascinates and bewilders us if we try to understand ourselves through it, even though we are nothing other than the totalizing movement which results in this particular objectification. (CDR 227tm)

To illustrate this, Sartre describes how female factory workers form a relationship of perfect symbiosis, or "trans-substantiation" (CDR 178) with the machines they work, wherein each "hosts" the other. Through the free movement of her project, the worker becomes a machine for the machine bringing to it her experience and creativity, even the fantasies, which its mechanisms demand. The machine then dialectically shapes the experience she invests within it to the point that even her sexual reveries are subjected to its rhythms: "The machine demands and creates in the worker an inverted semi-automatism which complements it" (CDR 233). From the dialectical mediation of the practico-inert comes the emergence of the "homme-machine" (CDR 191), a hybrid form of being definitively non-human but not inhuman either, rather a composite, or assemblage of "the totalizing movement which gathers together my neighbor, myself, and the environment in the synthetic unity of an objectification in process" (SM 155). Sartre depicts technology as one of shifting, mutually transgressive contexts that challenges any straightforward differentiation between humanity and the worked-upon material that surrounds it in the practical field since "man is mediated by things to the extent that things are mediated by man" (CDR 82). In the *Critique*, freedom no longer refers to a choice among possibles (as it had done in *Being and Nothingness*) but to the necessity of totalization and praxis in response to external exigencies within a transversal exchange of forces between different agencies. Within this relational assemblage, he posits only a small space for creativity as a "signature," or "trace" within the singularity that marks my making of being what has been made of me (CDR 330).

In an age of existential risk (as defined by the Future of Life Institute, for example), there are many risks that have the potential to kill large swathes of humanity and leave the survivors without sufficient means to rebuild their lives.[12] Not just natural risks—volcanoes, floods, tsunamis, droughts, viruses—but, new existential risks created by technology—global warming, pollution, chemical toxicity, nuclear radiation, war, artificial intelligence, and biotechnology. With Sartre's concept of "counterfinality" as guide, existentialism promotes a "Precautionary Principle" with which we can assess the ecological effects of different technologies and the concrete social relations, or practico-inert assemblages they give rise to. In the *Critique*, Sartre highlights the pitfalls of an "instrumentalist humanism," insisting that relations of modification and subjection are just one aspect of our multifaceted relationality to the world (CDR2: 316). In contrast to most scholars, however, who view Sartre's concepts of "practico-inertia," "trans-substantiation," and "counterfinality" as core elements of his deep-seated critique of technology and capitalist exploitation, Marcel Siegler (2023: 111, 147, 152–3) points out that there is another side to this negative judgment. The technological apparatus, institutions, *hexis* (habituated action), and the physical-chemical world are "needful structures and provide the framework within which praxis can take place at all. Technological artifacts manifest abstract structures of need in a concrete form." For Siegler, the practico-inert exemplifies the compromises individuals make to organize against inertia and scarcity with the restriction of practical freedom as its price. Also, contrary to the common negative evaluation of *hexis* as the opposite of praxis, Siegler emphasizes its social function, which enables a person to cultivate a way of life without much conscious thought. As

Emmanuel Levinas (1998: 94) remarks in rebuke of Heidegger's monolithic view of technology, technology is not just the will to power but also the price sometimes to be paid "by the high-mindedness of a civilization called upon to feed human beings and lighten their sufferings."[13] While Siegler's view is very much a minority one that fails to factor in Sartre's wider ethico-political aims, more than anything, Sartre's *Critique* alerts us to the fragile balance to be struck in mass society between freedom and ecological integrity on the one hand, and technological enframing and material comfort on the other.

## POSTHUMANISM AND TRANSHUMANISM

The Existentialists foresaw the dehumanizing effects of abstract thinking, leveling, and reification and prefigured much postmodernist thinking, such as Jean Baudrillard's concept of "the Mass" that, like Kierkegaard's "Crowd," pertains to everyone and no one within the Symbolic Code, a circulating interworld of significations that homogenizes and standardizes all things within it. It is fascinating to imagine what the techno-skeptical existentialists would have made of the "Computational Turn"[14] and the landscape of the algorithm[15] in the technological now of the second quarter of the twenty-first century.

The contemporary debate about technology is one often framed in terms of a posthumanist/transhumanist opposition. Inspired by Foucault's wake-up call to release us from our "anthropological sleep" (1973: 370), posthumanists have embraced a new direction in philosophical thinking that addresses itself to the pressing ecological and ethical issues of the Anthropocene present. As defined by Francesca Ferrando (2020: 118), philosophical posthumanism is a "non-hierarchical system of thought" in which alterity (human and non-human) is embraced as "an open and constantly evolving frame, not as the undisciplinable chaos to be normalized, otherized, or divinized." Posthumanism adopts an onto-epistemological approach, as well as an ethical one, "manifesting as a philosophy of mediation, which discharges any confrontational dualisms and hierarchical legacies" (2020: 22). Although it cannot be assimilated to it completely, philosophical posthumanism continues the postmodernist quest for proliferating difference and acknowledging "the voices of the subjectivities which have been historically reduced to the realm of the 'Other'" (2020: 24). By contrast, transhumanism can be characterized as anthropocentric and based on human exceptionalism with its roots in the Enlightenment, valorizing progress, linearity, science, technology, and rationality, a form of "ultra-humanism" (2020: 35). Transhumanists endorse the coming of the post-human condition brought about through a rapid technological and scientific acceleration, including computing, information, and media technologies, genetic engineering, nanotechnologies, artificial intelligence, virtual realities, prosthetic enhancements, robotics, and space colonization as common themes. Transhumanists hope for enhancements in all aspects of human beings, eliminating pain and suffering and enhancing pleasure and experiences.

In his many writings, Nietzsche does not mention technological items (and technological promise) very much, but his allusions to it tend to the phobic, complaining about typewriters, the empty, repetitive soulless "music" of a barrel organ, or disapproving of the enslavement of the worker to machines under capitalism. It is *nature* that attracts Nietzsche, where he found solace from the technological buzz and noise of the city. Scholars, however, have positioned Nietzsche on both sides of the posthumanism-transhumanism debate. Stefan Sorgner (2009: 38), for example, claims Nietzsche as an ally of transhumanism since he proposes a dynamic view of nature and values in which the cosmos undergoes endless change as well as a revaluation of all values in which a scientific form of thinking replaces the religious and the imperative to enhance human values and capacities: "The overhuman comes about via an evolutionary step which originates from the group of higher humans. Nietzsche does not exclude the possibility that technological means bring about the evolutionary step." In support of this, in his *Notebooks* Nietzsche suggests a strongly physiological/biological vision of the *Übermensch*: "I write for a species of man that does not yet exist" (WP 958). The "goal" of the higher human, he states, is the "evolution of the entire body and not just of the brain" (KSW 10.506). In the spirit of experimentation and adventure trumpeted by transhumanists, Nietzsche exhorts us to take chances and to "live dangerously!" (BGE 224) just like the tightrope walker who makes danger his vocation (Z P4).

Against casting Nietzsche as a transhumanist-in-the-making, Keith Ansell-Pearson (1997: 1) argues that becoming *übermenschlich* involves a state of being called "post-metaphysical," embodying a spiritualized physics that incorporates the truth and complexes of our natural drives and affects, as well as shareable practices that affirm human capacities and promote new forms of individuality. For Ansell-Pearson (1997: 144), "Nietzsche does not think this overcoming in terms of the abolition of the human but rather only in terms of the destruction of its anthropocentric determination as the superior point of evolution." The transhumanist overemphasis on technology often results in a technocentric transcendence of biology that ignores the situated aspect of the body, obscuring difference and plurality.[16] Pursuing radical life extension and immortality, transhumanist technophilia takes on the character of a religion in the form of an otherworldly striving for transcendence and salvation. From a Nietzschean perspective, according to Ansell-Pearson, transhumanism has become transformed into a classic expression of an ancient ideal: "it is no longer Christianity fulfilling the role of Platonism for the people, but rather a cyberspace cult" (1997: 2). By projecting a redemptive future and an ascetic ideal to overcome suffering, transhumanism takes the form of religious nihilism: "All that which Nietzsche regarded as providing fertile soil for an immanent process of continual self-overcoming is here treated as a condition that is to be escaped from" (1997: 32–3). In contrast to philosophical posthumanism, transhumanism employs simple dichotomies that Nietzsche's thought rejects (human/posthuman, organic/technological) and involves anthropomorphic projections onto nature. Evolution is conceived by Nietzsche as non-teleological and appears to be a highly contingent and random process, but in some forms of transhumanism, has become a grand narrative taking the form, in Ansell-Pearson's (1997: 4) words, of "a facile quasi-Hegelianism in which the rise of the machine is construed in linear and perfectionist terms."

Bernard Stiegler (2015) echoes these concerns about annexing Nietzsche's thinking to a transhumanist grand narrative. He charges transhumanism for being complicit, and serving as an ideological support, for capitalism and imperialism, which are seen as the culmination of a historical process geared toward progress, a "natural selection" of evolutionary processes. Contemporary information technologies bring nihilism to completion faster than Nietzsche prophesied because of the *leveling* effect. In his critique of the "last man" for which the *Übermensch* is his proposed antidote/solution, Nietzsche's principal target is the reactionary individualism of the calculating utilitarian shopkeeper. For Nietzsche, people have become slaves in the worship of the "god of machines and crucibles" (BT 18), constrained within the "spider's web of reason," and enslaved to labor under a "servitude of purpose" (Z 3.4). Like Marx, he recognizes the hardship of those subjected to the mechanical grind and indignities of the labor market and condemned the hypocrisy of the "pale religions" offered as a palliative to the slaves (BT 18). In Stiegler's (2015: 45–8) view, transhumanism is nothing but a wholesale embrace of this form of calculative rationality and thus a justificatory ideology for "cognitive capitalism." It seeks to reengineer the human being so that only averages are possible, and exceptions—those that escape algorithmic control—are eliminated. Since we are *constituted* by our technologies that condition our existence and our nature as human, technologies are paramount when considering what the human race is becoming. While the effect of technology is to reinvent and bring about changes in the function of human organisms that would otherwise risk enslavement to biological drives, Stiegler repeatedly refers to "the ambivalent therapy—toxicity of the technological object," both cure and poison, wherein the very technologies that "liberate," or "disautomate" us can also induce regression to pathological modes of automation.

Stiegler's critique of the leveling effects of cognitive capitalism has its roots in existentialist philosophy. As Sartre's analysis of the "homme–machine" (CDR 191) illustrates, neotechnic, and prosthetic technologies form a continuum with the human "body-machine" alongside a domain of virtuality and incorporeality that offers a potential space involving interrelations, interfaces, and autonomous becoming or, conversely, mystifications and impoverishments. Sartre's thinking points toward a view (consistent with posthumanism's "Precautionary Principle")[17] of the dangers of our "machinic becomings" for human projects of freedom. This signals a move away from a Faustian view of technology as a form of ultra-humanistic control to one of undecidability and non-calculability in relation to both our machinic enslavement and technics of becoming. As Sartre demonstrates with some prescience, our captivation by the practico-inert can often take the form of "dark magic" as in psychopathology and addiction. As technology advances in a digital society, the captivating powers of the image have intensified through advertising and consumer capitalism in a semiotic system of simulacra and hyperreal objects.[18] Sartre touches upon this in his early work on the imagination, where he describes the "statics of the image" (IM 16) and its poverty compared to the real-life inexhaustibility of things, their peculiar "*flesh*" or "intimate texture" (IM 16). Synaesthetic perception of the bloom of real objects is always more powerful than the imaginary and the one-dimensionality of the reproduced image (IM 144–5).[19]

To summarize, existentialism alerts us to the growing dangers of our technological age. According to Smith (2024: 240–2), for instance, Kierkegaard's "untimely meditation" on mass media can be placed alongside Simmel on money and Marx on capital as a "reflexive identification" of the very real agency of governing abstractions. His analysis encourages us "to think *hyper-empirically* about technology" avoiding technological determinism since he reflexively foregrounds the process of abstraction and aims to dispel it. Existentialists argue for an "open future" beyond the "pre-emptive control" of algorithmic science and cybernetic governance[20]—an undecidability of the yet-to-come which both instantiates and confirms our freedom in the face of humanly created external forces that grow ever stronger in a burgeoning age of quantitative reason and algorithmic governmentality. As Nietzsche (WP 610) and other existentialists warn, we must cast an existentially motivated critical reflection on science. Caught in a "giddy whirl of its products" that crucially neglects reflecting on itself in the determination of our ends, the human fascination with technology threatens, as Heidegger catastrophizes, to accede to forces that *have moved long since beyond his will and have outgrown his capacity for decision* (DT 51).

CHAPTER ELEVEN

# "I Am Not in Front of My Body, I Am in It, or Rather I Am It"

## (Merleau-Ponty, *Phenomenology of Perception*) THE BODY

*Does the body rule the mind, or does the mind rule the body?* This is a nagging question the existentialists devote much philosophical scrutiny to. It is fair to say that the body has not fared well in Western philosophy, starting with Plato and running in rationalist threads through Descartes' *cogito*, Kant's *noumenal self*, Hegel's *Geist*, and Husserl's *transcendental ego*. And yet, to existentialists, this is a strange position to hold since embodiment is an obvious fact and a necessary aspect of consciousness. As Marcel states: "To say 'I am a body' is in reality to utter a negative judgment: it is not true to say; there is no sense in saying I am other than my body" (EPC 34). Existentialists emphasize embodiment and connection to the physical world as crucial to selfhood. In place of Western philosophy's *odium corporis* and transcendentalism, existentialism celebrates and accepts the irrefragable fact of our sensual incarnation in the flesh of the world. As Beauvoir puts it, "men [are] not rarefied spirits but bodies of flesh and bone, racked by physical needs and crudely engaged in a brutal adventure that [is] life" (MDD 336). In this chapter, we look at the ways in which existentialism foregrounds the *wisdom of the body* as the indispensable matrix of our knowledge and comprehension.

## THE BODY'S GREAT WISDOM

"A single drop of blood too much or too little in the brain," Nietzsche surmises, "may render our life unspeakably miserable and difficult" (D 83). Nietzsche was perhaps the first philosopher to provide a "wild phenomenology" of the body and articulate the manifold dimensions of embodied subjectivity,[1] inverting Platonism by privileging the body over any transcendent conception of mind. In his rejection of "soul atomism"—"the belief which regards the soul as something indestructible, eternal, indivisible, as a monad, as an *atomon*" (BGE 112)—he values the "great wisdom" of the body. Nietzsche posits an intimate connection of transitive exchange between self and world, deploying the concepts of *incorporation* and *assimilation* to explain this. He conceives the body as a vehicle of assimilation that digests all kinds of material that are processed and modified into emotions and psychological states. Our character is susceptible and modifiable through the effects of inheritance, diet, exercise, and environment: "These small things—nutrition, location, climate, recreation, the whole casuistry of selfishness—are inconceivably more important than everything one has taken to be important so far" (EH 2.10). He connects environmental and dietary factors directly to certain psychological states. Too much rice in India leads to a lack of vigor and the nihilism of Buddhism, while the malaise of the German spirit is a result of poor air and winter sickness from spending excessive time indoors in front of burning stoves (JS 134).

Conceiving the self as a *psychosomatic continuum*, Nietzsche emphasizes the strong effects of physiology on judgments, feelings, moods, and tastes (JS 39). He recommends dietary change and physical labor for psychological disturbances or "distress of the soul" (D 269). His own physical ailments and sufferings made him sensitive to the "great reason" of his body and to decipher which foods and environments were conducive to well-being. He was preoccupied practically and philosophically with finding ways to improve health and recover from illness (HH P4). Reversing the transcendental conception of self as removed from earthly concerns, Nietzsche plunges us into the depth of matter: "The inorganic determines us through and through: water, air, earth, the composition of the soil, electricity, and so on. We are plants under such conditions." The denial and ignorance of the body is fueled by a misplaced arrogance on the part of humanity:

> How strange and superior we are towards the dead, the inorganic, and meanwhile we are three quarters a column of water, and have inorganic salts in us that probably have more influence on our fortunes than the whole of living society.[2]

In *Thus Spoke Zarathustra*, Nietzsche distinguishes two notions of self. The *Selbst* "lives in your body . . . is your body"; it's "a great reason, a multiplicity with one sense, a war and a peace, one herd and one shepherd." The *Ich*, by contrast, corresponds to the conscious self and, though worshipped by the metaphysicians, amounts to little: "Your small reason, what you call 'spirit' is also a tool of your body, my brother, a small work and plaything of your great reason" (Z 1.4). Ultimately, for Nietzsche, the *Selbst* rules the *Ich*: "The body is inspired, let us keep the 'soul' out of it" (EH 9.4). Although the body is the great intelligence of the self, Nietzsche does not conceive this in mechanical terms and distinguishes between the body as an object for medicine (*Körper*) and the living body as subjectively felt (*Leib*). Central to this is the notion of "affect" (*Affekt*) that always plays a role in perception, selecting and avoiding things or evaluating what is valuable for the overall growth and health of the organism (BGE 192). The *Selbst*, one's "for and against" (BGE 284), is, for Nietzsche, an active force whose physiological state, felt through sensory perception and mood, involves interpretation and the projection of value.

The body is axiological in Nietzsche's account of art and in his Dionysian affirmation of life. For Nietzsche, central to artistic experience is rapture (*rausch*), the intoxication of the senses and a heightened physiological state that increases the affective powers of the experiencing subject, felt at its most intense in the Dionysian force of music which hails the body directly. Even in the "*logic of dreams*" (HH 13), the mind is choreographed and guided by the sensory apparatus of the body—

hearing, touching, feeling, smelling—as it translates its experiences into mental imagery and narrative disclosure. The body also figures centrally in Nietzsche's reconstructive project "to give style to one's character" (JS 290) in which he sketches out the contours of a *positive asceticism*, a form of bodily self-discipline lodged between Stoicism and Epicureanism. Nietzsche's theory of the body reveals a process of fragmentation, of various forces each pulling in its own direction to establish provisional moments of stasis and assemblage. The Nietzschean self is constantly reinventing itself, releasing new energy configurations in which there is a multiplicity of drives vying for satiation—a single body inhabited by multiple selves. Like the French existentialists who follow him, Nietzsche elucidates a dynamic non-dualism where body and mind form an indissoluble psychosomatic unity. As he remarks in *Human All Too Human*: "*Embodiment of the spirit*. When a man thinks much and cleverly, not only his face, but also his body takes on a clever look" (HH 543). Through gesture, the body conveys meaning and wisdom in a language more primordial and direct than the spoken sentence or written word:

> *Gesture and language*. Imitation of gesture is older than language, and goes on involuntarily even now . . . The imitated gesture led the imitator back to the sensation expressed by the gesture in the body or face of one being imitated. This is how we learned to understand one another; this is how the child still learns to understand its mother. (HH 216)

## BODYING-FORTH

Surprisingly, bearing in mind the "thrown" and affective nature of Dasein, Heidegger scarcely mentions the body in *Being and Time*, leading some scholars to question whether he adopts a form of Docetism in this work.[3] It is worth remembering, however, that *Being and Time* was left incomplete—the third division and part two (which was to consist of three divisions) were unfinished (BT 64). Heidegger does at one point acknowledge Dasein's "bodily-nature" and the role it plays in spatial orientation but does not attempt to explain it, commenting parenthetically that our bodily nature "hides a whole problematic of its own though we shall not treat it here" (BT 143). In 1972, he admitted neglecting the body in *Being and Time* because "the bodily is the most difficult [problem to understand] and I was unable to say more at the time" (GA89: 292).

Heidegger's work before and after *Being and Time* does address different aspects of embodiment. In his *Freiburg Lectures*, he considers the body as a site of lived experience, and in his 1928 lecture course on Leibniz states that "Dasein is among other things in each case dispersed in a body" before discussing the problem of gendered embodiment (GA26: 173). In his lecture course *The Fundamental Concepts of Metaphysics* (1929/30), he elaborates at length on sense organs, moods, and Dasein as a "world-forming" animal while in his 1936/7 lecture course on Nietzsche, *The Will to Power as Art*, he presents the body as a living kinesthetic force:

> We do not 'have'a body in the way we carry a knife in sheath. Neither is the body a natural body that merely accompanies us and which we can establish, expressly or not, as being also 'at hand'. We do not 'have' a body; rather, we 'are' bodily . . . we are somebody who is alive. (GA6.1)

The most complete account of embodiment in Heidegger's work is found in the *Zollikon Seminars* (1959–69) delivered to psychiatrists and medical students. Reiterating Nietzsche's distinction between *Leib* and *Körper*, he argues that prior to any scientific claims about the body as a bounded biochemical entity that is physically present, as a corporeal object.

> I am already existing or 'bodying-forth' as a situated, affective and motile way of being-in-the-world. My body is not an enclosed self-contained thing for it is 'out there' stretching beyond my skin in the shared world of equipmentality in which it engages with others. (GA89: 112)

As a spontaneous mediating activity, my body orients me in the world and forms the "horizon" within which things are encountered: "The limit of bodying forth is the horizon of being within which I sojourn" (GA89: 113). Body and environment form a seamless kinesthetic bond where moods or emotions are not discrete sensations or "states of mind" that take place "inside" of us (GA2: 136–7) but are entwined with public contexts of meaning. In bodying forth, our fluctuating moods are "like an *atmosphere* in which we first immerse ourselves in each case and which then attunes us through and through" (GA29/30: 100). Our existence, Heidegger argues, "is necessarily a bodily comportment" (GA89: 258) since the body plays a crucial role in orientating space and conditioning consciousness: "The human has no body and is no body, but rather it lives its body."[4] Although he remains somewhat perplexed about the problem of incarnation, describing it in his 1966–7 Heraclitus Seminar as "the most difficult problem" (GA15), his idea of *bodying forth* after the 1930s was very much in line with the French existentialists—Marcel, Sartre, Beauvoir, Merleau-Ponty, and Fanon—who made it the starting point of any reasonable, non-idealist philosophy.

## BODYMINDS

Sartre's view of the body, both personally and philosophically, is complex. Beauvoir records how he revealed to her, "I found it hard to have a body" (FS 117). He first became acutely aware of his own body as seen by others when, at the age of seven, he was taken to have his long flowing locks cut off and experienced a severe "narcissistic wound" as a result. He had been a beautiful baby adored by his mother but, in the flash of the scissors, "I turned as ugly as a frog" (1983: 12). Alienated by his diminutive stature, he would imagine himself to be Pardaillan, a tall and athletic comic book hero, feeling "like a powerful warrior" as an imaginary "kind of compensation for my shortness" (1981a: 313). As an adult, he felt that people were unfriendly to him because of his ugliness: "if you are ugly, then asking the way to the Rue de Rome means inflicting a disagreeable presence on the person you ask" (FS 288). Up until his final months, Sartre's imaginary body had for all his life turned his interest away from his real body as a defense against vulnerability. His Stoicism was a form of sadism inflicted on his body that often turned into masochism and it was not until the severities of chronic ill health forced him to take notice in the 1970s that he grew more in touch with his body.

Sartre's philosophy was fully cognizant of the physical connections and neurological/pharmacological dimensions of consciousness. His early phenomenological works describe consciousness and body as intimately intermingled, such as they form a psychosomatic continuum or unity, showing how the body is intimately involved in belief. Emotion, for instance, is closely connected with physiological changes in the tensing of muscles, sobbing, clenching of fists and gesticulations: "during emotion, it is the body which, directed by consciousness, changes its relationship with the world so that the world should change its qualities" (STE 41). To believe in the magical behavior of emotions we must be physically upset since our bodies are the "instruments of incantation" through which emotions are lived out. In his description of anger, for example, the body is presented as a composite synthetic totality of life and action:

> Doubtless there is a cryptology of the psyche; certain phenomena are 'hidden'. But this does not mean at all that the meanings refer to something 'beyond the body' . . . these frowns, this blushing, this stammer, this slight trembling of the hands, these sly looks which seem to be at the same time timid and threatening do *not* express anger; they *are* the anger. (BN 462)

For Sartre, there is unequivocally no disembodied "pure knowledge." Consciousness, he insists, "exist[s] its body" (BN 441) and is body "in its entirety" (BN 412) since the body is its "sensory center of reference" (BN 437). Presenting consciousness and body as a living unity, he argues against the idea that "the psyche is *united* to a body" since "the body is its substance and its constant condition of possibility" (BN 452). Invoking the difference between *Leib* and *Körper*, he insists that "[t]he body is '*lived*, and not *known*'" (BN 435). "We do not employ this instrument," he argues, "for we *are* it" (BN 434). When there is a world, we are necessarily saying that there is a body (BN 413). In *Being and Nothingness*, Sartre details three layers of embodiment. First, the lived body, always reborn and reshaped by our projects, that constitutes the horizon of my possibilities "[m]y body as it is for me" (BN 327). Second, my body as it "is utilised and known by the Other" (BN 375), that is "the magic object par excellence" (BN 374), as the site inhabited by a free consciousness, never entirely predictable or incapable of surprise. And finally, Sartre investigates my body as an object as seen and scrutinized by the Other, a form of visceral alienation felt and inflicted by the objectifying Look.

Alongside judgments such as "groundbreaking," "multifaceted," "remarkable," "insightful," and "pioneering," Sartre's theory of the body has also been described as "puzzling," "multiply ambiguous," and "somewhat confusing."[5] In *Being and Nothingness*, Sartre says too little about bodily needs and what he says is inconsistent, maintaining that hunger, thirst, pain, and illness "*do not compromise* the very nature of the for-itself" (BN 511) and yet, in the case of sexual desire, stressing the indissolubility of consciousness and body, wherein both are reciprocally transformed: "in desiring, consciousness chooses to exist its facticity at another level. It no longer flees its facticity, but it attempts to submit to its own contingency" (BN 512–3). In the throes of sexual desire, Sartre recognizes the body as having *teloi* when it emerges as an alien presence that exerts upon us a *telic demand*. This is also the case with modes of bodily "dys-appearance," such as acute pain, which are affectively felt by the body as negative thematizations of the body demanded by the body itself, which affects an "internal disruption" and "spatiotemporal constriction" (as Sartre recognizes in our being-for-others).[6] In this respect, *Being and Nothingness* falls short of Merleau-Ponty's *Phenomenology of Perception* in showing fully how the body is an intrinsic element in the activities of consciousness. His examples of phantom limb pain and of brain damage (compared to Sartre's anodyne examples of stomach ache and eye strain) are indicative of the seriousness with which he takes the body. If, for Sartre, we can choose how to relate to the sick body, for Merleau-Ponty, it is only through illness that we exist at all.[7] In his subsequent work, Sartre irons out these inconsistencies, and takes a firmer view of the body's mandates, and makes *material need* the point of departure of his *Critique of Dialectical Reason*.

Rather than try to solve the mind–body duality and explain it away in metaphysical terms of exclusion and separation, the French existentialists bring to light the many conceptual ambiguities and paradoxes bound up with it, thus resisting a point of certainty or analytic closure. Both Beauvoir and Sartre espouse a form of naturalism in which they argue that we must assume our ambiguity (as facticity *and* transcendence) and not flee from it. Despite believing in conscious will, she found it alarming in the extreme that "[m]y body had its own whims, and I was powerless to control them; their violence overrode all my defenses . . . From the roots of my hair to the soles of my feet, a poisoned shirt was woven across my body" (PL 63). In *The Second Sex*, she is adamant that "I am my body" (SS 61), and although she contends that women have a greater predisposition to immanence in subordinating themselves to the exigencies of the body, men are also defined by ambiguity and subject to telic demands:

> man is, like woman, flesh, therefore a passivity, the plaything of his hormones and the species, the restless prey of his desires. And she is, like him, in the midst of carnal fever, consent, voluntary giving, activity; they live out, each in their own manner, the strange ambiguity of existence made body. (SS 737)

*How* we negotiate our body is contingent, but *that* we negotiate is necessary. Fiercely anti-dualist, Beauvoir and Sartre trace the ambiguity of psychosomatic unity and, following Nietzsche's original insight into the dynamic force of the body's "great wisdom" (Z 1.4), present the existentialist self not as any rational construct or disembodied consciousness, but as a dynamic and ambiguous *bodymind*.[8]

## BODILY INTENTIONALITY

Beauvoir, Sartre, and Merleau-Ponty were a phenomenological trio and their thinking on the body is very much the product of a collective praxis in which each pre-empts and guides the direction of travel of the others. In the first edition of *Les Temps Modernes* in 1945, Beauvoir wrote a glowing review of Merleau-Ponty's

*Phenomenology of Perception*, praising his idea of "the body as a generality" and developing this into her own philosophical framework of sexuality in *The Second Sex*. Despite the inconsistencies in Sartre's theory of the body in *Being and Nothingness*, it contains many insights that later philosophers, not least Merleau-Ponty himself, incorporated into their own view of embodied consciousness. For instance, Sartre anticipates the notion of *habit* or *motor skill* that Merleau-Ponty utilizes in his own work. Sartre recognizes that there are socially induced ways of moving the body, "techniques of the body" or "collective techniques" that "determine my membership of communities" (BN 666). He uses the example of skiing to illustrate how the skier appropriates such techniques (BN 667), and internalizes them (BN 680) before re-enacting them in the form of kinesthetic bodily movements. Although this is left undeveloped (on a physiological if not on a social level) by Sartre, it anticipates Merleau-Ponty's idea in *Phenomenology of Perception* that the body has its own "intentional arc" and modes of "proprioception" through which it incorporates the gestures and movements of others (PP 94). Furthermore, Sartre also introduces the concept of "the flesh" (*la chair*) integral to Merleau-Ponty's later philosophy where his delicate descriptions of the caress[9] show there are various non-instrumental ways of encountering the "magical behavior" (FI4 43) of one's own body and that of others, including the *aesthetic*, the *nurturing*, and the *sensuous*.

From his earliest thoughts in *The Structure of Behavior*, Merleau-Ponty makes it clear that there is no clear boundary between the "lived knowledge" of the body and the world of ideas, since consciousness emerges from the pre-conscious experience of the body as "a network of significative intentions which are sometimes clear to themselves and sometimes, on the contrary, lived rather than known" (SB 173). He acknowledges a debt to Marcel in his treatment of *incarnation* as a "new way of thinking" beyond the confines of the dominant idealism of the time. "My body," he says in *Phenomenology of Perception*, "is the fabric into which all objects are woven, and it is, at least in relation to the perceived world, the general instrument of my 'comprehension'" (PP 273). Orientating myself in the world and acting within it is all done as an embodied being. My body "is my point of view on the world" (PP 81), the "horizon of horizons" (PP 385), upon which my thoughts take form. It is that through which we can consequently be at home in that world, understand it and find significance in it (PP 275). The body is our permanent means of "adopting attitudes," as well as our "natural power of expression" (PP 187).

Employing a monistic ontology, Merleau-Ponty views subjectivity as engorged with the sensible, arising from the inter-corporeal exchange between self, environment and others. As an embodied carnal being, "the subject loses its purity and its transparency" (PP 350). Emotions, for instance, are not felt within the subject, but acquire meaning intersubjectively in a "between space" or "interworld." In the case of anger, "the location of my anger . . . is in the space we both share" (2004: 84). Emotions are bound up with corporeal articulations, the "expressive space" in which our body is thought to be "comparable to a work of art" (PP 151). Our everyday habits are not cognitive representations, but bodily dispositions: "it is the body that 'understands' in the acquisition of habit" (PP 167). The body comprises "stable organs and pre-established circuits" (PP 100) that operate beneath consciousness, carrying their own logic and driving force. Merleau-Ponty theorizes subject and object as "not two opposed domains to be somehow united; they are both aspects of the same flesh: the flesh seeing itself, turned upon itself, overlapping itself, folded upon itself, reversible" (VI 111). There is, he argues, "incipient significance" in the living body: "our gaze, prompted by the experience of our own body, will discover in all other "objects" the miracle of expression" (PP 197). Just as in Sartre's theory of sexual desire and the caress (BN 508), he shows how eroticism reveals the force of desire and the blind bodily links that cross over from one person to another (VI 264). In the conveyance of emotional meaning, it is "as if the other person's intention inhabited my body and mine, his" (PP 185). Experience is *transitive*, since what happens in me can pass over into the other. This first arises from an early affective spatiality of adherence or internal linkage between the child's body and the mother's expression in which their intentional encroachments and emotional apprehension overlap.

In the passage of his work from *Phenomenology of Perception* to *The Visible and the Invisible*, Merleau-Ponty shifts focus from a philosophy of consciousness to our unconscious bodily immersion in the world of "brute or savage being" (VI 200). The mind does not move the body as Descartes supposed since the mind is just an aspect of bodily intelligence that constantly negotiates its environment saturated with motor sense: "my body moves itself; my movement deploys itself" (1993: 124). In this world, "[a]ll flesh, even that of the world, radiates beyond itself" (1993: 145) and infuses with others (SNS 17). Existing as rhythms and durations, our bodies can coexist, communicate, synchronize, and when bodies meet, a "partial coincidence" (VI 122) occurs: "a sort of dehiscence opens my body in two, and because between my body looked at and my body looking, my body touched and my body touching, there is overlapping or encroachment" (VI 123).

## EXISTENTIAL BODIES

All existentialists take embodiment as the starting point of philosophical investigation. Against idealism, Marcel emphasizes the primary importance of the body which cannot be viewed purely instrumentally since "in the consciousness I have of my body, and of my relations with my body, there is a protest which is almost impossible to suppress: I do not *use my body*, I *am* my body" (EO 188–9). It is through embodiment that we are immersed in the world and always in situation. This is where Descartes went wrong. But, according to Merleau-Ponty, "no man can reject the *cogito* and deny consciousness, on pain of no longer knowing what he is saying and of renouncing all statements, even materialist ones" (SNS 79–80). The trouble with Descartes' cogito is that it has "exclusive reference to the interior" (SNS 78–9) and is purely epistemological. However, "[t]he *cogito* is false only in that it removes itself and shatters our inherence in the world." The only way to do away with it "is to fulfil it, that is, to show that it is eminently contained in interpersonal relations" (SNS 133).

The intersubjective character of the body (our bodies-for-others) is well understood by Fanon. Developing Sartre's theory of the Look, he brings to light the hypervisibility of the racialized body that is seen as "an object in the midst of other objects" (BSWM 109) and predetermined by others what it might become.[10] This causes an inner haemorrhage in consciousness, a temporal and spatial fragmentation of the racialized body in which an objectifying gaze gets incorporated into our own seeing causing a sense of alienation from one's self:

> At certain moments the black man is locked in his body. And yet for a being who has acquired the consciousness of self and body, who has achieved the dialectic of subject and object, the body is no longer a cause of the structure of consciousness; it has become an object of consciousness. (BSWM 200)

Existentialist insights, as Ada Jaarsma (2024: 252–8) contends, are crucial for critical disability studies in terms of the conceptual vocabulary they offer—*embodiment*, *objectification*, *becoming*, *lived experience*, *hodological space*. The social Other as developed by Beauvoir and Fanon is applicable to the disabled as otherized, objectified as deviant and unworthy, subject to neo-eugenic interventions and biomedical practices in the name of "health" that are predicated on an implicit ability/disability hierarchy. As *bodyminds* we are always entwined between the psychic and the somatic, between consciousness and embodied life, and no bodymind exists "apart from a network of connections or from the interplay of outside with inside, person with environment and present with evolutionary/historical time." This enables us to recognize we may not be inhabiting the same "spacetime" even if we are in the same place due to the "affordances" by which we move, interact and express ourselves, leading to an *ethos of hospitality* that spaces present by creating new affordances. Existentialism sensitizes us, as Jaarsma argues, to socially constructed system of norms and how what is deemed to be Other from another perspective represents human variation, plurality and biodiversity. It provides a useful framework for thinking through the complex terrain of social identity, especially the subjective experience of body image.

Although the body-as-seen can lock us into alienating spirals of self-alienation, it is also the site of Dionysian rapture (Nietzsche, Heidegger, Marcel) and revolutionary freedom (Fanon, Sartre, Beauvoir, Merleau-Ponty) for it remains a "living body" (GA6.1): "I am not, therefore, in Hegel's phrase, "a hole in being," but a hollow, a fold, which has been made and which can be unmade" (PP 215). Along with the influence of Spinoza and Bergson, existentialism inspired the French poststructuralists to develop concepts that liberate the full potential of the living body. Deleuze and Guattari's "bodies without organs" aims at freeing our bodies from capturing confinements, automatic reactions and habitual patterns and unleashing the intensive potentiality of the body beneath its traditional encoding. "Bodying forth" into the world is a mode of experience that allows new perceptions on the pre-reflective level of affective qualities and a scrambling of codes from the stratifying regimes of the socially accepted body. The ecstatic produces the highest possible intensification of experience in which, in Heidegger's words, "the entire emotional system is alerted and intensified so that it discharges all its powers of representation, imitation, transfiguration, transmutation, every kind of mimicry and playacting conjointly" (1987: 1.14). Incarnation might always remain "puzzling" to us as it did perennially to Heidegger. Our bodies will forever remain strange and magical to ourselves and to others as Sartre surmised, the site of ambiguity, as Beauvoir emphasized. But existentialism's polemic in favor of the body, articulated through Nietzsche's "great wisdom," Heidegger's "bodying-forth," and the "flesh" of the French existentialists, is a salutary reminder of embodiment in an age that sometimes conceives us abstractly as isolated minds, heavenly souls or complex formal computational systems.

# CHAPTER TWELVE

# "Hell Is . . . Other People"

## (Sartre, *No Exit*) SELF/OTHER

Existentialism is often voyeuristic and exhibitionist when portraying human behavior. Its fiction shines a lurid light on base, disreputable, and even brutal actions *in extremis*, but this is typically done in the interests of clarifying, by way of contrast, an underlying ethos of freedom and responsibility, generosity, and compassion. This is especially true of Sartre's play *No Exit* that is noted for its classic epithet "Hell is other people." Upon their deaths, three protagonists find themselves in hell where they see no instruments of torture or devilish tormenters, but only a permanently lit and distastefully decorated room in which they are subject to the permanent objectifying gaze of the other two. Here, "[t]here's no need for red-hot pokers. Hell is . . . other people!" (1982: 223). From this single line, and in combination with Sartre's account of the Look in *Being and Nothingness*, many scholars have drawn hasty fatalistic conclusions regarding existentialist accounts of intersubjectivity that, in Sartre's case at least, seriously misrepresent his overall philosophical view.

Existentialists strive to square the circle of individuality and sociality by differentiating between *healthy* and *unhealthy* forms of association. Different modes of intersubjectivity can enhance or degrade our freedom, confirm, or distort our subjectivity. Other people can be hellish, or they can be joyous and uplifting depending on environment, situation and the wider social relations that circumscribe their actions. The work of religious existentialist Martin Buber is indicative of this approach. His *I and Thou* (1923) emphasizes the *dialogical* nature of human existence and defines two types of relation that we can adopt with other people. Either we treat the other as "thou," respecting her freedom and subjectivity, or as an "it," an object to be manipulated and controlled in the instrumental pursuit of our goals. He recognizes that I-Thou relations can quickly calcify into I-It relations, which depersonalize and involve the denial of freedom, difference, and singularity. Existentialism brings to light the ambiguous dynamic between privacy and community. It shuns atomized individualism, but repudiates mass uniformity in a quest to resolve the paradox and to find true community that allows for true diversity, singularity in sociality.

As John Macquarrie (1973: 89) notes, existentialists often retreat to a form of individualism, as they view social relations as hugely distorted in modern society. The ways in which people are brought together is not deserving of the name of community as a harmonious "being-with" but is based on "being-for" others within a network of "I-It" relations. For existentialists, a true interpersonal relation does not collapse, or merge into a unified mass, but preserves the other in her otherness, her unique singularity. The quest to distinguish enriching forms of sociality that *enable* individuality from impoverishing ones that *diminish* it, as we will see in this chapter, begins with Kierkegaard's and Nietzsche's critique of mass conformity and finds its culmination in Sartre's theory of groups in the *Critique*.

## THE CROWD AND THE HERD

Though critical of it, both Kierkegaard and Nietzsche were influenced by Romanticism, especially the works of Hölderlin and Novalis, which advocated an aesthetic soulfulness of intoxication and a yearning to explore one's inner depths and share in the wonders of the mystery of the world. Like the Romantics, Kierkegaard holds a firm distrust of abstract rationality and social convention. To his mind, the modern age is marked by *reflection*, a form of calculative thinking and instrumental action in which there is a negative unifying principle between people based on envy, mutual selfishness, and superficiality. Becoming a true self, he argues in *Sickness unto Death*, involves responsibility, subjective truth, and commitment and is a difficult undertaking in modern mass society because it is "far easier and safer to be like the others, to become an imitation, a number, a cipher in the crowd." There is a fear of individuation since deep within every human being there still lives the anxiety over the possibility of being alone in the world. A person keeps this anxiety at a distance by looking at the many round about and immersing themselves in the deceptive consolations of the crowd. In *The Crowd is Untruth*, he criticizes society for being abstract and impersonal, quelling free thinking, passion, and individual expression and rendering individuals anonymous, fearful, and lonely. The crowd "in its very concept is the untruth, by reason of the fact that it renders the individual completely impenitent and irresponsible, or at least weakens his sense of responsibility by reducing it to a fraction" (2009: 193). As "an abstract void which is everything and nothing," the crowd is "the most dangerous of powers and the most insignificant. More and more individuals, owing to their bloodless indolence, will aspire to be nothing at all—in order to become the public" (1946: 267). A process of degeneration, leveling creates "an ever greater inorganic deposit in the body politic" (PJ 422), an abstract something formed so ridiculously "that every single participant is a third person," transforming "all reality most pleasingly into a theatre" (PJ 422). Kierkegaard cites the attractions on offer at Tivoli-Vauxhall as a prime example of public theater. An amusement park that offered mass entertainment in the form of fireworks, waxworks, pantomimes, restaurants, bazaars, and concerts, it is a soulless, shiny "glass-fronted world" that epitomizes "the culture of spectatorship."[1]

For Kierkegaard, true freedom must be an orientation toward oneself as a single individual. Taking a religious leap can often distance oneself from social mores and conventions, as exemplified by Abraham's willingness to kill his beloved son, Isaac on the commandment of God. Shunning the dissolute ways of the crowd, and appearing to disdain sociality altogether, Kierkegaard's individualism is explicit, conceiving fellowship as a lower category than the "single individual," which, in a direct relation to God, he recommends everyone should aspire to be. This was mirrored in his personal life that was riven with isolation and conflict. He broke off relations with his one-time good friend, Hans Christian Andersen,[2] as he did with his fiancée Regine Olsen because he felt these relationships impeded his inward connection to God. He was continually at loggerheads with the Danish Church and Press and became an object of public ridicule in wider Danish society during the *Corsair Affair*.[3] Rallying against Christendom, which he associates with the institutional rituals of the church, the secular public and Hegel's philosophy of *Geist*, he diagnoses his age as holding a "pantheistic contempt for the individual" and jests that if a man became sufficiently inured in Hegelian ideas he would become so anonymous that he could not even have a letter addressed to him.[4]

Kierkegaard's hostility to the crowd began as a small child, when he was told solemnly that it was the crowd that spat on Christ. The crowd "is the evil" that threatens chaos and lives in illusion, he wrote, and "there is rescue in one thing only, in becoming the single individual" (2009: 37, 69). Invoking the subversive power of martyrdom, Kierkegaard views "the single individual" (and himself) as "a solitary spruce, egoistically unfettered and pointing upwards" (PJ 109) and as "a thunderstorm . . . [that] goes against the wind" (PJ 106). "The Single Individual," he argues, stands at a narrow pass like at Thermopylae to prevent the hordes from forcing their way through (PJ 277). He announces his task as raising a polemic against "the numerical, the crowd, the inorganic, mass, the evil in society" (PJ 529). One of the tragedies of modern times is "to have abolished the 'I', the personal *I*," and he vows "to accustom contemporaries once more to hear an *I*, a personal *I* speak (not that fantastic pure *I* and its ventriloquism)" (PJ 282). For Kierkegaard, humanity progresses only by "a process of individualization brought about by 'the single individual'" (PJ 292). However, under the pretext of objectivity and the suffocating ways of the crowd, the aim has been "to sacrifice individualities altogether" (PJ 254).

Nietzsche was also familiar in his personal life with solitude and eremite detachment at various periods, especially after his romantic split with Lou Salomé in 1882, that caused him great distress and inner turmoil. "Now I am facing my task all alone," he despaired, "I need a bulwark against the unendurable" (KSB 6.306). His *free spirit*, the exemplar of his middle writings, is unfettered by social impediments as one "who thinks otherwise . . . [from] prevailing contemporary views" (HH 225). Equally, his Zarathustra is a hermit who "enjoyed and relished his solitude" (Z 4.10), shut away from the rest of humanity. Nietzsche too found the modern age to be soulless and bereft of individuality, its citizens ground down by the noise and machinery of capitalism (WP 890). His critique of forms of negative association in modern life is expressed through his analogue to Kierkegaard's crowd, the *herd*. The herd, he argues, exerts a gravitational pull toward the ordinary and mediocre—its tendency is "towards stasis and preservation; there is nothing creative in it" (WP 285). It has no spiritual aspirations, but simply longs for comfort, lack of danger, alleviation of suffering, and the state of "green meadow happiness" (BGE 44). Full of "the consistent growth of mediocrity" (WP 953), the herd represents a lower type of human.

Nietzsche's various comments on the herd, as John Richardson (2020: 468) comments, reflect a "predatory stance" which surfaces in certain passages in his writings and raises the worry of whether he cares at all about the herd[5] given his insistence on "rank-order": "*Basic error*: to place the goal in the herd and not in the single individuals! The herd is means, not more!" (WP 766). The fear is that Nietzsche is completely indifferent to the herd or, worse still, views it entirely as a slavish instrument for the elite (BGE 188, JS 377) to the point of immolation, imagining a large cleft between the highest and lowest types (WP 886). However, aristocratism is not the only card Nietzsche plays in his varied hand and there are other elements in his thinking (that surface mainly in his middle works) which signal a more egalitarian vision of Self and Other channeled through his idea of *positive agonism*.

## HEIDEGGER'S *MITSEIN*

The Lonely Dane, Kierkegaard set the vector for future existentialist thinking (as a quest to find authentic individuality) with his concept of the *Crowd*. Heidegger's *the They* (*das Man*) follows course, denoting the dangers of group-think or, social everydayness where we are thrown into a condition of inauthenticity in which we lose sight of our uniqueness as individuals. The They is no one in particular, a generic conception that only signals the uniform, where we read books and analyze art, for instance, as "they" do: "The 'They,' which is nothing definite and which all are, though not as the sum, prescribes the kind of Being of everydayness" (BT 164). This "Being of everydayness," Heidegger argues, breeds an atmosphere of mutual suspicion and alienation between people:

> Everyone keeps his eye on the Other first and next . . . Being-with-one-another in the "they" is by no means an indifferent side-by-side-ness in which everything has been settled, but rather an intent, ambiguous watching of one another, a secret and reciprocal listening-in. Under the mask of "for-one-another," an "against-one-another" is in play. (BT 219)

Although influenced by Kierkegaard, Heidegger's philosophy in *Being and Time* shows a greater appreciation of the dimensions of sociality. Even so, it walks an ambiguous line between the individual and the social and has been questioned by many for its coherence in this regard. *Being and Time* shows how existence is essentially a public phenomenon. Our lives are "fallen," sunken in social categories and concerns since *Mitsein* or "being-with-others" is more "proximal" than my experience of being an individual. Even a preoccupation of self is often bound to a concern with others in the form of envy, competitiveness or, seeking approval. He considers our being-with-others as a deficient mode of selfhood, characterized by fallenness, idle talk, everydayness and curiosity. The public lifeworld is punctuated by the anonymity of the They, which degrades intersubjectivity through leveling and the tyranny of public norms.

As in Kierkegaard's crowd and Nietzsche's herd, the They is a faceless anonymous power of conformity that governs us all, takes away choice, disburdens responsibility, determines norms and levels down to mediocrity by obliterating exceptionality.

In society, *Dasein* does not live from its own "ability-to-be" but from the They: "Everyone is the other, and no one is himself" (BT 165). Heidegger presents language and discourse, for instance, as a fundamental "existential" of human *Dasein* (BT 204). But the disclosive capacities of Dasein essential for uncovering our Being-in-the-world have been lost since our language has been so thoroughly infected by the They with its idle talk comprised of clichés, platitudes, dogma and empty truisms. In an individualizing move, Heidegger finds authenticity or, true conscience away from our social being, for "what else is it than the voice of the "they"?" (BT 323).

The overall mood of Heidegger's account of being-with others is gray. In his portrayal of public life, the harsh verdict he gives to worldliness and everydayness makes it hard to find where in his lifeworld authentic *mitsein* could prosper. The only form of positive sociality he hints at in *Being and Time* is in the idea of *solicitude*, which he briefly entertains as an authentic mode of being in our relations with others (BT 157). This amounts, Heidegger suggests, to authentic care "to the existence of the Other, not to a '*what*' with which he is concerned; it helps the Other to become transparent to himself *in* his care and to become *free for* it" (BT 159). In solicitude I "leap-ahead" of the Others and let them "'be' in their own most potentiality-for-Being" (BT 344). Whereas "leaping in" for the Other is the dominant mode where we take over him and close off possibilities, "leaping ahead" involves a kind of solicitude in which one opens up possibilities for the Other and enables him to realize his freedom. People can only be "*authentically* bound together," Heidegger suggests, when each "frees the Other in his freedom for himself" (BT 159).

Solicitude aside, however, avenues of reciprocal freedom are not generally explored by Heidegger's *Being and Time* which pursues authenticity as kind of decisionism that valorizes the radical will or heroic self-assertion. Where *das Man* experiences time emptily (non-ecstatically) as a succession of nows, authentic Dasein elevates itself above this temporal stasis in the "moment of vision" or, "suddenness," a secular epiphany that explodes and transcends the "fallen" character of routinized inauthentic temporality. Experiencing existential temporality, the call of conscience paves the way for authentic decision since it beckons our "ownmost potentiality-for-being" and "summons Dasein's self from lostness in the 'they'" (BT 319). Heidegger gives little clue as to where it emanates from, its specific content, or how it can be recognized: "it remains indefinite and empty in its 'what'" (BT 319). "The call," he states paradoxically, comes out of the depths "*from* me yet *from beyond me*" (BT 320). Owing to its "conspicuous indefiniteness" (BT 319), the call dispenses with any kind of utterance (BT 318) since it must not be confused with the linguistic distortions and platitudinous nostrums of the "They-Self."[6]

As Wolin (1990: 37, 55) observes, the logic of *Being and Time* oscillates indecisively "pro and contra the heritage of philosophical subjectivism." Selfhood and mineness are important parts of Heidegger's existential analytic (BT 365), but he warns against conceiving Selfhood as a Cartesian "self-positing subjectivity." In Division II of *Being and Time*, Heidegger turns his attention toward *historicity*. Despite advocating the free self-relationship of the individual, he does not understand this as individualism, but as the "factic" powers of *Dasein* in the community or nation. According to Heidegger, he who has accepted the thrownness of his own *Dasein* in a way that is freer from illusion (BT 446) realizes that fate ties him to his own people, an entanglement of individual *Dasein* with the "historizing of the community, of a people" (BT 436). Being free means participating in history and the lifeworld: "Resolve brings the Self right into its current concernful Being-along-side what is ready-to-hand and pushes it into solicitous Being-with-others" (BT 344). Seeking to relativize the non-relatedness of authentic Dasein, Heidegger urges Dasein to reach back into the past and "to choose its hero" (BT 437) to find a spur for its awakening.

In the 1930s, Heidegger perceives the National Socialist revolution as a collective breakout from inauthenticity, and maintains a steadfast antipathy for Publicness or democratic collectivity. His Logic lectures of 1934 investigate the transformation of "mineness" into "ourness." "The self," he argues, "is not a distinguishing determination of the 'I'"—what is important is the "we-ourselves" where loneliness and solitude disappear. The inauthentic we is the They, whereas the authentic We is in the nation that asserts itself as one: "A national whole, therefore, is a man on the large scale."[7] As Rector at Freiburg University, Heidegger put some of his ideas into action in his struggle for a "new university." On the surface, his Scholarship Camps share some similarity with the student groups of 1968. He announces his commitment to the Youth movement who are "on the march." Against the formal stiffness of the academic gowns, he appears in knee breeches and open-necked shirt. With the goal of abolishing the division between mental and manual work, he inveighs against the "idiot specialists," that is, the university professors in their positivist specialized academic disciplines.[8] However, as Safranski (2002: 263, 223) points out, his camps may have aimed for fusion and togetherness, but in reality, they were more like indoctrination events modeled on a military or scout structure with the aim of producing the perfect SA student. Based on the axial triad of "labor service, military service and service to knowledge," their authoritarian structure mirrored the hierarchical tripartite division of medieval society (peasants, knights, and priests).

If, as Hannah Arendt complains, Heidegger couldn't adequately grasp the difference between "being-together" and "being-alongside,"[9] this is a result of his "phony concreteness" where he never even gestures toward the question of the material constitution of historicity and to the reduction of possibility to actuality in the capitalist reified world. Concluding that "Heidegger doesn't know what freedom is,"[10] Jaspers notes an irony in his wilting critique of "the madness of the masses" since Heidegger himself was beguiled by the "deceptive mass intoxication" of the National Socialist revolution, announcing in prophetic tones how Being had at last arrived and how "[w]e are under the orders of a new reality."[11] With swift moves, Heidegger lurches from one pole (existential solipsism) to the other (extreme collectivism), either lacking concrete connections (*Being and Time*) or losing singularity (after the 1930s). Like Heidegger, other existentialists grapple with the problem of historicity and individuality, but take their conclusions in other directions. In *Sense and Nonsense*, Merleau-Ponty concludes that Heidegger

> lacks not historicity, but on the contrary, an affirmation of the individual: he does not mention the struggle of consciousnesses and that opposition of freedoms without which co-existence sinks into anonymity and everyday banality. (SNS 69)

## KIERKEGAARD'S EQUALITY AND NIETZSCHE'S POSITIVE AGONISM

Despite his invective against the evils of the crowd, Kierkegaard is not entirely anti-social and misanthropic since he does recognize the possibility (and desirability) of authentic human relations in the shape of the community. According to Kierkegaard, the key to authenticity is to find *authentic individuality*, which he differentiates from egoism or, selfishness. "Most people," he observes, "are subjective towards themselves and objective towards everyone else, sometimes frightfully objective—but the task is precisely to be objective to themselves and subjective towards all others" (PJ 264). He makes it clear that "isolated subjectivity . . . is indeed evil" and "the single individual . . . is always some one who operates with the help of the crowd" (PJ 468). The cure through objectivity is, however, "not a whisker better" for what we need is a "compelling subjectivity" anchored in the universal God (PJ 468). Kierkegaard advocates a form of equality as "fulfillment" within the divine totality, which he contrasts with leveling that "turns away from inwardness and wants to render equality in the negative, so that those who individually, each for themselves, are not essential and equality is in the external union" (PJ 251). Unlike "isolated subjectivity," "compelling subjectivity" is a kind of "heterogeneity [that] lies within particularity's point of departure but then tries to find its way back to the universal" (PJ 464). This reflects a difference between the "public" and "authentic community" and it is in the "humaneness" of community's equality rather than the inhumaneness of the leveling crowd that true humanity and freedom are found (PJ 271):

> In community the individual *is*; dialectically, the individual is crucial as the prior condition for forming a community . . . Every individual in the community guarantees the community; the public is a chimera. In community the individual is the microcosm who qualitatively repeats the macrocosm . . . Community is no doubt more than a sum, but is truly still a sum of units; the public is nonsense: a sum of negative units, of units that are not units, that become units with the sum, instead of the sum being a sum of units. (PJ 465)

Like Kierkegaard, Nietzsche isn't easy to fathom. With one eye fixed firmly on our singularity and the other eye focused on our interconnectedness, he is both a champion (and practitioner) of radical individualism yet also a concerned collectivist, vexatious about the well-being of the human species as a whole. Although his ethical paragons, like the Free Spirit and Zarathustra, seek their enlightenment away from the noise of others and the straitjacket of society, Nietzsche takes sociality to be the primordial dimension of existence and individuality a relatively recent historical invention: "To be alone, to feel separate, neither to obey nor to rule, to signify individuality—that was not a pleasure, but a punishment" (JS 117). Indeed, his early work, *The Birth of Tragedy*, eulogizes the power of community and "the destruction of the *principium individuationis*" (BT 2) within the Greek chorus that elicits Dionysian joy.

As Herman Siemens (2018: 329, 326) notes, the concept of the *agon* that is axiomatic to Nietzsche's social theory reminds us that "the individualistic pathos of his texts notwithstanding, he is a profoundly social thinker who addresses fundamental ethical questions in relational terms." In Nietzsche's *agon*, the relations of tension define the *relata*—each capacity, force and subject needs agonistic relations with another in order to become what it is. The resistance offered by others compels me to assert myself and, since the resistance I encounter is unpredictable, who I am and what I can do turns out to be highly dynamic and contingent. The community is constitutive of individual agency at the affective level of drives in sharp contrast to the capitalist society of possessive individuals who compete through egoistic drives. The meeting of forces gives rise to a process of assimilation, incorporation and expansion that aims toward "the feeling of increased power" (BGE 230). A dominant organization attempts to incorporate a suppressed organization but must bring itself closer and accommodate it in order to do so. The process of incorporation is not a simple submission, but is instead a shared becoming where each organization bends to form something new. This is understood by Nietzsche not in dualistic terms of submission and dominance but instead, as an *agonistic model of transformation* where striving between different and multiple forces allows intermingling and change to occur in each drive irrespective of which one is the incorporator.[12] Within relations of *agonistic indebtedness*, the other does not constitute a disabling threat to my identity but provides an alternative and enriching perspective through which I am able to grasp my own limits. Respect for others is based accordingly on a notion of indebtedness to those who prevent limits from congealing by sustaining contest between different ideas and identities. Through "a cultivation of care for difference,"[13] we are able to respect others by seeing them as living out some of the possibilities and richness of life that we had to forego in order to be who we are. Thus, it is important not to confuse the concept of equality presupposed by the *agon* with the kind of equality Nietzsche criticizes so vehemently in the context of modern democracy (TI 9.37). For one, it concerns equal forces or capacities, not equal rights or, equality as an ideal. Second, it does not exclude qualitative diversity in favor of uniformity.

The common view of Nietzsche as an extreme individualist solely preoccupied with the nature of an isolated individual is profoundly misleading. His political thought is characterized from beginning to end by a desire to transcend the atomistic basis of modern societies and its narrow, bourgeois individualism. He understands his politics as being neither individualistic nor collectivistic, since the former "does not recognize order of rank" and the latter fails to generate a notion of individual greatness (WP 859). Along with other existentialists, his ethics can be viewed as an attempt to square this circle through a dialectical analysis of the various ways and means by which individuality and intersubjectivity mutually implicate and reinforce (or diminish) each other, forming richer or, weaker expressions of subjectivity.

As Richardson (2020: 224) notes, the common trend in Nietzsche's thinking is toward a nuanced understanding of self and Other in which the operation of the common stands "in a certain dialectical relation to the individual." In spite of his predilection for solitude and individuality as lone wolf and outsider, Nietzsche does not want to abandon his social identity and argues for the indispensability of individual and herd: "one should *not* evaluate the solitary type by the herdish, *nor* the herdish by the solitary . . . both are necessary; equally their antagonism is necessary" (WP 886). Against the inverse relation that Nietzsche's predatory passages suggest, he thinks that progress depends on herds and individuals ascending together through a dialectical passage. This dialectic denotes an intimate relation of mutual involvements in which even the most exceptional individual is still really a mixture of herd and individual traits. The herd establishes the ground upon which the individual can flourish or flounder since common cultural practices are the essential springboard for individual singularity and excellence. The higher the herd, the more able the individual is to ascend even higher as their advances are in turn incorporated or absorbed into shared practices. There is a dialectical interplay between herd and individuals in which individuals, through their disenchantment and movement beyond the ethic of custom, generate new values and abilities that are in turn absorbed by the herd as new norms.

Exceptional individuals, in Nietzsche's view, "bear the seeds of the future, [as] the intellectual pioneers and founders of causes and federations" (JS 23). The herd in itself exerts a gravitational pull toward the ordinary and mediocre (WP 285). It simply longs for comfort, lack of danger, alleviation of suffering, and the state of "green meadow happiness" (BGE 44). For Nietzsche, the individual's "contempt" for the common is aimed at instituting a new common by changing and improving the common, within and against it, rather than opting out of it. Revisionary work is carried out in solitude since an active stance toward the common requires periodic estrangement from it. The purifying turn toward oneself is contained within an overall will to improve the community or group.[14] After leaving his hermitage, for instance, Zarathustra looks for a new community in order to make his individualized meanings into a new common and a new language. Equally, free spirits are the work of high culture. They cannot be reduced to individual egocentric endeavors, but are concerned with humanity and are interventions within a culture. Their stance against the group is just another way of serving it. By means of the individualizing turn, the individual is a device of the common to improve itself. All individual spirituality belongs to a collective spirit: "artists . . . orators, preachers, and authors . . . come at the end of a long succession" (JS 354). For Nietzsche, great experimenters realize a perfectionist demand that has a general orientation beyond the individual toward humankind.[15] Nietzsche "individualizes individuality" by aspiring to show us how to be an individual in a new way, a fuller and better way that can be incorporated into ongoing practice within groups.[16] He recognizes that in groups with shared social practices and norms we become a superorganism in which each member feels himself amplified by belonging to this greater power. This "communal power-feeling" numbs the individual's discontent with himself (GM 3.19).

Reading Nietzsche within a framework of positive agonism gives grounding for a dynamic conception of self and Other that brings him closer to a more democratic orientation. Even his advocacy of "*strong* selfishness" as "the deepest necessity for flourishing" (EH 4.7) is not simply self-absorption but rather a form of storing up for the purpose of enhancing expressive capacities and sharing them with others. In the "*right ideal* selfishness" we "care and watch for the *benefit of all*" (D 552) establishing a model for all to come as a pioneer for the whole type. There are, he argues, many kinds of selfishness that are "despicable" (UM 2.7), such as the "phantom" ego (D 105), the idea that one's self should become a universal law (JS 335) and the "tidal waves of selfishness" found in previous ages (BGE 212). Noble selfishness, by contrast, is entwined with magnanimity (JS 49), love and friendship (JS 14) and an extended sense of self for the growth of humanity (D 547), like the love and selfishness of a mother caring for her child (EH 2.9). The craving for equality, he argues, can take different forms, both negative and positive depending on the motivation involved:

> [it] can be expressed either by the wish to draw all others down to one's level (by belittling, excluding, tripping them up) or by the wish to draw oneself up with everyone else (by appreciating, helping, taking pleasure in others' success). (HH 300)

## EXIT OR NO EXIT?

Sartre's existentialism is often branded with a dystopian theory of interpersonal relations in which, as spoken by Garcin in *No Exit*, "Hell is . . . other people" (1982: 223). As philosophical evidence, interpreters hurry with haste to his account of the Look in *Being and Nothingness* to support this view. *Being and Nothingness* makes it clear that I can never be free of the Other who contaminates and infuses my whole existence. Even hatred "does not enable us to get out of the circle" (BN 543) and always fails for I can never truly abolish the Other. Responding to Heidegger, Sartre states that "[t]he essence of relations between consciousnesses is not *Mitsein*; it is conflict" (BN 564). Conflict arises from the fact that there is always (actually or potentially) a dissonance between how I see myself (my being-for-myself) and how others view me (my being-for-others). As objectified and as objectifier, a struggle for definition and meaning occurs on the level of the Look. When another person enters my situation, she brings with her an individual perspective of her own (in which I am an element) and represents for me a focal point of "counter-organization":

> The Other's appearing in the world corresponds, therefore, to a frozen sliding away of the universe in its entirety, to a decentring of the world that undermines the centralization I simultaneously impose. (BN 351)

A conflict is fought on the level of the gaze, where, as an "original presence," I am subject (*pour-soi*), directing it, or object (*en-soi*), constituted by it: "this original presence can only have meant as a being-looked-at or as a looking-being—in other words, according to whether the Other is an object for me or I myself am an object-for-the-Other" (BN 380). Our encounter is thrown into a circular conflict of the "Medusa's Gaze," where I "steal" the freedom of the other or lose my own to her objectifying glance:

> In this way, being seen constitutes me as a defenceless being for a freedom that is not my freedom. It is in this sense that we may regard ourselves as "slaves" in so far as we appear to the Other. (BN 365)

My image in the eyes of the Other is a fundamental shackle on my free consciousness in Sartre's view since the effect of being-looked-at is that "the Other teaches me who I am" (BN 374). Relations with others are founded in this way on conflict and objectification (domination and counter-domination): "all of men's complex ways of behaving toward each other are, in the end, only elaborations of these two primary attitudes" (BN 536). Even love in *Being and Nothingness* is a scene of appropriation and struggle, precluding synthesis or equilibrium—"a battle," as Iris Murdoch (1999) describes, "between two hypnotists in a closed room." Sartre casts heavy doubt on whether a state of unity among individuals is possible, for such assimilation "would lead necessarily to the disappearance of the Other's character of alterity" (BN 485). Common transcendence is seen at the outset to be problematic, or even antithetical, to subjective freedom:

> We are always . . . . in a state of instability in relation to the Other. We pursue the impossible ideal of simultaneously apprehending her freedom and her objectivity. (BN 538)

While it is true Sartre paints a bleak picture exploring the negative, objectifying aspects of human relations (in *Being and Nothingness* and *No Exit*), we should be careful not to ontologize this (as many scholars do).[17] He later described *Being and Nothingness* as his "eidetic of bad faith" (2008: 196), and in the text lodges a promissory escape from bad faith in a footnote that "would require corrupted being to reclaim itself. We will call this authenticity: its description does not belong here" (BN 117n27). Moreover, there are embryonic moments where Sartre suggests forms of intersubjectivity he would later develop to a higher sophistication, outlining a "We-Subject" where a plurality of subjectivities recognize one another as transcending subjectivities: "In the 'we' subject, nobody is an object. The *we* encompasses a plurality of subjectivities, each of whom recognizes the others as subjectivities" (BN 544). He returns to this later in the text, describing "the experience of the We-subject" as a kind of "collective rhythm" (BN 559).

In *Notebooks for an Ethics*, Sartre warns against drawing false conclusions from his early texts. Garcin's utterance in *No Exit*—"Hell is other people"—should not be taken at face value. "It has been thought that what I meant by that was that our relations with other people are always poisoned," he states, but "I mean that if relations with someone are twisted, vitiated, then that person can only be hell" (NE 199). Describing *No Exit*, Sartre underlines the fact that "other people are basically the most important means we have in ourselves for our knowledge of ourselves" (NE 199) and are not a priori enemies. If, as Jonathan Webber (2018: 107–11) comments, Sartre were arguing that conflict is a fundamental, irreversible state of permanence, this would contradict his central premise that "existence precedes essence." Although bad faith inevitably vitiates our relations with others as an attitude that is socially and culturally pervasive, we are not forever condemned to it. Unlike Christian Hell, which is everlasting, one always has the possibility of freely choosing to leave the hell of *No Exit* as the door always remains unlocked. Indeed, the central message of the play—"You are your life, and nothing else" (1982: 221)—is spoken by Inez and not Garcin. When she is challenged to exit the room and leave hell, she refuses, for without others she is nothing: "To forget about the others? How utterly absurd! I *feel* you there, down to my marrow. Your silence clamours in my ears" (1982: 200).

With this in mind, Edith Kern (1962: 91, 14) recommends that we should treat Sartre's plays as more a form of homeopathic treatment than a narcoleptic drug for the spectator. Although Sartrean man—as he looks and is being looked at—forever loses his Paradise when reduced like Matthieu in *The Reprieve* to "a particle in suspense within a glance," he may, if he lives authentically, still gain a world. Bad faith means closing off the dialectic between self (singularity) and Other (sociality) and associating exclusively with one of them.[18] In *Notebooks for an Ethics* and the *Critique*, Sartre embarks upon an ethical quest to exit bad faith and explore the pathways of authentic relations based on *recognition* and *reciprocity*.

Beauvoir's trajectory of Self and Other follows a very similar path to Sartre's in a passage from individualism to socialism, and though they strode in tandem, she often took the first steps to begin the motion toward the development of new concepts. Some of her earliest philosophical speculations are voiced in her novel *She Came to Stay* (1943), which revolves around a *ménage à trois* between Françoise, Pierre, and Xavière in which, citing Hegel, Beauvoir dramatizes how "[e]ach consciousness seeks the death of the Other." Social conflict is refracted through sexual jealousy arising from the triangular relationship that revolves upon the Hegelian master/slave dialectic in the struggle of recognition as both subject and object. Eaten by this jealousy, Françoise murders her rival Xavière exemplifying how, locked into patterns of bad faith, "ill will spreads like oil in water" (FC 661). In retrospect, Beauvoir judged, "I failed to achieve a properly balanced integration between daily life and tragedy" (PL 340) and acknowledged her conclusion that murder is the solution "is beyond any doubt the weakest aspect of the book" (PL 339). In *Pyrrhus et Cinéas* (1944), she argues that to be alone in the world would be nightmarish. Freedoms are separated, but they are also interdependent: "A man alone in the world would be paralysed by the self-evident vanity of all his goals; he undoubtedly could not bear to live" (PC 65). In order for what I have established to appear as good, the other must make it his good, and only then I am justified in having created it: "Only the freedom of the other is able to give necessity to my being" (PC 95–6). In order to extend my own freedom, I require the freedom of all others: "I need their freedom be available to make use of me, to preserve me in surpassing me" (PC 115). It is in this way, she states, that we are mutual partners: "[o]ur freedoms support each other like the stones in an arch, but in an arch that no pillars support" (PC 140).

Although it marked an improvement in exploring the positive dimensions of sociality alongside the less desirable ones as *She Came to Stay* had dramatically exploited, *Pyrrhus et Cinéas* was, she later thought, still too individualistic:

> An individual, I thought, only receives a human dimension by recognizing the existence of others. Yet, in my essay, coexistence appears as a sort of accident that each individual should somehow surmount . . . In truth, society has been all about me from the day of my birth: it is in the bosom of society, and in my close relationship with it, that all my personal decisions must be formed. (PL 549–50)

In *The Ethics of Ambiguity* (1947), Beauvoir sketches a social ontology, criticizing Hegelian and Marxist notions of the state that attribute to it a substance: "If the individual is nothing, society cannot be anything" (EA 106). But at the same time, she insists, "[s]eparation does not exclude relation" but implies it (EA 12). She therefore argues for "an intrinsic ontological interdependence" between human subjects: "I concern others and they concern me. There we have an irreducible truth. The me-others relationship is as indissoluble as the subject-object relationship" (EA 72). Others are essential to our material wellbeing and for our self-understanding. "It is this interdependence," she argues, "which explains why oppression is possible and why it is hateful" (EA 82). Authentic normative justification requires willing the freedom of others. Since all actions unfold in a social situation (EA 60), the social context provides the conditions for the possibility of expressing values and thus of offering justification (EA 71). Beauvoir situates *ambiguity* in the space between our subjective freedom and objective limits (including the subjectivities of other people). An ethics of ambiguity will be one which will refuse to deny a priori that separate existents can be bound to each other and that their individual freedoms can forge laws that are valid for all: "The precept will be to treat the other as a freedom so that his end may be freedom" (EA 142). In *The Second Sex*, she envisages an authentic mode of intersubjectivity based on the free recognition of each individual in the other, "each one positing both itself and the other as object and as subject in a reciprocal movement" (SS 159).

## SARTRE'S GROUPS: SERIALIZING AND FUSING

Although Sartre's phenomenological-existential individual is shot through with intersubjectivity, Sartre still thought that the section on "being-for-others" in *Being and Nothingness* was the weakest one: "What is particularly bad in *L'Etre et le néant* is the specifically social chapters, on the 'we,' compared to the chapters on the 'you' and 'others'" (1981b: 13). In Marcel's view, Sartre depicted a world that was sliding into chaos. His account of the Look is not a fiction but simply one-dimensional, dissolving the idea of grace "with such audacity and impudence" (PEX 79). In place of Sartre's *hostile* Look, Marcel offers a *confirming* look picturing a child gathering flowers in the meadow and running up to its mother, proclaiming "Look at what *I've* gathered!." The child seeks the other as a source of affirmation and recognition "resonating and amplifying" its original pleasure in its own being (HV 15). Marcel's ethics is straightforward—"I must somehow make room for the other in myself" (CF 88). Human existence is neither *en-soi* (like a natural object) nor *pour-soi* (a simple "upsurge of nothingness"), but *chez-soi* (a readiness "to receive [the other] in one's own prepared place of reception") (MB 118). This readiness he premises on *availability* (willing to put oneself at the disposal of the other, not closed off or preoccupied with self, a form of presence, or transcending toward the other) and *fidelity* (faithfulness to an other, or one's community as a form of pledge or statement of belonging). Merleau-Ponty echoes some of Marcel's complaints. In *The Primacy of Perception*, he argues for *transitivism*, a more primordial interrelation than the Sartrean Look which he illustrates with the mother/infant relationship. What Sartre lacks, he states later in *Phenomenology of Perception*, is the idea of a common interworld of mediations woven by intercorporeality and language (PP 354).

As Sartre later remarks (1974: 171), despite its best intentions to elucidate authenticity, *Notebooks for an Ethics* was stuck in an individualist problematic that led him eventually to abandon it. The second *dialectical ethics* that he formulates in the 1950s and 1960s heralds a more collective orientation that goes beyond the dyad of self and Other in his early philosophy and extends to wider groups and ensembles. In the *Critique*, Sartre identifies norms with customary morality, a function of the practico-inert that restricts spontaneity and creative moral praxis, producing inauthenticity and ingrained patterns of bad faith. This inert structure of social life can be found in the *serial group*. Seriality involves a certain ordering of people that "becomes a negative principle of unity and of determining everyone's fate as other by every Other as Other" (CDR 261). The series is a reified totalization maintained by "hexis" (habit) in which, rather than transforming a situation, individuals merely endure it. In this serial group, they are bound together from without by an object they do not control: "The series represents the use of alterity as a bond among men under the passive action of an object" (CDR 266). Serial existence is a common feature of social life found wherever individuals are brought together "horizontally" under the directing force of the practico-inert, through which their relations become structured. My individual characteristics are inessential in the series since, as just "one other" to the others, I am instantly replaceable by anyone else who might come along:

> In the series everyone becomes himself (as Other than self) in so far as he is Other than the Others, and in so far as the Others are Other than him. (CDR 262)

Examples Sartre gives of serial processes include a radio broadcast, elections and bus queues. Queuing for the bus, for instance, commuters are both united and separated by the collective object, the bus. It unites them by assembling them together in a demarcated space and by introducing a common interest between them—"improvement of public transportation, freezing of fares etc." (CDR 259)—but separates them by making each one an interchangeable and anonymous ordinal unit. Relations between them are not defined by a positive sense of reciprocity but by otherness and numerical equivalence since each person is viewed by the others in their relation to the position of the collective object, which they cannot control.

To counterbalance the negative gravity of the series, Sartre contrasts the *fusing group*. Where inertia forms the basis of the serial group, *praxis* is the constituent feature of the fusing group (CDR 418). In place of the objectifying third, Sartre introduces the *mediating third* that describes free organic praxis as constituting the fusing group in a network of reciprocity. In the fusing group, no individual sacrifices his freedom to the social whole since individual will coincides with the general will and each finds a confirmation of his own act in the actions of others. As a result, all signs of alterity between individuals dissolve: "everyone continued to see himself in the Other, but saw himself there as himself . . . everyone sees his own future in the Other" (CDR 354). The fusing group represents a state of genuine organic community since it encompasses "the individual discovery of common action as the sole means of reaching the common objective" (CDR 387). Since no praxis in the group serves to violate, or to obstruct any other, but only to enrich it, "the essential character of the group-in-fusion is the abrupt resurrection of liberty" (CDR 401). But, Sartre warns, while the fusing group becomes the prototype for authentic social relations, its existence is ephemeral and precarious. From the moment of its inception, the free praxis of the group "carries a destiny of seriality" (CDR 679). Since the group emerges as a defensive reaction against fear and imminent threat, once this is removed, the group falls into dissipation since the practical basis of its unity no longer exists. In order to stop this process of fragmentation, the group must impose stability by other means. This happens through the introduction of "fraternity-terror" that incorporates organization, function and the division of labor in addition to a pledge taken by the group for reciprocal protection against the relapse into seriality and indifference (CDR 422).

Following the political events of 1968, Sartre sketches out a third *dialogical ethics* in the course of a series of interviews. Expanding the concept of the fusing group, he speaks in 1976 of the establishment of a non-hierarchical society in which "a new form of freedom is established, which is the freedom of reciprocal relations of persons in the form of a we" (1980: 233). Key to this is the development of a form of fraternity no longer based on violence and terror but on reciprocal connection, "integral humanity" and the "interpenetration of consciousnesses," continuing the process of de-egoization and an "ethics of the gift" that he had initiated in *Notebooks for an Ethics* but then put on hold in the *Critique*. In Sartre's new ethical vision, a new era of "integral humanity" will replace the "subhumans" of the present deformed by the systematic processes and constitutive structures of capitalist society. Despite the constraints and alienations of social ensembles, Sartre does not lose sight of the intersubjective conditions for individual freedom and creative praxis:

> I think that an individual in the group, even if he is a little bit terrorized, is nonetheless better than an individual alone and considering separation. I don't think that an individual alone can accomplish anything. (1974: 171)

Mapping the passage from alienation to fusion (and back again), Sartre shows how connections in exteriority can transform into interior connections within the fusing group when the *mediating third* constitutes a potential regulatory third without becoming a transcendent other to the group. Fusion represents the archetype of a genuinely free, egalitarian and reciprocal community which has managed to overcome alienation and serial existence and effect "a transition from the Other to the same" (CDR 612). Within the reciprocal exchanges of the group, the Other no longer signifies the one who objectifies and steals my world, but one who enables, confirms, reflects and enlarges my possibilities as a partner in common action. Heralding "the beginning of the existence of men who live for each other" (HN 110), Sartre's later thinking of the "WE" pays testament to both the ontological interdependence of consciousnesses and the singularity of the individual, illuminating, in political terms, the complex and ambiguous dialectic of self and Other. In this respect, as Edith Kern (1962: 83) observes, Sartre had the last word over Marcel, eventually advancing beyond him in focusing attention on the collectivity and wider group ensembles rather than only on private relations (the family, local community, the couple) as Marcel did. Progressing beyond his dyadic framework in *Being and Nothingness*,

Sartre's dialectical account of groups in the *Critique* has proved influential as a matrix for understanding group interactions and variant modes of intersubjectivity, demonstrating how people can be together while remaining fundamentally apart.[19]

Blossoming from Kierkegaard's initial analysis of *the crowd* and *compelling subjectivity*, Heidegger's account of *Mitsein*, Buber's *I and Thou*, and Nietzsche's *positive agonism*, the French existentialists make us think deeply about the forms of association we create. This enables us to fully appreciate the mutually constitutive dimensions of individuality and sociality, providing a framework of intelligibility in which to decide (paraphrasing Beauvoir) which bits of me I should keep for myself, and which to devote to others in the dialectical dance of Self-Other we all act out each moment of our lives. Thus, in existentialism, hell *can* be a living reality between two antagonists, but is not so necessarily. It is bad faith, akin to Flaubert's "Operation Reflection," that leads to circular hostility. "I am indeed in hell," as Sartre says, "if I am situating myself in total dependence on someone else" (NE 199).

CHAPTER THIRTEEN

# "Man Is Always Congested, Drowned in Contingency"

## (Fanon, *Black Skin, White Masks*) FREEDOM/NECESSITY

Fanon's ideas of *congestion* and *contingency* lead us into another existentialist paradox: the paradox of freedom and determinism. Avoiding metaphysical closure, existentialists take a *compatibilist* view in which one cannot exist without the other. We are, as Beauvoir tells us, *ambiguous beings*, both free and unfree, contingent and necessary, transcendent and transcended. "This curious object, my life," she records in *All Said and Done*, "is both intimately known and remote; it defines me, and yet I stand outside it" (ASD 9). As we will see in Chapter 14, tracing the twin poles of objectivity and subjectivity through a "regressive-progressive" method, existentialism shows how contingency and necessity work together to form the *historical human subject*.

### LORD CONTINGENCY

Contingency, as Sartre vividly describes it in *Nausea*, makes us feel sick as we apprehend the superfluity, randomness, and raw existence of all things. For Beauvoir too, "[t]he idea of contingency terrifies me" (PL 361), since it is no mere notion, but "an actual dimension of real life" (MDD 343). It elicits anxiety as we realize we are abandoned in the universe and without ultimate purpose. Embracing ambiguity without metaphysical consolations or analytical closure, existentialism confronts the problem of freedom and existential meaning in a contingent universe without extrinsic purpose or design.

Nietzsche repudiated metaphysical philosophy chiefly for its "egypticism," turning concepts into dead mummies through its "hatred of the very idea of becoming" (TI 3.1). His genealogical philosophy, as Foucault (1977: 78–81) points out, is based on

> the *contingency of events*, the episodes of history, the games of chance outside any preconceived finality, demonstrating there is no secret atemporal essence lying behind things but revealing the accidents, the minute deviations—or conversely, the complete reversals—the errors, the false appraisals, and the faulty calculations which gave birth to those things that continue to exist and have value for us.

Like a dice game, even the origin of those things we take to be necessary (our mental categories, knowledge, reason) are the products of chance and historical circumstance (Z 1.16). Zarathustra celebrates the reign of "Lord contingency" (Z 3.4). The struggle against the dragon is the struggle for chaos against a fixed order since "one must have chaos within one still, in order to give birth to a dancing star" (Z P5). And yet, alongside this contingency, Nietzsche imposes an existential and ethical imperative. Humans must be liberated from chance as from priests (EH 3D2), from the diversion of the aimless and incidental (D 150) or from the rule of chance in human evolution (HH 24). Great culture must will some underlying necessity so that it becomes a willed achievement. There is an intimate relation between culture and the artist (BGE 62) such that, for instance, Wagner could not have come about by chance (UM 4.5). Nietzsche also views self-overcoming as a necessity not an accident by imposing a single taste or self-imposed law on the multiplicity of drives (JS 290). In the stage of higher spiritual liberation, "one should replace everything that is contingent-natural in relation to life with something that is chosen-necessary" (KSW 8.23). Freedom and necessity are thus not opposites that exclude each other but implicated in one another as dialectical partners. Knowledge of necessity becomes a form of freedom (Z 3.12.2), allowing us "to seize hold of chance by the forelock!" (BGE 274) and so avoid the impasse of nihilism.

Viewed from the outside, the existentialists were stuck in the paradox of meaning that their philosophy laid bare. We are inescapably condemned to meaning in an objectively meaningless universe. In such a Heraclitean universe of becoming and passing away without cosmic or moral purpose, the notion of progress seems a spurious concept since "becoming aims at nothing and achieves nothing" (WP 12A). However, such a view from above ignores the phenomenological perspective of the philosopher, the intentional and existential view *from the inside*, and the counter-cry of *active nihilism* that is the enduring hallmark of existentialist ethical thinking. Reflecting on "the chance" of her existence and how she became who she was, Beauvoir adduces "it seems to me that a thousand different futures might have stemmed from every single moment of my past" (ASD 9). Above all, however, the "leading thread" in explaining her self was her historical being: "Tossed into the world, I have been subjected to its law and its contingencies, ruled by wills other than my own, by circumstances and by history" (ASD 9).

## THROWNNESS

According to Nietzsche, to gain self-knowledge, direct self-observation is in itself insufficient. We require history "for the past continues to flow within us in a hundred waves: we ourselves are, indeed, nothing but that which at every moment we experience of this continued flowing . . . In many families, indeed in individual men, the strata still lie neatly and clearly one on top of the other" (AOM 223). Nietzsche identifies how we are "thrown" into a world of sedimented and established meanings of which the individual becomes a bearer. Culture's strata are both inside and outside the individual. In *Ecce Homo*, through the concept of *amor fati* (love of one's fate), he attempts to reconcile freedom and historical situation:

> My formula for greatness in a human being is *amor fati*: that one wants nothing to be different, not forward, not backward, not in all eternity. Not merely bear what is necessary, still less conceal it—all idealism is mendaciousness in the face of what is necessary—*but love it*. (EH 2.10)

Heidegger plots a similar path in *Being and Time*. In authentic temporality, past and future mutually inform one another: "Only insofar as it is futural can Dasein *be* authentically as having been" (BT 373). By projecting into the future, Dasein can reevaluate its past and, equally, can only understand the future in the light of its having been. "Renunciation" involves a critical attitude toward one's past where one becomes responsible for one's heritage through "retrieval" and "repetition" (BT 438). The radical individuation of authentic Dasein is modified by the category of *historicity* in which the self-referentiality of the call is conjoined with the transmission of a heritage that provides decisiveness with a concrete basis.

After *Being and Time*, Heidegger intensifies his account of thrownness and historicity. In experiencing the world, we are always struck by the "immediate vivacity" of the historical, a "living historicality, which, as it were, has eaten its way into our existence" (GA61: 32). He moves from viewing the thrown project as thrown by Dasein to being thrown by Being itself "as a destinal sending" (GA9: 327). In his Rectorial Address of 1933—"The Self-Assertion of the German University"—he welcomes the irresistible force of the thrownness of historical Dasein in the concrete form of National Socialism, encouraging submission to destiny in the shape of the *Führerprinzip*. In *What is Metaphysics?*, he reverses his existential-hermeneutical point of departure and endows historical Being with the characteristics of an all-powerful meta subject: "Being *indeed* essences without beings, but beings never are without Being."[1] In the middle phase of Heidegger's thinking, Dasein no longer possesses a world but it is the "work" that brings the world into unconcealment through the privileged disclosive status of the work of art *(Kunstwerk)*, the work of thinkers (*Denkwerk*) and the state-work (*Staatswerk*). As his work progresses, Heidegger dials up the weight of heteronomy and historical thrownness, describing language as the "Master of Man": "Man speaks only insofar as he *passively corresponds to language*" (GA10: 151). In his 1966 *Spiegel* interview, he searches atavistically for a lost condition of primordiality and a forgotten origin of blissful co-existence between mortals and gods while proclaiming the futility of human action:

> No human calculation and action can, in and of itself, bring about a turn in the present state of the world, if only because human dealings are molded by the state of the world and at its mercy . . . The sole possibility that is left for us is to prepare a sort of *readiness*, through *Denken* and *Dichten*, for the appearance of the god or for the absence of the god in an age of decline. (GA16)

Similarly, his approach to our historical thrownness in technology is fatalistic, prescribing inaction, and passivity and reinforcing, in the eyes of his critics, the reign of *Machenschaft* that he purportedly aims to criticize.[2] His post-*Being and Time* "philosophy of heteronomy" reduces human freedom to the force of historical thrownness: "Man does not decide whether and how things appear, whether and how God and the gods or history and nature come forward into the lighting of Being, come to presence and depart. The advent of beings lies in the destiny of Being" (GA 16). Heidegger enthusiastically proclaims the end of freedom as a viable philosophical category. Philosophy, practical reason, and praxis become mere hot air as Being essences itself without recourse to human will: "philosophy will not be able to effect any immediate change in the current state of the world. This is true not only of philosophy but of all purely human reflection and endeavor" (GA 16). For the French existentialists, although Heidegger alerts philosophy to the historicity and thrownness of our existential condition, his ontology lapses into obscurantism and become a philosophical dogmatism imprisoned in metaphysics. Heidegger loses sight of the fundamental contingency of the world and collapses into a form of determinism that dissolves human agency altogether and claims, in André Gorz's words, "to pronounce on Being in the absence of men."[3]

## SEDIMENTATION

Heidegger's concepts of historicity and thrownness influenced the French existentialists by foreshadowing and grounding their own key concept of *sedimentation* that emerged, as Jonathan Webber (2018: 128) notes, as one of French existentialism's most valuable insights in explaining the complex dialectic of freedom and necessity that forms the basis of the historical human subject.

For all of its emphasis on change and becoming, existentialism recognizes that there is much continuity that runs through a life and that it is childhood that deposits the deepest sediments in one's character. "*Parents live on*," Nietzsche writes, their "[u]nresolved dissonances . . . continue to reverberate in the nature of the child, and constitute his inner sufferings" (HH 379). Of all existentialist thinkers,[4] Beauvoir looks the deepest into the life shaping conditions of our earliest years. "Childhood," she avers is "the key to every life" (ASD 45). Even before birth, "[t]he child's situation is characterized by his finding himself cast into a universe which he has not helped establish, which has been fashioned without him, and which appears to him as an absolute to which he can only submit" (EA 35). In *All Said and Done*, she records:

> I am now more concerned than I was with the problems of childhood. For the longer I live the more I see the importance of the very first years in a human being's development . . . a great deal has already been either won or lost by the age of two [when] the gifts or the failings of the individual assume their definite shape." (ASD 160)

Citing her own life, "[m]ine is a striking example of how dependent the individual is upon his childhood" (ASD 39), she reports how each stage of life lives on and inveigles itself into the next: "When I was born, I was on the rails . . . the little girl of three lived on, grown calmer, in the child of ten, that of the child in the young woman of twenty, and so on. Of course, circumstances led me to develop in many ways. But through all the changes I still see myself" (ASD 36). She goes on to say

> I have noted a great stability in what is called people's character—the entirety of their reactions in analogous circumstances . . . Generally speaking, men and women, once they are settled into adulthood, remain consistent with themselves. Sometimes, indeed, they repeat their own conduct when they think they are being different. (ASD 36)

Freudian psychoanalysis is only concerned with children at the age of three or four when the Oedipus Complex appears, Beauvoir complains, but "the individual's earliest months have a decisive influence upon his future" (ASD 484). One's earliest experiences are vital for the evolution and coordination of one's abilities and faculties to the extent that "[a]t the age of three it is already too late to equalize opportunities" (ASD 485).

From the late 1940s onward, a growing recognition of the weight of situation informs Beauvoir's thinking. In her early work she echoes Sartre by insisting we are ontologically free and separate existents, distinguishing between ontological freedom *(liberté)* which "remains infinite" (PC 86) and power (*puissance*), the ability to act concretely in the world to pursue our projects which is "finite" in that others "can augment it or limit it from without" (PC 86). In *The Ethics of Ambiguity*, she argues that not everyone is capable of realizing freedom. This is not always due to bad faith as the power of the situation can emaciate one's experience of transcendence as a free human being:

> There are cases where the slave does not know his servitude . . . The slave is submissive when one has succeeded in mystifying him in such a way that his situation does not seem to him to be imposed by men, but to be immediately given by nature, by the gods, by the powers against whom revolt has no meaning; thus, he does not accept his condition through a resignation of his freedom since he cannot even dream of any other. (EA 85)

*The Second Sex* confirms the deep extent of our thrownness.[5] As values are constantly inculcated from childhood onward, projects become sedimented as in gender roles where specific traits become prevalent and identifiable. These fixed roles cause women to "wallow in immanence" (SS 653) and restrict the scope to pursue projects of transcendence.

Sartre too holds a mixed opinion about Freudian psychoanalysis, but becomes more appreciative of it over time. In *Being and Nothingness*, he is critical of the idea of the Unconscious and Freud's notion of the censor as a relay between the conscious and unconscious. In *Saint Genet* (1952), however, he takes a Freudian turn toward understanding the conditioning of childhood in the formation of Genet's character and aesthetic taste. Here (as Beauvoir says), Sartre now acknowledges the weight of sedimentation that gives projects their "temporal thickness" (MPPS 242–3). In Sartre's analysis, Genet the child "emerges in a world filled with meanings which impose themselves upon him" (MPPS 211). Sartre shows how a moral outlook was instilled in Genet through his childhood where he "progressively internalize[s] the sentence imposed by adults" (SG 37) with the effect that society's moral codes "have penetrated to the very bottom of his heart and installed a permanent delegate there which is himself" (SG 21).

In his later thinking, Sartre speaks of psychoanalysis as "the one privileged mediation" in understanding how a child lives his family relations inside a given society (SM 61). The examination of the individual within the family which psychoanalysis undertakes alone enables us, according to Sartre, "to study the process by which a child, groping in the dark, is going to attempt to play, without understanding it, the social roles which adults impose on him" (SM 60). *The Family Idiot* reiterates this Freudian view and sets out to show how, in the case of Flaubert, "the structures of [this] family are internalized in attitudes and re-externalized in practices by which the child makes himself be what others have made of him" (FI 3). Tracing this back to the very earliest stages of childhood, Sartre examines the way in which the infant Gustave is structured by the loving attention or by the indifference of his mother:

> To begin with, the baby internalizes the maternal rhythms and tasks as the lived qualities of his own body . . . His own mother, engulfed in the depths of his body, becomes the pathetic structure of his affectivity. (FI 57–8)

The lack of love shown by Gustave's mother who was only a mother "out of duty," formed a deep frustration that "penetrates him and becomes within him an impoverishment of his life—an organic misery and a kind of ingratitude at the core of experience" (FI 129–30). Inevitably, Sartre argues, Flaubert is pathologically impelled toward art by damage inflicted by his bourgeois upbringing: "[t]he prehistoric past comes back to the child like Destiny" (FI 55). To properly understand Flaubert we must refer back to his "proto-history," analyzing the ways in which prejudicial ideals, stories, histories, and expectations are transmitted, modified, and reinterpreted over generations. Psychological oppression within the family is connected to the structures of domination in the social macrocosm. This oppression may drive subjects to self-harming hexis (as with Genet and Flaubert) or to sadistic hexis (as with Lucien in *Childhood of a Leader* who compensates for his feelings of inferiority in his childhood by exploiting inferior groups as part of an oppressor group in society).[6] With Flaubert as his example, Sartre views the individual as formed predominantly by the forces of history and family destiny:

> [He is] a function of the society in which he lives, of the mode of production, of the technical knowledge available at the time, of the structure of the family, of antecedent circumstances, of the historic *future* which reveals itself as his destiny, but also of the singularity of his own previous history and of his biological characteristics, inherited or acquired.(IF3 442)

In Webber's view (2018: 202–3), "generational transmission" should be seen as complimentary to the process of sedimentation. By analyzing the mediations of family and society, French existentialism furnishes important insights into how prejudices are internalized and perpetuated. For the French existentialists, regimes of alterity have to be understood in terms of the circulation of the Third: "the group is not a reality which exists in itself separate from the 'transcendence-immanence' tension which characterizes the third party in relation to it" (CDR 409). Structures are "neither things nor ideas" (S 117) but elements of an interworld that organize a field of possibilities for future actions. Institutions are mediators of individual actions and bearers of intersubjective signification that individuals encounter as transcendent since they shape possibilities and sediment cultural norms. The economic substructure, as Merleau-Ponty argues, is the "schema and material symbol of the cultural order" (SNS 112) that expresses the generality of social being through the circulation of meanings.

In *Being and Nothingness*, Sartre suggests it is social pressure that causes us to adopt projects of bad faith. The example he gives of the waiter who scrupulously plays at being a waiter shows how "[s]ociety demands that he limit himself to his function as if we live in perpetual fear that he might escape from it" (BN 82–3). However, he leaves his explanation generally underdeveloped which subsequently gave him theoretical problems in *Anti-Semite and Jew* where he has difficulty accounting for the fact that authenticity is rare and bad faith widespread. By Sartre's early scheme, the prevalence of bad faith across Jewish communities amounts to "an unexplainable coincidence."[7] Since Sartre neglects the cultural sedimentation of Jewish identity promulgated through stories, histories, music, festivals, rituals and other facets of community (apart from the odd vague reference to "customs"), he could only explain social mores and cultural values in terms of projects or "ventures in behavior" (ASJ 93).

When analyzing racism in *Black Orpheus* a few years later, however, Sartre shows a growing awareness of the process of sedimentation where he argues the basic experience of black people is shaped by still fresh memory of a historical past of slavery. This presents itself as collective memory and nightmare that haunts the descendants of slavery and infects the sense of a black person's identity where self-image is an essence discovered as much as it is a project freely created. This central existentialist insight was, of course, developed to the full a few years later in Fanon's *Black Skin, White Masks* which replaces the Freudian focus on the family with the transmission of shared cultural meanings in the form of cultural imposition (BSWM 121–4).

## EXISTENCE PRECEDES SEDIMENTATION

Existentialism's most instantly recognizable catchphrase coined by Sartre in *Existentialism is a Humanism*—"existence precedes essence" (EH 20)[8]—should perhaps be replaced, as Webber (2018: 128) suggests, by the more appropriate "*existence precedes sedimentation*" in order to account for our historical thrownness. This thrownness, or facticity relates to my past, which, as Beauvoir states, conditions my present and future choices:

> My past is a datum, a base from which I project myself and which I must surpass: it has provided me with the mechanisms assembled in my body, the cultural tools that I use, my knowledge, my areas of ignorance, my tastes, my interests, my relations with others, my duties, and my occupations. (ASD 40)

"The past dwells in me and hems me about" (ASD 41), according to Beauvoir, but it is "a background on which new experiences and configurations emerge" (ASD 41). Wondering "[w]hat room does it leave my freedom?" (ASD 40), she later answers positively: "The miracle is within me, I know: the wonder-worker is myself" (ASD 154). For the French existentialists, "existence precedes essence"—humans are not determined by heredity and environment though we are strongly constituted by it. It always remains possible to make something out of what is made of us although this is an arduous, complex and sometimes seemingly impossible task, a "great and uncommon art" (JS 290) as Nietzsche calls it. We may be bound hand and foot by culture and history, but there are no timeless essences, only situations that constrain but also offer possible choices. "Man is elastic" (FC 599), as Beauvoir states. The past weighs heavy in our cultural consciousness that is deep within us, but is not eternal nature since the future remains a constellation of possibilities grasped or forsaken through resolute action in the present.

For existentialists, *we are condemned to be free*. However, freedom is by no means a simple freedom but one that is instigated and bound by nothing. It is easy to try escape this anxiety though bad faith and by blindly following customary values, but we must endure it and not evade it. Freedom is empty if not realized. It is a "power to refuse" released from the illusions of the They but "within the limitations of its thrownness" (BT 226), consisting of open confrontation with sedimented ways that have become inimical to the emergence of new meanings and creative practices.[9] In the "hyper-dialectic" of Merleau-Ponty, Being is One and inheres primordially in all existing things, but the subject as "a place of unrest" (SNS 65–6) doesn't wholly coincide in passive harmony with Being, Transcendence is a reciprocal movement beginning from either pole of the subject and the world (PP 169), we are *both transcending and transcended*. "My life," he writes, "is constantly thrown headlong into transcendent things and passes wholly outside me" (PP 369).

Human existence is the dialectic of transcendence and sedimentation. We create and become trapped by our own creations only to negate those creations by transcending them in an endless cyclical process. It is in this way that "the human dialectic is ambiguous" (SB 176). The influence of social conditioning can only be overcome through another process of sedimentation:[10] "By taking up a present, I recover possession of and transform my past . . . But I do so only by committing myself somewhere else" (PP 455). Hence, as Berdyaev observes, freedom seems to contain within itself the seed of its own degradation in the world-process: "The tragedy of the world process is that of freedom; it is born of the inner dynamic of freedom, of its capacity of changing into its opposite."[11] Out of the dialectic of freedom and necessity, new forms and patterns emerge in which the individual exists in tension between a sedimented past and an open future where "existence takes up, for its own purposes and transforms a (*de facto*) situation" (PP 169).

According to the theory of existentialism common to Beauvoir, Sartre, Fanon, and Merleau-Ponty, an individual's essence "is formed through the sedimentation of their projects chosen in their specific social environment."[12] Sartre's *Critique*, as Sonia Kruks (1990: 179) describes it, is "a somber and cautious reaffirmation of the values of freedom and rationality" that establishes spirals of totalization which demonstrate the dialectical emergence of social being from the starting point of individual praxis overcoming need. Although "circumstances determine the individual's powers" (CDR2: 219), even under conditions of scarcity, people will always "overflow" the objective historical task. Freedom, as Merleau-Ponty argues, is never an individual adventure but a collective task that must be taken up together: my "freedom cannot be willed without leaving behind its *singular* relevance" (PP 456). We cannot, in Sartre's words, "achieve the conversion from bad faith alone" (CM 16). Sartre thus seeks a concrete morality as a synthesis of the universal and historical: "it must find the universal within History and reappropriate it within History" (CM 14–5). For Beauvoir, the problem of ethics is how to reconcile individual freedom with a desire for universal equality. In *The Ethics of Ambiguity*, she takes a Kantian approach in which there is a universal recognition for the value of freedom. By valuing one's own freedom, one should therefore value the freedom of others since the human condition is universal and collective even though we remain as separate singularities. Concrete freedom, she argues ("[a]s a hope, and then at the end as a certainty"), can only come to pass as a "synthesis of socialism and liberty" (FS 357). But it is not automatic that socialism begets liberty for in the historical forms it has often assumed "we know it refuses liberty" (FS 359).

Despite their recognition of thrownness, sedimentation, and the force of circumstance, existentialists hold a strong aversion to the denial of freedom. We say "No," Fanon insists, "to the butchery of what is most human in man: freedom" (BSWM 222). "There is nothing above freedom" (FS 353), proclaims Sartre. Existentialism is the ethical theory that we ought to treat human freedom "as intrinsically valuable and as the foundation of other values" (EH 51–3). With freedom as existentialism's highest value that grounds all other principles, we are able to relativize relativism itself and, in Merleau-Ponty's words, "to recover an absolute in the relative" (AD 31). Nietzsche defines the true philosopher as a "liberator" and guardian of freedom (UM 3.1). In asking what philosophers have previously lacked, he gives a three-pronged answer: "(a) an historical sense, (b) knowledge of physiology, (c) a goal in the future" (WP 408). With these three in mind, we are in a position to demystify ourselves by identifying patterns of philosophical befuddlement, bad faith and asceticism with a view to eliminating them. We learn over the course of history "that iron necessity is neither iron nor necessary" (HH 514). Determinism "is only a *modus* of permitting ourselves to juggle our evaluations away" once they have no place in a mechanistically conceived world—"One must therefore attack determinism and undermine it" (WP 786). Congested by contingency, we humans are creatures of ingrained habit and sedimented ways, but ultimately "elastic" (FC 599), free in rare and privileged moments to follow our own path within the constraints we face.

CHAPTER FOURTEEN

# "You Shall Become Who You Are"

## (Nietzsche, *Ecce Homo*) THE SELF

When analyzing consciousness, subjectivity, personality, and selfhood, existentialists wrestle with paradoxes that readily emerge. "Ambiguity surrounding the question of an inner life," as Jennifer Gosetti-Ferencei (2021: 66, 224) comments, "haunts the tradition inherited by existentialist thinkers." As we will see, existentialist philosophers welcome *reflection* but not inwardness, *self-concern* but not egoism, *singularity* but not solipsism, *solitude* but not disconnection. *Mineness, continuity, reflection, multiplicity*, and *spontaneity* are all key themes in existentialism, but subject to qualification.

Existentialism inaugurated a "topological revolution"[1] in our conception of the self, and one in which there is no self that one may find but only what one can *become*. The self, in existentialism's post-Cartesian conception, is a *way* of being, not a "what" (thing) but a "how" (activity) that can modalize itself, in Heidegger's terms, authentically as a "living morality" (GA61: 164) or inauthentically through absorption in the fragmented ways of the They. Forensically examining the human psyche, existentialists endeavor to clear away philosophical misapprehensions regarding selfhood that have emerged in the shadow of Cartesian thinking, in particular the phenomenon of the *bewitched ego* that haunts Western philosophy. In this chapter, we look at the odyssey of the self in existentialism and follow the twists and turns of the deconstructive approach taken by existentialist philosophers as they explain the uniqueness and the multiple dimensions of the secret theater, speechless monologues, and social masks of what Beauvoir refers to as "me, myself" (MDD 60).

### WHAT IS THE SELF?

Academics trace the lineage of existentialism all the way back to Socrates (469–399 B.C) who attacked *the unexamined life* and made philosophy into a *living subjective truth* for the individual. Centuries later, St. Augustine of Hippo (354–430) explored the self as a placeholder for identity through which we are able to enact God's will and live a moral religious life. His care for the self was an inward exploration through the deepest chambers of one's innermost self and interior places. Following the Dark Ages, the Renaissance brought humanity out of God's shadow and thrust the human self into a hallowed spotlight. Pico della

Mirandola's *Oration on the Dignity of Man* (1486) was a new manifesto of the self, a plea to become "your own sculptor and maker, to fashion your form as you choose." In the sixteenth century, the French essayist Michel de Montaigne (1533–1592) composed a series of meditations where truth is sought through intense self-examination. Montaigne viewed selfhood as a process of becoming, a constantly changing and precarious unity formed through the activity of thinking it, fashioned by introspection, reflection, and activity. "I have no more made my book," he wrote, "than my book has made me."[2]

Inspired by Socrates and Augustine, and driven by his Lutheran upbringing, Kierkegaard was existentialism's first cartographer of the self. According to the Danish philosopher, "an existing individual is constantly in the process of becoming" (CUP 79). Existence is the process through which we realize our aspirations and possibilities, a relation to oneself through which our character emerges, always subject to change, or modification: "But what is the self? The self is a relation which relates to itself, or that in the relation which is its relating to itself" (SD 43). In the hectic flow of everyday life, it is easy to lose this sense of possibility and creative self-narrative, such that "the greatest hazard of all, losing one's self, can occur very quietly in the world, as if it were nothing at all." Moments of lucidity are rare and accessed through anguish, inwardness, and responsibility when we touch reality in events of intense choice and painful decision. When making a choice, it is not so much a question of choosing right as of the sincerity and pathos with which one chooses. The personality of the self is consolidated "when freedom looks down into its own possibility." Dismissing the fiction of a disinterested spectator "hovering in mystic suspension between heaven and earth and emancipated from every relation to an existing individual," he argues that such a conception "explains everything in its own terms but fails to explain itself" (CUP 278). It is false to suppose that the concrete real can be absorbed into the "shadow-play" of the abstract since it is "the most passionate interest" (CUP 155) that guarantees the living truth of subjective conviction. However, we should not equate Kierkegaardian inwardness with introspective reflection as a sort of detached contemplation rather than active involvement, but as a form of resolution, a "taking hold of oneself."[3] A maximally meaningful life involves a passionate, focused devotion to a single task through repetition, a leap into faith into the religious realm, and a commitment to God (as exemplified by Abraham).

Other existentialists take their cue from Kierkegaardian anxiety. Heidegger describes selfhood in *What is Metaphysics?* as Dasein becoming aware of its finitude and nothingness through the ontological experience of anxiety in the face of death. As an authentic response, resoluteness (the act of resolve) is Dasein's choice to redouble the structure of its existence by choosing it. Moreover, resolve, as the resolute anticipation of death, is an existential "interpretive process" (GA64: 52), that is to say, it is the way we effectively understand ourselves in terms of the radical absurdity of our mortal futurality. In so doing, we turn our everyday world into a "situation," a sphere of meaningfulness that is "opened up in authentic resoluteness to 'know yourself'" (GA31: 123). For Heidegger, the self is not an interior realm but an activity moving out toward the world. Always located in a particular space and time, and distributed among its entanglements with others, the self is always *ecstatic*, outside of itself interacting with the world and transcending toward its possibilities. Following Kierkegaard, however, he warns of the dangers of dissipation, of losing ourselves in the everyday preoccupations and distractions of the They:

> Proximally and for the most part, the Self is lost in the 'they'. It understands itself in terms of those possibilities of existence which 'circulate'" in the 'average' public way of interpreting Dasein today. (BT 435)

In *Being and Time*, Heideggerian authenticity involves "choosing one's hero" from the inherited past: "In one's coming back resolutely to one's thrownness, there is hidden a handing down to oneself of the possibilities that have come down to one, but not necessarily as having thus come down" (BT 435). This means freeing ourselves up "to the simplicity of its fate . . . a possibility which it has inherited and yet chosen" (BT 435). By retrieving desirable elements of our historical thrownness, we are able to disclose existence's "original and heretofore hidden possibilities" such that the retrieval transforms us by keeping our possibilities "free and alive" and available for re-appropriation in a present that reaches ahead into the future (GA3: 204).

Heidegger's philosophy, as Thomas Sheehan (2015: 153–5) argues, was not just about knowing something, getting the answer to a question, no matter how profound that question might be. In the spirit of Greek "existential wisdom," his thinking was at heart "an exhortation to self-transformation." The lifelong task that Heidegger set himself can be understood as a twofold movement: *analytic* and *protreptic*. The protreptic element of Heidegger's thinking was to show how we should personally embrace our finite and mortal "thrown-openness to Being," with the ultimate goal of transforming one's life. Although this transformation is somewhat subdued in his later writings, it remained his animating reason for teaching and writing at all. For Heidegger, becoming authentically what one already is means rendering oneself and others meaningfully present.[4] On his first day of teaching after First World War he regaled his students with the words of the German preacher Angelus Silesius: *Mensch, werde wesentlich!* "Become what you essentially are!." He repeats the same refrain eight years later in *Being and Time*: "Become what you are!" (BT 186). This protreptic message of self-transformation was voiced again in the late 1930s when he told his students:

> Over and over we must insist: In the question of "truth" as posed here, what is at stake is not only an alteration in the traditional conception of "truth", nor a complement of its current representation. Rather, what is at stake is a transformation in man's way of being. (GA45: 214)

## "KNOW THYSELF"

Nietzsche was obsessed with (his) self from a young age. Between the ages of thirteen and twenty-four, he produced at least six autobiographies, books he wrote in order to discover who he was in a bid to plot his existence as the sequential development of an autonomous self. In his final phase, he returns to this autobiographical task of discovery and projection in *Ecce Homo*. In notes written in 1867, he assesses the pros and cons of self-portraiture and self-observation: "it deceives . . . [it] inhibits energy: it separates and breaks apart"; "Self-observation as a developmental illness"; "Instinct is best," "our acts must occur unconsciously," "know yourself through actions, not by watching." The only advantage he lists for self-observation is as "a weapon against outside influences" (KGW 1.4.489). According to Nietzsche, one always invents, imagines or performs a self in a process of "mnemotechnics" (BGE 68) even as one attempts to remember it accurately. His later work advocates the idea of *becoming* as a kind of positing and creating: "Becoming as invention, willing, self-denial, overcoming of oneself" (WP 617). Metamorphosis must be embraced and we must renew ourselves like snakes that shed their skin (D 573).

Throughout his writings, Nietzsche exhorts us to "become who you are" (JS 270). Taken from Pindar's *Second Pythian Ode* (translated as "Become such as you are, having learned what that is"),[5] Nietzsche employs this phrase on several occasions to elucidate his philosophy of self-cultivation. Grappling with this phrase, however, we soon encounter a paradox. How can we become something we already are? Becoming implies change, the movement from one state to another, but how can we move into a space we occupy in the first place? Despite this surface paradox (or because of it), the German existentialists embraced what Georges Canguilhem described as this "apparently contradictory formula . . . full of contradictions."[6] According to Jaspers (1965: 369), we should read Nietzsche's exhortation as "an existential appeal" that is linked to *amor fati*, which is necessity but not of the causal kind:

> The necessity in question is not the category of necessity that applies to causal processes subsumed under natural laws and pertaining to mechanism . . . *Fatum*, for Nietzsche, is that necessity which, not being a category, is neither a law of nature nor a law of purpose, neither calculable compulsion nor intention. It *includes* accident and law, chaos and purpose.

For Jaspers (1965: 159), Nietzsche confuses the issue of becoming who you are by mixing the existential appeal with naturalistic claims involving biological or psychological facts whose determinism deprives the imperative of its meaning. Following Pindar's original recommendation, Jaspers (1957: 40) argues that the philosopher of *Existenz* must first learn what he is, and only then by means of self-elucidation, become who he is. Nietzsche, playful as ever, contradicts himself, declaring in *Ecce Homo*—"Becoming what one is presupposes that one does not have the slightest inkling what one is" (EH 3.9)—and dismissing the Socratic maxim *nosce te ipsum* as "the recipe for decline" (EH 3.31), while generally following Pindar's formula of learning + becoming. In his middle works, he considers it essential to seek to know oneself and to thereby engage in an active relation to oneself. In *Daybreak*, for example, he writes:

> Out of damp and gloomy days, out of solitude, out of loveless words directed at us, *conclusions* grow up in us like fungus: one morning they are there, we know

> not how, and they gaze upon us, morose and grey. Woe to the thinker who is not the gardener but only the soil of the plants that grow in him! (D 382)

Self-overcoming is possible by embracing historical thinking and making oneself an instrument of knowledge since knowledge frees the spirit (HH 288). Every pursuit of truth is considered worthwhile since knowledge makes us "gain awareness of our power" and allows us to "surpass older ideas" (HH 252). Nietzsche explains that the free spirit will be a mindful spirit, one who is conscious of the diverse forces that have formed her. Self-knowledge is the road to situated freedom:

> Alas, much boredom has to be overcome, much sweat expended, before we discover our own colors, our own brush, our own canvas!—And even then, we are far from being a master of our own art of living—but at least we are master in our own workshop. (WS 266)

But learning about oneself is only the first step. Nietzsche's free spirit is one who will experiment and will herself as an ambiguous multiplicity: "Active, successful natures act, not according to the dictum 'know thyself,' but as if there hovered before them the commandment: *will* a self and thou shalt *become* a self" (AOM 366). To *become who you are* means opening yourself up to the abyss of your own self and embracing a freedom that is not contrary to necessity but holds its own necessity: "it is as if the silkworm sought the freedom of its will in spinning" (WS 9). In loving one's fate, the strongest necessity and the highest freedom go hand in hand. "Letting necessity loose," Nietzsche posits freedom as the source of great responsibility in the feeling and force of creative power, a being whose essence, out of necessity, is to perpetually become.[7]

Rejecting idealist notions of free will as a human conceit, Nietzsche envisages us as less the heroic captains of our fate but more like oarsmen, capable of impressive self-movement but also swept along in a sometimes cruel but glorious sea.[8] Although Nietzsche avoids talk of conscious agency regarding intentional action and describes acts in terms of a "quantum of energy" that discharges itself within processes, such as "instinct," "drive," or other biological "agencies" (JS 360), he argued against the mechanization of such processes and believed that by cultivating ourselves we can become "a fellow worker in the construction of our character and our destiny" (D 115). By becoming "master in our own workshop" (WS 266) we can become a free spirit or sovereign individual, an instance of "rare freedom" and even a "master of free will" (GM 2.2). However much our natures are given, we are responsible for cultivating our character, though this, he recognizes, can be perilously difficult: "Giving style to one's character—a great and uncommon art" (JS 290).

In constructing new subjectivities, however, we must be wary of "the bewitched ego," a relic of Cartesian thinking (WP 484) that believes "in the ego as substance, and which projects its belief in the ego-substance onto all things" (TI 3.5). According to Nietzsche, the "I" is no more than a "synthetic construction" or "conceptual synthesis" (WP 371) and has become in the hands of metaphysicians a "rude fetishism" (TI 3.5), "a fairy tale, a fiction, a play on words: it has stopped thinking, feeling, and willing altogether" (TI 6.3). For Nietzsche, the self is the embodiment of the tensions within a subjective multiplicity—the "soul as a society constructed out of drives and effects" (BGE 12). The individual is a *dividuum*, that is, a multi-layered self that is an intentional embodied consciousness, that is unconscious and conscious, that is and can become, that is itself, in-the-world and with-others:[9] "The assumption of *one subject* is perhaps not necessary: perhaps it is just as allowable to assume a multiplicity of subjects, whose interplay and struggle lie at the basis of our thinking and of our consciousness generally" (WP 490). Although Nietzsche is praised by the poststructuralists for multiplying the subject and for shattering the unity of the ego, his philosophy plots a complex dialectic between multiplicity and unity. Despite the fact that "[a]ll unity is unity *only as organization and interplay*" (WP 561), he highlights the necessity of imposing a "singular taste" (JS 290) if only to provide a simplified version of oneself in public as an instrument of communication (D 182). He presents a positive characterization of the philosopher as comprehensive and multi-perspectival, a "wholeness in multiplicity" (BGE 212), not as a fragmented dissolution of identity. *Too much* fragmentation is decadence and "disintegration of the will" is crippling since "[o]ne loses one's power of resistance against stimuli" (WP 44).

Nietzsche comprehends the act of "becoming who you are" in terms of both centripetal and centrifugal movements, that is, as reflexive (moving toward the center) and as actional (moving toward the world). This manifests in Zarathustra's need for reflective solitude and his subsequent return from his hermitage. In *Ecce Homo*, Nietzsche boasts that his wisdom flows from "a constant self-overcoming" for which "I need solitude—which is to say, recovery, return to myself" (EH 1.8). Personally and philosophically for Nietzsche, solitude is a vital experience that we must seek actively in order to achieve free-spiritedness and remove ourselves from others who bring us down rather than elevate us. However, solitude should not be a permanent state and must be interspersed with episodes of active sociality. Ultimately, Nietzsche's repeated plea to become who you are (or are not) is premised on a philosophical view of the self as *performative*, that is, as activity or praxis. "Everyone *possesses inborn talent*," he writes in *Human All Too Human*, "but few possess the degree of inborn and acquired toughness, endurance, and energy actually to become a talent." For people "to *become* what they *are*," it effectively means they have "to release it in works and actions" (HH 263).

## BEING, BECOMING, AND NOT-BEING

Although Sartre confessed, that he had been tempted by the idealist teachings of his professors at the Sorbonne, he soon moved away from Husserl's philosophy because of its *idealist turn*. In *The Transcendence of the Ego*, he critiques the idealism of Descartes, Kant, and Husserl, arguing that they transform the real world of objects into the sanctuary of inner life, dissolving it into nothing but "contents of consciousness" and consuming it "with their eyes" (TE 87–9). According to Sartre, the transcendental ego of the idealists is neither necessary nor desirable (TE 7). The ego is simply the object of reflective consciousness, and it is only through a magical reversal that we think it to be the origin or owner of it. Pre-reflective consciousness has its own synthetic unity without a transcendental "I": it "constitutes a synthetic, individual totality . . . and the I can, clearly, be only an *expression* (and not a condition)" (TE 7). He gives the following example:

> When I run after a tram, when I look at the time, when I become absorbed in the contemplation of a portrait there is no *I*. There is a consciousness of the *tram-needing-to-be-caught*, etc., and a non-positional consciousness of consciousness. In fact, I am plunged into the world of objects. (TE 13)

Positing the *I* behind consciousness is obstructive to a true understanding of consciousness:

> this superfluous *I* is actually a hindrance. If it existed, it would violently separate consciousness from itself; it would divide it, slicing through each consciousness like an opaque blade. The transcendental I is the death of consciousness. (TE 7)

Since consciousness is pure activity, a transcending toward something it is not, to posit the *I* is to introduce "a center of opacity" (TE 8). In reality, the *I* comes to be purely through reflection: "The I only ever appears on the occasion of a reflective act . . . when reflected consciousness becomes the object of the reflecting consciousness" (TE 16). The *I* is therefore not originary but a transcendent existent that always accompanies acts of reflection. Sartre describes how "it is in exclusively magical terms that we have to describe the relations between the *me* and consciousness" (TE 26). Magic arises from "impure reflection" (TE 23) that reverses the real phenomenological order of things, making primary things derivative and secondary reflected-upon things primary. My actions are seen to flow from me, whereas in fact my *me* is the reflected synthesis of my actions. Unlike pure reflection that "stays with the given . . . [and] disarms unreflected consciousness by giving it back its instantaneous character" (TE 24), impure reflection effects a magical reversal whereby it carries out "an infinitization of the field" (TE 23), creating a transcendent object that serves as an imagined origin and cause "in the past and the future" (TE 23).

For Sartre, consciousness has no originary ego or contents within, but is "a sliding beyond itself" and "absolute flight" (1970: 4). Against the notion of interiority, he emphasizes the public nature of the ego and the fact that there are objective psycho-physiological aspects to ourselves of which we are most often consciously unaware. The fact that the nature of reflective consciousness makes itself an object for such consciousness means that the "I is *an other*" (TE 46). We are always obliged to view ourselves from another-person perspective, even when we use "I." The ego is a public phenomenon, conditioned, and shaped through interpersonal forces. In overemphasizing one's interiority, Sartre warns, the *I* is magically hypostasized which leads to bewitching and impure relations with oneself and others.

In *Being and Nothingness*, Sartre deepens his early phenomenological insights on consciousness and selfhood through what he calls "the circuit of ipseity" (BN 159). He presents consciousness as differing from itself through a temporal movement of deferral whereby the present can be what it is only through the mediation of the future. This gives the clue to his famous description of consciousness as "being what it is not and not being what it is" (BN 27). Since all consciousness is intentional (consciousness *of* something), it is nothing other than this activity of directing awareness toward an object. This awareness comes about by consciousness transcending the immediate appearance of the object and projecting toward the horizon of other possible appearances of the object. Sartre argues that human-reality is perpetually haunted by a totality, which it is without being able to be it. Consciousness is constituted by a temporal deferral, which means that it "has its being outside, in front of and behind itself" (BN 184), always caught between a future which is not yet and a "never present past" or "original contingency" (BN 202) that coincides with its facticity and thrownness. The temporality of consciousness means, for Sartre, that the subject is non-identical and non-contemporaneous with its present, a relation to self-grounded in self-difference and self-otherness. Hence, I am what I am not (future) and not what I am (past).

Sartre's three biographies—*Baudelaire* (Charles Baudelaire), *Saint Genet* (Jean Genet) and *The Family Idiot* (Gustave Flaubert)—all show how authentic selfhood is "a discovery of oneself that is possible at certain moments" (FS 355). According to Sartre, Baudelaire's dandyism is a self-imposed trap that prevents further self-growth and expansion. His project to become an aesthete meant that "his psychic becoming could only take the form of incessantly *working on himself*" (B 136). He inflicted suffering on himself because he concentrated his energies on self-possession rather than self-production, reproducing the past in the form of a "self-object." Baudelaire exhibits a circular process of self-cultivation in which he cannot become other than he is—a fixed, repetitious self in which "the loop was looped" (B 98). His characteristics are all entangled together and "are built into an indissoluble synthesis in which each of them expresses itself and all the others at the same time" (B 185).

Beauvoir summarizes *Baudelaire* as a "phenomenological description" that would ideally have afforded a greater emphasis on the role of the body, his lived history, and the objective socio-historical milieu in elucidating Baudelaire's self-inculcated Dandyism (FC 52). Sartre concurs with this judgment in a 1969 *New Left Review* interview in which he describes his first biography as "inadequate" due to its partial viewpoint.[10] He addresses this deficiency in *Saint Genet* where he traces a circular form of self-formation to Genet's childhood conditioning in which he was "condemned to theft" (SG 58). When caught thieving at the age of ten, his inwardness became associated with the shameful quality of the word "thief" (SG 18). After that, he is condemned to the damning judgments of society that "have penetrated to the very bottom of his heart" (SG 21). As Sartre's work evolves through his middle and later thinking, the freedom of the self steadily contracts (without disappearing altogether). In *Being and Nothingness*, conversion or change in one's character is seen as an "instant" in which a fundamental project is replaced by a new one (BN 621). This happens to Raskolnikov in Dostoevsky's *Crime and Punishment* when he decides to give himself up and experiences "extraordinary and marvelous instants in which the earlier project collapses into the past in the light of a new project which arises on its ruins" (BN 621). In *Saint Genet*, however, Sartre restricts our ability to change our fundamental project, replacing "instants" with "illuminations" where what we discover are familiar thoughts we haven't yet recognized, when original choices are modified and converted but not entirely dissolved (SG 406). In his psychoanalytic study of Flaubert, Sartre replaces his earlier idea of the "original project" to understand the total meaning of a person's life with the dialectical process of "personalization," a long and evolving process of assimilating, integrating, and transcending one's past, especially childhood (FI2 6). In the unfolding of a person's life, significant elements from childhood return in new forms and manifestations. Key stages are like spirals which the person revolves around, the deposited meanings of earlier experiences always developing, evolving, and forming richer aggregates: "we might well conceive of this movement in a three-dimensional space as a multicentered spiral that continually swerves . . . making an indefinite number of revolutions around its starting point" (FI2 7). For Sartre, dialectical development has a horizontal or a longitudinal dimension of spirals that unfold over time in an individual's life, as well as a vertical dimension that intersects with the cultural and historical epoch in which she lives. The self is thus a composite of the individual factors that conditioned the spirals of an individual's life (the experiences of childhood) with the social forces that unfold around them (and how they are internalized by the individual). As *singular universals*, individuals totalize a particular cultural and historical moment by expressing its values, detotalize it by challenging certain aspects of it, and retotalize it by producing changes that further impact future time and meaning.

Beauvoir views her own self-formation as incorporating *both* change and continuity. On the one hand, being a self is a process of perpetual change and irreversible becoming, a *living activity* open to transformation and not a thing fixed and immutable. Reading what she'd written the day before in her diary, she exclaimed, was like reading "mummies" of "dead selves" (2006: 57). We have to make an original choice and choose what we want to be not once and for all but continually "moment by moment for an entire lifetime" (EA 40). But, writing in *All Said and Done*, she also recognizes an enduring core to her personality and sense of self: "Of course, circumstances have caused me to develop in many respects. But through all my changes, I still see myself" (ASD 39). Her life has been the fulfillment of "a primary design" and at the same time "it has been the product and the expression of the world in which it developed" (ASD 40). Casting an analytical eye over her friends, she records, "I have also noted a great stability in what is called people's character—their reactions, taken as a whole, in analogous circumstances." Her friends evolve, but "I have never seen them undergo a radical change before my eyes" (ASD 46). The experience of becoming shifts with the passage of time. It becomes more difficult to forge new projects and beginnings as the years accumulate and the past becomes heavier and more sedimented. We realize with age that some of the dreams we have dreamt when younger are "infinitely remote from the dream made real," but we also realize that what gives life meaning is "reciprocal relationships" (OA 547) and our connections with what lies beyond us. Whilst retaining a strong sense of authentically living life as a unique singularity, Beauvoir's autobiographies are designed philosophically to show, as Kate Kirkpatrick (2022: 2) remarks, "how one's self is always shaped by others and related to others."

Hence, *being* and *becoming* are dialectical coordinates in existentialism. Continuity of self is a contentious issue, since existentialists extol becoming and change but eschew fragmentation and the disintegration of the will. To be a self involves a connection between past, present and future but memory can be fleeting, changeable, or broken. One is never a static or completed self but always in the process of becoming one. "I never stopped creating myself," Sartre writes in *Words*, "I was both giver and gift" (W 23).

## THE THREE ECOLOGIES OF SELF

The existentialist project to theorize what Nietzsche calls "new versions and refinements of the soul hypothesis" (BGE 12) presents a model of the self as an emergent "unity within a multiplicity" enmeshed in the social and material world. This is neatly represented in the *trivalent* model of selfhood proposed by Félix Guattari in *The Three Ecologies* (2000) of

(1) *a material environment in the process of being reinvented*

(2) *a constantly mutating socius*

(3) *a nascent subjectivity*

Like Guattari (who was heavily influenced by existentialism), the existentialists conceive the "circuit of ipseity" (BN) as involving transversal lines and connections between the three ecologies within a common ethico-aesthetic viewpoint. Existentialist descriptions of becoming are open-ended and allow for a notion of the subject that is precarious, shaped by the external world, the social sphere, and the individual's internal forces and critical reflection. Describing each of these forces as an "ecology" incorporates the idea of each as a living system that has a dynamism of its own, but which intersects transitively with the other two. The "new subjectivity" that existentialists advance is a living, evolving triptych of material, social, and psychological forces, a "psycho-social-somatic unity" that is able to install itself simultaneously, in Guattari's (2000: 69) words, "in the realms of the environment, in the major social and institutional assemblages, and symmetrically in the landscapes and fantasies of the most intimate spheres of the individual." Existentialism demonstrates the heaviness of material and social forces while providing the lightness required to elide them through "purifying reflection" (Sartre/Beauvoir/Fanon), the formation of the "intellectual conscience" (Nietzsche), "secondary reflection" (Marcel), or "resoluteness" (Kierkegaard/Heidegger).

The perpetual interplay of the three ecologies of self is clearly evident in the work of the French existentialists. As Beauvoir records in her diaries, when aged nineteen, she was confused by Nietzsche's existential imperative to "Become who you are?." She asks quizzically: "Do you know yourself? Do you see yourself?" (2011: 367). Her own sense of self is split into two parts, she observes, one "for others" and one "for myself":

> Certainly, I am very individualistic, but is this incompatible with the devotion and disinterested love of others? It seems to me that there is one part of me that is made to be given away, another that is kept and cultivated. The second is valid in itself and guarantees the value of the other. (2006: 12/08/1926)

Beauvoir's growing awareness of the conditioning "constantly mutating socius" led her to a *syncategorematic* view of the self in which "[w]e can only be who we are because of the others in our lives" (EA 71). Although authenticity requires us to tear aside the veil of our conventional self, to hear the call of freedom in ourselves, without heeding the call of freedom of others, it is a form of "spiritual death" in Beauvoir's eyes, a "refusal that stultifies our own becoming":[11] "A man who seeks being far from other men, seeks it against them at the same time as he loses himself" (EA 66). In the psycho-social-somatic unity that is the self, the existentialists formulate a *new subjectivity* and version of selfhood that is fully permeable to the world and to others.

## ME, MYSELF AND I

Existentialists never stop wondering about the amazing miracle of *singularity*, the *unique whatness* that makes me who I am, different from all other people. "In his heart," Nietzsche wrote in his *Untimely Meditations*, "every man knows quite well that, being unique, he will be in the world only once and that no imaginable chance will for a second time gather together into a unity so strangely variegated an assortment as he is." These sentiments of awe for singularity are repeated in Beauvoir's memoirs in which she recalls "I considered myself to be unique—the One and Only" (MDD 296). She didn't see herself as a child but as "me, myself" (MDD 60), the basis of her own apotheosis in which "I proudly imagined myself reigning alone over my own life" (MDD 57). Taking refuge in her innermost self, "I invoked a superior authority which would allow me to challenge outside judgments . . . and decided that my whole existence would be subordinate to it" (MDD 196). The wonder at the hidden depths and dimensions of one's own self never left her: "To be oneself, simply oneself, is so amazing and utterly unique an experience that it's hard to convince oneself so singular a thing happens to everybody else in the world" (PL 292).

But while existentialists vigorously promote self-concern, they do not license self-obsession or narcissism. Existentialism approaches *inwardness* with extreme caution for consciousness is always *out there* scattered in the world. Indeed, Nietzsche strongly disparages subjectivity centered wholly on itself: "is there anyone who has never been mortally sick of everything subjective and of its wretched ipsissimosity [self-fetishism]?" (BGE 207). "*Stop feeling like such a fantastic ego*," he admonishes, "[l]earn to throw off, step by step, *your alleged individuality*! . . . Go beyond 'me' and 'you'! *Experience cosmically*!" (KSA 9: 443). For all the talk of egoism, Nietzsche ruminates, "No one has yet asked: what kind of ego?" (WP 364). Against the ego, which is "only a conceptual synthesis" (WP 371) and leads to narcissism, existentialists promote, as Merleau-Ponty describes it, "a Being-self whose self-cohesion is also a tearing away from self" (S 184). "There is nothing more dangerous for a person, nothing more paralyzing," Kierkegaard writes, "than a certain isolating kind of fixation on oneself in which world history, human life, society—in short everything—disappears and, like the *ompfalopsuchitai*, one is constantly staring in an egoistic circle at one's own navel" (PJ 93).

Although they were prone, like all humans, to certain moments of vanity and self-publicity, existentialist philosophers tended to shun the bright lights of fame. Of course, in the mass proliferation of images that grew in the twentieth century, Sartre and Beauvoir courted popularity, posing for photoshoots in glossy magazines and appearing on film (*Sartre par Lui-Meme*). At the same time, Sartre is critical of self-glorification (expressed in Roquentin's distaste for the self-commissioned portraits of the burghers of Bouville in *Nausea*). He thinks his fame to be "ridiculous," an "unimportant game" or a "sort of shadow" (FS 163) and does not seek publicity for himself. Distrustful of the scandalizing tabloid press (which a hundred years or so earlier had viciously lampooned Kierkegaard in the *Corsair Affair*), Beauvoir also disliked the spotlight of public attention, declining some public appearances, such as the prestigious lunch for the winner of the Goncourt prize for literature in 1954 (which she won with her novel *The Mandarins*).[12] She rarely agreed to do anything on TV, or radio, but in 1974 participated in a documentary film on old age, where she contrasted the inhumane, sterile institutional settings of nursing homes with the personal space of her own flat surrounded by the artefacts of her life. "With the best will in the world, or the worst," she remarks, "publicity disfigures those who fall into its hands" (FC 328). She loathed showing herself in public and trained herself, when young "not to care for public opinion" (FC 664). It was with nostalgia and with anxiety that she discovered the full bloom of Sartre's celebrity and her own budding fame: "The carefree days were over the moment we became public persons . . . the adventurous side of our earlier trips was lost forever . . . we had to erect barriers" (FC 667).

The existentialist analysis of the bewitched ego stands as a warning against the narcissistic excesses of the age of the selfie. Critical of what Marcel referred to as "self-imitation" and "self-hypnotism," existentialism views objectification and a superficial preoccupation with appearances as a potentially negative aspect of our being-in-the-world, one, as recent studies have shown, that induces anxiety, leading to stress, eating disorders, bodily dysphoria and routine practices of corrective cosmetic surgery.[13] Kierkegaard began the investigation into how modern society degrades human forms of association, how individuals are trapped in a corrosive aesthetic sphere within the leveling gaze of the crowd. In *Either/Or*, he warns against the mode of modern "reflection" in which relationships are conducted through external presentation and lack any bond of inward commitment where the individual no longer belongs "to himself, to his beloved, to his art or to his science, he is conscious of belonging in all things to an abstraction." Heidegger also regards the modern vogue of "personality" as "insipid and disgusting" and as a "Big Lie" of a "rootless life."[14] In *The Age of the World*-Picture (1938) and *The Question Concerning Technology* (1954), he laments the deleterious effects of technological modes of pictorial representation that enframe the world and nature as a mere backdrop to self-presentation and human instrumentality. Nietzsche too was disapproving of the "Cult of Personality" since not only did it disfigure the famous but also those who worship it: "When the gratitude of many to one casts off all shame, the result is fame" (JS 171).[15]

The self is, in existentialist terms, a *Universal Singular*. For existentialists, self-reflection is not narcissistic, turning on an inner searchlight or involving the "extravagant grubbing about in one's soul" (BPP 160) but is contained in the "world of tasks" which is the "the image of what I am" (BN 281). As Heidegger says, Dasein "*finds itself . . . in things* because tending them, distressed by them, it always . . . rests in things" (BPP 159). When we say that Dasein understands itself, its own self, "we must not rest this on some fabricated concept of soul, person, or ego but must see in what self-understanding the factical *Dasein* moves in its everyday existence" (BPP 160). The self has no meaning in isolation but only in reference to others and what Beauvoir called its "reciprocal relationships" (OA 547) in the world. From his earliest moments of reflexivity, Sartre views the self as outwardly dispersed in the Other and not inwardly generated by any ego or soul:

> in vain we seek the caresses and fondlings of our intimate selves . . . like a child who kisses his own shoulder—for everything is finally outside; everything, even ourselves. Outside, in the world, among others. It is not in some hiding-place that we will discover ourselves; it is on the road, in the town, in the midst of the crowd, a thing among things, a human among humans. (1970: 5)

My proximal experience of the world always refers me to other people. The existence of others is not somehow added on in thought since things exude an "atmosphere of humanity." "*Dasein* in-itself is essentially Being-with," as Heidegger says: "even *Dasein*'s Being-alone is Being-with in the world" (BT 156–7). We are always in the presence of others, Sartre argues, even when they are absent: "in the form of an object when I'm alone in my room, in the form of some reminder, a letter lying on the desk, a lamp that someone made, a painting that someone else painted" (HN 71). However, just as my care for objects can take deficient forms, so can my being-with-others, resulting in degraded forms of association that inhibit possibilities for self-cultivation and restrict authentic expressions of singularity.

## A PLAYFUL WISDOM

It is in *play* that existentialists find the highest expression of the living truth of subjectivity and where freedom shines at its brightest. Play lies at the center of Nietzsche's affirmative thinking which he associates directly with creation, a cosmological game in which the events of the universe occur, like with a child who builds and scatters its playthings (BT 24). He associates the child with innocence and creativity (BGE 57) and urges us to emulate this—in the "genuine man, a child is hidden: it wants to play" (Z 1.18). The laughter of the child is an antidote to Christian seriousness, where to "*live joyously and laugh joyously*" (JS 324) is the mark of one who has learned to live without "metaphysical consolations" (BT A7). Indeed, "[i]t is strange," Nietzsche remarks, "to take everything so seriously" (KGW 4.1.6). In the passage "On the Three Metamorphoses," Zarathustra explains how the child's play makes possible a transvaluation of values and a passage to a higher level of moral thinking. Where the camel could only follow rules given to it (passive nihilism) and the lion was only capable of saying no (reactive nihilism), the child playfully creates its own values (active nihilism):

> The child is innocence and forgetting, a new beginning, a game, a self-propelled wheel, a first movement, a sacred Yes. For the play of creation, my brothers, a sacred Yes is needed: the spirit now wills its own will, and he who had been lost to the world now conquers his own world. (Z 1.8)

For Nietzsche, *Kinderspiel* denotes the play of the child. This is *serious play* but a kind of seriousness qualitatively different than that of the metaphysical comforters who preach salvation. The seriousness of the child is a form that recognizes the contingency of the world while fully affirming its own play (WP 797).

The French existentialists expand Nietzsche's critique of the *spirit of seriousness*. Beauvoir ranks the "serious man" among the "sub-men" in her existential moral scheme (EA 42). Sartre's *Being and Nothingness* "is in large measure a description of the serious man and his universe" (EA 46) analyzing the ploys of bad faith when we abdicate ourselves in favor of the world and bury our liberty by viewing ourselves as an object. Sartre too saw the ontology of *Being and Nothingness* in retrospect as "a pre-conversion ontology" (CM 13) in which seriousness "reigns over the world" (BN 810). The goal of existential psychoanalysis is "to abandon the spirit of seriousness" (BN 809) that places values on objects and social respectability in order to absolve the agent from authentic self-becoming and avoid the anguish of choosing. Seriousness is a false self-concept of fixity that obscures the ontological truth of being where we experience ourselves as passive in relation to objects and events that we could change. It "regards values as transcendent givens that are independent of human subjectivity, and it transfers the character of being "desirable" from the ontological structure of things to their simple material constitution" (BN 809). Authenticity, by contrast, must be understood in terms that do not collapse or conflate facticity and transcendence but take into consideration the interplay and "valid coordination" between them as a matter of degree. It embodies celebrating the perpetual and continuous play that is at the heart of transcendence and facticity and all decision-making.[16]

Beginning with Kierkegaard's idea of the self as "a relation which relates to itself" (SD 43) and culminating in Sartre's theorization of the *pour-soi* that is what it is not and is not what it is (BN 27), existentialism provides us with a radical version of subjectivity that avoids the falsity of the bewitched ego and the pitfalls of narcissism. Anticipating Guattari's (2000: 53) three existential territories, existentialists formulate a dynamic trivalent model of the self that confronts us as "not given, as an in-itself, closed in on itself, but instead as a for-itself that is precarious, finite, finalized, singular, singularized, capable of bifurcating into stratified and deathly repetitions or of opening up processually from a praxis that enables it to be 'habitable' by a human project." Their pioneering quest for new versions of selfhood promotes the depersonalization of subjectivity such that the subject identifies with the multiplicity while at the same time inventing and experimenting with re-singularizing subjectifications, rediscovering, in Nietzsche's words, "the seriousness one had as a child at play" (BGE 94).

CHAPTER FIFTEEN

# "To Be Dead Is to Become Prey to the Living"

## (Sartre, *Being and Nothingness*)
## DEATH

Philosophy rarely addresses the breakdown of the self and its disintegration into nothingness. But, as this chapter chronicles, existentialism is different and ponders at length the significance of our mortality, providing a variety of perspectives and moods that waver between anxiety and obsession (Kierkegaard, Heidegger), positive acceptance (Nietzsche), equanimity (Sartre, Fanon), and terrible dread (Beauvoir).

Kierkegaard theorizes the human being as a synthesis of two opposing qualities that form a paradoxical union but produce a split consciousness. We are forever torn between the desire for transcendence and eternity and the apprehension of our immanence and finitude. Mortality is hence a profound dimension of our lived experience. Making this basic recognition has opened existentialism up to accusations of morbidity but, as Beauvoir complains in her essay "Existentialism and Popular Wisdom" (1945), existentialism is not new in approaching the question of mortality, nor to ask why we are born and why we suffer. In turn, existentialists can accuse these critics of an unhealthy escapism since death-awareness is a major facet of human existence. Death must therefore be considered *existentially* as it is inwardly appropriated by the individual as a *being-toward-death*. As we will see, existentialists see death in all of its paradoxical dimensions. For Beauvoir, death is "a thing of fear" (FC 463) and yet without death "[o]ur lives would merge into universal indifference" and "there could be neither projects nor values" (PL 606). For Sartre, death is an absurdity with patrician hands that steals our freedom but is also a necessary condition for it:

> Death is the limit, but also a constituent of freedom . . . If a being were endowed with temporal infinity, he could realize all his possibilities . . . he would disappear with respect both to individuality (the realization of some possibilities to the exclusion of others) and to freedom (dangerous and irremediable choice of certain possibilities). (CM 338–9)

## HEIDEGGER'S SINGULAR DEATH

"Death," as Anne O'Byrne (2016: 263) observes, "is everywhere in *Being and Time.*" For Heidegger, it is the sense of temporality that distinguishes humans from other animals. Time is more than just successiveness moving from one instant to another but a unity of past, present and future, integrating perception of the now with memory of the past and projection into the future. This means fundamentally that all experience is shaped by the possibility of death: "when we speak of death, [it] does not signify *Dasein*'s Being-at-an-end . . . but a *Being-toward-the-end* . . . Death is a way to be" (BT 287–8). Dying is "something that every *Dasein* must take upon itself" (BT 284), an "existential phenomenon" that is "*Dasein*'s own most possibility" (BT 302). Death is at the hierarchy of Dasein's possibilities in the future, but different to other possibilities since death is "the possibility of the impossibility of any existence at all" (BT 307).

According to Heidegger, in feelings of dread, Dasein "draws back" from the nothing, which is not flight but the "calmness of wonder."[1] This movement "back from" is initiated by the nothing, the groundlessness being experienced, and directs Dasein to the very things experienced as slipping out of meaning (GA9: 114). Although the anxiety of death can cause us to become immersed in the distractions of the idle talk of the They, it is also a singularizing apprehension, "a way of disclosure in which Dasein brings itself before itself" (BT 226). The recognition of death gives Dasein its "moment of vision" and the sense of its possibilities, enabling "the possibility of a disclosure which is quite distinctive" (BT 235). Above all, Heidegger emphasizes the *mineness* of death, its individualizing aspect: "death is in every case mine" (BT 284). He rejects morbidity and suicide, but calls for an anticipation of death as a horizon of our worldly choice in order to live our mortal essence authentically. Like Nietzsche, Heidegger follows the Greek tragedians in recognizing the dual aspect of existence—the slow rotation of things, which suggests stable presence, alongside death and decay that underlie such ultimately transient stability. We are enveloped, in Sheehan's (2015: 114–5) words, "both by riotous becoming and by death-dealing entropy," struggling for a secure space where temporarily meaning staves off chaos for a brief stretch of time in the losing battle of life. Every living thing is stamped with possibility and having to become itself as possibility in order to stay alive. But whatever is alive is able to die at any instant and so in this sense, the living thing is always at-the-point-of-death. Hence, to live for Dasein is to live mortally, that is (consciously or not), always running up against its own ultimate possibility, which is to have no more possibilities and so to be dead (GA29/30: 343).

Scholars note that, for most of *Being and Time*, "Heidegger holds off the first-person plural"[2] when he delineates the "non-relational character of death" that "individualizes Dasein down to itself" (BT 308). Levinas, for instance, questions Heidegger's insistence on the singularity of death. Before our own death, we usually experience the death of others. This individualizes the self as responsible in such a way that the necessity of being in the world with others carries a different meaning. Individuation comes not from anticipatory resoluteness but from being called by the other as irreplaceable.[3] Despite recognizing that our experience is always a *being-with*,

Heidegger fails to fully acknowledge the collective dimension of death when he states, for instance: "the dying of others is not something which we experience in a genuine sense; at most we are always just 'there alongside'" (BT 282).

## BEAUVOIR'S BLACK ENLIGHTENMENT

No other existentialist, not even Heidegger, fixates on death quite as much as Beauvoir. Her autobiographies are replete with her horror of death or the prospect of it, describing how when it first dawned on her at a young age, she "was chilled to the marrow by the idea of personal extinction" (MDD 48), a "terror so violent" that it would catapult her to the point of tears and screams (MDD 207). Feeling utterly distraught that "death was slowly eating my life away," she would tremble, with clammy hands, and cry out: "I don't want to die!" (MDD 231). Vowing to "look reality in the face" (MDD 337), Beauvoir confronts mortality head-on in her writings, both her own finitude and those of her mother and Sartre. She explores the idea of immortality in her novels *All Men Are Mortal* and *The Mandarins* and examines ageing and mortality in her philosophical studies *Old Age* and *A Very Easy Death*. In her phenomenology of ageing, she charts new ground researching existing literature in addition to old people's letters, memoirs, diaries, inquiries, and statistical reports, undertaking "work that no one had done before me" (ASD 147).

In Beauvoir's memoirs, "the taste of death" (PL 604) is always palpably strong. Time, in one's youth, she regrets, is "a positive factor of accumulation" (ASD 22), but to grow old "is to set limits on oneself, to shrink" (FC 671). She complains that as she approaches old age "[t]here are no more oddities, madness is no longer holy, crowds have lost the power to intoxicate me; youth, which once fascinated me, seems now no more than a prelude to maturity" (FC 669). Although "every season has its beauty" (ASD 131) and ageing allows one to see the progress of certain lives in their continuity and their unexpected developments, senescence brings "the shrinking of the future" and "by lessening our vital strength, old age and disease often help us to tame the idea of the end" (ASD 44).

In *The Prime of Life*, Beauvoir dwells on the vanity of human endeavor and the imminence of death and reproaches Sartre "for allowing himself to be duped by that hateful mystification known as 'life'" (PL 207). In her thirties, she could not resign herself to the idea of her own mortality and suffered "brief mental crises induced by [the] horror of death" (PL 258–9). Aware of "the ghastly uncertainty of our mortal state" (PL 579), she could not bear to think of herself "as finite and ephemeral, a drop of water in the ocean" (PL 601–2). "I was afraid of growing old," she surmises, "not because my features would change and my powers diminish, but because of the ever stronger taste of death that would poison my every living moment" (PL 604). In *Force of Circumstance*, she describes with some turbulence how one's mortality seems like a living curse that colonizes one's consciousness: "Why? Why? Why must I wake up every morning filled with pain and rage, infected to the very marrow of my bones with a disease I could neither accept nor exorcise?" (FC 598). In *All Said and Done*, her final autobiography, she reveals "the taste of the void is deep within me" (ASD 144). After Sartre was seriously ill in 1954 with a severe attack of high blood pressure, she suddenly realized that, "like everyone else, he was carrying his own death within him." This came to her in the form of a "black enlightenment":

> death had closed its hand around me; it was no longer a metaphysical scandal, it was a quality of our arteries; it was no longer a sheath of night around us, it was an intimate presence penetrating my life, changing the taste of things, the quality of the light, my memories, the things I wanted to do: everything (ASD 319)

Although death had become an abiding presence up to this time, henceforth it completely "possessed" her: "I never stopped thinking about it now: about mine, about Sartre's" (FC 598). All day she teetered on the edge of that "impossible experience" of "touching the other side of my own non-being" (FC 497). "Our death is inside us," she vexed, "but not like the stone in the fruit, like the meaning of our life; inside us, but a stranger to us, an enemy, a thing of fear. Nothing else counts" (FC 463).

Despite her fear of death's hand, philosophically Beauvoir strives not to denigrate death but clears a space for it in life, since death, she argues, renders life ambiguous. We should assume our fundamental ambiguity and draw strength from it since death carries its own necessity: "The present must die so that it may live; existence must not deny this death which it carries in its heart" (EA 127). Death need not always be seen as violent for it alerts us to mortal fragilities that keep us open and attentive to the other in protecting them against violence.[4] There is the temporary freedom and peace of mind one achieves "the moment one stops running away from death" like when we sleep and dream and let ourselves "slip in a sort of glad abandon into the abyss of the Void" (PL 602–3). Following a bicycle accident near Grenoble in the early 1940s, she became intimately aware of death's absurdity and ever-present proximity: "in the most literal and precise sense, death is *nothing*. A *person* never is dead; there is no longer a 'person' to sustain the concept of 'death'" (PL 497). And yet, she concludes, "death is not always an absurd and lonely accident, but sometimes creates living bonds with other people, and then it has both meaning and justification" (PL 602). It exposes the ambiguity between self and other for "[d]eath is common to all of us, yet each individual faces it alone." Even if two people die together, their togetherness is illusory: "Between nothing and nothing there can be no bond" (PL 605). Death is thus paradoxical and should be viewed not only as a common link between the individual and mankind, but also as the major peril of loneliness and separation (PL 607). "I will die a death which is absolutely unique for me," she muses, "but it's the same for everyone" (1965: 78–9).

Compared to Beauvoir, Sartre rarely obsesses about death and it is true to say that his equanimity contrasts markedly with her vexation. His play *No Exit* illustrates how death makes us "prey to the living" (BN 706). The deceased male protagonist Garcin is in "hell" since he cannot influence how the living view him. He will be forever "a coward" in the eyes of the living and can no longer act to dispel or change it. Once dead, we are no longer able to retotalize ourselves and become something different by modifying the dialectical object that is our self which "remains between the Other's hands, like a coat that I have left him with" (BN 706–7). In this way, death involves the "transformation into otherness of the whole person," an act of "supreme generosity" in which I place myself completely at the disposal of others (CM 53–4). In *Being and Nothingness*, Sartre criticizes Heidegger's singularizing conception and "explication of death" in *Being and Time*, arguing that death accomplishes nothing but to "deprive [life] of all subjective meaning" (BN 707). It is just a brute fact like birth. In interview with Beauvoir not long before his death, Sartre maintains a calm serenity: "And up until the present, death has never weighed upon my life and probably it never will" (FS 433). Preparing us, old age disperses the self into "a mass of activities, of trifling things" before the ultimate dispersal of death arrives. "Death," he states calmly, "does not frighten me." As a serious matter that comes at an expected given moment "[i]t seems to me natural . . . It is after all the return to nature and the assertion that I was a part of nature" (FS 432). It is, in Sartre's mood of acceptance, "the final closing as birth was the opening," but a closure "accompanied by a continual broadening toward the universal" (FS 426). Posterity, he hopes, would arrive after death through his writing: "after death I survived in the form of my books; in my books I was found again. It was immortal life" (FS 413).

## VIBRANT DEATH

Kierkegaard was shaken to the core with paroxysms of profound sorrow at the death of his mother Anne in 1834. Reflecting on his own family, in *Works of Love* he writes about how love is inseparable from anxiety and loss. He offers *Either/Or* as material for "companionship of the deathbound" (PJ 664) but considers his death to be a blessing, releasing him from earthly suffering and allowing him "unceasingly, unceasingly [to] Speak with my Jesus" (PJ 657). For the sorrowful Dane, love for the deceased is the purest kind of love because it expects nothing in return but death is an adjunct of birth and something we have to look in the eye: "The Birth Cry—The Death Cry . . . the death scream is the scream at being born" (PJ 632). In her passage from personal horror to serenity, Beauvoir also learned how to see death in conjunction with birth, linking mortality with natality. Thinking through "the identity of birth and death" (BN 708), enables us to recognize these as plural, entangled events.[5] Natality points toward our being-with others making it *ur*-relational, an experience for others before it is our own. This opens us up to plural being since we are already with others, a dimension of intimate sociality Heidegger neglects in his account of historicity that passes from individual Dasein to the being of a people (*Volk*).[6] Death, as Derrida argues, is *relational* as we are deeply connected in virtue of our common finitude, a "kinship-in-the-same-darkness." Authenticity involves not only owning up to our own death but also to the death of others. Death and loss are existentially co-primordial and are essential facets of any partnership or friendship: "To have a friend, to look at him, to follow him with your eyes . . . is to know in a more intense way, already injured . . .. That one of the two of you will inevitably see the other die."[7]

Anticipating posthumanist theory, existentialism promotes the idea of *vibrant death*. This theorizes death not just from the viewpoint of the sovereign subject (philosophically, one's own death, as Sartre argues, is a "non-event") but on the basis of a "posthuman phenomenology of mourning" (of the kind Beauvoir provides) that disturbs Cartesian dualism and the idea of the corpse as abject, viewing life and death as a "flat continuum" rather than an opposition.[8] Materialized through auto phenomenological analyses and poetic explorations of death entangled with philosophical exploration from the viewpoint of the mourner, vibrant death is in this sense multi-perspectival. "Every time a man dies," Beauvoir writes, "a child dies too, and an adolescent and a young man as well; everyone weeps for the one who was dear to him" (ASD 497). Akin to Marcel's notion of "creative fidelity," in vibrant death the dead person is not a lifeless corpse but an intimate, co-present companion who continues to exert influence on the living. Mourning is a companionship that is sensitized to the vibrant assemblages of spectrally and materially metamorphosed remains of the departed in the form of dreams, memories, voices, imagined conversations and miraculated objects. This was felt by Beauvoir who recounts in *All Said and Done* "[a]llmost every night I saw my mother in my dreams" (ASD 134). In *A Very Easy Death* (1964), this entanglement is further evident as her confident subjective voice of the opening passages gradually gives way to the disappearance of her singular voice within the encounter of her mother dying where she describes how "someone other than me was crying in me" and how "I had placed mother's mouth on my face and despite myself I imitated its expressions" (1985: 43–4). As a flip side to Sartre's *self-other death dialectic*, this shows not only how the dead are prey to the living but also how the living are prey to the dead as they are assailed by dynamic inhuman forces and invading memories.

For the existentialist, mortality is an aspect of our *thrownness*, an inexorable given. As Macquarrie (1973: 154) comments, death and temporal finitude are so much a constitutive part of humanity "an unending human life would be a monstrosity." Death is tranquillized and sanitized in Western societies, presented as a common experience in the media but without its existential impact. Existentialism behoves us to maintain a steadfast gaze upon death as an authentic acknowledgement of our existential condition, a form of "death-affirmation,"[9] like Nietzsche's eternal return, that helps us to maximize the meaning of each moment and avoid the psychological emptiness of nihilism, hopelessness and suicide. For theistic existentialists (Marcel and Unamuno), death underlines the transcendent and immortal essence of humans. Love affirms the immortality of the beloved and the belief in a transcendent God as the source of that love.

Nietzsche's pagan wisdom of acceptance in *Thus Spoke Zarathustra* presents death as part of Nature's endless cycle of change as the wheel of time rolls inexorably on providing space for new things to grow: "Everything goes, everything comes back; the wheel of being rolls eternally. Everything dies, everything blossoms again, the year of being runs eternally" (Z 3.13). In its ubiquity, and under conditions that are oppressive, death can merge with life in a flat continuum. Loneliness and solitude can be, in Beauvoir's view, "a form of death" (FC 619), while for Fanon, death can be found in the minds of those who attempt to live in a society that militates against their humanity. The North African Syndrome that afflicted many psychiatric patients he treated in Algeria is a psychosomatic illness that manifests as a kind of "living death":

> Without family, without love, without human relations, without communion with the community, the first encounter with himself will be a neurotic mode, a pathological mode; he will feel empty, lifeless, in bodily struggle with death, a death on this side of death, a death in life, and what is more pathetic than this man with strong muscles who tells us in his truly broken voice: "Doctor, I'm going to die"[10]

In a letter on his deathbed to his friend Roger Taïeb, Fanon writes sanguinely: "death is always with us and the important thing is not to know how to avoid it but to make sure we do our utmost for the ideas we believe in . . . We are nothing on this earth if we do not first and foremost serve a cause, the cause of the people, the cause of freedom and justice."[11]

Existentialism teaches us how life and death are co-existent, each infusing, succeeding and surpassing the other in spirals of time. Every breath, as Camus argues in *The Myth of Sisyphus*, is an affirmation of life. As self-reflective agents, choosing to live means affirming existence as a universal value: "The moment that we recognize the impossibility of absolute negation—and merely to be alive is to recognize this—the very first thing that cannot be denied is the right of others to live." In thinking about life and death, like Camus, Beauvoir pondered the greatest existential question of all—suicide. For her, this remains an existential choice that each individual must decide with their loved ones and ultimately on their own: "I still retain the idea that freedom consists of being able to die. That is, if tomorrow some threat or other menaces my freedom, death is a way of preserving it" (FS 358). In her thirties, she attests, "I preferred the idea of a total, freely conceded sacrifice, which consequently does not limit the freedom of a being" to "a slow end with illnesses, aging, and even senility" (FS 358). Years later, on witnessing her mother's end of life suffering, she asks plaintively, "[w]hat is the basis of this savage code of ethics which insists upon reanimation at all costs? On the pretext of respecting human life doctors arrogate to themselves the right of inflicting any kind of torment and every kind of degradation upon human beings."

According to true existentialist precept, "[t]here should be as much right to a free death as to free love" (ASD 110). In Nietzsche's view, we should "practice the difficult art of—going at the right time" (Z 1.21). Why, he asks, is it "more praiseworthy for a man grown old, who feels his powers decrease, to await his slow exhaustion and disintegration, rather than to put a term to his life with complete consciousness? In this case, suicide is quite natural, obvious, and should by rights awaken respect for the triumph of reason" (HH 80). Above all, we should aim for a *good death* just as we do for a good life:

> That your death may not be a blasphemy against man and the earth, my friends: that is what I beg from the honey of your soul. In your death, your spirit and your virtue should still glow like a sunset glow around the earth: otherwise yours is a bad death (Z 1.21)

Nietzsche gives a firm message "To Those Who Dream of Immortality"—it is an impertinence to do so: "you petty dwellers on earth, with your narrow conceptions of a few thousand little minutes of time, you would wish to be an everlasting burden on this everlasting universal existence!" (D 211). Eternal life would, he avers, amount to "eternal tediousness" (D 211). In contrast to Heidegger's (and Beauvoir's) anxious preoccupation with death, Nietzsche follows the serene Sartre, urging us to quell "The Thought of Death" lest it dampen our love for life, which is "a hundred times *more worthy of our attention*" (JS 278). At the same time, Beauvoir's candid and pioneering work in *A Very Easy Death* and *Old Age* sensitizes us to the plights of old age and of the old as an Otherized group, extending existentialist care and concern for a good life and a good death to those who approach the grip of death's patrician hands.

Confronting death, existentialism lays bare our fundamental mortality with all of its paradoxes in the inescapable and mysterious passage from Being to Nothingness. Beauvoir in particular does not shy away from death's absurdity and violence—"All men must die: but for every man his death is an accident and, even if he knows it and consents to it, an unjustifiable violation" (1985: 92). In the end though, despite Beauvoir's *black enlightenment*, existentialism teaches us to be, in contemporary jargon, Death-Positive. Death is "a way to be" (Heidegger), "a constituent of freedom" (Sartre) and can "sweeten every life with a precious and fragrant drop of levity" (Nietzsche). Life and death, as Kierkegaard recognizes, are always conjoined for "the death scream is the scream at being born" (PJ 632). The only trouble is, as Nietzsche complains, "you strange apothecary souls have turned [death] into an ill-tasting drop of poison" that makes the whole of life repulsive (WS 322).

CHAPTER SIXTEEN

# "Existence Is One, Across and Through the Separation of Existents"

## (Beauvoir, *The Second Sex*) INTERCONNECTEDNESS

Existentialism is well known for valorizing a certain kind of ethical individualism, but scholars often pass over the reverse side of this—its wider theorization of *interconnectedness*. The fact, as Sartre says, that "everything is connected" (FS 65) feeds into existentialist theories of politics, history, self, ecology, and religion, and complicates simple unmitigated ascriptions of individualism. With the goal of comprehension, existentialists investigate both aspects of our lives—*singularity* and *relationality*—and offer a dialectical account of their mutual involvement. As Beauvoir states in *All Said and Done*, in understanding a thing or person, one must consider "the inexhaustible multiplicity of relationships that every element in an existence maintains with the Whole." "Like Einstein's universe," my life is "both boundless and finite." It stretches back to "the very beginnings of the world, incorporating our earthly inheritance and the state of the world at this moment" (ASD 10). And yet, she adds, it is also "a finite reality" bound in space and time with a beginning and an end, possessing "an inner heart, a center of interiorization, *a me* which asserts that it is always the same throughout the whole course" (ASD 10). Even Kierkegaard, the most individualistic of all existentialists, views the self as an active relation that is open to something that transcends itself in the form of God. This chapter brings into sharp focus existentialism's manifold insights into interconnectedness, beginning with Nietzsche's relational theory of the *will to power* before analyzing Heidegger's notion of the *fourfold* and Sartre's philosophical method of *emergent interactionism*.

## NIETZSCHE'S RELATIONAL WILL TO POWER

Humans have, in Nietzsche's view, a deep allegiance to their species, the closest in kind of all living things: "nothing in them is older, stronger, more inexorable, or invincible than that instinct" (JS 1). Each of us is an exemplar or representative of humankind, sharing a common link (TI 9.33). The human is not just an individual "but the living organic totality in one particular line" (WP 678): "the species is everything, the individual is always nothing" (JS 1). Nietzsche extends this insight of interconnectedness to his philosophical ontology. Formulating his *philosophy of forces,* he argues that events are not constituted by items but by the *interaction of things*. To view things discretely in isolation from their relations to other things is a philosophical error, since "there is no things without other things" (WP 557). Individual consciousness, for example, is the product of linguistic forces and not their origin (JS 354). A thing, Nietzsche argues, is "the sum of its effects, united by a concept, an image" (WP 551). If one removes other things, an object has no properties, therefore there are no "things-in-themselves" (WP 557). Since independently existing things are inventions "owing to the requirements of logic" (WP 558), if everything we projected onto the world in order to make it intelligible were eliminated, "no things remain but only dynamic quanta, in a relation of tension to all other dynamic quanta" (WP 635). The world is therefore "essentially a world of relationships" (WP 568). Nietzsche elucidates a *relational ontology of forces* that keeps open the tension between *relata* and *relations*. In this, the subject is a relational entity "designated by the effect it produces and that which it resists" (WP 634). Will to power is productive, not something the subject *has*, but the productive force of interpretation of which the delimited subject is an effect. In Nietzsche's philosophy of "originary multiplicity," things are derivative from a complex and rich multiplicity of forces:

> All unity is only as *organization and interplay* unity: not otherwise than how a human community is a unity: so, *opposite* of atomistic anarchy; therewith a *complex of rule*, which *signifies* One, but *is* not one. (KSW 12.2.104)

According to Nietzsche, the physiology of the human being "gives only an imitation of an astounding intercourse among this multiplicity, the subordination and integration of parts into a whole." However, he warns, "it would be false to conclude from a state the necessity of an absolute monarch (the unity of the subject)" (KSW 11.27.276). Self-organization is an *emergent play* among constituents, all seeking out the resistance of antagonists in order to overpower (subordinate and integrate, or functionalize) them.[1]

Life, in Nietzsche's existentialist universe, is a combination of forces that seeks assimilation, incorporation, and expansion, "the feeling of increased power" (BGE 230). The will to power is in this sense an assemblage both individually (in terms of inner drives) and collectively (in terms of its relation to other things), a variable and relational multiplicity that is kept together by "organization" understood in the sense of a verb and not a noun, since it is in continual movement, always reshaping.[2] Following Plank (1998: 395, 433), we may conceive this as a process of aleatory and recurrent patterns of the will to power "as non-teleologically locally maximized centers of the configurations of energy discharges," a series of recombinative particles/energy center/entities that are immanent in the system, not transcendent to it. In Nietzsche's ontology of "dissipative systems" there is no need for hidden variables, or metaphysical postulations, since reality is simply a process of combination, recombination, alignment, and dissonance between multiple centers of energy.

## THE FOURFOLD

In Richard Rorty's (1991: 52) estimation, the pragmatical young Heidegger is "the philosopher of inescapable relationality." In *Being and Time*, Heidegger shows our essential relatedness to others, both negatively in terms of the circulation of the They, and positively in the form of the historical culture of a people (*Volk*). His later work further develops his *relational thinking* and crystallizes in his concept of the *fourfold*, Heidegger's appellation for the interplay between *heaven* and *earth*, *mortals*, and *divinities*, adumbrated in essays such as "Building, Dwelling, Thinking" and in his *Bremen Lectures*. According to Wolin (2022: 354), the fourfold provides the ground for Heidegger's "postmodern pagan cosmology," or "earth mysticism," but what exactly is it, we may ask?

In general terms, the fourfold describes the existential context through which we comprehend the world, composed of the four dimensions of earth, sky, mortals, and divinities. The *earth* is materiality, not stable and fixed but a bearer of things that exist sensuously as materially apparent. It brings forth a "fructifying," a blossoming into sensuous appearance of things. As a "sensuous gleam," the earth is composed not of inert matter but of shining phenomenal radiance where, in Andrew Mitchell's (2016: 298) words, "[n]othing is inert, stones speak, rivers poetize, and both plants and animals move past any presumed encapsulation in an environment or 'disinhibiting ring.'" Heidegger's earth encapsulates a reverence for one's surroundings, the dynamic processes of materialization, and the *whatness* of things.

The *sky* is the space in which things appear, a complex or variable medium, a kind of "ether." Earth and sky are united in a "marriage" (GA7: 198) that comprises a space of movement and transience where the natural passage of day and night and of seasonal change determines how things appear. It affects everything within it and weathers them as time passes. The sky is not a void but a medium of relationality in which things are received "outside" of themselves, a textured space with a certain density and viscosity, full of passing patches of opacity (as clouds) and subject to occasional seizures of destructive power and outbursts (in the form of storms).[3] For Heidegger, the sky gives us appreciation of the wider cosmos that surrounds us in all directions. As *mortals* we are beings defined by openness and exposure to the world, living in anxiety within the strange nonpresence of death (when it is here, we are gone, and when we are here it is not). Our awareness of ourselves as finite, mortal beings brings *divinities* into our existential horizons, which symbolize our ethical being and our ability to reflect on our place in the universe. *Divinities* are "hinting messengers of godhood," a glimpse of a presence that is absent. They are conveyors of meaning in which things themselves are "messaged" to us, a promise between origin and destination, between those who have passed and those yet to come.[4]

Heidegger introduces the fourfold in the opening lecture of the *Bremen Lectures*, "the Thing." The thing is not self-enclosed but opens out and spills over into relations with what lies beyond it. Sustaining and sustained by relations, things are singular and unique owing to their place in this relation of mutually supportive connections. No thing is self-sustained and self-present but contextual and defined by what lies outside it. As the ground of relationality, the fourfold is the "mirror play of things" in which we must conceive the four dimensions as "belonging together" in a kind of "mirror-play" (GA79: 19): "the united four are already suffocated in their essence when one represents them only as individuated actualities that are grounded through one another and are to be explained in terms of each other" (GA79: 19). Together they constitute the "thinging of the thing" in which they are concentrated: "Each of the four in its way mirrors the essence of the remaining others again. Each is thus reflected in its way back into what is its own within the single fold of the four" (GA79: 18). Through appropriation, expropriation and interconnection, they form a composite relational whole:

> None of the four insists on its separate particularity. Each of the four within this bringing into ownership is much more expropriated to what is its own. This expropriative bringing into ownership is the mirror-play of the fourfold. (GA79: 18)

To Heidegger's deep dismay, technology has claimed this interconnected world, since it positions objects as standing-reserve within a network of unending circulation and interchangeability: "In positionality, the presencing of all that presences becomes standing reserve" (GA79: 32). No space is unclaimed or out of bounds, and tension exists between singularity and replaceability. For Heidegger, the fourfold represents the full actuality of all existence in its inexhaustible manifold richness, and to realize one's place poetically within the fourfold beyond the objectifying gaze of modern science and technological instrumentality is the mark of authenticity. In consonance with Buber, he judges that a person who lives in an I-it relation lives in severance and alienation without a home or dwelling in the universe.

Heidegger's esoteric redemptive promise for the advent of the "god to come" in the form of a poetic dwelling within the fourfold is indicative, as Michael Zimmerman (2007: 303) points out, of his "proximity to Buddhism." This is particularly so in his idea of the "mirror-play" (GA79: 19) of the four dimensions which establishes the doctrine of *dependent coproduction*, a relational ontology that emphasizes the interdependency of all things. This is metaphorically expressed by the example of the jewel net of the god Indra (advanced by the Hua-Yen Buddhist school). In a process of *dependent coproduction*, in an infinite net (the universe), an infinite amount of gems are set, each reflecting the light emitted by the others. The play of light is codetermined simultaneously by the presence of others, and no single gem stands in a superior causal relation to any other. All rise together in an event of reflection that is sentient though not self-conscious.[5] This insight of interconnectedness and dependent coproduction is one that the French existentialists develop further still in the theory of *emergent interactionism* elucidated most fully by Sartre in the *Critique*.

## EMERGENT INTERACTIONISM

As she grew older, Beauvoir tells how "a metamorphosis" within her took place: "I ceased to regard my life as an autonomous and self-sufficient project, I was obliged to rediscover my links with a universe, the very face of which I had forgotten" (PL 370). It was the outbreak of World War II that precipitated the sea change in her: "Then, suddenly, History burst over me, and I dissolved into fragments. I woke to find myself scattered over the four quarters of the globe, linked by every nerve in me to each and every individual" (PL 369). From then on, immersed in Spinoza and Bergson, she became fully aware of the interconnectedness of things and the relationality of her existence from which there was no looking back: "I had to aim at the universe in its totality if I was to possess the least grain of dust upon it" (PL 361).

Sartre experienced a similar transformation when history grabbed him by the scruff of the neck during the war, throwing him into a deeper recognition of historical and social entanglement: "As for the little well-scrubbed atom I believed myself to be, powerful forces seized him, and sent him to the front with others without asking his opinion" (2008: 24). Recognizing that "everything is connected" (FS 65), as far back as the 1930s Sartre had preached against social atomism, attributing it to the bourgeois analytical point of view that, as he would later argue in the *Critique*, is incapable of grasping collective realities or synthetic wholes, such as social class. He opposes this to synthetic or dialectical reason, which is totalizing and "thinks in terms of solidarity" (CDR 468). This difference "expresses itself as a conflict of rationalities" (CDR 802). Analytical reason, which constitutes bonds between individuals only "in the milieu of exteriority" (CDR 285), forms the basis of capitalist hegemony by reinforcing the "absolute separation between people which is so crucial to the continuing domination of the individualistic bourgeoisie" (CDR 297).

Unlike methodological individualism, Sartre's social theory of *emergent interactionism* appreciates the synthetic enrichment of social phenomena and their irreducibility to their parts. Such a theory of relationality had been suggested, though left underdeveloped, by Kierkegaard writing in his journals. Without other things to contextualize it, a thing itself is abstract and lacking concretization: "You always need one more light positively to identify another . . . Only when one more light appears can you fix the place of the first, in relation to it" (PJ 9). He describes intersubjectivity as "the transition from a quantitative to a qualitative determination" and wonders whether there is a synthetic enrichment of both parts within a relation—"Is mediation the zero point, or is it a third? Does the third emerge by itself through the immanent notion of the two, or how does it emerge?" (PJ 176). Viewing subjectivity and intersubjectivity as *emergent* explains how a higher order is founded on a lower one and in a sense contains it but at the same time takes it over and integrates it into new structures which cannot be explained by those that are taken over. This is not just a simple mixing of elements, but more a chemical reaction that yields a new substance with different qualities from its constituents. For Sartre, consciousness emerges on the intersubjective level as an ongoing totalization between subjectivities that becomes a "totality" but is always open to detotalization (CDR 404). Community is not a simple collection of separate individuals but is informed by a unity of existence that penetrates and transcends their private worlds. When two or more individuals enter into relationship, there is a reciprocity that is an existential modification of each (SM 45). This forms "inter-individual reality" which in turn transforms and conditions individual praxis. According broadly with a Spinozean ontologico-ethical position, Sartre articulates a subjectivity that is elaborated neither in terms of a monadic individual nor of a collective entity, but of an essentially self-creating, internally related multiplicity of singularities that interrelate according to intrinsic, spontaneous movements. When they move toward common ends, the singularities give rise to ontological dislocations—that is, the formation of more complex singularities in "constellations of reciprocities" (CDR 367).

In Sartre's universe, all of reality is a congregation of individual singularities freely configuring and reconfiguring themselves according to different, spontaneous modalities. His *pluralistic monism* is kaleidoscopic, composed of singularities in constant becoming that coalesce and merge together in the production of a composite whole. Free praxis becomes constituent power in this process, and it is within this continuous movement of becoming that the group discovers itself as subject. This gives us a rationality that goes beyond the dualisms of modernity, outlining a new form of thinking that represents itself in a logic of singularities-in-process, fusion, and continual surpassing. For the French existentialists, regimes of alterity have to be understood with a ternary logic in terms of the circulation of the Third: "the group is not a reality which exists in itself separate from the 'transcendence-immanence' tension which characterizes the third party in relation to it" (CDR 409).

Throughout his writings, Sartre makes clear his intention to steer a virtuous path between the metaphysics of idealists who "reduce matter to mind" and the materialist who "reduces mind to matter" (1995: 204). He holds an *emergentist* form of materialism where mind develops from matter but is irreducible to matter in its distinctive features, the chief of which is *intentionality,* which he consistently takes to be the defining characteristic of the mental.[6] A person is "wholly matter" (CDR 180), an organism symbiotically related to its environment through need, and engaged in a reciprocal dialectical process of "trans-substantiation" (CDR 178). It is this material process of exchange that establishes our interconnectedness: "[when something] has taken on the character of materiality it enters into relation with the entire Universe" (CDR 163). This is continuous with *Being and Nothingness* where Sartre seeks a "concrete ontology" of interconnections instantiated in the world.[7] Like the way quantum systems can become entangled and "get inside" each other to form a creative, internal relationship through which they further evolve,[8] in Sartre's philosophy interpersonal relations cause an "internal negation" for those involved. When fixed by the gaze of the Other, this decenters my world and causes me to experience "a new type of intraworldly haemorrhage" (BN 400) in which all the constituents of my world bleed into the Other. In an interview with Michel Sicard shortly before his death, Sartre focuses on the issue of interconnectedness and makes a quantum move by positing the existence of an internal *ontological* bond between human beings:

> Ontologically, consciousnesses are not isolated, there are planes where they enter into one another—planes common to two or to *n* consciousnesses . . . there are penetrations between consciousnesses. (1979a: 15)

The French existentialists' idea of "a duality that *is* a unity" (BN 125) provides a sophisticated mereology that avoids the Scylla of holism and Charybdis of methodological individualism. Avoiding analytical reason that fails to take account of numerous mediations and assemblages, they advance a dialectical worldview of parts and wholes in which parts acquire properties by virtue of being parts of a particular whole, properties they do not have in isolation or as parts of another whole. Parts and wholes evolve in consequence of their relationship, and the relationship itself evolves as a consequence of their interpenetration.[9] The existentialist universe is a dynamic, open-ended, integrative web of irreducible active connections and totalizations, a "totalization without a totalizer." Investigating the process of parts and whole in interaction, the dialectic, Sartre argues, is "not the study, not even the "functional" and "dynamic" study, of a unity already made" but "the real movement of a unity in the process of being made" (SM 69). Just like Nietzsche's *agonistic will to power* and the *codependent production* of Heidegger's fourfold, Sartre's *emergent interactionism* elucidates the productive entanglements and interconnections of Self and Other:

> If totalization is really an ongoing process, it operates everywhere. This means both that there is a dialectical meaning of the practical ensemble—whether it is planetary, or has to become even interplanetary—and that each individual event totalizes in itself this ensemble in the infinite richness of its individuality. (CDR2: 17)

*Interconnectedness* and *entanglement* are now key semantic signifiers in the contemporary mind brought to stark awareness by the impending dangers of the Anthropocene.[10] Existentialists were the progenitors to postmodernists like Derrida, Foucault, and Deleuze, who in turn inform contemporary posthuman theories that draw on Deleuze's and Guattari's ideas of the *rhizome* and the *intermezzo* to articulate *a philosophy of relations*. To this end, we should view existentialism in earnest as a pioneering philosophy of entanglement. Philosophical posthumanism has plundered the existentialist mereology passed down through poststructuralism and inspired by Spinoza—*relata* do not precede relations, but relations do not precede relata either: "relata and relations generate out of co-constitutive, embodied, agential processes, situated in specific spatio-temporal environments," therefore neither is primary (Ferrando 2020: 165). In her article "Transjectivity," Christine Daigle (2023: 149–51) draws upon Beauvoir's views of intersubjectivity in *The Second Sex* to elucidate the posthuman concept of *transjectivity*, a compound term that enmeshes the trans-subjective and trans-objective dimensions of existence. Out of this dynamic bundle of relations a "subjectivity-in-process" emerges, "constantly unfolding and dynamically becoming" within many quantitative and qualitative degrees of entanglement. This recognition makes possible an "ethics of flourishing" in which we develop a heightened responsibility with respect to our interconnectedness with others, adopting "a humble and careful attitude" as "the transjective ethos needed for our troubled times." Attentive to the fourfold that envelops us and to the singularity that defines us, existentialism lucidly presages contemporary (scientific) understanding of how "everything is connected" (FS 65) and how, in Beauvoir's words, "[e]xistence is one, across and through the separation of existents" (SS 57).

CHAPTER SEVENTEEN

# "The Question Is Not to Know Whether One Accepts or Rejects Violence, but Whether . . . It Tends Toward Its Own Suspension or Toward Self-Perpetuation"

## (Merleau-Ponty, *Humanism and Terror*) VIOLENCE

Violence figures ominously in existentialist literature. Famously, in Camus' *The Stranger*, the protagonist Meursault shoots an Arab man on the beach and offers no reason for his *acte gratuit* other than the overbearing sensation of the excessive heat he felt. In Dostoevsky's *Crime and Punishment*, Raskolnikov rationalizes his murderous crimes by his own exceptionality and by calculating the social benefit of his acts. Cross Damon, the protagonist in Richard Wright's *The Outsider* (1953), exercises his freedom to endow things with meaning, pursuing it through reckless and violent acts. Franz Kafka's Josef K in *The Trial* is arraigned for a crime that is never revealed to him and then shot dead in cold blood. Beauvoir's *She Came to Stay* and many of Sartre's plays, such as *The Flies*, *The Respectful Prostitute*, *Lucifer and the Lord*, and *The Dirty Hands*, feature murder and physical violence meted out by both oppressor and oppressed.

In this chapter, we analyze how existentialist philosophy theorizes violence. Nietzsche, Heidegger, Sartre, Beauvoir, Merleau-Ponty, and Fanon have all been accused of glorifying violence in some way, but is this an accurate assessment if we really follow the nuances of their argument? We begin with Nietzsche, existentialism's Man of Dynamite who addresses the themes of war, violence, and appropriation in cold reality in his volatile and explosive writings and end with Fanon's call to arms to the colonized in *The Damned of the Earth*. What, we ask, can existentialism illuminate about the violent times we live in?

## NIETZSCHE'S DYNAMITE

As a disciple of Dionysus (EH P2), there is no doubt Nietzsche was riven between barbarism and gentleness, torn in two between war and peace: "Dionysus possesses the dual nature of a cruel, barbarized demon and a mild, gentle ruler" (BT 10). He describes himself in *Ecce Homo* not as a man, but as "dynamite" (EH 4.1), an explosive force out to destroy all humanity holds precious, liable to ignite in your face and blow comforting thoughts into smithereens. And yet earlier in *The Joyous Science* he distances himself from all violent acts, following the example of Raphael by vowing to never paint another image of torture or seek the sublime "where it lives as a sister to cruelty" (JS 313). In *Human, All Too Human*, he gives a balanced judgment of war:

> *War*. One can say against war that it makes the victor stupid and the vanquished malicious. In favor of war, one can say that it barbarizes through both these effects and thus makes man more natural. (HH 444)

In his early school days, Nietzsche experienced the pecking order of male hierarchy and violence, teased, and bullied by his schoolmates at the *Gymnasium* for his seriousness and his withdrawn character, as well as for his zealous following of rules. He soon learned "how to philosophize with a hammer" and was known for his acerbic wit and sharp tongue, looking down from "a height where I speak no longer with words but with lightning bolts" (EH 6.3). At the age of fourteen, he left the family home in Naumburg for the elite boarding school Schulpforta, which was a conservative factory of masculine values, monastic austerity, and Prussian militarism. His toughening up continued into his university years. He competed in a fraternity dueling contest while at the University of Bonn (despite his physical frailty) from which he subsequently bore a small scar on his nose. After conscription into the army in 1867 for military service, he learned how to fire cannons and ride horses but was disbanded a year later after a serious riding accident. "My career as warrior," he wrote with some chagrin, "has not set the stage on fire" (KSB 2.292).[1] Despite this pugnacious veneer, however, he was well known for his gentleness and effeminacy (a fact that Wagner liked to spread in public through gossip and scandalizing).

Nietzsche's work exhibits the same ambivalence as his character. His early Bismarckian phase of thinking is unapologetically bellicose, describing the tenor of his *Untimely Meditations* as "warlike," reveling in the activities of "conquest" and "assassination" (EH 6.1). Modern humans, he complains, are no longer political animals in the Greek sense, for we are unwilling to organize ourselves as "material for society." He advocates war in order to reinstate the collective purpose and body of the state: "although it comes along like the night, war is nevertheless Apollo, the true divinity for consecrating and purifying the state" (G.S 15). In later texts, however, he is apt to present divergent perspectives. When reading *Ecce Homo*, for instance, it is hard to decide whether he wishes to present himself as a hawk or a dove (or just a confusing farrago of warring and peaceful instincts). Juxtaposing his professed belligerence as an "annihilator" (EH 4.2) near the beginning of the book—"I am warlike by nature. Attacking is one of my instincts" (EH 1.7)—with his peaceful declaration later "to be gentle and benevolent toward everybody" (EH 3.10.4), we are left with a Nietzsche of conflicting drives. Robert Solomon (2003: 7) highlights this paradox, contrasting the "Nasty Nietzsche"—the immoralist and Antichrist, the "mad-dog foaming at the moustache"—with the "Gentle Nietzsche"—a "quite respectable and house-trained lapdog, a defender of Good Things."

Often scholars overemphasize Nietzsche's warlike statements above his peaceful ones. In *Beyond Good and Evil*, for instance, he includes sympathy (*Mitgefühl*) as a basic virtue: "Courage, insight, sympathy, solitude" (BGE 284) and in *Daybreak* his list of virtues is anything but hawkish: "[h]onesty, courage, generosity, politeness" (D 556). Indeed, benevolence is considered by Nietzsche to be a key virtue. He praises small acts of kindness that people show (HH 49) and the way they contribute to a collective wellbeing (HH 111). In *Ecce Homo*, he proposes the virtues of magnanimity and veneration (EH 3.10.4). He makes it clear that social power does not necessarily dictate whether one adopts master or slave morality, and he warns time and again against confusing political power with strength and misfortune with weakness (D 413). While he advocates a pathos of distance (BGE 257) and argues that a certain form of cruelty is indispensable in which greatness means the ability to inflict great pain "to all that is old and feeble in us" (JS 26), he recognizes that some cruelties are "anti-life." Nietzsche may sometimes identify with Roman stoicism—brave tough, resilient, insensitive—but he shows only a qualified admiration for it and more readily aligns himself with Epicureanism (JS 306). Symbolically, the fourth book of *Thus Spoke Zarathustra* ends with the appearance of a laughing lion among a flock of doves. In a note of 1883, he discusses this symbol as combining strength and power with gentleness (KSW 21.2), and it is this dialectical tension between the two that he attempts to sublimate in his apparent contradictory thinking. Nietzsche's middle works are combative in challenging received opinion, but not violent and belligerent: "This war, but war without powder and smoke, without warlike poses, without pathos and stained limbs" (EH 7.1).

After the peaceful aura of his middle period, Nietzsche's later thinking reverts back to the theme of violent struggle. Influenced by Heraclitus' notion of strife as the basic motor behind change and becoming and a conception of existence as a battle of opposed forces, he places *agonism* at the heart of his social ontology. Just as trees in a jungle fight each other for power (WP 704), the will to power "seeks that which resists it" (WP 656). Aristocratic rule is justified by the will to power that strives to enhance its power, grow, and become predominant:

> Exploitation does not pertain to a corrupt or imperfect or primitive society: it pertains to the *essence* of the living thing as a fundamental organic function; it is a consequence of the intrinsic will to power, which is precisely the will of life. (BGE 259)

Nietzsche's last writings speak of a new revolutionary "grand politics" modelled in part on the violence of the French Revolution that would "break the history of humanity into two." Extolling the virtues of war and revolution that he had spoken disparagingly of in his middle period, he proposes heavy artillery, dynamite, and explosive terror. In a letter to August Strindberg in December 1888, he declares,

"I mean to have the young emperor shot," and to his friend Franz Overbeck in 1889, he extended this to haters of the Jewish people: "I am just having all anti-semites shot" (1969a: 344–6). After his death in 1900, this volatile dynamite was rediscovered by Nazi ideologues and deployed with explosive force in Heidegger's philosophy.

## HEIDEGGER'S STRIFE

Heidegger craved the military spirit (if not its grim reality) and lived "in the shadow of [Nietzsche's] sword" (EH 6.2). In 1914, he enlisted in the army, but was discharged for health reasons after two months. He rejoined the army in 1917 in Freiburg working for interior services as a postal censor and in 1918, he was sent to a meteorological station close to the Western front in the Ardennes to provide weather forecasts for the deployment of poison gas in the Marne-Champagne battle. In the last few weeks of the war he was promoted to corporal and reported that he had enjoyed his time in the military, especially the thrill of action: "the journey to the front was wonderful."[2] As Rector of the University of Freiburg, he was instrumental in the coordination of the German university with the party-state apparatus, but after 1934, his relationship with the party steadily deteriorated and restrictions were placed on his freedom to publish. In 1944, he was sent to dig trenches in the Rhine and then drafted into the People's Militia.

*Being and Time*, according to Herbert Marcuse, exudes the "spirit of the trenches" (*Frontesgeist*) that was a dominant theme in anti-Weimar conservative nationalist critique in Germany in the 1920s from which Heidegger took his political bearings. Heidegger's glorification of sacrifice and "choosing a Hero" in his "metaphysics of death" in the text keeps with the warrior ethos of World War I and reprises the theme of sacrifice as an end-in-itself. As Wolin (2022: 129) comments, this recalls "the battle cry of the fascist Futurists: *Viva la muerte!*" and marks his "regression to the *cult of death*," invoking the trench warfare imagery of authentic Dasein as "going over the top" and sallying forth. The spirit of the trenches also figures in Heidegger's reading of Hölderlin where he reiterates the ideology of war and links sacrifice to authentic sociality: "Death and a readiness for sacrifice produce the *space of community* from which camaraderie springs . . . Were it not for death as free sacrifice, camaraderie would not exist" (GA39: 74).

Heidegger conceives *strife* as the motor of change and as the midwife of Being, appropriating Heraclitus' fragment 53—"war is the father of all things"—as his guiding theme. In his discussion of Plato's cave analogy, he describes the philosopher qua liberator as a man of "violent action" who destroys comfortable worlds and illusions (GA34: 81):

> Violence against the preponderant power of Being must shatter against Being . . . Therefore the violent one knows no kindness and conciliation . . . To him disaster is the deepest and broadest affirmation of the overpowering. (IM 262–3)

To offset the groundswell of rootlessness, Heidegger advocates the "purification of Being" that would culminate in "the self-obliteration of the earth and the disappearance of contemporary humanity," which, he recommends, should be welcomed and not feared or misconstrued as a "misfortune" (GA96: 238, 281).

Presenting himself as "a prophet of total annihilation," Heidegger combines the "annihilationist edict" (GA96: 281) with the cleansing fantasies of Nazi race doctrine in which German Jews are a "domestic enemy" that pose a threat to the unity of community through a "Jewification of the German spirit" (GA36/7: 90–1). Against this threat, it is essential "*to keep oneself ready for attack*" for in order to avoid losing its edge, a people must find or fabricate its inner enemies and pursue them ruthlessly to the point of elimination (GA36/37: 91). In his 1940 lecture course on "Nietzsche and European Nihilism," he elevates *Macht* over *Moral*. Universal morality is little more than a "metaphysical tactic" and in order to bring about "active nihilism" there must be no half measures or compromises. One must consummate nihilism before overcoming it in accordance with the maxim "the worse the better" for "every power . . . has its own law, and only through impotence does it become illegal" (GA46: 264). For Heidegger, modernity has placed comfort and risk aversion above strength and force: "we believe it is no longer necessary in the fundament of our being to be strong." In the 1930s, he makes the move from "active nihilism" to "total mobilization" where violence becomes an ontological imperative, and in the eyes of his critics, a vehicle for authoritarian licentiousness.[3]

## DIRTY HANDS AND REDEMPTION IN FRANCE

If Heidegger views violence from the perspective of the oppressor and the strong who impose a culture on the weak, then the French existentialists reverse this and view it through the eyes of the oppressed and disenfranchized. In so doing, they journey to the heart of violence's paradoxes. It is unsightly, regrettable and self-defeating, but sometimes unavoidable. Also, it is paradoxical in that I must act materially in committing violence and, at the same time, become pure transcendence by treating the other as pure object and denying her transcendence. In a world of oppression, the oppressed may have to exercise violence against their oppressors in order to realize their freedom and bring about peace.

Although she became "a firm believer in pacifism" (MDD 238) after attending Alain's lectures as a student in the 1920s, Beauvoir sees violence as an aspect of our embodiment in a material world. In *Ethics of Ambiguity*, she shows how violence is always a possibility among competing transcendences. Conflict can arise even when we attempt to increase the field of freedom where "one finds oneself obliged to oppress and kill men who are pursuing goals whose validity one acknowledges oneself" (EA 99). She cites the example of anti-fascists in Europe during the Second World War who opposed liberation movements in British colonies, which would effectively weaken Britain in its struggle against fascism. Ambiguity often clouds political decisions for there is no "science of history": "at each particular moment we must in any case maneuver in a state of doubt" (EA 123).

Despite this, Beauvoir argues, we must act in such a way that the means do not undermine the end we aim for: "The means, it is said, will be justified by the end; but it is the means which define the end, and if it is contradicted in the moment that set it up, the whole enterprise sinks into absurdity" (EA 124) Stalinism is the consequence of not heeding the lesson that violence "must be legitimised concretely" (EA 148) if it is not to undermine its initial purpose for ultimately, oppression is self-defeating as the oppressor undermines his own freedom since, to be truly free, freedom needs to unfold in a world of free citizens. The oppressor largely ignores this though bad faith (EA 97) by seeing oppression as natural: "One of the ruses of oppression is to camouflage itself behind a natural situation since, after all, one cannot revolt against nature" (EA 83). Since, we cannot count on a "collective conversion" (EA 97) of the oppressors, resistance, revolt, and counter-violence is necessary for to bring about a society of equal freedoms. The oppressed "can fulfil his human freedom only in revolt" (EA 87). And yet, the oppressed live in an "infantile world" with no sense of past, future or possibility and often have "no instrument be it in thought or by astonishment or anger, which permits them to attack the civilization which oppresses them" (EA 38). Their freedom is unrealizable and the situation imposed on them is internalized as "immanent" or natural (EA 102–3) due to the mystifications, codes of signification and false narratives imposed on them by the oppressive class. Although Beauvoir contends "in a world at war every project is a matter of choice, and you must . . . consent to violence" (PL 549), violence in society is not an "unchangeable given." Violence takes root in societies that glorify it while tolerating oppressive relations, sexism and discrimination. Despite the phenomenon of Stalinism, she holds the faith that, at its best, Marxism is a "radical humanism" that "rejects the idea of an inhuman objectivity" (EA 18).

As Sonia Kruks (1990: 99) remarks, Beauvoir's work serves as a "prolegomenon" to Sartre's later Marxist existentialism and Merleau-Ponty's political thinking. In essays of the 1940s (e.g., "A Note on Machiavelli," 1949), Merleau-Ponty examines the question of political violence and follows a Beauvoirian logic. In doing violence to the Other I do violence to myself since I violate our common intersubjective space. Violence originates from my withdrawal into pure subjectivity in which I define the other as pure object, but can only be achieved by abandoning subjectivity and engaging with the other in relation as incarnate existents: "consciousness can do nothing without its body and can only act upon others by acting on their bodies" (HT 102). One is always compromised in an immoral world with soiled hands for although "[t]he moral man does not want to dirty his hands," under the Occupation "the garage mechanic had to repair German cars if he wanted to live" (SNS 147).

For Merleau-Ponty, the stance of non-violence can never amount to more than a tacit acceptance and endorsement of ruling-class violence (HT xviii). It is unavoidable in an oppressive society since inaction also leads to violence by leaving existing regimes of violence unchallenged. In *Humanism and Terror*, he argues that violence is a fact of life and endorses Bolshevism if "the violence it exercises is revolutionary and capable of creating human relations between men" (HT 18). The key question, he states, "is not to know whether one accepts or rejects violence, but whether the violence with which one is allied is "progressive" and tends toward its own suspension or toward self-perpetuation" (HT 1).

Merleau-Ponty makes it clear that all humanist projects can become adulterated by the conjunction of unforeseen events when contingency transforms *sens* into *non-sens* since "Marx himself pointed out that chaos and absurdity were one of the possible ways for history to end" (SNS 163). Freedom is always qualified and ambiguous: "The world is already constituted, but also never completely constituted" (PP 453). There exists "a sort of maleficence in history" (HT 94) that transcends individual intentions, deviates our original aims and becomes a source of violence. Merleau-Ponty wonders whether Marxism can transcend the paradox of humanism and terror and develop an ethics that is not subverted by the violence in which it entangles itself. Answering this, he turns to the developments in the Soviet Union where, instead of eliminating itself, violence increased and the intersubjective fabric was torn apart, a conflict between "the exigencies of realism and those of ethics" (HT 125). In the late 1940s, he believes that communism, despite all its flaws, still tends toward the suspension of violence and is more likely on a global level to reduce violence than capitalism, but in the 1950s he views Soviet violence as endemic and turns to a "new liberalism" as the least violent political option.

Like Nietzsche, Sartre first tasted violence at the hand of other boys at school. The bullying he suffered at La Rochelle made him take that violence into himself and implement "a physically confrontational masculinity" as one "who can endure hard blows" (1995: 175). Alongside learning how to box, his tough masculine sense of self was built around his heroic project of writing: "For a long while I treated my pen as a sword" (W 157). In 1939 he was conscripted into the French Army and served in the meteorological service, releasing weather balloons and taking readings just as Heidegger had done for the German army twenty years previously. He was captured by the German army in 1940 and sent to a prison camp, Stalag XIID at Trier from which he escaped in 1941. In his travels around the world with Beauvoir, he saw violence in its many guises. They witnessed "the happiness that had attained by violence" in Cuba immediately following the revolution whereas in Algeria they only saw its negative aspect: "the rejection of the oppressor" (FC 503). In the 1960s, Sartre was targeted with violence as his flat was bombed on two occasions by a right-wing French militia group (the OAS) for his outspoken support of Algerian independence. In his plays and novels, violence is a recurring theme, no more so than in *Dirty Hands* where he explores the world of political expediency, ideological powerplay and internecine murder.

Taken as a whole, Sartre's writings show some consistency, but also some variance concerning the question of violence. In *What is Literature?*, he views violence as a "setback" under whatever form it may show itself, but it is an inevitable setback because we are in a universe of violence and "if it is true that recourse to violence against violence risks perpetuating it, it is also true that it is the only means of bringing an end to it" (WL 214). In *Notebooks for an Ethics*, he makes a distinction between force (which is in accord with the law) and violence (which is defined in relation to the law that it violates) (NE 561). Oppressors can require through force the oppressed not to resort to violence, but the oppressed cannot require the oppressors to cease their violence since, the force they exert (e.g., slavery, labor–capital relations, colonialism) is not seen as violence under the law. Discussing the financial oppression of blacks in the South who could only register to vote if they paid heavy poll taxes, he wrote "[t]o change this situation, the oppressed has to use violence . . .

The union of the oppressed will come about, therefore, through violence" (NE 142). He identifies various forms of capitalist violence in the *Critique* and considers whether violence can overturn oppressive social relations and pave the way for new progressive social forms. Narrow conceptions of political violence misidentify acts of counter-violence as acts of original violence (e.g., industrial conflict) in order to exclude the structural violence that saturates society. In colonialism, for example, the "stickiness" of the past produced by colonial praxis has produced a "practico-inert hell" that degrades subsequent social relations (CDR 718).

Sartre's most incendiary and provocative text is the Preface that he wrote (at Fanon's request) for Fanon's *The Damned of the Earth* where he offers a new three-stage dialectic: colonial oppression (thesis), revolutionary action (antithesis) and decolonization (new syn/thesis). His notorious polemical statement "to shoot down a European is to kill two birds with one stone, to destroy an oppressor and the man he oppressed at the same time" (WE 19) caused great controversy (especially for the French Right) and led some, such as Hannah Arendt in *On Violence*, to accuse Sartre of assigning intrinsic value to violence. What such accusations disregard, however, as Michael Fleming (2020: 282–3) observes, is the initial violence that is embedded in the existing state of affairs. Sartre's Preface is not an endorsement of unrestrained violence, but rather a historically situated acknowledgement that colonialism leads to explosive contradictions that provide the victims of the colonial violence with few pathways to "full humanity" other than physical revolt. Sartre does not glorify violence, as Arendt supposes, but recognizes its ubiquity and the challenge it poses for freedom. Viewing the counter-violence of the oppressed as a form of self-defense, he is critical of preachers of universal non-violence: "this pseudo-universalist stance really means the following: 'I am in favor of the chronic violence the colonizers inflict on the colonized (overexploitation, unemployment, malnutrition, all held in place by terror)'" (1980: 409).

Rather than fetishizing violence, Sartre subjects it to a searching analysis. This is evident in his *Rome Lectures* of 1964 where he defines the limits of counter-violence that would be appropriate for achieving full humanity once the violence of oppression has been dissolved. He outlines four key conditions: 1. counter-violence does not produce an exploitative, alienating or repressive system; 2. it does not produce ideologies that function to designate or re-create a "sub-humanity"; 3. there is no other justification for violence than its contingent necessity; 4. it must originate in the masses, receive popular support and be continually critiqued.[4] Sartre's "temporal cap" on counter-violence illustrates how he was deeply concerned about the limits of violence, recognizing how, as well as breaking up "a certain state of enslavement" (HN 92), counter-violence can often reconfigure or intensify existing structures of violence. His criteria of legitimate counter-violence led him to support the claims of the Palestinians, but not the Baader-Meinhof group due to its lack of mass support. Even so, he and Beauvoir were horrified at the prospect of war breaking out between Israel and Egypt in 1968 and wished "some way of settling the conflict peaceably would be found" (ASD 431). They attached great importance to a peaceful and just resolution of the Israel-Palestine conflict, helping to organize conferences in France under the aegis of *Les Temps Modernes* in 1979 while vehemently condemning military and imperialist aggression (FS 113).

More than the other existentialists (whose infirmities excused them from the direct combat of war), Fanon tasted the blood of life-or-death battle in the raw. On 12 March 1944, he boarded the *Oregon*, a troop ship with 1000 men bound for a training camp in Morocco, joyfully singing "Hitler, we're going to knock you off your hilltop." His unit was the Bataillon de Marche des Antilles, a heteroclite force that would join up with the Free French forces and Allies. While Heidegger was digging military trenches for the German army, Fanon was near the German border in November 1944 loaded with artillery to blow the German trenches apart. Here, fighting in the Bois de Grappes he was hit in the chest by shrapnel from an incoming mortar round. After recovering from his injuries, he was awarded the *Croix de Guerre* by the French government with a bronze star for "distinguished service."[5] Upon recovering, he volunteered for another dangerous mission, but three weeks later the Germans surrendered. As a representative for the Algerian FLN in 1960, he suffered a near fatal car crash in Morocco, damaging several vertebrae. Recuperating in hospital in Rome, a gunman from a shadowy pro-colonial paramilitary group entered his room only to find that Fanon had transferred rooms as a precautionary measure.[6] Despite these lucky escapes, it was the slow violence of leukaemia that finally claimed his body at the tender age of 36 when, undergoing treatment in Maryland, United States, he succumbed to death in a hospital room.

In the psychiatric hospital in Algeria that he was in charge of in the 1950s, Fanon, the doctor from Martinique, treated the victims of colonial violence, both French oppressors and Algerian oppressed. At Blida-Joinville, he saw the debilitating effects of violence from all angles—traumatized victim, pathological and guilt-ridden perpetrator, and grieving relative. He dealt with a case in which a European police officer was increasingly prone to fits of violent rage against his wife and children caused in his own mind by his job as a torturer and elicitor of information in the colonial police force. On another occasion, he treated both a police torturer and one of his victims simultaneously in the hospital. The victim could not bear to see the face of the torturer and cowered in a room when he saw him while the torturer reported that his mind was plagued in recurring dreams by the sounds of screams growing ever louder and more desperate of men who were being tortured in front of his eyes.[7] Fanon's work as a practicing psychiatrist showed him how the confinement of the colonized in restricted zones stimulates "muscular dreams, dreams of action and of aggression." During colonization, "the native never stops achieving his freedom from nine in the evening until six in the morning" (WE 49). In waking hours, the aggressivity "deposited in the bones" as a form of possession is turned against his fellow colonized in displays of violence. This is why "[t]he native's muscles are always tensed" and he "is always on the alert" (WE 41), living as "a tonicity of muscles" that finds outlet regularly in "bloodthirsty explosions" (WE 42). Believing that violent resistance against the colonizing force is "a hopeless effort" and "suicidal" (WE 49), the native's relaxation "takes precisely the form of a muscular orgy in which the most acute aggressivity and the most impelling violence are canalized, transformed and conjured away" (WE 44). The muscular orgy of aggression Fanon describes and the everyday violence of colonial life is epitomized in an anecdote Beauvoir recounts in *Force of Circumstance*. Sitting reading on the corner of an avenue in Paris, she suddenly looked up to see two North African vendors start to fight—"How they fought . . . one of them had got his teeth firmly fixed in the other's shoulder . . . Then a cop strolled up, swinging his truncheon and smiling; but it was all over, he missed his chance of clouting anyone" (FC 421).

Arendt (1970: 65) labels Fanon as an "apostle of violence," one who glorifies "violence for its own sake." Sartre's polemical call for "the death of the colonizer" in the Preface is mirrored in Fanon's main text whose central thesis is "[t]he colonized man finds his freedom in and through violence" (WE 68). In Sartre's words, Fanon's *The Damned of the Earth* is a text through which "the Third World finds *itself* and speaks to *itself* through his voice" (WE 9). The "crime of colonialism" (WE 21) has produced a "primal situation" in which violence was produced and reproduced as the result of a set of violent practices, a form of "objective violence." In retaliation, the colonized practice counter-violence, "the moment of the boomerang" (WE 17) when the colonized "re-creates himself" (WE 18) and returns the violence he has suffered. This initial violence of the colonizer "has ruled over the ordering of the colonial world . . . [and] has ceaselessly drummed the rhythm for the destruction of native social forms," leading to the "petrification" of the colonized (WE 31). To escape the zone of non-being, counter-violence is the only means that negates and overturns the existing situation and opens out onto that which does not exist in the form of new possibilities. The project of the colonized responds to and negates the endemic and primal violence of colonization and allows a new situation to emerge. It is "absolute praxis" (WE 67tm) that negates the colonial situation in which the colonized is something "other than man" and allows his humanity to emerge. At the level of individuals, counter-violence is a cleansing force: "It frees the native from his inferiority complex and from his despair and inaction; it makes him fearless and restores his self-respect" (WE 74). It invests their characters with positive creative qualities and "binds them together as a whole" (WE 73). "*Revolution, at its core, is truth*," Fanon states, "*precisely because it changes man, renews and advances society. It is the oxygen that invents a new humanity*."[8]

As many scholars attest, the uncharitable readings of Fanon's life and thought as a valorization of violence are caricatures and ignore the "primal violence" and "embedded power" of the colonizer that sets the drama into motion. It is absurd to criticize Fanon for his advocacy of violence when, in Algeria in the 1950s, violence was everywhere and had seeped into the collective unconscious. Along with Sartre, the violence he evokes is *instrumental*, and he never dwells or gloats on its effects (unlike Nietzsche or Heidegger).[9] Although he argues the results of counter-violence "are not equivalent" to those of the colonizer since, the war machinery of the colonizer goes "far beyond in horror and magnitude any answer the natives can make" (WE 70), he recognizes violence and counter-violence is an infernal spiral and vicious circle: "The violence of the colonial regime and the counter-violence of the native balance each other and respond to each other in an extraordinary reciprocal homogeneity" (WE 69).

Violence, Fanon laments, is "a necessary evil" (WE 72) and "a disgraceful thing" (WE 73), but remains in a realist world the oppressed's only option other than petrification. At a conference in Accra in 1959, he spoke for the necessity of the value of insurrectionary violence and criticized "pacifist theses" but did so with some conflicted emotion, delivering a heartfelt and poignant speech spoken with accents that reduced him to tears.[10] All in all, the French existentialists were believers in *strategic violence* or *provisional counter-violence* as the only means, "like Achilles' lance" (WE 25), to cleanse humanity of violence's initial stain and heal the wounds it has inflicted. Violence is thus a kind of shock therapy in which the enlightened oppressed will resist pacification and the business of mystification. Although there are some contradictions in what they say, their overall tone is cautionary, but realist, bringing to light both the wretched and redemptive psycho-affective features of violence for victims, perpetrators, and humanity in general, but aiming, ultimately, toward violence's suspension. In this light, we can understand Aimé Césaire's powerful elegy for Fanon in *Jeune Afrique* as, paradoxically, a peaceful fighter for freedom:

> a theoretician of violence . . . his violence was non-violent, however odd this seems. I mean the violence of justice, of purity, of intransigence. It must be understood: his revolt was ethical, his approach one of generosity . . . Frantz Fanon was a paraclete. It's why his voice is not dead. Beyond the grave, it still calls people to freedom and man to dignity.[11]

## SLOW VIOLENCE

Existentialism sensitizes us to the many forms, overt or insidious, violence assumes. The French existentialists trace the contours of *structural violence*—the violence of the oppressor as entrenched in social inequalities, institutions, codes, and hierarchies. Oppression can include dyadic relations, but is usually a wider social situation practised against particular groups who, in Beauvoir's words, "are condemned to mark time hopelessly in order merely to support the collectivity . . . [as] the oppressor feeds himself on their transcendence" (EA 83). From the perpetrator to the victim and from the frightfully ugly to the therapeutically redemptive, violence refers us to our incarnation in the world. In this respect, existentialism's searching analysis of violence reveals the hidden capillaries of power in capitalist society and laid the groundwork for more detailed models of cultural and political appropriation, such as Michel Foucault's cratology and micropolitics of power.

Building on existentialist insights, Shela Sheikh (2021: 449) charts the phenomenon of "slow violence," a form of violence that is not time-bound or body-bound, but is attritional and of delayed effects. This is an insidious violence, mostly environmental, stemming from the "violent geographies of fast capitalism" that is "somatized in the cellular dramas" of the poor, remaining largely unobserved, undiagnosed and untreated. Beauvoir describes this vividly in her memoirs when she saw with her own eyes the injurious effects of poverty on those subjected to environmental toxicity: "but here I got a glimpse of a universe in which the air you breathed smelt of soot, in which no ray of light ever penetrated the filth and squalor: existence here was a slow death" (MDD 131). Such slow violence is a crime without a criminal or a witness, composed, in Sheikh's (2021: 450) words, of "force fields, causal ecologies that are nonlinear, diffused, simultaneous, and involve multiple agencies and feedback loops." What is required is a narrative of the "slow violences" of global capitalism that inflict material damage on the lifeworlds of indigenous, marginalized, and exposed peoples. Through his analysis of the practico-inert in the *Critique*, Sartre shows how material violences are inscribed in social structures (hierarchy, inequality, unemployment, exclusion, pollution), while in his biographies of Genet and Flaubert he demonstrates the slow violence of institutions with their symbolic and representational codes that permeate lives and condition choices. The State's restriction of violence to only the forms it recognizes and not to those it practices has curtailed a deeper understanding of the slow violence and its myriad forms.

All in all, surveying existentialism presents us with a double-capture of violence—the perspective of the perpetrator (Heidegger's "strife," Nietzsche's "dynamite") and that of its victims and redemptive recruits (Sartre, Beauvoir, Fanon). More than any other topic, we thus find a sizeable schism between its German and French proponents and it is with Sartre, Beauvoir, Fanon and Merleau-Ponty that we are able to decode those situations in which, as Merleau-Ponty says, "[violence] tends toward its own suspension or toward self-perpetuation" (HT 1). By widening the terms of the discourse, French existentialism gives us the tools to fully decipher the violences endemic to our times and therefore perhaps a means for their atrophy.

CHAPTER EIGHTEEN

# "Yes to Life. Yes to Love. Yes to Generosity"

## (Fanon, *Black Skin, White Masks*) LOVE

*Love* is the hidden soil of existentialist thinking, lying beneath the grasses of miserabilism that interpreters often sow on its surface. Violence and hatred are ever-present possibilities in human relations, but it is loving that existentialist philosophers value most of all. According to the Russian existentialist philosopher, Nikolai Berdyaev (1947: 121, 146–8), the central concern of existential philosophy is "personality," a process of creative change that is "best revealed in love" and "the relationship of one personality to another." For Marcel, love involves one's willing "subordination of the self to a superior reality" and embodies the authentic core of human relations that takes us beyond alienation: "love as the breaking of the tension between the self and the other, appears to me to be what we might call the essential ontological datum" (BH 167). As a transcendent relation beyond mere "desire," love is the most intense of I-Thou relations where hermetic boundaries are disrupted and there is "a sort of fertile indistinction where beings communicate, where they *are* in and through the very act of communication" (EPC 59). Furthermore, love acts as antidote against the larger dehumanizing structures of political society, helping the individual to maintain resolute spiritual purity (MAMS 244). This can extend to "community love" and foster togetherness but, according to Marcel, it is "only within groups that are fairly restricted in size and animated by a spirit of love that the universal can embody itself" (MAMS 267).

Even Kierkegaard, the individualist for whom "the sole ethical interest is in one's own reality" (CUP 288) is not immune to love's special powers in helping one "to become an entire man" (CUP 309). "A love affair" he affirms, "is always an instructive theme regarding what it means to exist" (CUP 222). His resolute individualism is mitigated to some extent by his text *Works of Love* where love of one's fellow human beings—"Those We See" (WL 153)—is said to be "the only blessed consolation" and something without which one "is not really living": "to love human beings is still the only thing worth living for; without this love you do not really live" (WL 344). In *Works of Love*, Kierkegaard shows a more positive orientation to other people, in which the singularity of each individual binds us together as fellow humans and faith allows us to recognize each individual in their "human similarity" before God.

To this end, he advocates loving one's neighbour in an abstract sense as a generalized other stripped of their individual characteristics (which might seem to contravene his arguments against Hegelian abstraction). Indeed, in his early journal he notices that "fear and trembling (c.f. Phil 2:12) is not the primus motor in the Christian, for that is love; but it is what the balance is in a clock—it keeps the Christian life ticking" (2008: 9). Although faith requires individuation, it is the love for one's neighbour that succours the Christian heart. On a similar note, *Either/Or* asks "[w]hat, after all, is a human being without love?" (EO 518), and a loveless life is compared to entering the labyrinth of the Minotaur without Ariadne's thread.

As Skye Cleary (2015: 2) argues, the existentialist perspective lends itself perfectly to the analysis of the complexities, knowledge, and expressions of our being-with-others in romantic loving because it deals with everyday interactions and relationships. Building on the insights of Nietzsche's observations into the social construction of gender roles, the French existentialists set out to adumbrate and practically live an authentic form of intersubjectivity by achieving equilibrium between devotion and egoism and, as Beauvoir (2006: 66) said, creating a reciprocity that can "found a true love." In this chapter, we begin with Nietzsche's ruminations on the complexities of amorous love before looking at the Beauvoir-Sartre love story and their "necessary," open relationship based on transparency, honesty, respect, and the reciprocal exchange of "erotic generosities" (SS 781). From here, we move on to wider manifestations of love with a more universal reach as we look at the importance existentialists give to the ideas of *the gift* and *friendship* in connecting us lovingly to others.

## EXISTENTIALISTS IN LOVE

When we look at the personal love lives of existentialist thinkers, we find great diversity. Kierkegaard broke off his engagement with his young fiancée Regine Olsen,[1] as he could not commit to a bourgeois life of marriage that would compromise his project of writing or temper his commitment to God, as did Kafka to Felice Bauer for similar reasons. Rilke abandoned his wife Clara and infant daughter for the sake of literary greatness while Camus was notoriously unfaithful to both of his wives, causing them considerable distress and unhappiness. Jaspers, by contrast, faithfully stood by his Jewish wife in Nazi Germany. Nietzsche generally lived the life of a solitary bachelor, with some suspicions of homosexual tendencies, although he did propose marriage to Mathilde Trampedach and Lou Salomé. Heidegger, Fanon, and Marcel lived within a family structure with children to care for, but, in the case of the former two, their marriages were "open" or adulterous and able, in Nietzsche's words, to "tolerate an 'exception" (HH 402).[2] Marcel was the only existentialist philosopher whose writings provide the perspective of a parent and its transformative effects in terms of love, selflessness, belonging, and becoming.[3]

In existentialist folklore, it is the enigmatic relationship between Simone de Beauvoir and Jean-Paul Sartre that is held up as the exemplar of authentic loving. Described by Carlo Levi as "the great love story of the [twentieth] century," their relationship was, in Annie Cohen-Solal's (1987: 86) words, "a model to emulate, a dream of lasting complicity, an extraordinary success since, apparently, it seemed to reconcile the irreconcilable: the two partners remained free, equal, and honest with each other." A legendary couple, like Abélard and Héloïse, they are buried in a joint grave, their names sempiternally linked.[4] Their dual allegiance "to life, to the here-and-now reality" (PL 145) meant that their relationship elicited "utter respect or radical rejection" (Cohen-Solal 1987: 518) according to whether one valued the active pursuit of freedom or the dictates of conventionality. As Beauvoir records in her memoirs/diaries: "Sartre corresponded exactly to the dream companion I had longed for since I was fifteen: he was the double in whom I found all my burning aspiration raised to the pitch of incandescence" (MDD 345). Her love for her "Leprechaun," "storytelling Playboy," "husband," and "little man" (2024: 191–221) flowed from the "perfect union of two human beings" finding a definite meaning in existence in the other's need, discovering the world together and making a gift of their discoveries to one another (MDD 143). Decades later, she reaffirms the thoughts of her younger self: "Sartre is for me the *incomparable*, the *unique* one" (2018: 349). Throughout, Sartre remained her "main source of encouragement"[5] and the "one undoubted success in my life" (FC 659). Sartre echoes Beauvoir in fulsome praise for their relationship, stating in a 1975 interview with Michel Contat for *Le Nouvel Observateur*, that although there were significant women in his life, Beauvoir was "in a sense" the only one "because she was the only one [with] knowledge of myself, of what I wanted to do. For this reason she was the perfect person to talk to, the kind one rarely has. It is my unique good fortune."[6] In a 1970 interview with John Gerassi, he conceives theirs as a profound kind of love: "we fell in love with each other's intuition, imagination, creativity, perceptions, and eventually for a while bodies as well . . . Do you know that I would never allow any writing of mine to be published, or even made public to anyone, until Castor approved?" (2009: 32).

In the place of a conventional bourgeois marriage, Beauvoir and Sartre embarked upon a "morganatic marriage" (PL 19) with a dual identity. They would role-play and pretend to be M. and Mme. Organitique, penurious civil servants, unambitious and easily satisfied or Mr and Mrs. Morgan Hattick, an American millionaire and his wife. We "wriggled into their skins," Beauvoir muses, "in order to emphasize our difference from them" (PL 20). Polyamorous, open and transparent, their love would be "an *essential* love" that was not possessive but allowed them "to experience *contingent* love affairs" and "the fleeting riches" (PL 22) to be gained from intimate and erotic experiences with others. According to the famous pact they created in the Luxembourg Gardens in the autumn of 1929, "we would never lie to one another, but neither of us would conceal anything from the other" (PL 23). They agreed that is no timeless formula that guarantees all couples achieving a perfect state of understanding since "it is up to the interested parties themselves to decide just what sort of agreement they want to reach" (PL 25). The comradeship that welded their lives together "made a superfluous mockery of any other bond we might have forged for ourselves" (PL 25). Marriage would only "double one's domestic responsibilities, and, indeed, all one's social chores" (PL 77), Beauvoir commented. The desire for children, "this we did not possess" and although she found "slightly older children slightly charming," small babies "had never interested me" (PL 77). Feeling such "absence of affinity" with her own parents, she fears she would have regarded them in advance as strangers and so "I never once dreamed of rediscovering myself in the child I might bear." So great had been her aversion to family life that childbearing seemed no more than a purposeless and unjustifiable increase of the world's population (PL 77-8). "[W]e had no children, no families, no responsibilities," she enthused, "we were like elves" (PL 362). Just two lovers, as T.S Eliot (1969) expresses, "whose bodies smell of each other/Who think the same thoughts without need of speech/And babble the same speech without need of meaning."

## NIETZSCHE, THE RELUCTANT CELIBATE

Nietzsche did not enjoy a happy life in affairs of the heart. He led, for the most part, a reluctant celibate's life. Indeed, it might be accurately said in his case: "What Love Life"?[7] The breakdown of his embryonic amorous relationship with Lou Salomé in 1882 dealt him a serious blow that left him reeling and feeling utterly alone. Beguiled by her intelligence, ebullience, and beauty, he thought of her as his "twin brain," and the days they spent together—like their "holy" walk up the path to Monte Sacro in Italy in 1882—as "the most enchanting dream of my life."[8] After this rupture (for which in large measure he blamed the interference of his sister and mother), his general attitude toward women and view of amorous love deteriorated to the extent that, in places, he appears as the misogynistic "enemy of women" (D 346) he warns against in less embittered times.

Generally, Nietzsche characterizes heterosexual love as adversarial, since men and women understand love differently. Love for men is a game of "*having* and *possessing*" (BGE 194), a site of appropriation where they quench "a desire to possess" (JS 363) women, ranging from "the simple disposal of her body and sexual gratification" (BGE 194) to "the unconditional and exclusive possession of the person he longs for" (JS 14). Asserting dominance, men treat women like exotic birds that need to be caged and so will not escape (BGE 237). By contrast, women view love as "a full *bestowal* of herself body and soul" (JS 363). Conscious of man's feelings toward her, a woman "assists his efforts at idealization by adorning herself, walking beautifully, dancing, expressing delicate thoughts" (WP 806). Her muscular strength increases as soon as a man comes into her vicinity (WP 807). "Inspired by her finery" (WP 807), a woman performs her role like an actor by "deliberately *closing one's eyes to oneself*" (WP 806) and uses her feminine charms for her gain. According to Nietzsche, women are corrupted by men but are complicit in the gender power dynamic in which they act as both slaves and tyrants. Their will to slavery is simultaneously an expression of their will to power.

Carol Diethe (2007: 112–3, 157) flags Nietzsche's split personality on the question of gendered love. On the one hand, he appears to be "less than dynamite," an "ultra-conservative" of the old guard who defends the status quo of patriarchal society. He acknowledges men both idealize and oppress women but argues that women should play the game and cultivate their feminine powers of mystery and seduction, which are their weapons in the powerplay. At the same time, he alludes to "The Problem of the Actor" (JS 361), praising women for their artistry but condemning them as "empty shells" for their lies and artifice. And yet, Nietzsche knew several emancipated women as friends and voted in favour of admitting female students to the University of Basel. He saw that women are "The Chain-Wearers" (D 227) whose intellects are restricted, bound, and channelled into "delicate thoughts" (WP 806). There are many clever women, he says, "who have been banished by fate to narrow and dull surroundings" (D 227). Although he recognizes the societal chains that bind women, he thinks it a mistake for women to imitate men by "compromising themselves through enlightenment" (BGE 232). The emancipation of woman is a movement of "*stupidity*," he reckons, for "this dangerous and beautiful cat" (BGE 239). Women have plenty of the "eternal boring" (BGE 232) and when they argue on principled matters, forget their "arts and best policy: those of charm, play, the banishing of care" (BGE 232). Emancipation diverts women from the more important task of raising strong, healthy children, and scholarly inclinations imply a problem in a woman's sexuality since it makes them "unfruitful" (BGE 144). He refuses women access to his "epicurean Garden" of free spirits and ennobling friendship because he thinks society has rendered them incapable of cultivating the requisite virtues.

On the topic of marriage, Nietzsche very much follows Kierkegaard who accords himself special status. Like Diana, the goddess of birth who did not give birth herself, Kierkegaard composes "one of the most gifted defences of marriage" (PJ 452) but felt it inappropriate for his own life, as it would compromise his commitment to God and to his writing. Judge William in *Either/Or* advises marriage as the perfect home for faithful love, an ethical commitment and resolution renewed through repetition. He compares marriage to a gentle stream flowing into a lake, constant yet full of life—"quiet, modest, humming," a smooth melody that is not "showy" (1988: 144). This is contrasted with the dissolute lothario Don Giovanni who leads a shallow aesthetic existence, the slave of his passions and biological urges; he is impulsive, whimsical, superficial, and lacking seriousness. In a letter penned in 1877, Nietzsche also states that marriage would not suit his independent life of free-spiritedness but nevertheless expresses the desire for a female companion to share intellectual and sensual pleasure with.[9] On the whole, Nietzsche is sceptical of marriage, as it generally involves mutual renunciation (JS 228).[10] He suggests marriage is a form of prostitution for women that "has even corrupted concubinage" (BGE 123), which is more honest. "The Hazard of Marriages" means that individuals are wasted: "the married man hangs his humanity on a peg where any female may pick it to pieces for him" (D 150). Hence, in marriage, "our trees do not grow so high now owing to the ivy and vines that cling around them" (D 503). Sexual attraction is a poor foundation for a marriage since passion is ephemeral. Sensuality grows too quickly and therefore is an easy root to pull out (BGE 120). Warning against the strong allure of desire when one is led astray by "blue eyes or heaving bosoms" (WP 981), Nietzsche declares marriage "is not a matter of love" (WP 732), but one that should keep the interests of society in view. It requires "patience, compatibility, care for one another" (WP 679) to produce a strong family in which children can thrive and benefit future generations. In *Of Marriage and Children*, Zarathustra advises, "You should propagate yourself not only forward, but upward!" (Z 1.20). The "garden of marriage" elevates love to greater nobility when you "build beyond yourself" (Z 1.20).[11]

Nietzsche's split thinking on love reveals an implicit tension between a masculine "economy of the proper" (denoting property, possession, mastery, self-aggrandizement) and a feminine "economy of the gift" (involving "squandering," generosity, "letting be") that reflects the ambiguity of will to power as mastery and domination versus a will to let be and let go.[12] When he castigates women for seeking emancipation and forsaking motherhood, one must remember that pregnancy and childbirth are things that he venerates as elements of women's creativity (JS 361) and "fruitfulness" (BGE 144). Academic work is boring and sterile by contrast in Nietzsche's view and so can only lead to her becoming "unfruitful." Nietzsche recognizes that although both sexes are complicit in the perpetuation of existing gender roles, it is men primarily who should feel the guilt and make amends. "Men need to be better educated," he argues, to atone for his corruption of woman who "moulds herself according to this image" (JS 68). He also scolds men for their cruelty and stupidity in promulgating female chastity and calls for the liberation of female sexuality through education which, up till now, has been to educate them "with as much ignorance as possible *in eroticis* and, and their souls filled with a deep sense of shame about such things" (JS 71). Although he warns against outright licentiousness and giving free rein to the "raging demon" (JS 14) of "unbridled urge" (WP 777),[13] he recognizes that "[t]he degree and kind of a man's sexuality reaches up into the topmost summit of his spirit" (BGE 75). The sexual act is a rare, privileged moment when "we meet with such a benevolent arrangement in nature . . . where one being gratifies another by the pleasure he enjoys" (D 76). He complains about "the diabolisation of Eros" (D 76) when "Christianity gave Eros poison to drink" (BGE 168) and speaks out "Against the Disparagers of Nature," in whom "every natural inclination immediately becomes a disease, something disfiguring, or even disgraceful" (JS 294). Chastity is vainglorious and sexuality irrepressible: "These people abstain, it is true: but the bitch Sensuality glares enviously out of all they do" (Z 1.13).

Nietzsche is sceptical of amorous harmony between the sexes, but like other existentialists, he views love as "the greatest stimulus of life" (WP 808). "The most angelic instinct," love is the most astonishing proof of "how far the transfiguring power of intoxication can go" (WP 808). It is a bestowal flowing from a superabundance of personality, since "[o]nly the most complete persons can love" (WP 296). Making the lovers "stronger, richer, more perfect" (WP 808), love creates a virtuous bond whereby, when we unlearn to love others, we end by finding nothing lovable in ourselves (D 401). In *Untimely Meditations*, Nietzsche compares love to a bridge that runs between "I's," enabling there to be moments and the bright sparks of love "in whose light we cease to understand the word 'I'," something "beyond our being which at these moments moves across into it" (UM 161).

Akin to Marcel's *creative fidelity*, Nietzschean love is an active undertaking and "must be learned" by "those who love themselves" (JS 334). Just as we learn to hear music by lending it our "hospitality" and becoming accustomed to it, we learn about love when we exercise "its irresistible magic" more and more (JS 334). For Nietzsche, there is a difference between "slavish love" that is decadent and weak and that "idealizes, and deceives itself" and a "divine love" that respects autonomy and "reshapes and elevates the beloved" (WP 964). In *The Joyous Science*, he argues that friends strive toward a higher ideal beyond the incorporating drives that make lovers want to possess or be possessed (JS 14). The greatest recognition that men and women can achieve is a kind of esteem experienced through the fulfillment of gender roles.

Thus, Nietzsche's view of love switches between two different economies that vie with one another through different texts. Teetering between androcentrism and gynophilia, ultimately Nietzsche shows how male and female gender roles dominate "slavish" love relationships and prevent them from becoming "divine" friendships. Power dynamics stifle female autonomy and accordingly, woman's love for her partner becomes a form of over-identification and faith in the unreal (JS 363). Stuck in "the most abysmal antagonism" (BGE 238), men and women "never cease to misunderstand each other" (BGE 85). But, Nietzsche's overall aim, as he states in *Ecce Homo*, is a therapeutic one: to take the path of the "noble individual" to lessen "the deadly hatred between the sexes" (EH 3.5) and find a way to love divinely.

## TO MERGE AND NOT TO MERGE

In ecstatic and idealistic moments, lovers feel *as if* they are merged, and yet come to realize this feeling is deceptive and ephemeral. Love's deception is recognized by Goetz in Sartre's play *Lucifer and the Lord* when he is perplexed by the impossibility of merging with his lover Hilda: "you *are not myself*. It's intolerable. I cannot understand why we are still two people. I should like to become you, and still remain myself" (1982: 142). In many of her writings, Beauvoir criticizes the idea of "merging" (where we obliterate the "I" to become a "we") as a common womanly delusion. *She Came to Stay* and *Les Belles Images* both revolve around the shattered delusions of unity felt by Françoise and Laurence. In *The Blood of Others*, Hélène replaces her previous religion and invests all her meaning in loving Blomart to make her feel that she "must exist." This theme of shattered unity is revisited in *All Men are Mortal* where the vain and anxious Regina believes she can achieve immortality by existing in a man's eyes (who has gained immortality). It steadily dawns upon her this is a foolish vanity as his immortality makes everything meaningless and insignificant for him. In Beauvoir's *philosophy of ambiguity*, consciousnesses are connected while remaining separate. It is bad faith to think of ourselves as entirely transcendent to the other just as it is to show complete devotion by assigning absolute value to them.

The recursive dialectic of singularity and interconnectedness was fully at play in the Beauvoir-Sartre relationship where each was deeply affected by the other, bringing about an "intraworldly haemorrhage" (BN 400) in each other's very being and thoughts. According to Lionel Roulet (Beauvoir's brother-in-law), "through their constant talking, the way they shared everything, they reflected each other so closely that one just could not separate them."[14] This "twinship transference"[15] between them grew as they fused together looking at the world in unison and sharing its enchantment. In his letters to "the beaver," Sartre describes her as "my dear little you who are me" (1983: 501), "my little self" (1983: 169), "my little moral consciousness" (1983: 180) and "little paragon" (1983: 95). He states that "[w]hatever I thought, it seemed as though I was saying it to you or rather that you were thinking it with me," that "[y]ou seem to have a surer sense of me than I do." Sensing an internal link between them, he had "the feeling of two consciousnesses melted into one" (1983: 417, 157). In her memoirs, Beauvoir reports how when with Sartre she would not distinguish between "I" and "we" (ASD 235). But the fusion they felt was emergent upon their interaction, "worked for continually" (PL 208) and always liable to splinter into singularity or lapse into bad faith. Indeed, total assimilation is impossible and would signify the loss of individuality.[16] As Beauvoir argues in *The Second Sex*, lovers find comfort in the illusion of harmony and the feeling of oneness but true love in an existential sense would need to be always open to the other's becoming, and involve recognition on the part of each individual of their responsibility to the love that is their common creation. Authentic love is founded on the mutual recognition of two liberties, where difference is maintained and supported.

In a quest to keep love authentic, Beauvoir supports "the abolition of the family" (FW 210) as it engenders relations of inequality and devalues the unpaid "invisible work" carried out by women in the home and in childrearing. Trapped in immanence and devalued in patriarchal society, some women attempt impossibly to live their immanence as a choice (through narcissism, all-consuming love, or mysticism), but "this ultimate effort—sometimes ridiculous, often pathetic—of imprisoned woman to transform her prison into a heaven of glory, her servitude into sovereign liberty" (SS 680) is futile since all-consuming love involves "an unreal relation with a real being" (SS 734). Like Nietzsche, Beauvoir saw a cognitive dissonance between the sexes: "The word 'love' has not at all the same meaning for both sexes and this is a source of the grave misunderstandings that separate them" (SS 699). A man wishes to "annex" his lover and "integrate her into their existence, not submerge their entire existence in her." By contrast, love for the woman is "a total abdication for the benefit of a master" (SS 699). Without a master, she is "a scattered bouquet . . . losing herself body and soul in the one designated." She exalts the one she loves as a supreme reality: "Love is a religion for her" (SS 700). The vicious adversarial circle is so difficult to break here because "each sex is victim both of the other and of itself" (SS 771). Ultimately, since all oppression creates a state of war, in a patriarchal society where marriage is an institution, "[t]wo transcendences confront each other; instead of mutually recognising each other, each freedom wants to dominate the other" (SS 770).

Some Beauvoir scholars[17] have questioned whether "the greatest love affair of the century" has been over-romanticized down the years both by Sartre and Beauvoir, and by others intent on bestowing it with legendary status. Toril Moi (1993: 17) wonders, for instance, why Beauvoir tended to present a rose-tinted view of her relationship with Sartre in public (particularly, in her published memoirs) while in private (in her diaries) she was much more critical of him as a lover. Moi comments "it is as if Beauvoir's relationship to Sartre remains the one sacrosanct area of her life, to be protected even against her own critical attention." In *Becoming Beauvoir* (2022), Kate Kirkpatrick questions whether the centrality of Sartre in Beauvoir's heart/mind (and of Beauvoir in Sartre's) was eclipsed at other times by the other lovers whose arms they fell into and who to some extent shaped their lives. Although she later repudiates aspects of her first novel, *She Came To Stay*, in which a sexual *ménage à trois* degenerates into murderous jealousy, the pact between Beauvoir and Sartre of "contingent and necessary love" came with some anxieties for both parties, who were not *always* totally transparent and honest as they lived their philosophy of free love. Reflecting on such anxieties that arise from polyamory, Beauvoir wonders: "Is there any possible reconciliation between fidelity and freedom? And if so, at what price?" (FC 133). Complete fidelity "[o]ften preached, rarely practiced," she says, "is usually experienced by those who impose it on themselves as a mutilation" (FC 134). However, when a third person enters the relationship and becomes more special to one of the others, asymmetry and jealousy set in. The main risk to polyamory is the feeling of betrayal. When "contingent" lovers become "necessary" partners, in the place of two free persons "a victim and a torturer confront each other" (FC 134).[18]

In *Being and Nothingness*, Sartre criticizes Heidegger's "existential analytic" for not concerning itself at all with sexuality, with the result that "his '*Dasein*' strikes us as sexless" (BN 506). Generally, Sartre painted a bleak picture of amorous relations in his writing of that period (*Being and Nothingness* and *No Exit*). Repeating Nietzsche's idea of sexual love as a battleground for appropriation (BGE 194), Sartre's amorous scenario is one locked in a circular struggle of the objectifying Look. In this struggle of consciousnesses that is "doomed to failure" (BN 523), I am sent back from "transfiguration into degradation, and from degradation to transfiguration" (BN 402). The lover wants a contradiction and so will never be satisfied, as each wants to wholly limit the freedom of the other and yet to be loved by someone who is free. Through an objectifying look, the other "models my body in its nudity, gives birth to it, sculpts it, produces it as it *is*, sees it as I will never see it" (BN 483). Sexual desire is the attempt "to take hold of the other's free subjectivity through her objectivity-for-me" (BN 505). This is "a specific mode of appropriation," Sartre argues, in which "it is the other's freedom as such that we want to seize" (BN 486). In a sexual union, each lover "wants to possess a freedom as freedom" (BN 486).

Sartre lists three responses to this circular situation—sadism, masochism and indifference—all of which he views as destined to fail as projects. A lover may become a sadist and seek complete control of the other by "forced incarnation" (BN 526) through physical coercion and violence. The object of sadism is "immediate appropriation" to "presentify flesh" of the other through pain (BN 527), treating the other's body "obscenely" (as a passive object) rather than "with grace" (as a "psyche in situation"). But the sadist cannot completely control the other as object, because the other is always a potential threat, an "explosive instrument" (BN 402). Sadism is a failure because the freedom of the other "remains necessarily out of reach"

(BN 534). When the victim "return[s] her gaze" (BN 502), the sadist "discovers his mistake" (BN 534). An alternative ploy is masochism through which one consents to control by the other and become a "me-object" (BN 500) or "thing." This is ultimately futile, as "the Other is only a qualified object for me to the extent that I can be that for him" (BN 400). One cannot completely be an object, as one is always a "transcended-transcendence" (BN 538), both objectivity and subjectivity: "the masochist's objectivity escapes him . . . in seeking to grasp his objectivity he finds the objectivity of the other, thereby liberating his subjectivity, in spite of himself" (BN 501). The third way—indifference—means evading the conflict completely, an attitude Sartre believes cannot last since I try to practise "a sort of *defacto* solipsism" (BN 503). Lost in a kind of "bewitchment" (BN 498), being indifferent involves "*blindness* in relation to the other" (BN 504) where, to relieve me from the danger of being possessed by the other's freedom, I falsely believe myself to be "an absolute and unique subjectivity" (BN 504).

According to Sartre, there is something special about sexuality: "a huge gulf separates sexual desire from our other appetites" (BN 512). More so than other bodily states, "desire *compromises* me" (BN 512). Made heavy by desire, "[o]ur weighed-down consciousness swoons, and slides into a state of languor comparable to sleep" (BN 512). The "terrifying effects" of desire induce torpor in one's consciousness and tranquillize resistance (BN 512). Sexual desire reveals the indissolubility of consciousness and body, wherein both are reciprocally transformed, revealing the incarnation of consciousness: "in desiring, consciousness chooses to exist its facticity at another level. It no longer flees its facticity, but it attempts to submit to its own contingency, in so far as it apprehends another body . . . as desirable" (BN 512–3). What many scholars miss in Sartre's account of love in *Being and Nothingness* when they depict it as hopelessly negative is his description of flesh in the sexual *caress* that overflows his other more negative descriptions of incarnation and promises an escape from the vicious circle of "degradation and transfiguration" (BN 402).[19] The truest caress, Sartre argues, "consists in the contact made by the most carnal parts of the two bodies" (BN 522). Through "the contact of two epidermises" (BN 514), a caress does not attempt "to *appropriate* someone else" but "is a set of rituals that *incarnates* the Other": "In caressing the other I give birth to her flesh, through my caress, beneath my fingers" (BN 514). The "tingle of pleasure" (BN 522) that runs through her in that moment elicits a "thickening" of consciousness' that actualizes the other's incarnation (BN 516). The caress has as its only aim "to impregnate the other's body with consciousness and freedom" (BN 525). Motivated by desire, the point of the caress is to give rise, through the pleasure it occasions, to the other's body: "she is born to herself and to me" (BN 515). In such relations, the body of the other becomes a "moving image of necessity and freedom" (BN 528) and is viewed, not obscenely, but with grace: "The most gracious body is the naked body, whose acts surround it with an invisible garment while robbing it of its flesh, even though its flesh is wholly present" (BN 528).[20]

Sartre's account of sexual relations in *Being and Nothingness* thus incorporates both negative and positive horizons. Ensnared in bad faith, where one attempts to be absolute subject (sadism) or absolute object (masochism), love is doomed to failure and the spiral of appropriation. Through the notion of "the caress" and "the graceful body," however, he begins to sketch the contours of an authentic love that explores love's ecstasy in forming a unity of being-with the other that encompasses "the basis of love's joy, when it exists: to feel ourselves justified in existing" (BN 491). *Notebooks for an Ethics* is an exploration of Sartre's promise in *Being and Nothingness* to "devote a future work" (BN 811) to elucidate an "ethics of reciprocity" that overcomes the appropriative model of bad faith that locks love into conflict. He points to the necessary role of (non-dominative) objectification in reflective self-knowledge as an affirmation and recognition of our singularized material embodiment and our individual consciousness, a form of mutually fulfilling recognition unfolding "in the dimension of otherness" (NE 280).

Around the same time, Beauvoir was mapping out her own version of authentic love that would likewise avoid "the traps of bad faith and the mystifications of seriousness" (SS 680) that lie in wait for all amorous partners. Her "ethics of generosity" requires us to respect the singularity of the Other and "to love him in his otherness and in that freedom by which he escapes" (EA 67). In *The Ethics of Ambiguity* and *The Second Sex*, she advances a concept of authentic love centered on a number of key elements and themes, such as *respecting each other's freedom*, *appreciating oneself as subject and other*, *transcending together*, and *mutually creating meaning*.[21] Based on the criteria of reciprocity, mutual need, legal, and economic equality, shared obligation, and subjects serving as both subject and object for each other, authentic love creates a generative tension (seen in both friend and enemy relations) but does not result in the subordination of one group or the other.[22] Through the mutuality of generosity and friendship that "must be worked for continually" (PL 208), a sense of harmony between partners can be realized existentially.

## THE GIFT

Although it is often associated with the poststructuralist philosophy of Derrida, the concept of the *gift* (as an ethical model) was birthed in existentialist thinking. Marcel was the first of the French existentialists to propose the model of the gift. Like many interpreters, he saw only the negative aspects of Sartre's account of interpersonal relations in *Being and Nothingness*, overlooking his move toward authenticity and promissory goal of dissolving bad faith. In two essays, "Existence and Human Freedom" and "Testimony and Existentialism" (1946), Marcel criticizes the narrowness of Sartre's phenomenological narrative of our relations with others for failing to capture the sacred nature of the gift. In "Testimony and Existentialism," Marcel introduces the idea of "creative receptivity" linked to the act of generosity and gift-giving that leads to "an accretion of being" for both giver and receiver where one finds enrichment and communion rather than domination. Marcel refers to this disposition as "creative fidelity" or "presence." To be present means to be available to the other in all their complexity, singularity, and mystery, an open attitude or affirmation of the other in a form of selfless generosity that avoids the reduction of the other to mere object or function.

In the late 1940s, Sartre made good on his promise and produced his own elaborations on the idea of the gift as a cornerstone for authentic morality. In *What is Literature?*, for instance, he argues that a work of art is both a gift and exigence. Literature involves a "dialectic of reciprocity" and collaborative effort between reader and author, in which the writer expresses "an act of confidence in the freedom of men" (WL 67). His "Essai sur le don" in *Notebooks for an Ethics* makes the distinction between authentic giving and the subjugating gift where the former "presupposes a reciprocity of recognition" (NE 369) in contrast to the latter, such as the Potlatch ceremony, which involves debt and the alienation of freedom bound up with proprietorship where "[t]he act of gift-giving installs my freedom in the other as a subjective limit to the other's freedom" (NE 376). Sartre extends his notion of deep recognition to love where "[t]he ego exists to lose itself. It is the gift" (NE 418). Love is not an appropriation but an unveiling or creating: "In pure generosity, I assume myself as losing myself, so that the fragility and finitude of the other exists absolutely as revealed within the world" (NE 507).

As Guillermine de Lacoste (1999: 285) observes, Sartre's "Zen and Derridean" tone when discussing the gift shows him deconstructing himself three decades before poststructuralists took up the cause of "deconstruction." He did not return to the themes of gifting and authentic love until the interviews of the 1970s, but in *Saint Genet* he gives a strong (Cixousian) conception of love that involves a total acceptance of the loved one, including the most contingent dimensions of the body.[23] Genet loves Decarnin unprovisionally, in even the body lice he receives from him. "[O]ne loves nothing, if one does not love everything" (SG 532) since love, Sartre stated in interview with Francis Jeanson in 1965, is "the acceptance of the total person, including his viscera."[24] As it matures, Sartre's thought pivots more and more toward a "feminine economy of reciprocal abandon" that reverses his earlier masculine economy and ontology of sadism and masochism in *Being and Nothingness*. He replaces the hostile look of independent consciousnesses with the *fraternity* of "people bound to each other in feeling and action" (HN 91). This involves a form of abandon as not a negative purely passive thing but as an activity of "de-selfing" or "de-egoisation" (NE 507).

In his later phase, Sartre revisits the theme of the gift and posits a new intersubjective ideal in which selfhood is "necessarily linked to and often is even engendered by the presence of another" (HN 71). A "feeling" for the gift, he argues, leads to the notion of "open" fraternity that extends beyond closed groups to include all of humanity. In *Hope Now*, he articulates (against Lévy's pressing) a new ideal of non-violence and fraternity based on the birth from a common Mother (HN 87). He tells Lévy that woman is a giver of gifts since she has "the womb that gives life, the breasts that nourish and the back that carries," establishing a relationship where "the motivations for an act come from the affective realm" (HN 89). In interviews, he articulates the project first voiced in *Notebooks for an Ethics* of "getting rid of one's ego," reaffirming and reinforcing the notion of reciprocal giving: "Tenderness one receives, tenderness one gives, the two are linked and there exists only a general tenderness, both given and received" (1977b: 81). Loving is a project to choose oneself as one who does loving acts and to allow "oneself to be overcome by one's love" (NE 477). In *The Family Idiot*, he refers back to his earlier consideration of "the true caress" describing the love of a mother as "woman making herself flesh in order to nourish, nurture, and caress the flesh of her flesh" (IF1 47). This echoes Beauvoir's call toward the end of *The Second Sex* for the emergence of a politics of reciprocity, where she looks to the erotic as an experiential ground and means of political transformation. Within a transformed culture of *erotic generosities*, "new carnal and affective relations of which we cannot conceive will be born between the sexes" (SS 781) and, in a relationship of equal to equal, "eroticism and love would be a free surpassing and not a resignation" (SS 778).

Of course, over fifty years earlier, before Marcel, Beauvoir and Sartre had spoken of their "ethics of the gift," Nietzsche had pronounced the ethical value of *gift-giving* as a framework for a new morality. The virtues of giving and bestowing are constant themes in his thinking and integral to his ideal of higher friendship. The abundance of the world, he writes in *The Birth of Tragedy*, is a feature of the Dionysian where "freely nature offers her gifts" (BT 1). Wagner's "true music," he states in his *Untimely Meditations*, is a gift to those who hear it (UM 4.6). In his later work, he speaks of finding "a sublime way of letting gifts befall" (BGE 265) and enacting a form of giving without gratitude or debt that does not shame either giver or receiver. His book of poetic philosophizing *Thus Spoke Zarathustra* is his "greatest gift" (EH P4) ever given to humankind, a complex and enigmatic gift, difficult to understand, "a sacred book," or a "fifth Gospel" intended to challenge all religions.[25] Through "Ideal Selfishness," in cultivating our skills to pass onto others, we bestow "the noblest gifts of our soul" (D 552).

Nietzsche conceives an authentic gift as a fully altruistic gift free from the dynamics of giving in order to take. Following Seneca's distinction, the truest gift is generous and gratuitous, a selfless gift (*beneficium*) rather than one that incurs obligation (*munus*). Without a guarantee of repayment, the selfless gift is one that is given in order to create or nourish the social bond between people and represents a new paradigm of the gift beyond utilitarianism.[26] After filling himself with wisdom in the mountains in solitude, Zarathustra needs to find people again to become a donor and empty himself of that overflowing wisdom (Z 1.1). The subject of the gift is the gift itself, since it bestows a wisdom that acts both on the donor and the recipient. The knowledge Zarathustra has modifies him and compels him to pass it on to others, forming a sort of universal bond that holds all together and expresses the dynamics and strength inherent in the gift. The gift is therefore not a simple transfer of energy but enables the recipient to rediscover the richness in herself that has been forgotten and lies dormant. It awakens the awakening of love, as illustrated in "The Night Song" where, Zarathustra says, "I drink back into myself the flames that break from me" (Z 2.9). As Emilio Corriero (2023: 46) remarks:

> Rather than the strengthening of the individual, the Overman foreshadows the abandonment of individuality; what is worthy of love in man is not his capacity to strengthen himself, but rather his capacity to give up that power, to renounce coming to an end in order to become a means of overcoming

"[T]o *give* is more blessed than *to have*" (Z 2.9), Zarathustra affirms, and it is within *friendship* that we can truly find a model of *bestowal* that captures the essence of the loving, joyful gift. Through "the joy of giving" (Z 2.9), we are able to create the great expenditure of energy that is required to cross over into the *Übermensch*.

## FRIENDSHIP: A SURROGATE LOVE

In a 1948 letter to Nelson Algren, Beauvoir tells him that her relationship with Sartre has become purely platonic: "[Sartre] does not care much for sexual life. He is a warm, lively man everywhere, but not in bed. I soon felt it, though I had no experience; and little by little, it seemed useless, and even indecent, to go on being lovers" (1998: 208). Was it the case, as Kate Kirkpatrick (2022: 13) asks, that "the great love story of the century" of Simone and Jean-Paul was ultimately "the story of a friendship"? Their shared narrative was, as they both acknowledged, and above all else, one of mutual bestowal. With this in mind, it is perhaps surprising that they did not address the topic of friendship more directly in their writing as part of their "ethics of recognition."[27]

Renouncing Christian love for the sake of Greek friendship, Nietzsche valued his friendships as a vital part of his self-growth,[28] a release valve from the suffocating solitudinous life he lived after his break with Lou Salomé. Bereft of a soulmate—the Russian kind of soul "I lust after"[29]—he found surrogate love in friendship and explored the philosophical dimensions of what friendship is in his work thereafter. *The Joyous Science* behoves free spirits who seek "one's own way" to separate themselves from society and to "live in seclusion" but also encourages them to have friends and help others (JS 338). Nietzsche argues that friends strive toward a higher ideal beyond the incorporating drives that make lovers want to possess or be possessed (JS 14). Within the three types of higher friendship, Nietzsche outlines (*joyful*, *agonistic*, and *bestowing*), he promotes the virtues of shared experiences and mutual becomings. Joyful friendship in which we "share not suffering but joy" (JS 338) is a healing agent against the "preachers of pity" and the anxiety of death. When friends experience a "*fellowship in joy*" (JS 338), they foment affirmative energy by expressing their drives within a shared creative movement. In agonistic friendship, friends can exchange a kind of meta-perspective on each other that challenges beliefs and ingrained habits (JS 355). They provide a "secret path" for self-overcoming by exposing parts of oneself of which one is unaware: "The actual stronghold is inaccessible to him, even invisible, unless friends and enemies turn traitor and lead him there by a secret path" (HH 491). As a mirror of recognition, friendship can provide a form of sobering external critique that helps us to renew ourselves (JS 307) and conduct a revitalizing daily battle against our own thoughts (D 370).

Revealing the compatibility of egoism and friendship (JS 14), agonistic friendship involves a form of "spiritualized *cruelty*" (BGE 229) that provides the opportunity for self-examination and growth through cooperative competition: "In one's friend one should have one's best enemy. You should be closest to him in your heart when you strive against him" (Z 1.14). Enmity is transformed into a tool for mutual growth and self-overcoming where friends engender qualities that we hope to accrue through shared endeavor and striving. Despite the importance of joyful sharing and agonism in friendship, Nietzsche places the highest worth of all on the bestowing friendship: "the highest virtue is a bestowing virtue" (Z 1.22.1). The bestowing friend offers potential and wisdom to others to use for their own growth, believing that "to *give* is more blessed than to *have*" (WS 320). His own attributes and wisdom are offered in the form of a gift to others who in turn reciprocate their own bestowing: "I teach you the friend and his overfull heart . . . in whom the world stands complete, a vessel of goodness—the creating friend, who always has a complete world to bestow" (Z 1.17).

Using the criterion of reciprocity/non-reciprocity, Nietzsche distinguishes between *higher* and *lower* forms of friendship. Lower ones inhibit the expression of free-spiritedness, such as honesty, knowledge-seeking and individualism, and invalidate one's "own source of experience" (HH 292). Zarathustra disparages those who have nothing to bestow or offer in a friendship, suffering from greed or weakness, acting like "secret thieves" who manipulate situations for their own ends: "With the eye of a thief it looks at everything that shines; with the greed of hunger it measures him who has plenty to eat; and it is always skulking around the table of those who bestow" (Z 1.22.1). Zarathustra's first friend is the corpse who weighs heavily on his shoulders and drags him down. His second is the jester, a companion who ridicules and pokes fun, ready to deceive at any moment.

For Nietzsche, love of oneself is essential for any flourishing friendship. His notion that selfishness is not inimical to friendship breaks with traditional conceptions—Kant, Aristotle, Montaigne—that associate it with noble sentiments. Good friendship involves respect for the other and self-love (AOM 241) that relations of non-reciprocity debar. As bestowing agents, "the greatest lovers are so from the strength of their ego" (WP 362). In the hands of the bestower, "ideal selfishness" becomes "a balm which spreads far around us and on restless souls too" (D 552). However, higher friendship flounders on "the stormiest waters and flood-tides" (BGE 212) of egoistic selfishness that is parasitic and calculating. Friendship is part of the process in which "one belongs to the whole, one *is* the whole" (TI 6.8). In the love I have for a friend I joyously affirm the existence of someone who is not me. This extends to a social program of justice, in which Nietzsche says, we "love with seeing eyes" (Z 1.19). By loving we participate in "an ecstatic affirmation of the total character of life" (WP 539). A healthy creature "being alive, loves life" (BGE 24) for the core of life is love, a creative force that keeps life alive: "We love life not because we are used to life but because we are used to loving" (Z 1.7). In *The Joyous Science*, he tells us to cultivate the disposition of "learning to love" (JS 334) before introducing his existential test of "eternal recurrence" (JS 341). Rüdiger Safranski (2003: 278) describes Nietzsche's existentialist position on love eloquently:

> Once we have familiarised ourselves with love, we take the rest of our life into our bargain. Only the will to love can enable man to discover the potentially lovable sides of life; otherwise man is likely to focus on its repulsive, ugly, and torturous aspects. We ought to use our will to love to enchant the world around us as well as ourselves. We need to fall in love with love

Although there are some problems with Nietzsche's theory of friendship,[30] through it he seeks a positive form of evolving *communitas*, a paradoxical community of solitary people geared toward the birth of the *Übermensch* who loves life.[31] His call for friendship, to "teach the friend" (Z 1.14), was subsequently adopted by Derrida (in *The Politics of Friendship*) who firmly linked friendship with a political destiny orientated toward a new form of democracy governed by equality and freedom. Guided by Nietzsche's idea of bestowing, French existentialism theorized an "ethics of reciporocity" based on availability, openness, and creative fidelity (Marcel), as well as recognition, solidarity and fraternal love (Beauvoir/Sartre/Fanon). Acknowledging both our interconnectedness and singularity as twin poles in constant dialectical tension, and echoing the existentialist economy of the gift, Fanon characterizes our human ethical dimension as essentially a *movement of love* and a *gift of the self to* the other:

> The person that I love will strengthen me by endorsing my assumption of my manhood, while the need to earn the admiration or the love of others will erect a value-making structure on my whole vision of the world (BSWM 41)

Construed authentically, in the existentialist way, love can be divine, rise above spirals of conflict and become no longer slavish where each makes a gift of their discoveries to the other. Moreover, love is extendable beyond amorous partnerships to friendship and existence itself. In his journals, even the solitary, saturnine Dane, Søren Kierkegaard, extends love universally, loving life and taking joy in the simple fact of a cosmic existence for which "the moon begins to shine and the stars are lit" (2016: 78–9).

CHAPTER NINETEEN

# "Ambiguity Is the Essence of Human Existence and Everything We Live or Think Has Always Several Meanings"

## (Merleau-Ponty, *Phenomenology of Perception*) PARADOX/AMBIGUITY

Existentialist literature is full of ambiguity, and Franz Kafka is likely its greatest illustrator. Kafka approaches ambiguity through a literature of magical realism in which ordinary life is reconfigured in absurd ways and casts doubt on our ability to exercise our freedom as exterior forces condemn the protagonists. In *The Transformation*, Gregor Samsa awakes one morning to find himself transformed into an insect. He is eventually killed by a wound from an apple thrown at him before being swept out with the rubbish by the maid. As an insect, he worries more about his ability to carry on working as a travelling salesman to support his family than his own mortality and grotesqueness. In *The Trial*, Josef K is arraigned for a crime he never learns the details of and is eventually "killed like a dog" by external authorities. In "A Country Doctor," one of Kafka's short stories, the protagonist attends a sick patient, is undressed by the villagers and placed in bed with the boy whose mysterious and noxious wound he cannot heal. He makes for home pulled by unearthly horses that move so slowly he might never make it back.

Absurdity and ambiguity are intrinsic to existentialist philosophy. Like Buddhist "koans" or word-paradoxes, they cast us deeper into thought attuning us to existence, presenting logical puzzles (such as a "one-hand clap") that problematize simple logic and highlight our radical groundlessness. Sartre, for instance, tells us in *Being and Nothingness* "I am what I am not and I am not what I am," while Nietzsche describes *Thus Spoke Zarathustra* as a book "for all and none." In his biographies of Jean Genet and Gustave Flaubert, Sartre examines how, paradoxically, "he who loses wins" (SG 430, FI3 369). Genet does not begin writing as a means to positive change but in order to infect his audience with the contempt they hold for him and take pride in their mockery. It is his failure in life that impels him to write and writing becomes his success. His transcendence is not a vertical movement or original arising but is diverted, warped, contaminated, or negated by the weight of situation. Similarly,

Sartre identifies "Loser Wins" as Flaubert's life philosophy that enables him to find "hope in the depths of [his] desperate soul" (FI5 7) and to continue to live. At the Pont-l'Evêque in 1844, in a Damoscene moment he makes himself "the loser who wins" by magically transforming "his being" (FI3 369), cultivating his madness to "cut himself off from his future being by a moment of irreversibility" (FI4 70). Becoming a "man-failure" and "losing" allows Flaubert to win by becoming an artist (FI5 3). His neurosis provoked by failure becomes a ploy, "an intentional adaptation of the whole person to his entire past, to his present, and to visible forms of his future" (FI 168).

Existentialists probe these paradoxes in the quest to unlock a greater wisdom, a kind of sapience that has filtered through to many channels of human life. Gurus of success preach that achievement requires failure since we learn and evolve through making mistakes. "Black Box Thinking" is vaunted as a justification for experimentalism showing the paradoxical manifestations, as Sartre demonstrated, of "Loser Wins" and "the failure of failure." This chapter delves to the bottom of existentialist paradox, examining the role of contradiction within the wider strategic thinking of deconstruction elaborated through Nietzsche's *historical philosophy*, Beauvoir's *tragic ambiguity* and Sartre's *ternary logic*.

## PERSISTENT PEDLARS OF PARADOX

According to Kierkegaard, *paradox* "is the intellectual life's authentic pathos" (PJ 115) that lies at the very heart of existence: "One should not think slightingly of the paradoxical; for the paradox is the source of the thinker's passion, and the thinker without the paradox is like a lover without a feeling" (PF 46). Paradox is the catalyst that makes possible "leaps to faith" between the three stages of the aesthetic, ethical and religious. Each stage is viewed as paradoxical from the viewpoint of the other. From the ethical point of view, the aesthetic phase bears no discrimination or commitment, all is possible and each event elicits only a fleeting feeling ensuing in indifference and boredom. The religious stage is that of contingency converted into and experienced as necessity, things lived as though they are necessary in a form of unconditional commitment even though there is no more justification in this other than faith.[1] Although he is staunchly anti-Hegelian, Kierkegaard is "by nature a dialectician" (PJ 552) and works within a Hegelian framework of thesis-antithesis-synthesis that the French existentialists also employ. In *Sickness unto Death*, he analyzes the dialectic in terms of the negative relation and positive relation (SD 43–4). In a negative unity one set of factors within a dualism—body/mind, immanence/transcendence—is denied and the other posited as if it were the essential one, such as in Plato's view of the body as the tomb of the soul. The positive relation, by contrast, is the attempt to express both sets of factors in thought and action but this is impossible and doomed to frustration. If one opens up to make possibility absolute, this forecloses what is stable and necessary, for the self is a hopeless tension unable to resolve its contradictions: "the self cannot by itself arrive at or remain in equilibrium and rest" (SD 44).

Presenting himself as "*Contradiction Incarnate and Animated*" (D 263), Nietzsche thrives openly on uncertainty and paradox. Not only does he regularly contradict himself, he takes delight in doing so: "Does the good historian not, at bottom, constantly *contradict*?" (D P2). By his own admission, he needs nobody to refute him since "for that he suffices himself" (WS 249). He casts doubt on whether he is playing games of dissimulation with his readers, preferring to keep his true thoughts disguised (BGE 290). Like Kierkegaard, who describes himself as "a Janus bifrons" (PJ 111) who laughs with one face and weeps with the other, Nietzsche has "a 'second' face in addition to the first" and access to separate worlds (EH 1.3). Moreover, he believes that one must make a virtue out of contradiction as it is essentially a sign of spiritual abundance. He views the inability to tolerate contradiction—to contain or negotiate opposites in the right way—as an aspect of cultural illness (JS 297). His dual optic of contradiction abounds at every corner of his work. In *Ecce Homo*, he declares, "I contradict as has never been contradicted before" (EH 4.1) and presents his earthly prophet Zarathustra as a paragon of contradiction:

> The ladder he climbs up and down is enormous; he has seen further, willed further, had further abilities than anyone else. This most affirmative of all spirits contradicts with every word he speaks; all oppositions are combined into a new unity in him. (EH 3Z6)

Negotiating contradiction, in Nietzsche's view, is a fundamental requirement for any form of anti-metaphysical thinking that seeks to overcome "*the faith in antithetical values*" (BGE 2). In this light, he contrasts his own "historical philosophy" with the dualist thinking of "metaphysical philosophy":

> how can something arise from its opposite—for example, reason from unreason, sensation from the lifeless, logic from the illogical, disinterested contemplation from covetous desire, altruism from egoism, truth from error? Until now, metaphysical philosophy has overcome this difficulty by denying the origin of the one from the other, and by assuming for the more highly valued things some miraculous origin, directly from out of the heart and essence of the 'thing in itself'. Historical philosophy, on the other hand . . . has discovered . . . that they are not opposites . . . and that this opposition is based on an error of reason. (HH 1)

In his more self-reflective moods, Nietzsche calls into question his own pretensions as a philosopher-legislator, disclosing his identity grandiosely as a historical "destiny" but reminding his readers that this "little piece of dynamite" may turn out to be a buffoon (EH 4.1). Nietzsche's avatar of discontinuity is the figure of Dionysus, who was the God of masks. Nietzsche presents himself as a philosopher of masks who, in line with his philosophy of becoming, did not particularly want to be fully understood, pinned down and thereby exhausted of future possibilities: "Every profound thinker is more afraid of being understood than of being misunderstood" (BGE 290). We should always wonder, Nietzsche warns, "whether, behind each cave, there is not another deeper cave . . . Each philosophy *conceals* another philosophy; each opinion is also a hiding-place, each word also a mask" (BGE 289). Contradiction and paradox are, in this sense, modalities of Nietzsche's perspectivism. Since "there are no eternal horizons or perspectives" (JS 143), ambiguity arises from the multiplicity of perspectives when each person sees only from their own corner or space. Nietzsche hopes to heighten our awareness and attention, guided by the insight, as Safranski (2003: 208) puts it, "that all of our so-called consciousness is a more or less fanciful commentary on an unknown, perhaps unknowable, but felt, text." Our intentions and drives are thus a form of directedness toward the world. An object is never registered in neutral terms but is grasped with an emotional valency in terms of our moods. Contemplation without interest, Nietzsche claims, is a "nonsensical absurdity" (GM 3.12).

Nietzsche defines his perspectivism as the ability to multiply our perspectival affects: "the more affects we allow to speak about one thing, the more eyes, different eyes, we can use to observe one thing, the more complete will our "concept" of this thing, our "objectivity," be (GM 3.12). The free spirit must "be able to gaze with many eyes and consciences from the heights into every distance, from the depths up to every height, from the corner onto every expanse" (BGE 211). This he contrasts with "Socrates' one great Cyclopian eye" that can only see the world through the optics of rationality and so is unable to appreciate "the lovely madness of artistic enthusiasm" (BT 14). Affirming the multiplicity of perspectives reformulates our notion of objectivity in opposition to the Kantian "disinterested spectator." Nietzsche posits Argos, the hundred-eyed monster, as a paradigm of perspectivism, a master of interpretation who "places each thing in the best light and walks all around it with an attentive eye" (HH 636). He presents the "new philosopher" as a "manifold plurality" who looks with many kinds of eyes and consciences from the corners into every wide expanse (BGE 211). In Nietzsche's perspectivism, one must know how to employ a variety of perspectives and affective interpretations in the service of knowledge (GM 3.12).

Traditional logic, Nietzsche argues, is a clumsy tool that can "handle only formulas for what remains the same" (WP 517), whereas the world of becoming is self-contradictory. The law of non-contradiction might have limited application in the field of logic but does not apply to value or to truth in general where opposites evolve out of prior evaluations, such as "evil" out of the noble concept of "good" and "truth" out of "error." Certain opposites play a strategic role in Nietzsche's analysis. Apollonian and Dionysian are described as opposites (BT 1–2) but he conceives their relationship as co-compositional since both of these artistic drives are required to unfold their energies in reciprocal proportion. They are necessarily interdependent and "Apollo could not live without Dionysus" (BT 4). He describes himself and Dionysus as opposite to Christ and Christianity (EH 4.9), and he praises new philosophers as the stimuli for "opposite values" (BGE 203). Denouncing the "hemiplegia" of the "good human" who separates off one side of a dualism and insists on it alone, teaching "that it is a higher thing to be efficient on only one side" (WP 351), Nietzsche proclaims that the greatest are those like Zarathustra who combine opposites (EH 3Z6).

## TRAGIC AMBIGUITY

From its very beginnings, Beauvoir proposes, "existentialism defined itself as a philosophy of ambiguity" (EA 9). "Contradiction," she states in her memoirs, "presented no terrors for us" (PL 361). The duality of self/Other and transcendence/immanence ultimately makes ethics possible since "a being who, from the very start, would be an exact coincidence with himself, in a perfect plenitude, the notion of having-to-be would have no meaning. One does not offer an ethics to a God" (EA 10). To be authentically free I need others to be genuinely free so they can open the future for me and make possible a morality of reciprocity. Unfolding in the space between unbounded individuality and ossifying sociality, an ethics of ambiguity "will be one which will refuse to deny a priori that separate existents can, at the same time, be bound to each other, that their individual freedoms can forge laws valid for all" (EA 21). In an essay for *Les Temps Modernes*, "An Eye for an Eye," Beauvoir argues that the execution of Nazi war criminals was morally justified owing to the *tragic ambiguity* of existence to exist as both consciousness and material thing. Through dehumanizing practices, victims became pure objects in the exercise of the Nazi's pure subjectivity. Violent reprisal reverses this situation—the victim reasserts their own freedom and subjectivity while the perpetrator viscerally experiences their own materiality. For Beauvoir, reciprocity demands we recognize that "an object for others, each man is a subject for himself" (PW 249). Such reciprocity forms "the metaphysical basis of the idea of justice" (PW 247). The tragic ambiguity of being human "is at the same time [to be] a freedom and a thing, both unified and scattered, isolated by his subjectivity and nevertheless coexisting at the heart of the world with other men" (PW 258).

Beauvoir develops this theme further in *The Ethics of Ambiguity* where she demonstrates the inextricable connection of consciousness and the world in which a human being "is still part of the world of which he is a consciousness" (EA 7). Humans are from the moment of conception dependent on others in a state of "original helplessness" (EA 12), and although we assert ourselves as "a pure internality against which no external power can take hold," the body can always be "crushed by the dark weight of other things" (EA 7). According to Beauvoir, past, present and future are all dimensions of a single experience. The present is always predicated on the possibility of the future: "Only the future can take the present for its own and keep it alive by surpassing it" (EA 116). Oppression effectively closes off the future and reduces its victims to a life of pure repetition. Ambiguity shows up in the impossibility of acting morally in an immoral world. As those in power will not give up their privileges and repressions voluntarily, violence is required to bring about a moral society, and dirty hands are always a reality: "others will here have to be treated like things, with violence . . . in order to win the freedom of all" (EA 97).

In *The Second Sex*, ambiguity appears in Beauvoir's thick descriptions of human experience in which the subject/object distinction is blurred. Her phenomenological descriptions of women's lived experience detail a movement across and through the states of transcendence and immanence in which transcendence is denied both by oneself (in the form of bad faith) and to others (through patriarchy). A significant proportion of *The Second Sex* consists in extended discussions of how, trapped in immanence and suffering and locked in "a degradation of existence," women are unfree in a world of constraints (SS 654). Where some see only contradiction and inconsistency in Beauvoirian ambiguity, others find value and insight. Women's subordination is not a contingent fact or a necessary structure but somewhere *in between*, showing how there is an intimate connection but at the same time an irreconcilable tension between our transcendence (freedom) and our facticity (embeddedness in the world).

Along with Beauvoir, Merleau-Ponty is characterized as a *philosopher of ambiguity*. For Merleau-Ponty, we are embodied beings of the world, but nonetheless not reducible to it, both constituted and constituting. Ambiguity is a condition of being a perspective on the world and yet being blind to that perspective as a kind of unconscious-conscious. He rejects epistemological transparency in favor of phenomenological richness and diversity and denies epistemological primacy to our first-person viewpoint. Ambiguity arises since we all inhere in the One where our experiences intersubjectively overlap to create an "interworld" (PP 357), but at the same time, we do not have identical perceptions as we are all uniquely situated: "Both universality and the world lie at the core of individuality and the subject" (PP 406). This is exemplified by language, which demonstrates how meaning is subjectively constituted and objectively interpreted:

> In the experience of dialogue, there is constituted between the other person and myself a common ground . . . [we] are inserted into a shared operation of which neither of us is the creator . . . We are collaborators for each other in perfect reciprocity . . . we coexist through a common world. (PP 354)

Although we have different perspectives from our situated viewpoint, in perception, we can still make distinctions of truth and falsity because of the common experience we share. Hallucinatory perception is "closed," solipsistic, totally subjective, and not confirmed by others or in action (PP 339). In the common world we create when we converse with another, there is a *third existent* that emerges—the dialogue—which escapes us both in its generality and which becomes the ground of ambiguity (as words and speech are open to different and discordant interpretations).

As "the moralist of paradox,"[2] Sartre is the third of the phenomenological trio to show the ambiguity inherent in human existence by collapsing the fixed polarities of dualisms—mind/matter, finitude/infinity, unconscious/conscious, immanence/transcendence. He follows Beauvoir's musings concerning the difficulty of acting morally in an immoral world. Although he agrees with the Kantian imperative never to treat people as means rather than ends (in *Existentialism is a Humanism*), in practice this is shown to be impossible in a congealed world, as shown by Goetz's compromised actions in *Lucifer and the Lord*. In a world of need, scarcity, and material inequality, the task of the artist is to demonstrate the paradox that "morals are *for us* both unavoidable and impossible" (SG 185). Paradox, tension, and dilemma are key elements, according to Istvan Mészáros (1979: 88), in understanding the work of "Sartre the adventurer":

> He is a man who perceives the contradictions of the world around him in the form of dilemmas, antinomies and paradoxes. His praise of the 'adventurer' is not a temporary lapse but an expression of his inner tensions which remain a permanent dimension of his lifework. He is the man who 'keeps together the unbearable tension' of the perceived contradictions as insuperable antinomies.

In his personal life, Sartre's tendency for discontinuity is manifest in the way he takes an almost religious pleasure in battling against himself. "Each moment of my life," he writes, "detaches itself from me like a dead leaf" (1995: 126). Throughout his life he never ceases calling himself into question, trying hard, as Beauvoir says, to "break bones inside his head" (FS 3–4). *Words* is littered with accounts of Sartre's self-transfigurations enacted through the regular shifting of perspective: "I never stopped creating myself; I was both giver and gift" (W 23); "Above all, I had to renounce myself" (W 102); "I have often written them against myself" (W 103); "I came to think systematically against myself to the point of weighing the evidence for an idea by how much I disliked it" (W 156). He was always reluctant to be cornered into sharp dichotomies when pressed by Raymond Aron's analytic approach into either/or choices: "As there was more imagination than logic in his mental processes, he had his work cut out" (PL 31). Like other existentialists, Sartre attacks the dichotomous logic of Western metaphysics and commits himself to logical contradiction. In the Introduction to *Being and Nothingness*, for instance, he asserts that the "principle of identity" has only "regional validity" for the *en-soi* but not the *pour-soi*

> This formulation appears to be strictly analytical . . . For a start, it refers to a particular region of being, that of *being-in-itself*. We shall see that the being of for-itself is defined, on the contrary, as being what it is not and not being what it is. (BN 27)

Paradox is for Sartre woven into the ambiguities of existence in which we encounter a kind of overflowing in the world of things: "There is, at every moment, always infinitely more than we can see; to exhaust the richness of my current perception would take an infinite time" (I 9). However, his thinking very much aims toward the sublimation of contradiction conceived non-metaphysically—the truth of an act as "a complex movement of contradictions which are posited and surpassed" (SM 98–9n4). He seeks dialectical intelligibility in the place of metaphysical closure by exploring the "paradox" of concrete singularity and concrete universality. The laws of dialectical intelligibility are "individualized universals" (CDR 49) where singularity and universality blend together and in which it is pointless to ask which is primary. Every singular act is thus part of a gestural whole. In Deleuzian (2004: 74) terms, we might say Sartre approaches paradox interrogatively through an *index of equivocity* where two contradictory elements generate a tension that allows us, in a movement of comprehension and sublimation, "to be present at the genesis of the contradiction."

## CONTRADICTION AND DECONSTRUCTION

There is a wider purpose to existentialist paradox—the promotion of active thinking—a form of deconstruction that unblocks sedimented patterns of thinking and discloses Being in the *closed-openness* that we are. Identity thinking locks us into fictions that calcify into metaphysical misapprehensions. Logic, in Heidegger's view, is flawed since it holds *assertion* as the locus of truth, where more primordially, unconcealment must occur prior to this: "Being as unconcealment . . . is precisely what was lost due to 'logic'" (GA40: 124). In a footnote in *What Is Literature?* Sartre signals his interest in the development of dialectical history, an area that his earlier phenomenology had left untouched: "Some day I am going to try to describe that strange reality History, which is neither objective, nor ever quite subjective, in which the dialectic is contested, penetrated, and corroded by a kind of antidialectic, but which is still a dialectic" (WL 333–4). He continues this dialectical search in *Notebooks for an Ethics*, where he proposes an "existential dialectic" or a "dialectic with holes in it" (NE 449), a historical process where individual agency and moral responsibility can produce "an irrational leap into another dimension of being, a new dialectic and a new leap" (NE 458).

Sartre's version of the dialectic in the *Critique*, as Alain Badiou (2009: 167–8) describes it, "is not the synthetic neutralization of two pre-existing but contradictory terms, but the discovery of the articulation that deploys the dimension along which they suddenly emerge as 'sides.'" It designates "the active unity of an operation as a preliminary to any determination of a duality." The dialectic is hence "never a dualized sequence of concepts . . . [but] is the polarization of a space that is articulated." The Sartrean dialectic establishes an "index of complementarity" between opposing pairs that requires a ternary logic of comprehension in which, in Ally's (2020: 373) words, "[c]ontradictions abound, and paradox lurks in the nearby ternary shadows." Following the threefold stages of "contradictions, surpassing, and totalization" (SM 34), Sartre's dialectical method offers a way out of metaphysical dualism and protection against analytical closure by transforming opposing pairs into a displaced or sublimated third. Within his surpassing of opposites, for example, *real-imaginary* becomes *possible*, *pour-soi/en-soi* becomes *for-others*, *praxis-practico inertia* becomes *praxis-process*, *totality-totalization* becomes *totalization of envelopment* and *need-scarcity* is sublimated into *abundance*. As Ally (2020: 365) explains, in Sartre's thought, ternary logic continually infuses and surpasses binary categories:

> We might call this the immanent imminence of the ternary, both immanent and imminent. The third is always coming and always nearby and always already there. When we think with Sartre, if we look for a Third, we will find one.

Rich in contradiction, existentialist paradox serves a strategic philosophical purpose to steer us away from dualist metaphysical thinking and direct us toward a sublimating *ternary* logic or Nietzschean "third face" (EH 1.3). In this respect, Sartre's working method of ternary logic—"Contradictions, surpassing, and totalization" (SM 34)—pre-empts Derrida's postmodern method of deconstruction as a tool for dismantling dualisms. By bending dualisms, the existentialist philosophers of tragic ambiguity have bequeathed a new kind of posthumanist dualistic thinking, "an explicit duality expressing an implicit unity" (Ferrando 2020: 22) that is shifting, intra-changing, and scalar. In this sense, we may contend, along with Nietzsche, that when investigated closely, "[t]he so-called paradoxes of an author, which a reader objects to, are often not at all in the author's book but rather in the reader's head" (HH 185). Hence, we should not think disparagingly about paradox, as Kierkegaard warns, for it remains the source of a greater totalizing wisdom, "the intellectual life's authentic pathos." Great thinkers are prone to paradoxes, which, after all, "are nothing but grand thoughts still wanting completion" (PJ 115).

CHAPTER TWENTY

# "There Must Be a Concept of Man, a Concept about the Future of Mankind"

## (Fanon, *The Damned of the Earth*) HUMANISM

*Humanism* is a great concern for existentialists, but do they embrace it or reject it? Not surprisingly, there is some ambivalence in their thinking on this matter despite the claims of some scholars, such as David Cooper (1990: 3), that existentialism is uncomplicatedly humanist. Cooper's assurances apart, however, we will see that existentialism is a curious and complex constellation of *humanist*, *antihumanist*, and *posthumanist* intensities that ebb and flow in the twists and turns of their thinking that make a simple humanist ascription misleading. The schizophrenic mood of existentialists in reality vacillates between lionizing and lambasting humanity, but all thinkers desire to transform it radically from what it has become under the iron cage of modernity. Although intensely critical of human foibles, they share St. Augustine's wonder at the inexhaustible mystery of the human being, a restless self of great depth that goes out from and beyond its self. From a Nietzschean "abortion" to a Heideggerian "messenger of Being," existentialism has given humanity a searching self-examination that contains a wide spectrum of pros and cons. This chapter looks in detail at our human, all too human condition as existentialism theorizes it, beginning with Nietzsche's *ambivalent humanism* before examining the *renewed humanism* of Beauvoir and Fanon and the *posthuman humanism* of Heidegger and Sartre.

## HUMAN, ALL TOO HUMAN

Nietzsche is in no doubt that "man is something that should be overcome" (Z P3). His view of humanism veers between Lutheran contempt and the Renaissance promissory faith in human perfectibility, of a Goethian god-in-the-making. Deflating human conceit and arrogance, he conceives humanity as both an unfortunate aberration of nature and as a creature of unparalleled possibilities. Nietzschean philosophy forges a qualified humanism that stresses our continuation with the rest of nature while both decrying and celebrating our distancing ourselves from it as an emergent evolutionary bundle of values, experiments and self-overcoming.

This conveys a certain love–hate relationship, a mixture of adulation and contempt (that mirrors his self-relationship as one of affirmation and denial).

Nietzsche is often scathing about our human, all-too human features and grants no quarter to his own species: "*Most ugly*. It is to be doubted whether a well-traveled man has found anywhere in the world regions more ugly than in the human face" (HH 320). The danger of metaphysical thinking as religion, the state, or science is always ready to deform humanity and turn its will to power into a reactive force against itself and others. Turned against its animal instincts and drives, "the human is *the* sick animal" (GM 3.13) tormented by its own self-consciousness. Even its finest notions, such as reason, are "a mere idiosyncrasy of a certain species of animal, and one among many" (WP 515). Religion has debased the concept "human" by placing all that is good in the realm of God (WP 136). This imperils the human condition for "[t]here is not enough love and goodness in the world for us to be permitted to give any of it away to imaginary things" (HH 129). Modern man "is *diminished*" (WP 866), and has become "a manifold, mendacious, artificial and untransparent animal" (BGE 291), the heir "of the conscience-vivisection and self-torture of millennia" (OGM 2: 24).

As a result, humanity, imprisoned in an iron cage of errors, became a caricature of itself, sick, wretched and ill-disposed, "a walking picture of misery: this artificial, arbitrary, *recent* abortion" (WP 397). A "little, eccentric species of animal" (WP 303), humanity has assumed the form of "something scarce half made up, weak and awkward" (JS 352). Nietzsche urges us not to be deceived about human progress (WP 90). Confounding anthropocentric arrogance, he adjudges: "man as a species does not represent any progress compared with any other animal" (WP 684).

And yet, despite this litany, Nietzsche shares Renaissance ideals of the "dignity of man" and the human adventure to fly to greater heights (D 573). He holds the comfort that "above the steam and filth of human lowlands there is a *higher, brighter humanity*" (WP 993). To replace the humanism of the "last man" he proposes a form of humanism in which the *Übermensch* radicalizes humanist principles and avoids nihilistic dead-ends. This is to think the human but also to think *beyond* the human—from the inside and the outside—within a theory of action and responsibility that crosses the human–non-human divide. Throughout his writings, Nietzsche offers several paragons to fit this radical humanism, including musical Socrates (a productive synthesis of Dionysian art and Apollonian science), the free spirit (wandering lonely beyond social conformity and boundaries), Zarathustra (connected and true to the Earth), Dionysus (the god of masks, intoxication, rapture, and wholeness), and the *Übermensch* (the re-evaluator of all values who drags humanity into a new dawn).

## IS EXISTENTIALISM REALLY A HUMANISM?

We should not be too easily misled by the unequivocal published title of Sartre's *Existentialism is a Humanism*, which was, as originally intended by Sartre, (the more skeptical) *Is Existentialism a Humanism?*.[1] Sartre's early work is also liberally peppered with anti-humanist sentiment. In *Nausea*, Roquentin dryly lists the many types of humanists he has known—the radical humanist, the Communist humanist, the Catholic humanist among them who all hate each other "as individuals, naturally, not as men" (N 117). Sartre voices his "theoretical opposition to humanism" (WD 87) and warns against the idea of a human nature or essence as a universalized "species" whose destiny is to conquer and order the world: "The religion of man conceived as a natural species: the error of 1848, the worst error, the humanitarian error ... The notion of human species has made incredible ravages" (WD 21–2). In *Mallarmé*, he describes humanity deflatingly as no more than "[a] volatile illusion flittering over matter in movement" (1988: 135).

After the war, Beauvoir and Sartre renounced their individualistic anti-humanism and "learned the value of solidarity" (PL 433). During this period, Sartre alludes to a number of possible radical humanisms that might replace the abstract humanism of Enlightenment thinking and give the term a "modern meaning" (WD 25), but nonetheless remains skeptical at heart. He refers variously to a "humanism of work," a "humanism of need" and, in his final years, to a "flourishing humanity" while simultaneously rejecting bourgeois humanism and insisting "[h]umanity *is not* and corresponds diachronically to no concept" (IF3 346) and, most brutally, "humanism is shit" (EM 32). In Merleau-Ponty's view, Sartre's thinking shifted from the anti-humanism on display in *Nausea* to a "difficult" humanism[2] in his subsequent writings and it is true that, like Nietzsche, he displays some ambivalence on the topic, regretting what humanity has made of itself but holding on to the promise of what it can become under a different system of values and collective orientation. As Beauvoir observes, "Sartre detested certain specific social groups, but never turned his back on the human race as a whole: his severity was directed solely at those who professed to fawn upon it" (PL 149). Torn between dismantling humanism and reconstructing it, "[h]e jeered at all human shibboleths" and thought it was impossible "to cherish an entity called 'Man', or indeed to hate it either" (PL 148). "Society as then constituted we opposed," she recalls, "[b]ut there was nothing sour about this enmity: it carried an implication of robust optimism. Man was to be remoulded, and the process would be partly our doing" (PL 15). In this process of resculpturing, Sartre warns, we must take utmost care not to use a logic of substitution in which the cult of Man supplants the cult of God as another form of value hypostatization, a "self-enclosed humanism" that ends in fascism by erecting humanity as an abstract timeless ideal and thus detracting from human freedom as a not-yet realized immanent historical value (EH 92).

## *LETTER ON HUMANISM*

Of all existentialists, Heidegger is probably the most inimical toward humanism. In *Letter on Humanism*, he traces humanism's origin and development: "The first humanism, Roman humanism, and every kind that has emerged from that time to the present, has presupposed the most universal "essence" of man to be obvious. Man is considered to be an *animal rationale*." This definition "is not simply the Latin translation of the Greek *zoon logon echon* but rather a metaphysical interpretation of it" (LH 243). Although this is considered as a "universal essence," it was not applied to all humans since only those who embodied Roman virtue and Greek *paideia* (education, culture) qualified as human, the rest were simply "barbarians" unworthy of moral consideration: "*Homo humanus* was opposed to *homo barbarus*" (LH 224).

Heidegger asks "whether the essence of man primordially and most decisively lies in the dimension of animalitas at all?" (LH 227). The thinking in *Being and Time* "is against humanism" but does not "deprecate the dignity of man" since humanism "does not set the *humanitas* of man high enough" (LH 233–4) by ascribing an essence to him. Heidegger fears that the word "humanism" has lost its meaning and become "a mere empty sound" (LH 247) and wonders "Can we restore meaning to [it]" (LH 216) or "is the damage caused by all such terms still not sufficiently obvious?" (LH 219). Insisting that he in no way advocates the inhuman, he asks whether we should show "open resistance" to humanism or should "we still keep the name "humanism" for a "humanism" that contradicts all previous humanism?" (LH 248). As Karsten Harries (2012: 197) comments, Heidegger's critique of humanism is not born out of distaste, but "of a care for our humanity." Heidegger ultimately falls short of abandoning humanism completely by holding on to the ontological uniqueness and exclusive status of the human. Throughout his writing, he reserves a special place for human existence (as uniquely reflexive):

> Man alone exists. A rock is, but it does not exist. A tree is, but it does not exist. A horse is, but it does not exist. An angel is, but he does not exist. God is, but he does not exist. (EB 15-16)

Because plants and animals "lack language," they are "lodged in their respective environments but are never placed freely in the clearing of Being which alone is 'world'" (LH 230). To understand Being "an analytic of Dasein must remain our first requirement in the question of Being" (BT 37). The inquirer must be "transparent in his own being" (BT 27), and it is Dasein that "has ontological priority over all other beings" (BT 34) due to its great disclosive power which burdens it with unparalleled responsibility to care for Being. By "letting beings be," this does not mean leaving them untouched and unknown, but enabling them be present as "endlessly engageable."[3] Hence, although Heidegger dismisses humanism as a dead duck (as it culminates in a destructive "will to will"), he nonetheless bestows upon humanity a godlike status as Being's interlocutor and steward with a care "*for the sake of beyng*—not the being of the human being but of the beyng of beings as a whole" (GA65: 16). Outlining his relation to Buddhist thinking, for instance, he states:

> In contrast, I believe, to Buddhist teachings, in Western thinking an essential distinction is made between human being and other living things, [namely] plants and animals. Human being is distinguished by having language, that is, by the fact that he stands in a relationship of knowing to being. (GA16: 590)

Where (some schools of) Buddhism and Eastern philosophy either endow all sentient beings with the possibility of reaching supreme enlightenment or do not require a guardian for the clearing,[4] Heidegger is resolute in his conception of "[t]he human being . . . [as] the placeholder of the nothing" (GA9: 118). With the disclosive power to gather and preserve things as they are manifest in their Being, he maintains the especial singularity of the human: "it is very important to me that the human being is a *human* being."[5]

## HOPE OR APOCALYPSE?

Existentialism is often charged with dwelling on the tragic sense of life, incubating a negativity bias like a depressive, pessimistic or melancholic type who, in Nietzsche's words, gives us "only the shadows, the grey and black images of what the day before had arisen in his soul" (JS 90). By telescoping the negative emotions—fear, anxiety, nausea, alienation, dread—as primary ontological feelings, do existentialists neglect the positive emotions—joy, hope, happiness—that harbour a sense of belonging? Three notorious protagonists in existentialist literature—Dostoevsky's Raskolnikov in *Crime and Punishment*, Camus' Meursault in *The Outsider* and Sartre's Roquentin in *Nausea*—all constitute "a veritable incarnation of absurdity,"[6] with the former two easily given to *actes gratuits* and murderous deeds. They exhibit what Heidegger called "uncanniness," a feature of ontological dislocation, of feeling not at home in the world prompted by the recognition that the world will carry on being when they exist no longer. Roquentin expresses this feeling of repulsion as a sense of distance where he finds himself at odds with a world of bare contingency, a form of "negative enlightenment" (Marcel) where we are deprived of illusions and feel a stranger in the "unreasonable silence" of the world.[7] The futility of life is captured in Camus' *The Myth of Sisyphus* where purpose seems meaningless and life a huge expenditure of effort and repetition that ends in catastrophe. For the existentialist, when illusions shatter, one must learn to look reality in the eye.

But the heavy, violent mood of existentialist literature doesn't always mirror the temper of existentialist philosophy and we should be careful about automatically drawing direct parallels between the two.[8] Alongside existentialism's bare realism we find exuberant affirmation as new unexplored possibilities are born when old ways of thinking are dismantled. Even anguish and the apprehension of death are propadeutics to freedom. To dispel the labels of pessimism and nihilism that were attached to existentialism by its critics, in 1945 both Beauvoir (in "Existentialism and Popular Wisdom") and Sartre (in *Existentialism is a Humanism*) define existentialism as a *positive philosophy* of action, hope, authenticity, intersubjectivity, commitment and freedom:

> Existentialists are so far from denying, friendship, and fraternity that in their eyes the only way for each individual to find the foundation and accomplishment of his being is in these human relationships. (Beauvoir, PW 213)

> [Existentialism] can not be taken for a philosophy of quietism, since it defines man in terms of action; nor for a pessimistic description of man—there is no doctrine more optimistic, since man's destiny is within himself. (Sartre, EH 35–6)

Beauvoir's memoirs traverse the range of human despair and joy. In *Force of Circumstance*, she often wallows critically in the negative. Following De Gaulle's return to power, for example, she is overwhelmed by pessimism: "The future has no face. We feel unemployed, useless, abashed" (FC 463). As she contemplates her existence and powerlessness, everything tears at her heart: "this poverty, this unhappiness, this city, the world and life, and death" (FC 497). Decrying the historical present, she judges the future to be slipping from our grasp (FC 636) as we sink in the nihilist malaise of Capitalist modernity:

> For now I know the truth of the human condition: two thirds of mankind are hungry. My species is two thirds composed of worms, too weak ever to rebel, who drag their way from birth to death through a perpetual dusk of despair. (FC 670)

Elsewhere in her writings, however, Beauvoir strikes a more optimistic note, though still despondent about the state of the world. "Against sluggish reason, and the void, and everything else," she says, "I set up the incontrovertible evidence of a living affirmative" (PL 550). With eyes cast to the dark blue sky of the Roman night, she lyricizes the joy of living, the "moment of perfection" when "once more, life sinks its teeth into my heart" (FC 440). Even politics offers some hope. Experiencing the honeymoon period of post-revolutionary Cuba "restored a pleasure in just being alive that I had thought I had lost forever" (FC 503). For Beauvoir, freedom carries the highest worth in life: "Liberty is the very modal essence of existence" (PL 549). From her earliest years, she felt a joyful bond of solidarity with the rest of humanity that compelled her to act: "I heard an imperious voice inside me saying: 'My life must be of service to humanity'" (MDD 181).

For existentialists, *affirmation*, *freedom* and *hope* are key themes in creating a meaning to live for in an objectively meaningless world. In Camus' (1975) famous phrase, "we must imagine Sisyphus happy." Hope is not a kind of "listless waiting," according to Marcel, "it underpins action or runs before it . . . that is to say, rooted in being."[9] Sartre voices this sense of a hopeful, committed, and positive existentialism in his final philosophical text *Hope Now*:

> I know I shall die in hope. But this hope must be grounded. We must try to explain why the world of today, which is horrible, is only one moment in a long historical development, that hope has always been one of the dominant forces of revolutions and insurrections, and how I still feel hope is my conception of the future. (HN 110)

*The Birth of Tragedy*, Nietzsche states in his notes, is an "anti-pessimistic" book in the sense that "it teaches something that is stronger than pessimism, 'more divine' than truth: *art*" (WP 853). In *Daybreak*, "pessimistic opinions" rank alongside the premature approach of old age and ugliness as an illness to avoid (D 409). *Thus Spoke Zarathustra* is perhaps the most consistently optimistic of all existentialist texts in which the joy of living is celebrated and rhapsodized, and the future is redeemed by the advent of the *Übermensch* and a radical shift in direction for humanity. Even catastrophic ecological damage is reversible. Beneath the scorched skin of the ravaged earth lies a vein of gold that can eventually replenish it once the "last man" has disappeared: "Truly, the earth shall yet become a house of healing!

And already a new odour floats about it, an odour that brings health—and a new hope!" (Z1.22).

Metabolizing its rage against the errors of humanity, existentialism strikes an even balance between critique and affirmation, striving for the creation of a critical spirit that can say No and act No without puncturing the delicate membrane of its joyous Yes.[10] "It is my good fortune that after whole millennia of error and confusion," Nietzsche writes, "I have rediscovered the way that leads to a Yes and a No" (WP 54). For Heidegger too, No and nothing are the mysteries of freedom and the prelude to a Yes: "Without the original revelation of the nothing, no selfhood and no freedom" (1949: 37). Although existentialists favor optimism, this is not blind optimism. Hope, Nietzsche remarks, can be the worst evil of all in Pandora's Jar "because it prolongs man's torment" (HH 71). The future, as Merleau-Ponty states, is "only probable" and never certain, but not wholly unshaped or random: "it is not any empty zone in which we can construct gratuitous projects: it is sketched before us like the beginning of the day's end, and its outline is ourselves" (HT 95). Sartre leaves the dialectic open and recognizes, along with Nietzsche, that "[i]f the world had a goal, it must have been reached" (WP 1062), but "there is no final state" (WP 1064). Ethics is always bound up with the possibility of failure, circumscribed by material limitations and the potential lapse into bad faith:

> Tomorrow, after my death, some may decide to set up Fascism, and the others may be cowardly and muddled enough to let them do it. Fascism will then be the human reality, so much the worse for us. (EH 31)

In the *Critique*, Sartre leaves history as a series of "broken sequences," each in relation dialectically to the prior ones, leaving open the possibility that history might end badly. In Nietzsche's view, cultures and societies evolve through a dialectic of regression/progression. The free spirit triggers change and helps the movement forward to occur, which is not straightforward but comprises many backward steps. However, progress, if it occurs at all, is not strictly circular but *helical*; it takes the form of a series of loops where the backward movement of the circle (when drawn from right to left) propels us forward to a point that is beyond the starting point.[11]

For existentialists, the past acts as a spur to the future if we view it critically. In Heidegger's *Being and Time*, the present gathers itself from the future and out of the past. He argues that "the call" is a moment of transformative self-reckoning that retrieves and repeats the past in an authentic mode. In *Repetition*, Kierkegaard calls for a repetition of the past in light of the present. But where inauthentic repetition merely repeats the past as a kind of effigy, authentic repetition reaffirms it over and over again as a form of praxis and renewal (as in marriage, friendship or faith). Similarly, Beauvoir argues that we must creatively engage the past in our choices and acts: "The creator leans upon anterior creations in order to create the possibility of new creations. His present project embraces the past and places confidence in the freedom to come."[12] The ambiguity of our existential situation, however, is revealed by the temporal complication of freedom in which our acts create new situations that contextualize and potentially limit our freedom. Nietzsche warns against revering the past (like Kierkegaard's inauthentic repetition) since an over-ripened sense of the past can kill the present and prevents creative possibilities and imaginings for the future. For Nietzsche, we should cultivate a healthy sense of forgetting in order to escape the customary weight of the past in order to seize and live in the moment (as expressed in the eternal return of the same). Real generosity toward the future consists in fully living the present.

In the hands of Nietzsche and Heidegger, existentialism assumes a prophetic tone and a higher eschatological task. In *Ecce Homo*, Nietzsche predicts cataclysms and upheavals as purging mechanisms that will create "wars the like of which have never yet been seen on earth" (EH 14.1). He conceives the *Übermensch* as a "reverse movement" against the "dwarfing and adaptation of people to an increasingly specialized utility as finely adapted cogs" to the tremendous clockwork of total administration (WP 463). Heidegger adopts Nietzsche's *accelerationist* view (in BGE 176) where embracing catastrophe is a precondition for "another beginning" of cultural and spiritual regeneration that makes way for the *Übermensch*. Heidegger's inverted Hegelianism views modernity as heightened catastrophe rather than progress in the consciousness of freedom. The history of the West is a destiny of decline, a fall from origins that can only be reversed by the redemptive powers of the German *Volk*. The *Black Notebooks* codes the theme of "downfall" not as something that should be feared, but welcomed as "the essential precondition for historical greatness" in "the transition to another Beginning" (GA94: 484, 502) away from an age of darkness: "a technological monstrosity in which . . . a sense of what is truly historical is lost and what is rootless takes on the most variegated and contradictory forms, unable to recognize itself as the monstrosity it is" (GA95: 96–7).

## POSTHUMANIST HUMANISTS

If we are to adequately describe existentialist philosophers, we should probably view them as "posthumanist humanists."[13] They strip bare and deconstruct the building of humanism while still keeping it standing. As Derrida said, humanism cannot simply be erased or avoided. A complete break is impossible since "the end of Man" is destined to be written in the language of Man. There is no pure outside to which we can leap for to oppose humanism by claiming to have left it behind is to overlook the very way that opposition is articulated. It does not follow, however, that this means confirming the status quo, for Derrida's work repeatedly shows how systems are always self-contradictory, forever deconstructing themselves *from within*.[14] Heidegger's *Contributions to Philosophy* is one such attempt at "overcoming metaphysics" and deconstructing from within as it sets out to bridge "ontological difference"—the "barrier that blocks a path" (GA73.2: 1330).

Existentialists do not erase human agency but deconstruct its epistemological primacy and present it in a relational form. Presaging posthumanism, they present the *human*, not as something to be taken for a static notion, but to "be accessed as a process and as a verb (humanizing), for its dynamic, and also reiterative and performative, modes of proceeding" (Ferrando 2020: 52). It therefore points toward what it will become as *praxis*. This gives us a conception of humanity, in Rosi Braidotti's (2013: 82) words, no longer as the rational species but as a "transversal entity encompassing the human, our genetic neighbors the animals and the earth as a whole." The existentialist idea of interconnectedness in which "[e]verything is always revealed as united to everything" (CDR 360) gives us the resource to transform humanism into an *anthropism*, "an immanent humanism" that demands the recognition of a shared humanity in the now, eschewing the exclusionary mechanisms of the past in a process of self-critique and articulation. Where previous humanisms define humanity by a set of properties essential to Man—rationality, autonomy, language, etc.—the agential character of posthumanist subjects "arises from their material affects (their ability to affect and be affected by others within the assemblages they co-inhabit)."[15] In Heideggerian terms, a new beginning will occur only when humanity ceases to regard itself as the master or ground of entities. A transformed humanity would acknowledge its radically receptive, dependent, mortal, and finite status, thereby allowing itself to be appropriated as the site required for the presencing or being of entities to occur.[16]

Like no other philosophy, existentialism vivisects the human psyche and its all-too-human foibles, providing a deep understanding of emotion, internalization, creativity, immorality, hubris, and the intentional drives of conscious/unconscious. Of this, Nietzsche above all, was the most brilliant detective—examining, probing and tracking human exploits, vanities, and achievements from the dawn of civilization into the mists of the future. Existentialism undertakes a post-mortem of humanity in both an analytic and protreptric sense, offering us a vital set of tools to reformulate our humanity through recognition of the deep and diverse forces that enter and shape it. This leads to a "new humanism" of intersubjective possibilities and an "open future" where, as Merleau-Ponty says, "one is not free alone" (SNS 142) and where, as Fanon argues, the human struggle against oppression "*is the oxygen that invents a new humanity*."[17] In a real sense, existentialism is *anthropometric* rather than anthropocentric. Human reality is the closest to us and, as Nietzsche acknowledges, "all the products of [one's] thinking are bound to reflect the condition he is in" (D 42). An *open humanism* represents a process of becoming within the twin poles of our singularity and our interconnectedness in ways that mutually enhance both. That is, to recognize our morganatic part in the affective and agential assemblages of the material world and to preserve the human in an increasingly de-humanized and inhuman technological world.

"Existentialism," as Sartre famously remarks, "never admits that the chips are ever down (1974: 163–4), that is, hopelessly condemned to repeat past mistakes. For Fanon, a new humanism of collective praxis undergirds the hope of a new society: "people must know where they are going and why" (WE 135). Hence, "there must be a concept of man, a concept about the future of mankind" (WE 143) in order to bring about progressive change. It is only when we turn over a new leaf and work out new concepts that we will be in a position to "set afoot a new man" (WE 255). Humanity simply is, in Sartre's view, as humanity *does*: "We experience humanism only as what is best in us, in other words, our striving to live beyond ourselves in a society of human beings. We can prefigure people in that way through our best acts" (HN 69). The essential question is, what sort of human shall we choose to project and invent in a world already historically constructed by humans? Each person is an individual adventure in the dimension of the universal shot through with possibilities: "[b]ut my destiny is me coming to myself as an image. What is more, humanity is an individual adventure that takes place in the dimension of the universal. The individual coming to himself in terms of the features of the universal, this is humanity's destiny" (NE 422). In his ethical vision of "a flourishing humanity," Sartre equates moral growth with intersubjectivity and reciprocity (NE 407). In *Hope Now*, he considers a *post-humanist* view of society that goes beyond previous humanisms but still preserves the human:

> We are struggling to establish human relations and arrive at a definition of what is human. At this moment we are in the thick of the battle, and no doubt it will go on for many years. But one must define the battle: we are seeking to live together like human beings, and to be human beings so it's by means of searching for this definition in this action of a truly humankind—beyond humanism, of course—that we will be able to consider our effort and our end. In other words, our goal is to arrive at a genuinely constituent body in which each person would be a human being and collectives would be equally human. (HN 67)

Influenced by Augustine's view of humanity as caught in a wretched, troubled state between the glory of creation and the final redemption of salvation,[18] as we have seen, it is too simplistic and even misleading to ascribe an unqualified humanism to existentialism. As Heidegger remarks, the word "humanism" has lost its meaning and become "a mere empty sound" (LH 247). Along with the other existentialists, he wonders "can we restore meaning to [it]?" (LH 216) and create a renewed humanism "that contradicts all previous humanism" (LH 248). This is always possible, existentialism insists, because humanity "is elastic" (Beauvoir, FC 599), nothing more than "a leak of gas slipping into the imaginary" (Sartre, 2008: 46), and so remains an open question to be answered through action alone.

CHAPTER TWENTY-ONE

# "Animals. As I See It They Are a Philosophical Problem"

## (Sartre, *Adieux: A Farewell to Sartre*, 316) ANIMALS

If existentialism is a humanism, how does it conceptualize other forms of life? Existentialists have long held a fascination with the human-animal divide, sometimes seeking to confirm it and on other occasions to dissolve it, though never simply assuming it without questioning.[1] In this final chapter, we take a close look at how existentialist philosophers view animals and other organisms—those who grant them a secondary or inferior status (Kierkegaard, Heidegger, Beauvoir) and those who ascribe to them what we imagine to be distinctively human qualities, such as morality, consciousness and reason (Nietzsche, Merleau-Ponty, Sartre). To breathe life back into animals as they were conceived dynamically in ancient times before the onslaught of anthropocentrism, and to re-animalize the human, was a task that Nietzsche first took squarely on his broad philosophical shoulders well before the findings of contemporary science that now detail the complex activities, intricate psychologies, and sophisticated, goal-oriented behaviors of organic life.

## THE SICK ANIMAL

Of all modern philosophers, Nietzsche mentions the largest number of animals in his writings, a diverse collection of no fewer than 120, some encountered on his walks in nature and others discovered in his reading. Animals are vital sources of nourishment for his philosophical thinking, and no more so than in *Thus Spoke Zarathustra*. When Zarathustra is despondent and lost in the human world, animals enable him to find the right track toward happiness. After leaving the ugliest human being, he is cold and lonely but feels "warm and lively" when he stumbles across a herd of cows huddled together on a knoll, finding a beggar in the midst of them who is there "to learn from these cows" (Z 4.8). The cows teach him to "chew the cud," to ingest food slowly and gather his thoughts gradually rather than be dazzled by a superabundance of impressions as in life in the city. During the course of conversation with his animals, Zarathustra learns much from them. Significantly, after conversing with the "higher men" in his cave, he chooses to slip outside to talk to his animals (Z 4.14.1). As the *Übermensch* appears only on the distant horizon, Zarathustra can only feel at home with his animals, which provide him with philosophical solace. The eagle and the snake accompany him at all times. The eagle represents a view from above, seeing what's ahead, "the tree called future" with its clear vision and sharp eyes, while the snake, "the wisest animal under the sun," symbolizes the eternal return and the circularity of time, keeping its body close to the earth.

Along with Charles Darwin and other naturalists, Nietzsche was a major voice of the nineteenth century in dissolving the firm Christian distinction between humans (as possessors of souls or rationality) and animals (as creatures of pre-programmed instinct and desire). His concept of *will to power* is conceived as a natural motivation or creative force that applies to *all* organisms: "every animal . . . instinctively strives for an optimum of favourable conditions under which it can expend all its strength and achieve its maximum feeling of power" (GM 3.7). "To understand what life is," Nietzsche argues, "the formula must apply to trees and plants as well as to animals" (WP 704) and "for each of these there is a small corner from which it measures, is aware, sees and doesn't see" (LN 129). Indeed, he emphasizes, "*[t]he organic process constantly presupposes interpretations*" (WP 643). All organisms have "a biological intentionality or perspectivity," a minimal consciousness that forms "the foundation of the affects" (BGE 258). He even extends this beyond animals and plants to include all organic and inorganic things: "the will to power . . . guides the inorganic world as well. Or rather, that there *is* no inorganic world" (LN 15).

In Nietzsche's view, it is an error to think we are different to other animals. What we think of as the protocols of "social morality" can be found everywhere in a simple form "even down to the deepest depths of the animal world" (D 26). This includes the drive to truth as well as other values that we think are uniquely human, such as morality: "The beginnings of justice, as well as of prudence, moderation, valour . . . are *animal* in nature . . . it is not improper to describe the entire phenomenon of morality as animal" (D 26). Like humans, animals have self-consciousness motivated by sociality. The animal observes the effects it produces upon the representing of other animals, from this it learns to look back upon itself, to take itself objectively, "it has its degree of self-knowledge" (D 26). Animals can show "sympathy" or "empathy" and are capable of representing what another is experiencing (e.g., in the predator's interpretation of the prey), making them capable of pity or cruelty. This also gives them a sense of cause and effect, the ability to see "intentions in *all* happening" (WP 550). Indeed, Nietzsche talks of "the sagacity of plants" (WP 660) and attributes memory to all organisms due to the intelligence and intentionality of their drives. He assigns the power of recognizing and concluding, and even finds the origin of logic in the protoplasm which "makes what it appropriates equal to itself and fits it into its own forms and files" (WP 510). Just like animals and other organisms, human conscious experience is shaped by bodily drives that carry their own intentionality and interpretations. It is nature, that is to say, the neediness of our bodies that constitutes our basic existential situation.

Adopting philosophical perspectivism in which "[t]here are many kinds of eyes" (WP 540), Nietzsche reverses the anthropometric gaze by viewing the human perspective from the outside and imagining what animals actually think about humans: "We do not regard the animals as moral beings. But do you suppose the animals regard us as moral beings?—An animal that could speak said: 'Humanity is a prejudice of which we animals at least are free'" (D 333). Humanity, he surmises, must appear very strange indeed to the rest of the animal kingdom:

> I fear that the animals regard man as a being not unlike themselves, but who has lost his sound animal understanding, in an extremely dangerous way—thinking him the silly animal, the laughing animal, the weeping animal, the unfortunate animal. (JS 224)

According to Nietzsche, it is through "esteeming" that humans have become the "undetermined animal" (BGE 62) since they are able to gain some latitude from the play of their biological drives in accordance with created and assumed values. He identifies humanity as the bearer of a multiplicity of drives that have been created through history: "The Human has, in contrast to the animal, bred large in himself an abundance of *opposite* drives and impulses; by this synthesis he is master of the earth" (WP 966). The human creation of "bad conscience" within Christianity is a dramatic turn in animal development, "an animal soul turning against itself," internalizing a morality based on guilt before God for one's biological drives, body and earthly existence: "Oh this insane, pathetic beast—man! What ideas he has, what unnaturalness, what paroxysms of nonsense, what *bestiality of thought* erupts as soon as he is prevented just a little from being a *beast in deed!*" (GM 2.23). This has made humanity sick, in painful denial of its animalistic and biological nature: "human is sicker, less certain, more changing, more unsettled than any other animal. Of this there is no doubt—he is *the* sick animal" (GM 3.13). Hence, there is an ambiguous sense in which Nietzsche makes a distinct place for humanity while simultaneously closing it. He tries to deflate our pride in these human values and suggests they are less reliable guides than our animal drives and affects but he also sees the possibility for change, conceiving the human as a bridge that threatens to disintegrate in modernity but which at the same time "*can transform itself* from a *moral* to a *wise* humanity" (HH 107tm). Whatever differences Nietzsche suggests in his writings, it is clear that the general thrust of his thinking is toward effacing or diminishing human/animal differences for which he always gives a *genealogical* rather than metaphysical explanation. Just like animals, our conscious experience is shaped by bodily drives that carry their own intentionality and interpretations and it is foolish conceit to think we are essentially different:

> For to translate man back into nature; to master the many vain and fanciful interpretations and secondary meanings which have been hitherto scribbled and daubed over that eternal basic text *homo natura*; to confront man henceforth with man in the way in which, hardened by the discipline of science, man today confronts the *rest* of nature, with dauntless Oedipus eyes and stopped-up Odysseus ears, deaf to the siren songs of old metaphysical bird-catchers who have all too long been piping to him 'you are more! you are higher! you are of a different origin!' (BGE 230)

Nietzsche uses dynamite to explode the hubris of anthropocentrism. He outlines one of humanity's four great errors as thinking itself in a false position to animals and nature (JS 86). "[M]an is absolutely not the crown of creation," he argues, for "every creature stands beside him at the same stage of perfection" (A 14). Indeed, it is within this skewed anthropocentric gaze that man cruelly condemns animals to both sentimentality and inferiority:

> Could there be anything more repugnant than the sentimentality which is shown to plants and animals—and this on the part of a creature who from the very beginning has made such ravages among them as their most ferocious enemy—and who ends by even claiming affectionate feelings from his weakened and mutilated victims! (D 286)

## ANIMALS AS "WORLD-POOR"

Existentialists provide a range of answers to the question of the human–animal divide. Kierkegaard is adamant there is a sizeable qualitative chasm between the two sides:

> Materialistic physiology is comical . . . spread[ing] out over the plant world and animal world, showing analogies, analogies which are nevertheless not meant to be analogies inasmuch as human life from the beginning, from the first germ, is qualitatively different from the plant kingdom and the animal kingdom (PJ 238)

It is such "dreadful sophistry," he bemoans, that collapses the distinction by ignoring the ethical dimension of humanity (PJ 238). Unlike humans, animals do not have a heightened temporal sense and therefore don't experience dread and anxiety:

> As far as I know, natural scientists agree that animals do not suffer anxiety, just because they are by nature not qualified as spirit. They fear the present, tremble, etc., but are not anxious. They no more have anxiety than they can be said to have presentiment (PJ 184)

Furthermore, because animals lack spirit or critical reflection, they are naïve and controlled by bodily appetites: "Naïvety. Only the animal can remain naïve in the sexual relationship; man is unable to because he is spirit, and sexuality, as the extreme point in the synthesis, promptly rebels against spirit" (PJ 185). This means animals are very simple creatures since they lack language. This gives them a certain advantage over humans (Kierkegaard comments with ironic jest) in that they therefore cannot become "a babbler or a hypocrite" (PJ 632). According to Kierkegaard, "[e]very person is a synthesis, animal-spirit" (PJ 605) and suffering is needed "to get the animal properly knocked out of the one who is to become spirit" (PJ 605). It is, above all, solitude and the ability to endure being alone that differentiates us from animals: "Sociality belongs to the animal side of being human" (PJ 612).

Alongside Kierkegaard, Beauvoir is also firmly anthropocentric and exclusivist. Overwhelmed by "the wonders of Nature" (MDD 55) and its "infinite variety" (MDD 23), she restricts this love to flora and does not extend it to the fauna of the earth. Organic phenomena very soon ceased to interest her: "I cared very little for the softness of fur or feather. I have never liked animals" (MDD 56). When asked "Do you like animals?" later in life at a social event, her response was still an unequivocal and brusque "No" (FC 247). In her memoirs, she fondly recollects a trip to Spain with Claude Lanzmann and writes about her fascination for bullfighting: "I can appreciate the value of these trials in which a man engages his body in this hand-to-hand grapple with death" (FC 341). Her view is unwaveringly anthropometric as she admits her *one* reservation with the event is that "the will of the exploited is never free under the defects of capitalism." Nonetheless, she protests against the protesters, arguing "moral attacks are without foundation" for "they pay no attention to the needs, defections, resources, limits, strength and fragility" of the human body. Oblivious to the mortality of the "dumb beast," she exclaims "as for death, it is less present in a bullring than on an airstrip" and describes the bullfight as a fair fight in which "an intelligent animal fights and overcomes an animal that is more powerful but less mentally skilled" (FC 341). She neglects to mention, of course, that (non-human) death is actually constantly present in the bullring, as well as the fact that the matador is armed with a razor-sharp weapon that proves even more decisive than his superior "mental skill" in turning the conquest in his favor.

Such insouciance toward the needs and consciousness of animals is also evident in *The Prime of Life* when, describing a trip to Greece in the late 1930s, Beauvoir remarks with some cold annoyance and heartlessness: "I had taken an active dislike to the sheep themselves after seeing them in the Athenian markets, with their idiotic profiles, and their penchant, as wretched as it was indecent, for displaying their sourly anaemic bodies" (PL 304). In *The Second Sex*, Beauvoir makes clear the human–animal divide. One cannot transfer data about female behavior between species "because animals constitute given species and it is possible to provide static descriptions of them . . . but humanity is constantly in the making" (SS 45). Humanity "cannot be deduced from biology" since "it transcends itself toward the world and the future" (SS 48). As a "historical reality," she contends, "[h]umanity is not an animal species . . . Human society is an anti-physis: it does not passively submit to the presence of nature, but rather appropriates it" (SS 63). With her eye fixed inflexibly on the human realm, Beauvoir rarely addresses or considers the issue of animal consciousness, desire, or emotion, and this can be viewed as a significant blind spot in her thinking.[2]

By a more circuitous route, Heidegger reaches the same end-point of human exclusivism as Beauvoir and Kierkegaard. In *Being and Time*, he cements the breach between Dasein and nonhuman nature to such an extent that, as one of his students, Karl Löwith remarked, human existence is lifted completely out of its corporeal and natural preconditions.[3] Dasein, Heidegger insists, "has ontological priority over all other beings" (BT 34). Always asking questions about itself, "Dasein is ontically distinctive in that it *is* ontological" (BT 68) and is an "exemplary being," different from all others, since it understands, discloses and questions Being (GA2: 9): "being human, as such, is distinguished by the fact that to be, in its own unique way, is to be this openedness" (GA2: 216). Care, absent in animals, is Dasein's distinctive "way of being" and points to the reflexive structure of the "self" (GA2: 162).

The essence of the human, Heidegger argues, lies in its *ek-sistence* (ec-static, always ahead of itself and futural). The human is outside of itself not in some void but within the truth of Being (GA9: 330). Exposed to and standing within Being, "he stands in the dispensation of being" (GA9: 336) as an "open expanse" or "clearing" (GA9: 332). Dasein is a way of being, not a what (thing) but a how (activity) that can modify itself into different modes of authentic and inauthentic temporality. Heidegger thus distinguishes between human praxis (*Arbeit*) and animal action. Humans project themselves toward the future in a way that transcends the purely instrumental whereas

> [s]tones, animals, and plants are themselves not temporal, as we are. They assume no mandate, they possess no mission, *they do not work*—not because they are carefree, but because *they are incapable of work*. The horse may be said to work only insofar as it is incorporated into a human work-event (GA38: 133)

Ontologically impoverished, a stone is "worldless" since it occurs in the world without being able to establish a relation on its own with that world. Animals are "world-poor" as their environment is a "surround-ring" in which their urges are "benumbed." Certain patterns and aspirations are triggered and "unlocked" from the stimuli it receives (GA29/30: 347). World is environment for the animal and one that it cannot separate from: "the way in which the animal is bound to its environment is almost as intimate as the unity of the body itself" (GA29/30: 375). Although animals possess reactivity they do not have reflexivity, perceiving the world around them but not aware of perceiving. This implies openness to the world, but the world does not manifest itself to the animal as the world since it lacks a second-order awareness. Heidegger calls this confinement to behavior "captivation." He also calls it "putting aside"—that is, the animal does not recognize those appearances as what and how they are but rather "leaves those meanings aside." The objects as such remain withdrawn from animal perception, unable to be apprehended as something intelligible. Thus, he concludes

> We can see more and more clearly in particular respects the essential contrast between the animal's being open and the world-openness of man. Man's being open is a being held toward . . . whereas the animal's being open is a matter of being-taken-by . . . and thereby a being absorbed in its encircling ring (GA29/30: 498)

To "have a world" is the hallmark of authentic selfhood that involves authentic temporality and projection toward the future. On the basis of this, Heidegger concludes, "(1) The stone (material object) is *worldless*; (2) The animal is *poor-in-the-world*; (3) Man is *world-forming*" (BT 91–147). Humans can differentiate themselves from the world and from other things. They have an "open dimension" that liberates a locked-up existence and it is through humans that nature erupts into self-visibility and notices that it exists:

> Man is that inability to remain and yet is unable to leave his place . . . And only when there is the perilousness of being seized by terror do we find the bliss of astonishment—being torn away in that wakeful manner that is the breath of all philosophizing (GA29/30: 531)

In *Letter on Humanism*, despite his professed anti-subjectivist and anti-humanist stance, Heidegger maintains his position on worldless stones, world-poor animals and world-forming humans and argues that there is an "abyss of essence" separating humanity from animality (LH 230). Dasein is unique and qualitatively different to all other animals since it forms a clearing in which Being becomes aware of itself: "The human body is something essentially other than an animal organism" (LH 228).

As Peter Trawny (2019: 36) comments, although Heidegger abandons Cartesian thinking, he does not entirely escape its clutches by dint of the human-animal divide he employs.[4] In fact, his persistence in holding on to his world-poor/world-rich distinction goes against the movement of his later deconstructive thinking in the "fourfold" where, in Andrew Mitchell's words (2016: 298), "[n]othing is inert . . . both plants and animals move past any presumed encapsulation in an environment or 'disinhibiting ring'." It was left to other existentialists—Sartre, Merleau-Ponty and one of Heidegger's students, Hans Jonas—to fully grasp Nietzsche's mantle and further scrutinize human exclusivity.

## ANIMAL PRAXIS

Although Sartre does not devote any lengthy treatment to animal consciousness in his philosophical writings, he does express an interest in the subject. "Basically," he states, "I see [animals] as a philosophical problem" (FS 316) and one he would have liked to give more attention to in his work. Although he never got over his fear of crabs and the view that insects and crustaceans seem like they "belong to another world" with "that same degree of life and doubtful consciousness that I find so irksome" (FS 332), he reveals that he likes animals, especially dogs and cats (FS 316). Like Nietzsche, he dabbled with vegetarianism because eating meat "made me too conscious of eating part of an animal" (FS 333). It is often repeated how Sartre configures praxis in exclusivist terms as a distinctly human activity. His lecture "morale et histoire," for instance, discusses the example of a monkey in terms of its being an actor and rearranging its environment in a purposeful way in order to satisfy a need, but doesn't call this praxis. He reiterates this viewpoint in the *Critique*:

> The whole complex of behavior patterns of certain insects and mammals may be called action or activity. It can even be noted that activity on earth begins with single-celled creatures themselves. At all events, the questions posed by such activity have nothing in common with those . . . posed by the existence of practical multiplicities . . . equal or superior to our own (CDR2: 384)

For Sartre, the distinguishing human feature of praxis is "constituent interiority," the "motive force of everything" (CDR 322). This, he states, is "phenomenologically temporalizing," "dialectically totalizing" and uniquely human:

> We affirm the specificity of the human act, which cuts across the social milieu while still holding on to its determinations, and which transforms the world on the basis of given conditions. For man is characterized above all by his going beyond a situation, and by what he succeeds in making of what he has been made (SM 91)

Sartre's transitional essay of the 1940s "Materialism and Revolution" explicitly rejects Engels' dialectic of nature and argues for the specificity of human acts: "it is obvious that the notion of *natural history* is absurd . . . only human history is possible" (1995: 192). Adopting an analytical viewpoint (that he later rejects in the *Critique*), he argues that biological change across time is "of a mechanical and not dialectical order" (1995: 192–3). In *Search for a Method*, this exclusivism is still, albeit more subtly, at play in his thinking: "What we call freedom is the irreducibility of the cultural order to the natural order" (SM 152). Considering only *Anthropos* as relevant for his social ontology, he poses the fundamental question, "[d]o we have today the means to constitute a structural and historical anthropology?" (SM xxxiv).

As Matthew Ally (2017: 153, 224) observes, despite Sartre's increasingly dialectical sensibilities, his propositions "carry the burden of a familiar supposition that humankind and nature are somehow radically distinct *from* each other—even if they are, and at the same time, fundamentally wrapped up *with* one another." Sartre's reflex position is to ascribe value singularly to human beings, and his "anthropogenesis of the ought" is evident throughout all of his scattered ethical writings. In other passages and parts of his writings, however, his view is more nuanced and parenthetical, suggesting more of a continuum with the rest of nature rather than a separation from it. In the *Critique*, for example, he defines his "monism of materiality" as

> the only monism which makes man neither a molecular dispersal nor a being apart, the only one which starts by defining him by his praxis in the general milieu of animal life, and which can transcend the following two true but contradictory propositions: all existence in the universe is material; everything in the world of man is human (CDR 180–1)

The *Rome Lectures* marks something new in Sartre's thinking where he takes up our animality not simply as an ontological structure but as a positive region of ethical investigation. The bond between our lived animality and our lived moral experience is, he argues, *felt need*, something common to all living organisms. When commenting directly on animals in 1943, he follows Merleau-Ponty's lead in *The Structure of Behaviour* and takes a resolutely anti-Cartesian view: "I do think that animals exist as consciousness, and as such, nihilate . . . I am not at all Cartesian on this point, I've always believed in the intelligence and passions of animals' (2014). He reiterates this view in interview in the 1970s—"I think animals have consciousness. In fact I have always thought so" (1981b: 28)—and extends this provisionally to plants—"A plant that is growing is no longer altogether in-itself. It is more complex. It is alive" (1981b: 40)—but considers gauging the extent and advent of consciousness to be "an extremely difficult problem":

> consciousness exists where we notice it; and there are animals that do not have it, protozoa, for example. Consciousness appears in the animal kingdom at a certain moment: in men; surely also in monkeys. But how does it appear and what is it?' (1981b: 28)

All in all, Sartre's exclusivism is one of *degree*, not one of kind, despite the fact that it returns as a "bad habit" or as "a cognitive spasm" in his thinking.[5] His ecosophical insights remain, as he himself contends, "absolutely open-ended" (1981b: 24) and it is incorrect, as Damon Boria (2022: 273) complains, to accuse him flatly of being "anthropocentric, instrumentalist, and ecologically tone-deaf." After speculating about the origins of Flaubert's persistent boredom in the *Critique*, for instance, he considers the question of animal boredom and the effects felt by domesticated animals: "It seems clear that household animals are bored: they are *homunculae*, the dismal reflection of their masters. Culture has penetrated them, destroying nature in them without replacing it" (CDR 137). Prefiguring the notion of *zoochosis* (a common psychological condition that affects encaptured animals), Sartre argues "[w]ithout culture the animal would not be bored—he would live, that is all":

> Boredom with life is a consequence of the oppression of animals by man; it is nature grasping itself as the absurd end of a limiting process instead of realizing itself as biological spontaneity (CDR 138–9)

Sartre's philosophical insights, as Boria (2022: 281) notes, signal "a path toward non-oppressive relations with animals such that they are able to live as the wild beings that they are." They are compatible with attributing facticity, including Nietzschean drives, to at least conscious nonhuman animals and, additionally, that such beings, just like us, "create meaningful *worlds*." Along the way, he shows the question of bio-consciousness to be a complex sliding scale that is ethically and philosophically problematic.

## THE PHENOMENOLOGY OF LIFE

Subsequent thinkers refined the insights of Heidegger, Sartre, Merleau-Ponty and Nietzsche. In his existentialist *phenomenology of life*, Heidegger's former student, Hans Jonas applies Heidegger's concepts within human experience to life itself. Taking "Heidegger beyond Heidegger," Jonas pursues Heidegger's (unfulfilled) logic to consider the organic and non-organic "in a deconstructing fashion" (GA29/30: 371). Breaking apart Heidegger's exclusivism, Jonas develops a scientifically informed existentialist perspective that explores the deep continuity between life and mind. He combines Darwinism and phenomenology to argue that all organisms are affected by interiority and caring: "*all forms of life, even the simplest, have interiority and they all have a world.*" It is our own living experience that grants us access to life in general as "only life can know life." Against the idea of substantial identity, Jonas develops the concept of *metabolism* in which the individual organism is established as "a self-affirming precarious process of constant regeneration of form within a flux of matter and energy." Each organism experiences "*a needful freedom*," in which choosing among possibilities is bound up with strict material needs. Jonas' "freedom of mediation" that extends existential categories to all life has been instrumental in shaping recent cognitive scientific approaches and is a forerunner to *enactive cognitive science* developed by Francisco Varela based on the notion of *life as poiesis*.[6]

Posthumanism leans heavily on existentialism's insights in erasing strict separations between humanity and the rest of nature. Developing Nietzsche's concept of affectivity, Brian Massumi (2015: 8–9) compares animal instinct to how a musician plays improvisational variations on a theme as "a spontaneous excess of creative self-consistency," a force not of impulsion or compulsion but of "*affective propulsion*." Deleuze and Guattari (1994: 185) draw on Nietzsche to propose "a melodic, polyphonic and contrapuntal conception of nature," emphasizing the musical character of complex evolution. This replaces a teleological conception of nature with a *melodic* one in which the boundary between art and natural technique is arbitrary. They point to relations of "counterpoint" in nature, such as that of the hermit crab and the shell of the dead mollusc, which join planes together as "a double articulation" and form blocs of sensation and longitudinal/latitudinal lines of becoming. To view the world in this way is to construct "[n]ature as music" and to recognize that artifice is fully a part of nature.[7] Such an *involutionary* perspective, according to Deleuze and Guattari (1987: 318), carries not "the slightest risk of anthropomorphism." This is fully in accord with Nietzsche's observations that also conceive nature as an *aesthetic* network of becoming and animals as artists:

> Art does more than merely imagine; it even transposes values. And it is not only that it transposes the *feeling of values* . . . In animals, this condition produces new weapons, pigments, colors, and forms; above all, new movements, new rhythms, new love-calls and seductions. It is no different with man (WP 808)

One can also see the imprint of existentialism in Derrida's *The Animal That Therefore I Am* which urges us to move beyond "the ends of man" to "the crossing of borders" between human and animal (2002: 372). In an extension of Sartre's account of the Look and Nietzsche's approach of reversing the perspective, Derrida ponders being seen naked by his cat: "it can look at me. It has its point of view regarding me" (2002: 380). It is "violence" and "stupidity," he concludes, to think of "depriving the animal of every power of manifestation" (2002: 387) and seal the borders between human life and animal life.[8] Utilizing existentialist insights, Derrida deconstructs the dichotomy of the human and animal so entrenched in Western thought and offers an alternative posthumanist perspective.

Existentialism's speculations on the human-animal divide, especially those of Nietzsche, contain a radical and far-reaching overturning of anthropocentric naïvety. They prefigure a posthuman subject that is, in Deleuze's (2004: 107) words, a "free, anonymous, and nomadic singularity which traverses men as well as plants and animals independently of the matter of their individuation and the forms of their personality." By "thinking the animal" and raising "the question of the plant," existentialism strongly prefigures a posthumanist perspective that allows for a more flexible understanding of our age, a greater generosity in our moral considerations toward non-human life based on the phenomenology of life we share, and a more "expansive imaginary" of the world's possibilities.[9] As Sartre reflects, animals remain for us "a 'philosophical problem' (FS 316), a conundrum we can no longer dismiss with Cartesian hubris and one we are better placed to properly comprehend as a 'biological spontaneity'" (CDR 139). By reversing the gaze, imagining life through the eyes of Derrida's cat, Nietzsche's butterfly or Sartre's domesticated pet, and exploring the undiscovered phenomenological depths of animal consciousness, existentialism broke virgin philosophical territory that modern science is only just beginning to catch up with many decades later in the twenty-first century.

# NOTES

## *Preface*

1. See Ferrando (2023).

## *Introduction*

1. See Kirkpatrick (2022: 211–16).
2. See Beauvoir (FC 242).
3. See Marcuse (1983: 174) where he accuses Sartre's philosophy in *Being and Nothingness* of sharing a deep affinity with the egoic individual of classical liberalism as they both appear "with all the attributes of absolute autonomy."
4. Reportedly, Sartre felt that the Anglo-American world was never existentialism's true home. When he learned the staging of *No Exit* in New York had been turned into a gross comical farce, he remarked "Americans will never understand anything about existentialism." See Bentley (1962: 73).
5. See Ryle (1978), Ayer (1945), Murdoch (1999), and Warnock (1989).
6. Quoted in Safranski (2002: 3).
7. See McBride (2012: 62–3) and Wicks (2020: 184–208) for a quick overview of some of these wider cultural manifestations of existentialist ideas. Although the influence of existentialism on the Arts and Literature has been seismic, there is a temptation to turn all literature into existentialism from Shakespeare to Herman Melville to T.S. Eliot. For this reason, it is useful to demarcate "existential" (dealing with existence) from "existentialist" (referring to a particular philosophical attitude or core set of beliefs) in order to avoid applying the term too profligately. See Malpas (2012: 293).
8. Kaufman (2016: 7).
9. See Kirkpatrick (2024: 196).
10. See Bianco (2024: 528n).
11. See, for instance, Ansell-Pearson (2024), Daigle (2021) and Bergoffen (2009). As Keith Ansell-Pearson (2024: 315) observes, in dissociative accounts of Nietzsche and French existentialism it is often a "straw man of existentialism that is being denounced."
12. See Joseph and Reynolds (2024: 14).
13. On the one occasion Sartre met Heidegger in person, he spent much of the time apologizing to him for Marcel's play *La Dimension Florestan* in which Marcel openly parodies the German philosopher. Interestingly, Marcel was better disposed towards Beauvoir's work than Sartre's. He actively encouraged her to write an existentialist ethics ("you must write it!" (FC 75)) at a lecture in 1945 when she

was defending the moral possibilities of Sartre's *Being and Nothingness*. Sartre, with good grace, did not return Marcel's attacks of "diabolical debasement," showing "deferent friendship" towards him in a 1943 letter where he also cites Marcel's theory of embodiment and situation as influences on his own philosophy.

14. In "Overcoming Metaphysics," cited in Wolin (1992: 250).
15. Heidegger's positive reference to Marxism here is read suspiciously by some scholars as a way of "playing it safe" with the impending advance of the Soviet army. See, for instance, Wolin (2022) and Safranski (2002).
16. See Safranski (2002: 347). Heidegger takes issue with Sartre's use of the terms "existence" and essence" in *Existentialism is a Humanism* charging Sartre with using "existence" in the traditional Cartesian sense relating to the empirical presence of something in contrast to his own definition in which he does not use it to mean pure "being-at-hand" or facticity but the transitive meaning of existence as a self-relationship.
17. Sartre initially agreed when Towarnicki assured him that Heidegger had protected Jewish university teachers against Nazi reprisals. They eventually met in 1952 after which Heidegger spoke more positively about their ninety-minute conversation than did Sartre.
18. See Towarnicki (1993: 83–5).
19. Heidegger (1990: 251). Cognizant of Hannah's Arendt's judgment that Heidegger was an inveterate liar, some accuse Heidegger of ingratiating himself with Sartre purely strategically in order to help his personal cause in his denazification tribunal. See Safranski (2002: 348) and Bernasconi (2016: 369).
20. See Richmond (2018) for a concise overview of Heidegger's influence on Sartre's early philosophy.
21. Wicks (2020), Raffoul (2024) and Gosetti-Ferencei (2021) are recent examples of this kind of Sartre bashing repeating the "pseudo-Sartrism" Beauvoir complains of in their narratives of existentialism where Sartre is cast as its individualist and Cartesian arch-villain. As early as 1962, Edith Kern warned about portraying "a stereotyped and obliquely lighted image of Sartre" (1962: 2), a warning which, it seems, has been left unheeded by many scholars.
22. In *Force of Circumstance*, she writes of her relationship with Merleau-Ponty—"though we both felt great friendship for each other, our differences of opinion were often violent" (FC 332).
23. Beauvoir (FC 341), (MP 2082).
24. See Caeymaex and Cormann (2020).
25. See Kirkpatrick (2024: 185) and Cormann (2023: 1).
26. See Webber (2018: 149).
27. See Neimanis and Hamilton (2023: 19–21) and Webber (2018: 189). In Webber's view, existentialism greatly informs developments in moral philosophy, empirical psychology, psychotherapy, and literary criticism that can in turn test and modify existentialist philosophy. Within an "integrative perspective," new findings can strengthen and refine existentialist insights further, evolving through critical engagement supported by experimental methodologies.

28. Matthew Ally (2020) speaks of the "Sartre of the footnotes" where, in both of his two major works of philosophy, he raises questions and suggests alternative approaches in footnotes that to some measure go against the grain of the main text, such as famously in *Being and Nothingness* where he places the possibility of "a morality of deliverance and salvation" and a "radical conversion" (BN 543) from bad faith in a footnote towards the end of the book having devoted much of the book to explaining the ubiquity of bad faith.
29. Ferrando (2023: 47). Francesca Ferrando and Christine Daigle are two scholars that link posthumanism closely to existentialist concerns. Unlike Daigle (2023), however, who cites Beauvoir as an influence on her theory of "transjectivity," Ferrando (2023) makes no explicit reference to French or German existentialism as influential in the formulation of her "Existential Posthumanist Manifesto" although it clearly resonates in tune with them and could easily read as a Beauvoir-Fanon-Sartre-Nietzsche Manifesto.
30. See Braidotti et al. (2023: 21–2).
31. This phrase is David Macey's (2012: xxii) who uses it in relation to Fanon.
32. See Wolin (1992: xvii–xviii).
33. See Safranski (2002: 264).
34. See Wicks (2020: 209–11).
35. Nietzsche to Joseph Paneth, May 1884 cited in Wolin (2022: 190).
36. The American philosopher William Barrett (1946: 239) described Sartre's *Being and Nothingness* in the 1940s as "the Bible of existentialism."
37. See Solomon (2003) for an analysis of Nietzsche's split personality torn between peaceful and warring instincts.
38. In his defense, Heidegger cites February 1934 when he resigned from his rectorship as a gesture of protest against the anti-intellectual foundations of the emerging National Socialist worldview, daring to do, as he said, what "no one in our universities . . . dared to do." See Ott (1994: 29).
39. See Wolin (1990: 129, 8, 21).

## *Chapter One*

1. See Macquarrie (1973: 6).
2. Cited in Solomon (1988: 89).
3. See Carlisle (2020: 13).
4. "I am a dialectician by origin, by nature a dialectician" (PJ 552). Unlike Hegel's dialectic where opposition gives rise to a renewed synthesis, however, Kierkegaard leaves the dialectic in a tension-ridden situation, a disjunctive either/or.
5. See Carlisle (2020: 14, 130).
6. His nephew Henrik Sigvard Lund protested at his uncle's funeral service at the Church of Our Lady, speaking without permission at the graveside and accusing the Church of ignoring his uncle's writings and failing to honor his reputation.
7. See WP, p. 53.
8. This is a theme already discussed and prepared by Nietzsche in *Daybreak* (D 93, D 95).

9. See, for example, Megill (1985: 347) and Corriero (2023: 70). According to Corriero, Nietzsche modifies Christianity rather than eliminates it. He argues Dionysus is "a god who somehow prepares and anticipates the coming of Christ" and points to the fact that Nietzsche offers his *Zarathustra* to humankind as a "sacred text" or "Fifth Gospel" (2023: 11, 27).
10. Howells (1981), Kirkpatrick (2017), Wicks (2020) and Richmond (2018) are four among several Sartre scholars who assign to him a "crypto-Christianity" highlighting his frequent use of theological vocabulary (incarnation, deliverance, salvation, emanation, grace and passion), the predominance of the theological idiom of sin in his phenomenology of interpersonal relations in *Being and Nothingness*, and the parallels between the mystical conception of God and the transcendent *néant* of Sartrean consciousness.
11. Essentially, the concept of freedom is the transcendental moral absolute for Sartre: "the Good is that which is useful to human freedom . . . Evil is that which is harmful to human freedom" (FS 439).
12. See Gillespie (2013: 82–5).
13. See Gillespie (2021: 134).
14. See Kirkpatrick (2022: 73–5).
15. Hamilton and Altizer (1966: ix).
16. See Woodward (2011: 174).
17. Karl Löwith describes Heidegger as "[a] Jesuit by education, he became a Protestant through indignation; a scholastic dogmatician by training, he became an existential pragmatist through experience; a theologian by tradition, he became an atheist in his research, a renegade to his tradition cloaked in the mantle of its historian." Cited in Ott (1994: 120).
18. See Corriero (2023: 70, 45–7, 59).
19. Sartre describes his *War Diaries* as a "proud, pagan journal" (WD 69).
20. See Safranski (2002).
21. Cited in Safranski (2002: 144).
22. Cited in Safranski (2002: 181, 433). His friend Max Müller reported that whenever they came to a church or chapel on their hikes, Heidegger always dipped his finger in the stoup and genuflected. When asked why, he answered: "One must think historically. And where there has been so much praying, there the divine is present in a very special way."
23. As Hugo Ott (1994: 18) comments: "Heidegger beat a path back to the door of his Catholic origins where he knocked but did not cross the threshold to return as a penitent."
24. Cited in Wolin (2022: 364).
25. See Burnham (2015: 34).

## *Chapter Two*

1. See Macquarrie (1973: 129).

2. "Dasein" is Heidegger's term for human consciousness or awareness which Heidegger framed in order to avoid a lapse into Cartesian subjectivity. It is often translated as "being-there," but Sheehan (2015) finds "openness-disclosedness" to be a more appropriate translation as Heidegger takes humanity to be a "clearing" in which Being can be grasped rather than a "subject–thing" as Descartes conceived it.
3. Cited in Wicks (2020: 175).
4. See Stolorow (2016: 451–3).
5. Cited in Safranski (2002: 405).
6. See Safranski (2002: 351–2).
7. See Zimmerman (2007: 310).
8. As Mary Edwards (2023: 34) notes, Sartre's concept of psychological well-being is different from standard conceptions that prioritize the self's adaptation to the social environment. Lucien Fleurier and Baudelaire are both highly adaptive and successful in society, but their "real Self" is eliminated by their bad faith.
9. See Welch (2021: 168).
10. See Detmer (2013: 122).
11. See Webber (2018: 201, 157).
12. See Cormann (2023). In 1926–27, Sartre was particularly concerned with the *Journal de psychologie normale et pathologique* (*Journal of Normal and Pathological Psychology*). The ENS borrowers list recorded him as having requested the 1924, 1925, and 1926 numbers on several occasions. In the following years, he became more focused on the *Revue française de psychanalyse* (*The French Review of Psychoanalysis*, founded in 1927) and *Recherches philosophiques* (*Philosophical Research*) published from 1931 to 1937.
13. Quoted in Cohen-Solal (1985: 200).
14. See Klaw (2019: 7). By practicing positive thinking in her memoirs and diaries—asking oneself what she wants and how she wants to feel—Beauvoir, Klaw argues, attracts what she had wished for.
15. See Safranski (2002: 152).
16. Cited in Wicks (2020: 183).
17. "Neither Freud, nor Adler nor even the cosmic Jung took the black man into consideration in the course of his research" (BSWM 130).
18. See Gordon (2015: 8).
19. See Macey (2012: 148).
20. See Gordon (2015: 79).
21. In conversation in 1953, Métraux disapproved of Fanon's practice of administering ECT (shock therapy) to his patients. Fanon also regularly used narcotherapy in which patients were kept for sustained periods in darkened rooms. In Fanon's defense, as Macey points out, these practices were standard procedure in many psychiatric hospitals at the time, but nonetheless they do seem to conflict with Fanon's wider humanistic and revolutionary approach. See Macey (2012: 208, 318).
22. See Macey (2012: 322) and Gordon (2015: 82).
23. Cited in Shatz (2025: 130–4).

24. Cited in Shatz (2025: 203–4).
25. Cited in Carlisle (2020: 101, 125).
26. Cited in Carlisle (2020: 110).
27. See Carlisle (2020: 53, 244).
28. See Hayman (1982: 341).
29. See Safranski (2003: 371).
30. See Macey (2012: 231, 41).
31. Cited in Shatz (2025: 135).
32. Cited in Gordon (2015: 84).

## *Chapter Three*

1. See Gosetti-Ferencei (2021: 173, 165, 143).
2. Cited in Gosetti-Ferencei (2021: 173).
3. Cited in Ott (1994: 125).
4. See Farrell Fox (2023: chapter 2) for criticisms (especially Derrida's) of Heidegger's appropriative reading of Nietzsche.
5. Cited in Glazebrook (2016: 437).
6. Matthew Ally's *Ecology and Existence* (2017) is by far the most systematic investigation in both a deconstructive sense (of interpreting his range of writings) and a reconstructive manner (of seeing through some of his blind spots and developing his fledgling ecology to the full). Ally shows how Sartre's philosophy is rife with ambiguity where nature is concerned but far from the purely negative view many scholars all too readily ascribe to him through a superficial reading. See also Boria (2022) and Farrell Fox (2023).
7. See Ally (2017: 364, 392).
8. In her early diaries, Beauvoir aligns Sartre with the God Pan, who is "not only Sartre" but "all of earth" (2024: 168).
9. In her diaries, Beauvoir scarcely develops any sort of Green consciousness aside from the odd lyrical reference to nature's abundant and diverse beauty. In *All Said and Done*, she welcomes the pedestrianization of squares in Moscow and Rome, for instance, but also the construction of the motorway leading down to the South of France—"One of my greatest pleasures was to go out in a car" (PL 55). Displaying some ambivalence, she takes an admiring view of the aesthetic splendor of the world from the window of the airplane but does not at any point consider the footprint of her extensive travels by plane and car on that world (ASD 328).
10. See Mirvish (1996: 65, 69).
11. See Mussett (2020: 518).
12. Sartre first penned the idea of the tree experience (that appears in *Nausea*) in a letter to Beauvoir from an experience he had on the Avenue Foch in Paris which he describes glowingly, and not with the slightest distaste: "And I sat there staring at the tree. It was extremely beautiful" (PL 106).
13. See Böhme (1995: 119).

14. Elaborating her theory of *Philosophical Posthumanism*, Ferrando (2020: 140–1) elects the term "sympoiesis" as it better conveys the fundamental exchanges between organism and environment since no system is self-producing or organizing.
15. See Baudrillard (2003: 3).
16. See Abram (1997: 54).
17. See Asberg (2023: 145–7).

## *Chapter Four*

1. As Shatz (2025: 214) comments: "Let's be clear: Fanon was in no way a feminist." He once told a colleague that he could not bear not being a God to his wife Josie. He was unfaithful to her many times when he was away from home, and let her take the lion's share of parenting and homemaking duties. In his defense, he has been praised for his celebration of Algeria's female freedom fighters and was deeply shocked by the level of domestic violence in Martinique when he set up a practice at Le Vauclin in 1952 helping in the arrest of some men for murdering their wives. He has also been criticized for viewing homosexuality as an aberration to be cured in *Black Skin, White Masks* but in his clinical practice, he would always listen to his homosexual patients and displayed a compassionate bearing toward them. See Shatz (2025: 104, 7).
2. See Bair (1990: 355).
3. See Kirkpatrick (2022: 16, 401, 2).
4. Cited in Belle (2024: 97, 109).
5. See Rowbotham (2011: x).
6. See Kirkpatrick (2022: 228).
7. Altman (2007: 212) describes Beauvoir's claims about gender as "a sandwich with an essentialist or essentializing filling in the middle between outer layers of social constructionist bread."
8. See Belle (2024: 26, 286).
9. See Jones (2024: 338).
10. See Hengehold (2024: 334).
11. In *Beauvoir and Belle* (2024), Kathryn Belle takes issue with Beauvoir for not implanting her insights of the *Social Other* fully enough and forsaking proper intersectionality for a flattening and sometimes misleading analogical method. Her recognition that not only one group has been made Other but multiple is, in Belle's view, "the place of both interesting insight and oblivious oversight for Beauvoir" (2024: 10). Unfortunately, Beauvoir puts white woman in the epistemic default position and marginalizes the "othered Other," consistently missing the chance to engage with Black women and other ethnicities in *The Second Sex* (2024: 25, 290). Beauvoir's comparative and analogical approach to competing frameworks of oppression means not only she collapses diverse systems of oppression as the same, but also privileges gender oppression as a more significant and constitutive form of subordination above other forms of identity. As Patricia Hill Collins (2017: 329) comments, "Beauvoir herself recognizes the limits of analogies, but cannot seem to extract herself from them," thus undermining herself and sabotaging her own insights by rendering invisible the interlocking effect of multiple oppressions.

12. See Kirkpatrick (2022: 357).
13. Schwarzer (1984: 62).
14. Cited in Schwarzer (1984: 16).
15. See Rowbotham (2011: xvii) and Schwarzer (1984: 113).
16. Cited in Kirkpatrick (2022: 364).
17. See Gerassi (1976: 82).
18. See Simons & Benjamin (1979: 342–3).
19. Cited in Kirkpatrick (2022: 400).
20. Cited in Kirkpatrick (2022: 386).
21. This is not to say however that *The Second Sex* lacks an economic dimension for it represents a main source of women's oppression in her explanatory framework. Beauvoir maintains that in eliminating prostitution, for example, women "must be granted a decent job" along with customs that "must not place any obstacles to free love" (SS 624).
22. Cited in Kirkpatrick (2022: 222, 76).
23. Cited in Thomas (1983: 88–91).
24. As Burnham (2015: 34) notes, it is likely Nietzsche was influenced by the work of Swiss anthropologist Johann Bachofen, a source of the Apollo/Dionysus account who argued that the Dionysian was a transitional phase between matriarchal societies (Gaia and Demeter) and the patriarchal stage of the Apollonian which included the formation of states and the "male lust for struggle" (BT 21).
25. See Derrida (1979) and Richardson (2020).
26. Sartre fully endorsed Beauvoir's idea of gender equality in *The Second Sex* and apparently made suggestions to Beauvoir on reading the unpublished manuscript. See McBride (2009: 195).
27. Cited in Lacoste (1999: 293–4).
28. Cited in Boulé (2005: 5).
29. Cited in Hayman (1986: 23).
30. See Gerassi (1976: 84).
31. See Belle (2024: 323).
32. See Braidotti et al. (2023: 460).
33. See Simons (1999: 19).
34. Cited in Belle (2024: 34).

## *Chapter Five*

1. See *Daybreak*, p. 74n.
2. See Wolin (1990: 4–5, 85, 102).
3. See Wolin (2022: 149).
4. Wolin (1990: 109) describes this as the passage from his previous transcendental solipsism in *Being and Time* to one of a national solipsism after it.
5. Cited in Wolin (1990: 129–30).
6. Cited in Wolin (1990: 110).
7. Cited in Wolin (2022: 227).
8. Cited in Wolin (2022: 59).

9. See Wolin (2022: 78).
10. In Wolin's (2022: 85) view, Heidegger exaggerated the differences between his own "spiritual National Socialism" and the "vulgar National Socialism" of the Nazi Party. First, in Nazi race-thinking there was a broad trend to avoid crude biologism and the narrow limitations of bourgeois materialism and scientism. Heidegger's differences with other Nazi ideologues were largely the result of internal petty squabbles and powermongering rather than over issues of substantive theory. Second, although he criticized the cultural vulgarity of National Socialism through its endorsement of technology and its propaganda machinery, this didn't disincline him from praising the military might of Germany or from zealously instituting the *Führerprinzip* at Freiburg University as Rector.
11. See Wolin (2022: 81).
12. See Macey (2012: 462) and Shatz (2025: 361).
13. As Jonathan Webber (2018: 123) notes, in Sartre's analysis there is "unexplainable coincidence" as to why bad faith is so endemic among Jewish people as he has not yet developed the concept of *cultural sedimentation* (that he later theorizes as "practico-inertia" in the *Critique*).
14. See *Le Nouvel Observateur* (10.3.80).
15. Cited in Gosetti-Ferencei (2021: 128).
16. Beauvoir (1998: 113).
17. See Macey (2012: 155–7).
18. See Macey (2012: 159–60).
19. See Romdenh-Romluc (2024: 55).
20. According to Komarine Romdenh-Romluc (2024: 58), Fanon was very sympathetic to Césaire's view of negritude, in particular his therapeutic method of *nekyia*. Adopted from Jung, a nekyia is a kind of inner journey into the depths of the Unconscious and its horrors in order to release oneself from them. This must be undertaken by black people to liberate themselves from harmful cultural impositions but is a perilous journey that can also lead to mental fracture and madness.
21. The term *lived experience* denoting an experience that is deeply lived through derives from the term *Erlebnis* used by Husserl and Heidegger and developed by Merleau-Ponty before being adapted by Fanon in *Black Skin, White Masks* and Beauvoir in *The Second Sex* to describe racialized and gendered experience.
22. See Macey (2012: 323).
23. See, for instance, Webber (2018: 145) and Bernasconi (2023: 258).
24. See Bernasconi (2023: 192).
25. In Fanon's view, however, the Whites shirked their responsibilities (BSWM 84–5), citing Sartre's statement in *Anti-Semite and Jew*: "there is not one of us who is not totally guilty and even criminal; the Jewish blood that the Nazis shed falls on our heads" (ASJ 136).
26. *Les Damnés de la Terre* (1961) is most often translated as *The Wretched of the Earth*. However, I follow Lewis Gordon (2015) in preferring *The Damned of the Earth* as a more suitable rendering, reminding us of the subtle force, shifts of meaning, and "inconspicuous furrows" left by language.

27. See Bernasconi (2023: 251).
28. See Jules-Rosette (2020: 392) who discusses the *antinégritude* arguments of the Haitian poet René Depestre in this context.
29. See Bernasconi (2023: 118).
30. See Macey (2012: 466).
31. See Braidotti et al. (2023: 49–50).
32. See Braidotti et al. (2023: 18–9).
33. See Braidotti et al. (2023: 126–7).
34. Jules-Rosette (2020: 389).
35. See Braidotti et al. (2023: 29).
36. Patricia Hill Collins (2017: 328, 337) distinguishes between analogies that present *oppositional difference* and *relational difference*. Instead of asking how are racism and sexism are alike and unalike within an oppositional framework, it is more revealing to ask relationally "what do racism and sexism reveal about the separate systems and how do they shape one another?". Understanding oppression in this way through a properly intersectional analysis of race, class, age, ethnicity, sexuality and other marginalizations can provide "a new angle of vision on freedom" in the struggle against it.

## *Chapter Six*

1. See Gosetti-Ferencei (2021: 289–90).
2. See Lemm (2021: 84–5).
3. Lemm (2021: 94) also identifies a second dimension of contingency in Nietzsche's idea of creation in his notion of *forgetfulness* where "strength lies in forgetting himself," a giver of gifts "whose soul is overfull so that it forgets itself" (Z P4). This construes creativity not as a conscious decision but as an active force of life.
4. See Wolin (1990: 110).
5. In his notebooks, Nietzsche colorfully describes *L'art pour l'art* as "the virtuoso croaking of shivering frogs, despairing in their swamp" (WP 808).
6. Cited in Wolin (1990: 110).
7. See Macey (2012: 18, 122).
8. Cited in Gordon (2015: 88).
9. See Ellison (1964: 78–9).
10. See Gordon (2015: 89–90).
11. See Gordon (2015: 91).
12. Noudelmann (2012: 132, 44) notes how in this composition Sartre took his inspiration from Debussy rather than from Chopin, making some use of Debussy's innovative and extended spacings but ultimately sticking to the sonata form instead of trying, through Debussy, to use intervals capable of disrupting traditional forms.
13. Cited in Flynn (2014: 388).
14. See Noudelmann (2012: 42) and Hayman (1986: 42).
15. Cited in Danto (1980: 50).
16. See Noudelmann (2012: 55, 63).
17. Cited in Thomas (1983: 138–9).

18. Cited in Wood (2005).
19. See Wood (2005: 10).
20. See Noudelmann (2012: 44, 31, 18, 136, 140).
21. Cited in Noudelmann (2012: 143).
22. Cited in Hayman (1982: 341).
23. See Macey (2012: 229).

## *Chapter Seven*

1. See Plank (1998: 102).
2. Cited in Wolin (1990: 152).
3. Cited in Wolin (1992: 4).
4. See Wolin (2022: 94) and (1990: 122).
5. See Landes (2024) for a full exposition of this in relation to Merleau-Ponty.
6. Cited in Kruks (1990: 26).
7. See Wild (1962) and Kruks (1990: 32).
8. Or, as Nietzsche puts it: "However far man may extend himself with his knowledge, however objective he may appear to himself—ultimately he reaps nothing but his own biography" (HH 513).
9. Cited in Kruks (1990: 32).
10. As William Plank (1998: 256, 352) argues, Nietzsche recognized that humans, animals, and plants use unconscious systems of difference to achieve individuation, for example, by pheromone. This can be compared to Deleuze's "autoproductive unconscious" that generates desire and comprehension below the level of reflective consciousness through a productive synthesis of the senses.
11. See Macquarrie (1973: 220–1).
12. See Wood (2005: 36).
13. See Gordon (2015: 72).

## *Chapter Eight*

1. See Thomas (1983: 18, 56).
2. Cited in Thomas (1983: 49).
3. See Thomas (1983: 103). Carol Diethe (2007) also questions the veracity of this rumor.
4. See Thomas (1983: 93, 128).
5. Cited in Safranski (2002: 300).
6. See Connolly (1988) and Hunt (1993).
7. See Safranski (2002: 166) and Wolin (2022: 23, 204).
8. Cited in Wolin (2022: 381).
9. Cited in Wolin (2022: 277).
10. Heidegger's academic summer camp in Todtnauberg October 1933 amounted to "the lively inculcation of a National Socialist revolution" that followed Nazi camp discipline. The participants marched on foot as a body from Freiburg University were required to wear SA or SS service uniform, and adhered to a rigorous military daily routine (e.g., reveille at 06.00 a.m., tattoo at 10.00 p.m). See Ott (1994: 229).

11. Cited in Wolin (1990: 4) and Ott (1994: 156).
12. Cited in Wolin (2022: 233, 206–7).
13. See Safranski (2002: 94).
14. In 1848 Kierkegaard visited King Christian VIII (who admired his writings) at Amalienborg Palace on three occasions where they discussed mainly politics, voicing concern of possible uprisings and a mutual fear of communism. In his journal, he pours scorn on democracy: "Of all tyrannies, a people's government is the most excruciating, the most spiritless, unconditionally the downfall of everything great and sublime . . . A people's government is the true picture of hell . . . [where] 'the others' tyrannize over one" (PJ 302). He views the state as "a useful, expedient evil rather than a good" that is "cunningly composed so that individual egoisms intersect one another correctively" (PJ 621). Above all, as David Sherman (2024: 55–7) comments, as the self-styled "champion of subjectivity," Kierkegaard's thought "tends towards political quietism." For Kierkegaard, the political and economic realms are characterized by the purely quantitative (force of number and majoritarianism) that effaces qualitative distinctions. He endorses liberty, equality and fraternity but these are "before God" and rejects these in political terms: "I have to serve a religious cause, and above all, to keep myself away from politics and from political considerations."
15. Schmitt (1985: 9).
16. Cited in Wolin (1992: 99, 101).
17. See Wolin (1990: 141).
18. Cited in Wolin (2022: 305).
19. Cited in Ott (1994: 35).
20. See Kruks (1981: 97).
21. Sartre's "conversion" occurred in the reverse direction when in 1952 the arrest of the Communist leader Jacques Duclos on trumped-up charges led him to pledge support for the French Communist Party.
22. In *Memoirs of a Dutiful Daughter*, Beauvoir describes how as a youngster she would regurgitate her father's rampant nationalism with pride: "'Simone is an ardent patriot', they would say" (MDD 27). She went out of her way in her commitment to the national cause by "perform[ing] my duty as a loyal daughter of France" (MDD 26). By her twenties, however, her feelings had drastically changed, now viewing patriotism and nationalism as the perfect means "for a child to become a sedulous ape" (MDD 27).
23. In Gerassi (2009: 44).
24. See Heter (2020: 532) and Eshleman (2020: 20).
25. See Thomas (1983: 56).
26. Deleuze and Guattari (1994: 102).
27. See Staal (2021: 404).
28. See Macey (2012: 384–5). As Macey notes, elsewhere Fanon takes a different view of pan-African unity, vowing to drag it out of its "woolly minded swamps" and use it as a stepping-stone to the creation of a United States of Africa that bypasses the "national chauvinist bourgeois phase." In 1958, he wrote an article that advocates *creole* as a basis for a "West Indian consciousness" that would crystallize social

developments, such as the rehabilitation of local traditions and non-Christian religions (especially in Haiti) and a newly found pride in being black (2012: 411–2).
29. See Macey (2012: 479). Contrary to Fanon's wishes, the Code of Nationality adopted by the Algerian state in 1962 defined Algerian nationality in both religious and ethnic terms and made Islam the official state religion.
30. Cited in Shatz (2025: 373).

## *Chapter Nine*

1. See Wolin (2022: 115–6).
2. See Rorty (1991: 3). Although he views Heidegger as "one of the great synoptic imaginations of our century," Rorty quips "Heideggerese is only Heidegger's gift to us, not Being's gift to Heidegger" (1991: 67, 65).
3. See Rorty (1991: 17) and Sheehan (2015: xix). The phrase "Heidegger cackling" (*Heideggergegacker*) was coined by Karl Jaspers. Sheehan (2015: 5–8, 136), for instance, highlights the difficulties in translating and understanding Heidegger's key philosophical terms, such as *Sein* (Being) or *Dasein* (openness/disclosedness), painstakingly documenting the numerous variants he employs in a bid to define them.
4. See Edwards (2023: 158).
5. As Clare Carlisle (2020: 187) puts it, none of Kierkegaard's many pseudonyms are him directly but "they are paths which converge at the question of his own existence."
6. See Wolin (1990: 19).

## *Chapter Ten*

1. Despite the fact he declares "[o]f all tyrannies the tyranny of the daily press is the most wretched and mean" (PJ 228), this didn't stop him from using the press to mount a counter-offence against the *Corsair* for all its "gossiping small-talk" and "piffle about my legs and trousers!" (PJ 323). With the stroke of a pen he hurled himself "against mob vulgarity" (PJ 481) and in June 1855 he published the first issue of his own broadsheet, *The Instant*. Among other targets, it pilloried the state church in a satirical diatribe that went through nine issues before he fell ill in October.
2. See Ortega Y Gasset (1962: 152–3).
3. See Smith (2024: 244).
4. This position of non-activism, he affirms, "in spite of appearances to the contrary, is an active role" (MAMS 263). He later records in his "An Autobiographical Essay," however, that Nazism troubled him deeply from 1932 onward and colored his experience, fracturing his sense of hope of inner grace—"How could I be happy in a world so menaced?." He describes himself as "a liberal who has become more and more painfully aware of the limits of liberalism." Cited in Kruks (1990: 195, 47).
5. See Sheehan (2015: 258).
6. Cited in Wolin (1990: 161).
7. Cited in Sheehan (2015: 290).
8. See Ruin (2016: 354–5).

9. By annexing technology to "world-Judaism," as Trawny (2019) notes, Heidegger constructs a Manichean narrative in which technology always appears as an evil.
10. Cited in Wolin (2022: 242).
11. See Sheehan (2015: 276).
12. See Smith (2024: 247).
13. Fanon highlights the dual nature of the technological object as both poison and cure when he discusses the use of radio technology in the Algerian War in the 1950s. Official radio for the colonized Algerians, *Radio Alger* was viewed as "an evil object, anxiogenic and accursed," but the FLN broadcast, the *Voice of Algeria* became "the only means of entering into communication with the Revolution, of living with it . . . Almost magically . . . the radio receiver lost its identity as an enemy object." Cited in Shatz (2025: 228).
14. See Parisi (2021).
15. See Goldberg and Ng (2021) and Rouvroy and Klumbyté (2023).
16. In the passage *On Redemption*, for example, Zarathustra tells a gathering of cripples who surround him that the redemption we should seek are opportunities to transform our experiences of earthly time rather than to try to escape it or reverse its marks.
17. See Ferrando (2020: 135).
18. See O'Shiel (2019: 33) for a discussion of how the "magic of experience" can, through modes of impure reflection, become "dark forms" that lead to bad faith, addiction, prejudice and madness.
19. See Farrell Fox (2023: 227n10).
20. See Rouvroy and Klumbyté (2023: 11).

## *Chapter Eleven*

1. Christine Daigle (2021: 2, 23) describes Nietzsche's philosophical method as "wild phenomenology," a phenomenology *avant la lettre* that incorporates phenomenological concepts, such as intentionality (in anticipation of Husserl), without naming them.
2. Cited in Manschot (2021: 30).
3. See, for instance, Macquarrie (1973: 85).
4. Cited in Russon and Jacobson (2016: 351).
5. See Morris (2020: 233–7) and Howells (2011: 26–46).
6. See Morris (2020: 234).
7. See Howells (2011: 46).
8. See Jaarsma (2024: 256).
9. See, for instance, BN 522 and, in *The Family Idiot*, IF1: 47.
10. See Ngo (2024: 296–8).

## *Chapter Twelve*

1. See Carlisle (2020: 172).
2. In response to Kierkegaard's acidic review of Hans Christian Andersen's novel *Only A Fiddler* for lacking a world-view, Andersen caricatured him for his quirky hairstyle and melancholia in the play "Vaudeville in One Act" performed at

Copenhagen's Royal Theatre in 1840. In spite of this, the relationship later became amicable according to Andersen. See Carlisle (2020: 120) and PJ 664.

3. In July and November 1845, the *Corsair* showed admiration for Kierkegaard's work, praising Victor Eremita and Hilarius Bookbinder from *Either/Or* and *Stages on Life's Way*. But when Peder Ludvig Møller became editor, he embarked on a character assassination of Kierkegaard, linking his productivity to an unwholesome and unmanly sickly nature in which he was wont to "expose his whole inner development to the public eye." Møller accuses Kierkegaard of mistreating women in his life and in his writing—"the feminine nature placed on the experimental rack." After the *Corsair* affair, as Carlisle comments (2020: 200), Kierkegaard's "ambivalent suspicion of the world" hardens into "a wholehearted, militant opposition." He regards newspapers as "a form of evil" spreading "demoralization," "envy, caprice, pettiness," and "disintegration," bemoaning the "indignities" he suffered due to the comic lampooning of "my thin legs and my ridiculed trousers." Scurrilous journalism, he snipes, is a "nasty dog" kept by the public for its amusement as "just a bit of fun" attacking "superior" victims. See Carlisle (2020: 189–201).
4. See Solomon (1988: 89).
5. For example, in *Ecce Homo*—"[m]y danger is disgust with people" (EH 4.6) and "I never speak to masses" (EH 4.1). Also, in *Thus Spoke Zarathustra* "let Zarathustra not talk to the people, but to companions! Zarathustra shall not become shepherd and dog to a herd!" (Z 1.9).
6. Wolin (1990: 51–2, 183) describes Heidegger's "call" as "an uncognizable will-o'-the-wisp" and his ethic of "resolve" as "normatively impoverished" since it seems to openly glorify the irrationalist bases of decision. Allowing of no general criteria for distinguishing it, Heideggerian resolve represents the "formalism of decisionism where decision as such becomes the highest virtue."
7. Cited in Safranski (2002: 266).
8. See Safranski (2002: 258).
9. See Safranski (2002: 266).
10. Cited in Wolin (1990: 131).
11. See Safranski (2002: 231).
12. See Verkerk (2020: 88).
13. See Connolly (1991: 64).
14. See Richardson (2020: 232–8).
15. According to Plank (1998: 128–30, 389), Nietzsche proposes a cosmology in his dialectic of self-Other that conjoins the scientific moral. Individuality in the form of genetic diversity and variation is essential for the biological integrity of the species (since rigid encodement is evolutionarily degenerate) just as it is for the moral integrity and advance of humankind (since conformism is morally degenerate).
16. See Richardson (2020: 237).
17. To cite a recent example, Gosetti-Ferencei (2021: 21, 139) argues that Sartre laid out only "stark oppositions" in our relation with others predicated on "struggle and hostility" where other existentialists provide mystery, ambiguity, reverence, and availability. "Yet identifying such a structure as a universal feature of the human

condition as Sartre does," she concludes, "neglects the crucial factors of actual oppression that motivate domination or objectification of the individuals of some groups by those of others."

18. In his later work on Flaubert in *The Family Idiot*, Sartre shows how Flaubert's I is an Other to him because he takes his being-for-others as his primary mode of existence. Flaubert's fascination with mirrors after the Fall—he needs to see himself as others see him—causes him to embark upon "Operation Reflection" (FI2: 107) which was doomed to fail as one cannot truly apprehend oneself in the mirror as each gesture is apprehended and anticipated in advance. He escapes into the imaginary in the company of his sister Caroline by acting out different roles in front of her to amuse her and thus transform his "passive constitution" into a positive experience of agency. Although he quickly abandons acting (due to his family's silent disapproval), this is a manifestation of his original "*choice of the unreal*" (FI2 10) which he later reconfigures in his choice to become a creative writer. See Edwards (2023: 105–7) for a fuller elucidation of this.
19. Deleuze and Guattari, for instance, both credit Sartre with inspiring their notion of the "subject-group" (in *A Thousand Plateaus*) as a basis for the production of richer modes of subjectivity (which they later modified to the "collective assemblage of enunciation"). See Young et al. (2013: 148).

## *Chapter Thirteen*

1. Cited in Wolin (1990: 148). As Wolin notes (1990: 199), just to confuse matters, Heidegger *reverses* this formulation in the fifth edition of *What is Metaphysics?* (1949)—"Being *never* essences without beings, beings are never without Being."
2. See, for instance, Wolin (2022) and Smith (2024).
3. Cited in Wolin (1992: 145).
4. As William McBride (2009: 201–2) comments, it is ironic given the weight Merleau-Ponty attributes to personal history in the formation of individual, such as facial expressions, bodily dispositions, and psychological states, he doesn't allude to his own childhood in his philosophical expositions.
5. As Matthew Eshleman (2009: 67–9) observes, Beauvoir's view of freedom undergoes similar modification by the effects of social conditioning to Sartre's. Her view of freedom in *Pyrrhus et Cinéas* looks like Sartre's "absolute view" (in the first half of *Being and Nothingness*), while her more nuanced view in *The Ethics of Ambiguity* very much mirrors Sartre's "considered view of freedom" (in the second half). Equally, the view of freedom in Sartre's *Saint Genet* (1952) is very close to Beauvoir's in *The Second Sex* (1949). Indeed, Sartre acknowledges his debt in *Saint Genet* to Beauvoir's idea of sedimentation in her 1949 book (SG 37, 57, 291).
6. See Edwards (2023: 202).
7. See Webber (2018: 123).
8. Of course, it was this very phrase that caused a rupture between Heidegger and Sartre and provoked Heidegger to distance himself from the existentialist label. It is not entirely clear why he criticized Sartre for this in *Letter on Humanism* since in *Being and Time* he also assumes "*the essence of Dasein lies in its existence*"

(BT 67) and proclaims "the priority of '*existentia*' over *essentia*" (BT 68). However, he accuses Sartre of remaining in metaphysics through simply inverting Plato by prioritizing existence: "the reversal of a metaphysical statement remains a metaphysical statement" (GA9: 250).

9. See Cooper (1990: 156).
10. See Webber (2018: 128).
11. Cited in Macquarrie (1973: 140).
12. See Webber (2018: 11).

### *Chapter Fourteen*

1. This is how François Raffoul (2016: 280) describes Heidegger's theorization of Dasein.
2. Cited in Gosetti-Ferencei (2021: 67).
3. See Gardiner (1991: 92).
4. See Sheehan (2015: 170).
5. See Brusotti (2022: 253).
6. See Brusotti (2022: 249).
7. See Daigle (2021: 145).
8. See Solomon (2003: 180).
9. See Daigle (2021: 12).
10. See Edwards (2023: 84).
11. See Kirkpatrick (2022: 241, 401).
12. Beauvoir explains her rationale for not attending the lunch—"if you accepted the prize, you should have played the game . . . [but there was] no obligation on my part toward the television, the radio and the press, nor why it should have induced me to smile at the camera . . . In my view, the relations a writer entertains with the truth make it impossible for him to acquiesce to such treatment; it is quite enough that it should be inflicted on him by force" (FC 326). Of course, Sartre went one step further when he refused the Nobel Prize for Literature in 1964 for his autobiography *Words*, justifying his decision by repeating Beauvoir's rationale that collusion with institutions is incompatible with the free pursuit of truth.
13. See Gosetti-Ferencei (2021: 230, 225).
14. Cited in Safranski (2002: 21).
15. It was hence with some irony that Nietzsche became the pawn (as a museum exhibit) in his own Cult of Personality orchestrated by his sister for financial gain after he became incapacitated in the 1890s.
16. See Sawyer (2015: 46).

### *Chapter Fifteen*

1. See Sheehan (2015: 166).
2. See O'Byrne (2016: 264) and Stauffer (2016: 393–6).
3. See Stauffer (2016: 394–5).
4. See Marovich (2021: 149–51).

5. According to Beatrice Marovich (2021: 149–50), the foetus captures the inextricable entanglement of birth and death. Defenseless and helpless, it is a reminder that the human is both mortal and natal. There is a misogynistic bias at play in the denial of death as fear of death is also a form of woman's abjection as the giver of life.
6. See O'Byrne (2016: 263–5).
7. See Derrida (2001: 107).
8. See Lykke (2023: 155).
9. See Wicks (2020: 73).
10. Cited in Gordon (2015: 77).
11. Cited in Gordon (2015: 140–1).

### *Chapter Sixteen*

1. See Siemens (2015: 97–8).
2. See Aydin (2007: 30).
3. See Mitchell (2016: 299).
4. See Mitchell (2016: 299–300).
5. See Zimmerman (2007: 306).
6. See Flynn (2014: 250).
7. As Eshleman (2011: 33) points out, his philosophy never talks about different kinds or types of being but always different *modes* of being. For Sartre, the universe contains only one kind of being that can be divided into different modal categories. Understood in this way, he subscribes to a version of substance monism (materialism) conjoined with a modal pluralism (in a way influenced by Spinoza and Bergson).
8. See Zohar (1991: 59).
9. See Farrell Fox (2023: 107–8).
10. A shining example of this is Merlin Sheldrake's *Entangled Life* (2022).

### *Chapter Seventeen*

1. Kierkegaard's military career was even less spectacular. In 1830 after matriculation at the University of Copenhagen, he enlisted in the King's Guard, but was declared unfit for service after four days when failing to report for duty. See Carlisle (2020: 5).
2. Cited in Safranski (2002: 84, 87).
3. See, for instance, Wolin (1990: 74–5, 126).
4. See Fleming (2020: 382–3).
5. Fanon's subsequent rejection of the motherland would be that of a disappointed son. According to his brother Joby, France's treatment of its ethnic soldiers (black soldiers were excluded from the victory march into Paris) "wounded him to the core of his being" and ignited his sense of revolt. See Shatz (2025: 29, 36).
6. See Macey (2012: 100, 390).
7. See Macey (2012: 292). Reportedly, Fanon showed professional concern and care for his torturer patient despite his visceral hatred of the colonizing power and his growing everyday experience of the misery it caused in the traumas and pathologies

of the colonized. It is also true, however, as Macey remarks, that Fanon would soon have found *himself* in the torture chair if his cover as a supporter and operative for the Algerian FLN were to be blown.

8. Quoted in Gordon (2015: 105).
9. See, for instance, Gordon (2015), Macey (2012), and Fleming (2020).
10. See Macey (2012: 367–8).
11. Cited in Shatz (2025: 346).

## *Chapter Eighteen*

1. Kierkegaard first met Regine at a party given by his friend Peter Rordam in May 1837 when she was still only fifteen. He wrote her a letter three years later telling her that her love "rescued" and "liberated" him and asked her to marry him. But by the summer of 1841 he had resolved to break off their engagement. Like Abraham on Mount Moriah—"fearfully painful, having to be so cruel and loving her as I did," he made the break. Terribly hurt, she told him—"So after all, you have played a terrible game with me." After Regine returned the engagement ring he gave to her, he had it re-fashioned, the diamonds set in a small cross (a memento of his hopes and mistakes) and wore it on his finger when he died after sunset on 11 November 1855. In a written will (1849) that he kept locked in his desk, he left his estate to Regine (now, Schlegel) since he considered engagement to be binding just as marriage is. See Carlisle (2020: 16, 24–5) and PJ 657.
2. As a younger man, Fanon dreaded marriage and the family table—"that larval, stocky, obsolete life." After a relationship with a younger white woman, Michelle Weyer, in Lyon, Mireille Fanon was born in 1948 but Fanon abandoned the relationship, as he was also involved with Marie-Josephe Dublé (Josie) whom he married in 1952. He was not known for fidelity and espoused "parallel love." He thought jealous people to be "dangerous paranoids" and jealousy was "an evil to be eliminated so that humans could be truly adult." When his absences grew more frequent Josie took a lover but fiercely defended his legacy without compromise, keeping a photo of him by her bed "like a bodyguard." See Shatz (2025: 51, 237, 361). Heidegger also had several affairs (notably, with his former Jewish student, Hannah Arendt). His wife, Elfride, was also promiscuous, resulting in the illegitimate birth of a second child, Hermann Heidegger (who became Martin's literary executor).
3. Marcel and his wife Jacqueline Boegner adopted a son (Jean-Marie) and, in "Phenomenological Notes on Being in a Situation," he presents marriage as freely giving oneself to the other as a form of generosity. This does not involve possessing the other or sacrificing one's own freedom, but is freedom's greatest expression, he argues, achieved by maintaining one's presence and openness to the other.
4. See Kirkpatrick (2022: 6).
5. See Schwarzer (1984: 110).
6. Cited in Kirkpatrick (2022: 370).
7. See Cleary (2015: 72).
8. See Salomé (2001: xlvi).
9. Cited in Kofman (1998: 47).

10. In his journals, Kierkegaard also shows some scepticism, viewing erotic love and marriage as "really just a deeper corroboration of self-love, with two people involved in self-love" (PJ 267). Although the whole business of man and woman "is a very intricately laid plot, or a practical joke designed to destroy man *qua* spirit" (PG 591), in marriage the different gender characteristics tend to balance out one another. Intellectually, compared to man, woman is "something of a little goose," but in practical wisdom, man "is a great clod" weighed down "by a thousand reflections" and "the stupidly pompous idea of his own dignity in being a man" (PJ 591). Woman is more readily suited to zeal and commitment because of her devotional nature but "she throws no light on anything." Her devotion supplemented by "an eminent masculine intellectuality," however, in Kierkegaard's view, is a perfect combination (PJ 617).
11. A lifelong exclusive love for a single person, he states, "is a piece of barbarism: for it is practised at the expense of all others" (BGE 67). Cleary (2015: 87) argues that, in place of conventional marriage, Nietzsche advises serial monogamy, that is, "planetary friendships" (JS 279) that do not involve mutual renunciation and are destined to part ways.
12. See Ansell-Pearson (1994: 191–2).
13. In *Daybreak*, he warns against the helpless yielding to instincts, impulses and drives. Instead, we should "act as the gardeners of our impulses" (D 560).
14. Cited in Kirkpatrick (2022: 127).
15. See Boulé (2005: 130).
16. Their perceived oneness did at times proved to be a limiting factor. Feeling she could have done more in protesting against the situation in Algeria, Beauvoir opined: "Sartre pointed out exactly what I had always told myself: that I can't very well go around mimicking him all the time; our names are so closely linked we're almost thought of as only one person" (FC 659).
17. See, for instance, Kirkpatrick (2022), Moi (1993), Altman (2020).
18. "The third person question" was often problematic for Beauvoir and Sartre. The fact that they wouldn't allow a "contingent" third to become a primary priority over their "necessary" pact made their other relationships unsustainable and unromantic. This led to considerable trauma for the "thirds" (e.g., Bianca Bienenfeld and Evelyne Rey) and caused the breakdown of Beauvoir's relationship with Nelson Algren (who emotionally withdrew from her once she told him she would never abandon Sartre and live with him permanently in America).
19. Katherine Morris (2020: 231) is an exception to this and notices the seamless mix of phenomenology and ontology in *Being and Nothingness* where Sartre's "often beautiful descriptions" of the caress show there are various non-instrumental ways—the aesthetic, the nurturing, and the sensuous—of encountering one's own body and that of others.
20. Sartre's concept of the caress dovetails with his own preferred way of loving which, as Noudelmann (2012) notes, was one of surface where he was a "masturbator of women" rather than "penetrating Hussar." According to Nietzsche's aphorism, this lends him a certain wisdom: "All profound men find bliss in being like flying fish for once, and playing on the highest crests of the waves; what they regard as best in things is the fact that they have a surface: their skinnedness" (JS 256).

21. See Cleary (2015: 141–7).
22. See Belle (2024: 201).
23. According to Cixous (1994: 133), there are two different criteria that mark masculine and feminine economies—*the relation to pleasure* and *the attitude toward giving*. She explains the relation to pleasure through the story of the quest for the Holy Grail. On one side is the law "which is absolute, verbal, invisible" and which is not and, on the other, "the apple which is, is, is." Perceval (who seeks the Holy Grail) is a mother's son with no father on the side of innocence and happiness, but after he is educated, he becomes "phallicized" and falls prey to the law, which is "anti-pleasure" (1994: 135). One"s path in life and participation in either or both economies is not determined by anatomical sex but by history—by "the cultural schema and the way the individual negotiates with these schema . . . adapts to them and reproduces them, or else . . . goes beyond them" (1994: 135). In many respects, Nietzsche and Sartre were two archetypal Percevals, raised by feminine hands on the side of "innocence and happiness," "phallicized" by institutions and male violence, but eventually negotiating a path out of this through their proposed economy of the gift.
24. Cited in Lacoste (1999: 286).
25. See Corriero (2023: 27).
26. See Corriero (2023: 15–17).
27. This deficiency can be seen as an oversight of the social theory that Sartre develops in the *Critique* since he stays on the historical level of explanation and neglects the local level where friendships develop and emerge. Ideally, Peter Diers (1999: 255, 263) argues, we need to build a bridge between the two levels in order to explore friendship as "a source of revolutionary praxis."
28. c.f. "*Collective mind*. A good writer possesses not only his own mind but also the mind of his friends" (HH 80).
29. Cited in Safranski (2003: 250).
30. Verkerk (2020: 49, 164), for instance, is critical of Nietzsche for providing an *androcentric* conception by denying friendship to women, deeming them to be incapable of it (due to their lack of "free spiritedness"). She also questions the emphasis he gives to agonism in friendship that encourages traditionally masculine values, such as competition and toughness at the expense of other values, such as intimacy, rest and enjoyment.
31. See Corriero (2023: 96).

### *Chapter Nineteen*

1. See Smith (2024: 238).
2. See Flynn (2014: 361).

### *Chapter Twenty*

1. It is unclear whether the title was changed by Beauvoir (who helped edit the original paper for publication) or the publisher.
2. Merleau-Ponty (2016: 239).

3. See Zimmerman (2007: 319).
4. See Zimmerman (2007: 311) and Davis (2016: 465–66).
5. Cited in Davis (2016: 466).
6. See McBride (2012: 55).
7. See Gosetti-Ferencei (2021: 157).
8. Colin Davis (2024) warns against a direct assimilation of existentialist literature to existentialist philosophy, for example, Roquentin to Sartre. See also Boulé (2005) and Farrell Fox (2023) for a reiteration of this point.
9. Cited in Gosetti-Ferencei (2021: 276).
10. See Farrell Krell (2003: 35).
11. See Daigle (2021: 120).
12. Cited in Gosetti-Ferencei (2021: 250).
13. This is how Elizabeth Butterfield (2012) describes (the later) Sartre.
14. See Badmington (2000: 9).
15. See Bignall (2023: 104)
16. See Zimmerman (2007: 301).
17. Cited in Gordon (2015: 105).
18. See Carlisle (2020: 20).

### *Chapter Twenty-One*

1. Kafka's literary fiction epitomizes this scrambling mechanism. In his story "Report to an Academy," an ape evolves to the intelligence of the average European man. In "Investigations of a Dog," Kafka is a young dog who is "filled with a premonition of great things" while in *The Transformation*, human and insect are conjoined in hybrid form in the figure of Gregor after a phantasmagorical overnight metamorphosis.
2. Given that Beauvoir states (somewhat parenthetically) when in conversation with Sartre in the 1970s that insects "are endowed with consciousness" (FS 332), her omission on this matter, as well as her generally dismissive attitude towards animals, is somewhat surprising and can be contrasted with Sartre's more questioning approach.
3. Cited in Safranski (2002: 198).
4. See also Sheehan (2015: 143) who criticises Heidegger for maintaining this divide in the light of contemporary studies into the intelligence of animals, as well as Zimmerman (2007: 312) who charges Heidegger with an ingrained anthropocentrism.
5. See Ally (2017: 363).
6. See Wheeler and Di Paolo (2024: 204–15).
7. Deleuze and Guattari (1987: 51, 314). They describe *scenopoetes dentirostris*, a bird in the Australian rainforest, as "a complete artist" (1994: 189).
8. Derrida (2002: 372, 380, 387).
9. See Boria (2022: 282).

# BIBLIOGRAPHY


Abram, David (1997) *The Spell of the Sensuous* (Vintage Books).

Agamben, Giorgio (1999) *The Man without Content*, tr. G. Albert (Stanford University Press).

Agamben, Giorgio (2019) *Creation and Anarchy: The Work of Art and the Religion of Capitalism*, tr. A. Kotsko (Stanford University Press).

Ally, Matthew C. (2017) *Ecology and Existence: Bringing Sartre to the Water's Edge* (Lexington Books).

Ally, Matthew C. (2020) "The Logics of the *Critique*" in *The Sartrean Mind*, eds. M. Eshleman & C. Mui (Routledge), pp. 362–375.

Altizer, Thomas J.J. (1966) *The Gospel of Christian Atheism* (Westminster Press).

Altman, Meryl (2007) "Simone de Beauvoir and Lived Lesbian Experience," *Feminist Studies, 33:1*, pp. 207–232.

Altman, Meryl (2020) *Beauvoir in Time* (Brill).

Ansell-Pearson, Keith (1994) *An Introduction to Nietzsche as Political Thinker: The Perfect Nihilist* (Cambridge University Press).

Ansell-Pearson, Keith (1997) *Viroid Life: Perspectives on Nietzsche and the Transhuman Condition* (Routledge).

Ansell-Pearson, Keith (2024) "New Directions: Nietzsche" in *The Bloomsbury Handbook of Existentialism*, eds. 313–320.

Arendt, Hannah (1970) *On Violence* (Harcourt, Brace & Co.).

Arendt, Hannah (1971) "Martin Heidegger at Eighty," *New York Review of Books*, October 21.

Aronson, Ronald (1995) "Sartre and Marxism: A Double Retrospective," *Sartre Studies International, 1:2*, pp. 21–36.

Asberg, Cecilia (2023) "Toxic Embodiment" in *More Posthuman Glossary*, eds. R. Braidotti, E. Jones & G. Klumbytė (Bloomsbury), pp. 145–147.

Aydin, Ciano (2007) "Nietzsche on Reality as Will to Power: Towards an 'Organization-Struggle' Model," *The Journal of Nietzsche Studies, 33*, pp. 25–48.

Ayer, Alfred J. (1945) "Novelist Philosophers v—Jean-Paul Sartre," *Horizon, 12:67*, pp. 12–25.

Badiou, Alain (2009) *Pocket Pantheon: Figures of Postwar Philosophy*, tr. D. Macey (Verso).

Badmington, Neil (2000) *Posthumanism* (Palgrave).

Bair, Deirdre (1990) *Simone de Beauvoir: A Biography* (Vintage).

Barrett, William (1946) "Talent and Career of Jean-Paul Sartre," *Partisan Review, 13:2*, pp. 237–246.

Baudrillard, Jean (2003) *Passwords*, tr. C. Turner (Verso).

Belle, Kathryn Sophia (2024) *Beauvoir and Belle: A Black Feminist Critique of the Second Sex* (Oxford University Press).

Bennett, Jane (2017) "Vibrant Matter" in *Posthuman Glossary*, eds. R. Braidotti & M. Hlavajova (Bloomsbury), pp. 447–448.

Bentley, Eric (1962) "Sartre's Struggle for *Existenz*" in *Sartre: A Collection of Critical Essays*, ed. E. Kern (Prentice-Hall), pp. 73–79.

Bergoffen, Debra (2009) "Getting the Beauvoir We Deserve" in *Beauvoir and Sartre: The Riddle of Influence*, eds. C. Daigle & J. Golomb (Indiana University Press), pp. 13–29.

Bernasconi, Robert (2016) "Heidegger and Sartre: Historicity, Destiny, and Politics" in *The Bloomsbury Companion to Heidegger*, eds. F. Raffoul & E. Nelson (Bloomsbury) pp. 369–375.

Bernasconi, Robert (2023) *Critical Philosophy of Race* (Oxford University Press).

Betschart, Alfred (2022) "Deconstructing Sartre," *Sartre Studies International*, *28:1*, pp. 85–105.

Betschart, Alfred (2024) "Sartre's Reading in His Formative Years in the 1920s" (paper presented at the UK Sartre Society Conference, July 2024).

Bianco, Giuseppe (2024) "The Concrete and the Abstract in Modern French Philosophy" in *The Oxford Handbook of Modern French Philosophy*, eds. M. Sinclair & D. Whistler (Oxford University Press), pp. 524–539.

Bignall, Simone (2023) "Posthuman Agency" in *More Posthuman Glossary*, eds. R. Braidotti, E. Jones & G. Klumbyte (Bloomsbury), pp. 104–105.

Böhme, Gernot (1995) *Atmosphere: Essays on the New Aesthetics* (Suhrkamp).

Boria, Damon (2022) "Reading Nietzsche and Sartre toward an Eco-Existentialism" in *Nietzsche und der französische Existenzialismus*, eds. A. Betschart, U. Sommer & P. Stephan (De Gruyter), pp. 271–282.

Boulé, Jean-Pierre (2005) *Sartre, Self-Formation and Masculinities* (Berghahn).

Braidotti, Rosi (2013) *The Posthuman* (Polity Press).

Braidotti, Rosi, Jones, Emily & Klumbyté, Goda (2023) "Introduction" and "Convergences" in *More Posthuman Glossary*, eds. R. Braidotti, E. Jones & G. Klumbyte (Bloomsbury), pp. 1–6, 21–23.

Braver, Lee (2016) "Later Essays and Seminars" in *The Bloomsbury Companion to Heidegger*, eds. F. Raffoul & E.S. Nelson (Bloomsbury), pp. 249–254.

Brusotti, Marco (2022) "'Choice' or 'Gift'? Nietzsche, Jaspers and Ricoeur in a Text by Georges Canguilhem on Becoming Oneself" in *Nietzsche und der französische Existenzialismus*, eds. A. Betschart, U. Sommer & P. Stephan (De Gruyter), pp. 249–269.

Burnham, Douglas (2015) *The Nietzsche Dictionary* (Bloomsbury).

Butterfield, Elizabeth (2012) *Sartre and Posthumanist Humanism* (Peter Lang).

Caeymaex, Florence & Cormann, Gregory (2020) "Sartre and Merleau-Ponty" in *The Sartrean Mind*, eds. M.C. Eshleman & C.L. Mui (Routledge), pp. 475–486.

Camus, Albert (1975) *The Myth of Sisyphus*, tr. J. O'Brien (Penguin).

Carlisle, Clare (2020) *Philosopher of the Heart: The Restless Life of Søren Kierkegaard* (Penguin).

Cixous, Hélène (1994) *Hélène Cixous Reader*, ed. S. Sellers (Routledge).

Cleary, Skye (2015) *Existentialism and Romantic Love* (Palgrave Macmillan).

Cohen-Solal, Annie (1985) *Sartre, 1905–1980* (Gallimard).
Cohen-Solal, Annie (1987) *Sartre: A Life* (Heinemann).
Cohen-Solal, Annie (2023) "Qui a encore peur de Sartre?" *Le Monde*, March 12.
Connolly, William (1988) *Political Theory and Modernity* (Blackwell).
Connolly, William (1991) *Identity/Difference: Democratic Negotiations of Political Paradox* (Cornell University Press).
Cooper, David E. (1990) *Existentialism: A Reconstruction* (Basil Blackwell).
Cormann, Grégory (2023) "Plea for a Collective Genetics: Another Reading of Sartre's Early Texts, 1926–27," tr. J. Gillespie, *Sartre Studies International*, *29:1*, pp. 1–21.
Corriero, Emilio Carlo (2023) *"The Gift" in Nietzsche's Zarathustra: Affirmative Love and Friendship*, tr. V. di Stefano (Bloomsbury).
Crenshaw, Kimberlé (1991) "Mapping the Margins: Intersectionality, Identity Politics, and Violence against Women of Color," *Stanford Law Review* 6, pp. 1241–1299.
Crowell, Steven (2012) "Existentialism and Its Legacy" in *The Cambridge Companion to Existentialism*, ed. S. Crowell (Cambridge University Press), pp. 3–24.
Daigle, Christine (2021) *Nietzsche as Phenomenologist: Becoming What One Is* (Edinburgh University Press).
Daigle, Christine (2023) "Transjectivity" in *More Posthuman Glossary*, eds. R. Braidotti, E. Jones & G. Klumbyte (Bloomsbury), pp. 149–151.
Danto, Arthur C. (1980) *Nietzsche as Philosopher* (Columbia University Press).
Davis, Bret W. (2016) "Heidegger and Asian Philosophy" in *The Bloomsbury Companion to Heidegger*, eds. F. Raffoul & E.S. Nelson (Bloomsbury), pp. 459–471.
Davis, Colin (2024) "Existentialism and Literature" in *The Bloomsbury Handbook of Existentialism*, eds. J. Reynolds, A. Woodward & F. Joseph (Bloomsbury) pp. 113–125.
Deleuze, Giles (1987) *Dialogues* (with Claire Parnet), tr. H. Tomlinson & B. Habberjam (Athlone Press).
Deleuze, Giles (1988) *Spinoza: Practical Philosophy* (City Lights Books).
Deleuze, Giles (1992) "Postscript on the Societies of Control," *October*, *59*, pp. 3–7.
Deleuze, Giles (2004) *The Logic of Sense*, tr. M. Lester (Continuum).
Deleuze, Giles & Guattari, Félix (1987) *A Thousand Plateaus* (University of Minnesota Press).
Deleuze, Giles & Guattari, Félix (1994) *What Is Philosophy*?, tr. H. Tomlinson & G. Burchell (Columbia University Press).
Derrida, Jacques (1979) *Spurs: Nietzsche's Styles*, tr. B. Harlow (University of Chicago Press).
Derrida, Jacques (1981) *Positions*, tr. A. Bass (University of Chicago Press).
Derrida, Jacques (1982) *Margins of Philosophy*, tr. A. Bass (University of Chicago Press).
Derrida, Jacques (1992) *Points… Interviews, 1974–1995*, tr. P. Kamuf and Others (Stanford University Press).
Derrida, Jacques (2001) *The Work of Mourning*, eds. P. Brault & M. Naas (University of Chicago Press).
Derrida, Jacques (2002) "The Animal That Therefore I Am (More to Follow)," *Critical Inquiry*, *28*, pp. 369–418.

Detmer, David (2013) "Bad Faith" in *Jean-Paul Sartre: Key Concepts*, eds. S. Churchill & J. Reynolds (Acumen), pp. 118–130.

Diers, Peter (1999) "Friendship and Feminist Praxis: Insights from Sartre's *Critique of Dialectical Reason*" in *Feminist Interpretations of Jean-Paul Sartre*, ed. J. Murphy (Pennsylvania State University Press), pp. 253–271.

Diethe, Carol (2007) *Nietzsche's Sister and the Will to Power* (University of Illnois Press).

Edwards, Mary L. (2023) *Sartre's Existential Psychoanalysis: Knowing Others* (Bloomsbury).

Eliot, T.S. (1969) *The Complete Poems and Plays of T.S. Eliot*, ed. V. Eliot (Faber and Faber).

Ellison, Ralph (1964) *Shadow and Act* (Vintage).

Eshleman, Matthew C. (2009) "Beauvoir and Sartre on Freedom, Intersubjectivity, and Normative Justification" in *Beauvoir and Sartre: The Riddle of Influence*, eds. C. Daigle & J. Golomb (Indiana University Press), pp. 65–89.

Eshleman, Matthew C. (2011) "What Is It Like to Be Free?" in *Reading Sartre: On Phenomenology and Existentialism*, ed. J. Webber (Routledge), pp. 31–47.

Eshleman, Matthew C. (2020) "A Sketch of Sartre's Life" in *The Sartrean Mind*, eds. M. Eshleman & C. Mui (Routledge), pp. 8–21.

Farrell Fox, Nik (2003) *The New Sartre: Explorations in Postmodernism* (Continuum).

Farrell Fox, Nik (2022) "Nietzsche and Sartre: Twin Philosophers of Paradox" in *Nietzsche und der französische Existenzialismus*, eds. A. Betschart, U. Sommer & P. Stephan (De Gruyter), pp. 7–33.

Farrell Fox, Nik (2023) *The Parallel Philosophies of Sartre and Nietzsche: Ethics, Ontology and the Self* (Bloomsbury).

Farrell Krell, David (2003) "General Introduction: The Question of Being" in *Basic Writings: Martin Heidegger*, ed. D. Farrell Krell (Routledge), pp. 1–35.

Ferrando, Francesca (2020) *Philosophical Posthumanism* (Bloomsbury).

Ferrando, Francesca (2023) "Existential Posthumanism: A Manifesto" in *More Posthuman Glossary*, eds. R. Braidotti, E. Jones & G. Klumbyte (Bloomsbury), pp. 47–49.

Fleming, Michael (2020) "Political Violence" in *The Sartrean Mind*, pp. 376–386.

Flynn, Thomas R. (2006) *Existentialism: A Very Short Introduction* (Oxford University Press).

Flynn, Thomas R. (2014) *Sartre: A Philosophical Biography* (Cambridge University Press).

Foucault, Michel (1973) *The Order of Things: An Archaeology of the Human Sciences*, tr. A. Sheridan-Smith (Random House).

Foucault, Michel (1977) *Language, Counter-Memory, Practice: Selected Essays and Interviews*, ed. C. Gordon (Blackwell).

Foucault, Michel (2001) *Dits et écrits, Vol. 1* (Gallimard).

Gardiner, Patrick (1991) *Kierkegaard* (Oxford University Press).

Gardner, Sebastian (2009) *Being and Nothingness: A Reader's Guide* (Continuum).

Gerassi, John (1976) "Simone de Beauvoir: *The Second Sex* Twenty-Five Years Later," *Society*, *13*, pp. 79–85.

Gerassi, John (2009) *Talking with Sartre: Conversations and Debates* (Yale University Press).

Gillespie, John (2013) "Sartre and God: A Spiritual Odyssey? Part 1," *Sartre Studies International, 19:1*, pp. 71–90.

Gillespie, John (2021) "Sartre and Agamben: Confronting Nothingness and the (Apparent) Death of God" in *Agamben and the Existentialists*, eds. M. Norris & C. Dickinson (Edinburgh University Press), pp. 115–135.

Glazebrook, Trish (2016) "Heidegger and Environmental Philosophy" in *The Bloomsbury Companion to Heidegger* (Bloomsbury), pp. 433–440.

Goldberg, David & Ng, Jenna (2021) "Algorithmic Studies" in *Posthuman Glossary*, eds. R. Braidotti & M. Hlavajova (Bloomsbury), pp. 26–27.

Gordon, Lewis R. (2015) *What Fanon Said: A Philosophical Introduction to His Life and Thought* (Hurst & Co.).

Gosetti-Ferencei, Jennifer Anna (2021) *On Being and Becoming: An Existentialist Approach to Life* (Oxford University Press).

Guattari, Félix (2000) *The Three Ecologies*, tr. I. Pindar & P. Sutton (Athlone Press).

Guicharnaud, Jacques (1962) "Those Years: Existentialism 1943–1945" in *Sartre: A Collection of Critical Essays*, ed. E. Kern (Prentice-Hall), pp. 15–20.

Hamilton, William & Altizer, Thomas J.J. (1966) *Radical Theology and the Death of God* (Bobbs-Merrill).

Hansberry, Lorraine (1995) "Simone de Beauvoir and *The Second Sex*: An American Commentary" in *Words of Fire: An Anthology of African American Feminist Thought*, ed. B. Guy-Sheftall (The New Press), pp. 128–142.

Haraway, Donna (2016) *Staying with the Trouble: Making Kin in the Chthulucene* (University of Minnesota Press).

Harries, Karsten (2012) "The Antinomy of Being: Heidegger's Critique of Humanism" in *The Cambridge Companion to Existentialism*, ed. S. Crowell (Cambridge University Press), pp. 178–198.

Hayman, Ronald (1982) *Nietzsche: A Critical Life* (Penguin).

Hayman, Ronald (1986) *Writing Against: A Biography of Sartre* (Weidenfeld & Nicolson).

Hengehold, Laura (2024) "New Directions: De Beauvoir" in *The Bloomsbury Handbook of Existentialism*, eds. J. Reynolds, A. Woodward & F. Joseph (Bloomsbury), pp. 330–338.

Heter, Storm T. (2020) "Sartre and Anarchism" in *The Sartrean Mind*, eds. M.C. Eshleman & C.L. Mui (Routledge), pp. 528–540.

Hill Collins, Patricia (2017) "Simone de Beauvoir, Women's Oppression and Existential Freedom" in *Blackwell Companion to Beauvoir*, eds. N. Bauer & L. Hengehold (Wiley-Blackwell), pp. 325–338.

Howells, Christina (1981) "Sartre and Negative Theology," *Modern Language Review, 76: 3*, pp. 549–555.

Howells, Christina (1992) "Sartre and the Deconstruction of the Subject" in *The Cambridge Companion to Sartre*, ed. C. Howells (Cambridge University Press), pp. 318–352.

Howells, Christina (2011) *Mortal Subjects: Passions of the Soul in Late Twentieth-Century Thought* (Polity Press).

Hunt, Lester (1993) *Nietzsche and the Origin of Virtue* (Routledge).

Irigaray, Luce (1985) *Speculum of the Other Woman*, tr. G. Gill (Columbia University Press).

Jaarsma, Ada (2024) "Existentialism and (Dis)ability" in *The Bloomsbury Handbook of Existentialism*, eds. J. Reynolds, A. Woodward & F. Joseph (Bloomsbury), pp. 252–268.

Jackson, Zakiyyah (2020) *Becoming Human: Matter and Meaning in an Antiblack World* (New York University Press).

Jaspers, Karl (1965) Nietzsche: *An Introduction to the Understanding of His Philosophical Activity* (Gateway).

Jones, Rachel (2024) "Irigaray and Feminism in French Philosophy after Beauvoir" in *The Oxford Handbook of Modern French Philosophy*, eds. M. Sinclair & D. Whistler (Oxford University Press), pp. 334–352.

Joseph, Felicity & Reynolds, Jack (2024) "Existentialism, Phenomenology and Method" in *The Bloomsbury Handbook of Existentialism*, eds. J. Reynolds, A. Woodward & F. Joseph (Bloomsbury), pp. 14–29.

Jules-Rosette, Bennetta (2020) "Recasting Négritude: Jean-Paul Sartre and black intellectuals in post-war France" in *The Sartrean Mind*, eds. M.C. Eshleman & C.L. Mui (Routledge), pp. 387–401.

Kaufman, Eleanor (2024) "Literature and Modern French Philosophy" in *The Oxford Handbook of Modern French Philosophy*, eds. M. Sinclair & D. Whistler (Oxford University Press), pp. 661–679.

Kaufmann, Walter (2016) *Existentialism from Dostoevsky to Sartre* (Pickle Partners Publishing).

Kern, Edith (1962) "Introduction" in *Sartre: A Collection of Critical Essays* (Prentice-Hall), pp. 1–14.

Kirkpatrick, Kate (2017) *Sartre and Theology* (Bloomsbury).

Kirkpatrick, Kate (2022) *Becoming Beauvoir: A Life* (Bloomsbury).

Kirkpatrick, Kate (2024) "Early Existentialisms" in *The Oxford Handbook of Modern French Philosophy*, eds. M. Sinclair & D. Whistler (Oxford University Press), pp. 183–200.

Klaw, Barbara (2019) "On Reading Beauvoir's Early Writings, 1926–1930, as a Philosophy of Self-Help" in *Diary of a Philosophy Student, 1928/9, Volume 2*, eds. B. Klaw, S. de Beauvoir, S. Le Bon de Beauvoir, M. Simons & M. Timmermann (University of Illnois Press).

Kofman, Sarah (1998) "Baubo: Theological Perversion and Fetishism," in *Feminist Interpretations of Friedrich Nietzsche*, tr. T. Strong, eds. K. Oliver & M. Pearsall (Pennsylvania State University Press), pp. 21–49.

Kruks, Sonia (1981) *The Political Philosophy of Merleau-Ponty* (Harvester Press).

Kruks, Sonia (1990) *Situation and Human Existence: Freedom, Subjectivity, and Society* (Unwin Hyman).

Lacoste, Guillermine de (1999) "The Beauvoir and Lévy Interviews: Towards a Feminine Economy" in *Feminist Interpretations of Sartre*, ed. J.S. Murphy (Pennsylvania State University Press), pp. 272–298.

Laing, Ronald D. (1960) *The Divided Self* (Penguin).

Landes, Donald A. (2024) "Merleau-Ponty: A Bergsonian in the Making" in *The Oxford Handbook of Modern French Philosophy*, eds. M. Sinclair & D. Whistler (Oxford University Press), pp. 219–236.

Lemm, Vanessa (2021) "The Work of Art and the Death of God in Nietzsche and Agamben" in *Agamben and the Existentialists*, eds. M.A. Norris & C. Dickinson (Edinburgh University Press), pp. 83–99.

Levinas, Emmanuel (1974) *En Découvrant l'existence avec Husserl et Heidegger* (J. Vrin).

Levinas, Emmanuel (1998) *Entre Nous: Thinking of the Other*, tr. M. Smith & B. Harshaw (Columbia University Press).

Lykke, Nina (2023) "Vibrant Death" in *More Posthuman Glossary*, eds. R. Braidotti, E. Jones & G. Klumbytė (Bloomsbury), pp. 155–156.

Macey, David (2012) *Frantz Fanon: A Biography* (Verso).

Macquarrie, John (1973) *Existentialism* (Penguin).

Malpas, Jeff (2012) "Existentialism as Literature" in *The Cambridge Companion to Existentialism*, ed. S. Crowell (Cambridge University Press), pp. 291–321.

Manschot, Henk (2021) *Nietzsche and the Earth: Biography, Ecology, Politics*, tr. L. Waters (Bloomsbury).

Marcuse, Herbert (1968) *Negations* (Beacon).

Marcuse, Herbert (1983) *From Luther to Popper*, tr. J. de-Bres (Verso).

Marovich, Beatrice (2021) "Death and the Negative in Agamben and Beauvoir" in *Agamben and the Existentialists*, eds. M.A. Norris & C. Dickinson (Edinburgh University Press), pp. 139–154.

Massumi, Brian (2015) "The Supernormal Animal" in *The Nonhuman Turn*, ed. R. Grusin (University of Minnesota Press).

McBride, William L. (2009) "Taking a Distance: Exploring Some Points of Divergence between Beauvoir and Sartre" in *Beauvoir and Sartre: The Riddle of Influence*, eds. C. Daigle & J. Golomb (Indiana University Press), pp. 189–202.

McBride, William L. (2012) "Existentialism as a Cultural Movement" in *The Cambridge Companion to Existentialism*, ed. S. Crowell (Cambridge University Press), pp. 50–69.

Megill, Alan (1985) *Prophets of Extremity: Nietzsche, Heidegger, Foucault, Derrida* (University of California Press).

Merleau-Ponty, Maurice (2016) *Entretiens avec Georges Charbonnier* (Verdier).

Mészáros, István (1979) *The Work of Sartre: Search for Freedom* (Harvester Press).

Mirvish, Adrian (1996) "Sartre and the Problem of Other Embodied Minds," *Sartre Studies International*, 2:2, pp. 65–84.

Mitchell, Andrew J. (2016) "The Fourfold" in *The Bloomsbury Companion to Heidegger*, eds. F. Raffoul & E.S. Nelson (Bloomsbury), pp. 297–302.

Moi, Toril (1993) *Simone de Beauvoir: The Making of an Intellectual Woman* (Wiley).

Moorehead, Caroline (1974) "A Talk with Simone de Beauvoir," *New York Times*, June 2, pp. 16–34.

Morris, Katherine (2020) "Sartre on the Body" in *The Sartrean Mind*, eds. M.C. Eshleman & C.L. Mui (Routledge), pp. 225–238.

Murdoch, Iris (1999) *Sartre: Romantic Rationalist* (Vintage).

Mussett, Sharon (2020) "Nature as Threat and Escape in the Philosophies of Sartre and Beauvoir" in *The Sartrean Mind*, eds. M.C. Eshleman & C.L. Mui (Routledge), pp. 515–527.

Neimanis, Astrida & Hamilton, Jennifer Mae (2023) "Composting" in *More Posthuman Glossary*, eds. R. Braidotti, E. Jones & G. Klumbytė (Bloomsbury), pp. 19–21.

Nelson, Eric S. (2016) "Heidegger's *Black Notebooks*: National Socialism, Antisemitism, and the History of Being" in *The Bloomsbury Companion to Heidegger*, eds. F. Raffoul & E.S. Nelson (Bloomsbury), pp. 483–494.

Ngo, Helen (2024) "Existentialism and Racism" in *The Bloomsbury Handbook of Existentialism*, eds. J. Reynolds, A. Woodward & F. Joseph (Bloomsbury), pp. 290–305.

Noudelmann, François (2012) *The Philosopher's Touch: Sartre, Nietzsche and Barthes at the Piano*, tr. B. Reilly (Columbia University Press).

Noudelmann, François (2021) *Un Tout Autre Sartre* (Gallimard).

O'Byrne, Anne (2016) "Birth and Death" in *The Bloomsbury Companion to Heidegger*, eds. F. Raffoul & E.S. Nelson (Bloomsbury), pp. 263–267.

O'Shiel, Daniel (2019) *Sartre and Magic: Being, Emotion and Philosophy* (Bloomsbury).

Ott, Hugo (1994) *Martin Heidegger: A Political Life*, tr. A. Blunden (Fontana Press).

Parisi, Luciana (2021) "Computational Turn" in *Posthuman Glossary*, pp. 88–91.

Plank, William (1998) *The Quantum Nietzsche: The Will to Power and the Nature of Dissipative Systems* (Writers Club Press).

Raffoul, François (2016) "Dasein" in *The Bloomsbury Companion to Heidegger*, eds. F. Raffoul & E.S. Nelson (Bloomsbury), pp. 275–281.

Raffoul, François (2024) "Heidegger in Modern French Philosophy" in *The Oxford Handbook of Modern French Philosophy*, eds. M. Sinclair & D. Whistler (Oxford University Press), pp. 471–486.

Richardson, John (2020) *Nietzsche's Values* (Oxford University Press).

Richmond, Sarah (2018) "Translator's Introduction" in *Being and Nothingness* (Routledge), pp. xix–xxxvii.

Romdenh-Romluc, Komarine (2024) "Black Orpheus, Fanon and the Négritude Movement," *Sartre Studies International, 30:1*, pp. 47–63.

Rorty, Richard (1991) *Essays on Heidegger and Others* (Cambridge University Press).

Rouvroy, Antoinette & Klumbyté, Goda (2023) "Algorithmic Governmentality" in *More Posthuman Glossary*, eds. R. Braidotti, E. Jones & G. Klumbyté (Bloomsbury), pp. 10–12.

Rowbotham, Sheila (2011) "Foreword" in *The Second Sex*, S. de Beauvoir, tr. C. Borde & S. Malovany-Chevallier (Vintage), pp. ix–xix.

Ruin, Hans (2016) "Technology" in *The Bloomsbury Companion to Heidegger*, eds. F. Raffoul & E.S. Nelson (Bloomsbury), pp. 353–359.

Russon, John & Jacobson, Kirsten (2016) "Space: The Open in Which We Sojourn" in *The Bloomsbury Companion to Heidegger*, eds. F. Raffoul & E.S. Nelson (Bloomsbury), pp. 345–352.

Ryle, Gilbert (1978) "Review of Heidegger, *Sein und Zeit*" in *Heidegger and Modern Philosophy*, ed. M. Murray (Yale University Press).

Safranski, Rüdiger (2002) *Martin Heidegger: Between Good and Evil*, tr. E. Osers (Harvard University Press).

Safranski, Rüdiger (2003) *Nietzsche: A Philosophical Biography*, tr. S. Frisch (Granta Books).

Salomé, Lou (2001) *Nietzsche*, tr. S. Mandel (University of Illnois Press).

Sawyer, Dane (2015) "Playing Seriously with Bad Faith: A Derridean Intersection," *Sartre Studies International*, *21:1*, pp. 34–52.

Schmitt, Carl (1985) *The Crisis of Parliamentary Democracy*, tr. E. Kennedy (MIT Press).

Schwarzer, Alice (1984) *Simone de Beauvoir Today: Conversations 1972–1982* (Hogarth Press).

Shapiro, Gary (2016) *Nietzsche's Earth: Great Events, Great Politics* (University of Chicago Press).

Shatz, Adam (2025) *The Rebel's Clinic: The Revolutionary Lives of Frantz Fanon* (Head of Zeus).

Sheehan, Thomas (2015) *Making Sense of Heidegger: A Paradigm Shift* (Rowman & Littlefield).

Sheikh, Shela (2021) "Violence" in *Posthuman Glossary*, eds. R. Braidotti & M. Hlavajova (Bloomsbury), pp. 449–450.

Sherman, David (2024) "Existentialism and Politics" in *The Bloomsbury Handbook of Existentialism*, eds. J. Reynolds, A. Woodward & F. Joseph (Bloomsbury), pp. 52–68.

Siegler Marcel (2023) *Needful Structures: The Dialectics of Action, Technology, and Society in Sartre's Later Philosophy* (Transcript Publishing).

Siemens, Herman (2015) "Reassessing Radical Democratic Theory in the Light of Nietzsche's Ontology of Conflict" in *Nietzsche and Political Thought*, ed. K. Ansell-Pearson (Bloomsbury), pp. 83–105.

Siemens, Herman (2018) "Nietzsche's Agon" in *The Nietzschean Mind*, ed. P. Katsafanas (Routledge), pp. 314–333.

Simons, Margaret (1999) *Beauvoir and The Second Sex* (Rowman & Littlefield).

Simons, Margaret & Benjamin, Jessica (1979) "Simone de Beauvoir: An Interview," *Feminist Studies*, *5:2*, pp. 330–345.

Smith, Dominic (2024) "Existentialism and Technology" in *The Bloomsbury Handbook of Existentialism*, eds. J. Reynolds, A. Woodward & F. Joseph (Bloomsbury), pp. 236–251.

Solomon, Robert C. (1988) *Continental Philosophy since 1750* (Oxford University Press).

Solomon, Robert C. (2003) *Living with Nietzsche: What the Great "Immoralist" Has to Teach Us* (Oxford University Press).

Sorgner, Stefan (2009) "Nietzsche, the Overman and Transhumanism," *Journal of Evolution & Technology*, *20*, 29–42.

Staal, Jonas (2021) "Stateless State" in *Posthuman Glossary*, pp. 404–406.

Stauffer, Jill (2016) "Heidegger and Levinas" in *The Bloomsbury Companion to Heidegger*, eds. F. Raffoul & E.S. Nelson (Bloomsbury), pp. 393–399.

Stiegler, Bernard (2015) *La Société automatique: L'Avenir du travail* (Fayard).

Stolorow, Robert D. (2016) "Heidegger and Post-Cartesian Psychoanalysis" in *The Bloomsbury Companion to Heidegger*, eds. F. Raffoul & E.S. Nelson (Bloomsbury), pp. 451–458.

Thomas, R. Hinton (1983) *Nietzsche in German Politics and Society, 1890–1918* (Manchester University Press).

Towarnicki, Frédéric de (1993) *À la rencontre de Heidegger* (Gallimard).
Trawny, Peter (2019) *Heidegger: A Critical Introduction*, tr. R. Therezo (Polity Press).
Verkerk, Willow (2020) *Nietzsche and Friendship* (Bloomsbury).
Warnock, Mary (1989) *Existentialism* (Oxford University Press).
Webber, Jonathan (2018) *Rethinking Existentialism* (Oxford University Press).
Weheliye, Alexander (2014) *Habeas Viscus: Racializing Assemblages, Biopolitics, and Black Feminist Theories of the Human* (Duke University Press).
Welch, Andrew (2021) "Endless Ontology: Agamben and Sartre on Death" in *Agamben and the Existentialists*, eds. V. Lemm & B. Marovich (Bloomsbury), pp. 155–173.
Wheeler, Michael & Di Paolo, Ezequiel (2024) "Existentialism and Cognitive Science" in *The Bloomsbury Handbook of Existentialism*, eds. J. Reynolds, A. Woodward & F. Joseph (Bloomsbury), pp. 203–218.
Wicks, Robert L. (2020) *Introduction to Existentialism: From Kierkegaard to the Seventh Seal* (Bloomsbury).
Wild, John D. (1962) "The New Empiricism" in *Sartre: A Collection of Critical Essays*, ed. E. Kern (Prentice-Hall), pp. 136–141.
Wolin, Richard (1990) *The Politics of Being: The Political Thought of Martin Heidegger* (Columbia University Press).
Wolin, Richard (1992) *The Terms of Cultural Criticism: The Frankfurt School, Existentialism, Poststructuralism* (Columbia University Press).
Wolin, Richard (2022) *Heidegger in Ruins: Between Philosophy and Ideology* (Yale University Press).
Wood, Robert E. (2005) "Introduction" in *Music and Philosophy*, G. Marcel, tr. S. Maddux & R.E. Wood (Marquette University Press), pp. 10–39.
Woodward, Ashley (2011) *Understanding Nietzscheanism* (Acumen).
Young, Eugene, Genosko, Gary & Watson, Janell (2013) *The Deleuze & Guattari Dictionary* (Bloomsbury).
Zimmerman, Michael E. (2007) "Heidegger, Buddhism, and Deep Ecology" in *The Cambridge Companion to Heidegger*, ed. C. Guignon (Cambridge University Press), pp. 293–325.
Zohar, Dina (1991) *The Quantum Self* (Flamingo).

## *Primary Texts*

Beauvoir, Simone de (1944) *Pyrrhus et Cinéas* (Gallimard) **[PC]**.
Beauvoir, Simone de (1952) *America Day by Day*, tr. P. Dudley (Gerald Duckworth & Co. Ltd).
Beauvoir, Simone de (1955) "Merleau-Ponty et le pseudo-Sartrisme," *Les Temps Modernes*, *114–115*, pp. 201–272 **[MPPS]**.
Beauvoir, Simone de (1963) *Memoirs of a Dutiful Daughter*, tr. J. Kirkup (Penguin) **[MDD]**.
Beauvoir, Simone de (1965) *Que peut la littérature*? (Union Générale d'Editions).
Beauvoir, Simone de (1976) *Force of Circumstance*, tr. A. Deutsch (Penguin) **[FC]**.
Beauvoir, Simone de (1977) *All Said and Done*, tr. P. O' Brian (Penguin) **[ASD]**.
Beauvoir, Simone de (1983) *The Prime of Life*, tr. P. O' Brian (Penguin) **[PL]**.

Beauvoir, Simone de (1985) *Adieux: A Farewell to Sartre*, tr. P. O' Brian (Penguin) **[FS]**.
Beauvoir, Simone de (1985) *A Very Easy Death*, tr. P. O'Brian (Pantheon).
Beauvoir, Simone de (1994) *The Ethics of Ambiguity*, tr. B. Frechtman (Citadel) **[EA]**.
Beauvoir, Simone de (1997) *Old Age*, tr. P. O' Brian (Penguin) **[OA]**.
Beauvoir, Simone de (1998) *A Translatlantic Love Affair: Letters to Nelson Algren* (New Press).
Beauvoir, Simone de (2004) *Philosophical Writings*, eds. M. Simons, M. Timmerman & M. Mader (University of Illnois Press) **[PW]**.
Beauvoir, Simone de (2011) *The Second Sex*, tr. C. Borde & S. Malovany-Chevallier (Vintage) **[SS]**.
Beauvoir, Simone de (2011) *"The Useless Mouths" and Other Literary Writings*, eds. M. Simons & M. Timmermann (University of Illinois Press).
Beauvoir, Simone de (2015) *Feminist Writings*, eds. M. Simons & M. Timmerman (University of Illnois Press) **[FW]**.
Beauvoir, Simone de (2018) *Mémoires 1*, eds. J.-L. Jeanelle & E. Lecarme-Tabone (Gallimard).
Beauvoir, Simone de (2019) *Diary of a Philosophy Student, Volume 2 1928–9*, eds. B. Klaw, S. Le Bon de Beauvoir & M. Simons (University of Illnois Press).
Beauvoir, Simone de (2024) *Diary of a Philosophy Student, Volume 3 1926–30*, eds. B. Klaw, S. Le Bon de Beauvoir, M. Simons & M. Timmermann (University of Illnois Press).
Berdyaev, Nikolai (1947) *Solitude and Society*, tr. G. Reavey (Geoffrey Bles).
Fanon, Frantz (1969) *Pour la revolution africaine: Écrits politiques* (Maspero).
Fanon, Frantz (2001) *The Wretched of the Earth*, tr. C. Farrington (Penguin) **[WE]**.
Fanon, Frantz (2008) *Black Skin, White Masks*, tr. R. Philcox (Penguin) **[BSWM]**.
Fanon, Frantz (2015) *Écrits sur l'aliénation et la liberté*, eds. J. Khalfa & R.C. Young (La Découverte).
Heidegger, Martin (1949) *Existence and Being*, ed. W. Brock (Regnery-Gateway) **[EB]**.
Heidegger, Martin (1949) *Was ist Metaphysik?* (Frankfurt).
Heidegger, Martin (1950) *Holzwege* (Frankfurt).
Heidegger, Martin (1958) *Introduction to Metaphysics*, tr. R. Mannheim (New Haven) **[IM]**.
Heidegger, Martin (1962) *Being and Time*, tr. J. Macquarrie & E. Robinson (Basil Blackwell) **[BT]**.
Heidegger, Martin (1966) *Discourse on Thinking*, eds. J. Anderson & E. Freund (Harper & Row) **[DT]**.
Heidegger, Martin (1971) *Poetry, Language, Thought*, tr. A. Hofstadter (Harper & Row) **[PLT]**.
Heidegger, Martin (1972) *What Is Called Thinking?*, tr. J. Glenn Gray (Harper & Row) **[WCT]**.
Heidegger, Martin (1973) *The End of Philosophy*, tr. J. Stambaugh (Harper & Row) **[EP]**.
Heidegger, Martin (1977) *The Question Concerning Technology and Other Essays*, tr. W. Lovitt (Harper & Row) [QCT].
Heidegger, Martin (1978–) *Martin Heidegger's Gesamtausgabe* (Vittorio Klostermann) **[GA]**.

Heidegger, Martin (1981) "Only a God Can Save Us" in *Heidegger: The Man and the Thinker*, ed. T. Sheehan (Precedent Publishing) **[OG]**.

Heidegger, Martin (1982) *The Basic Problems of Phenomenology* (Indiana University Press) **[BPP]**.

Heidegger, Martin (1990) *Kant and the Problem of Metaphysics*, tr. R. Taft (Bloomington).

Heidegger, Martin (1993) *Basic Writings*, ed. D. Farrell Krell (Routledge) **[BW]**.

Heidegger, Martin (2009) *Heidegger-Jahrbuch, Vol. 4* (Karl Alber) **[HJ]**.

Heidegger, Martin (2016) *Martin Heidegger's "Black Notebooks"* (Columbia University Press).

Jaspers, Karl (1951) *The Way to Wisdom*, tr. E. & C. Paul (London).

Jaspers, Karl (1957) *The Philosophy of Karl Jaspers*, ed. P.A. Schlipp (New York).

Jaspers, Karl (1966) *Nietzsche: An Introduction to the Understanding of His Philosophical Activity*, tr. C. Wallraff & F. Schmitz, (Gateway).

Kierkegaard, Søren (1941) *Concluding Unscientific Postscript*, tr. D. Swenson & W. Lowrie (Princeton University Press) **[CUP]**.

Kierkegaard, Søren (1946) "The Present Age" in *A Kierkegaard Anthology*, ed. R. Bretall (Modern Library).

Kierkegaard, Søren (1962) *Philosophical Fragments*, tr. D.F. Swenson (Princeton University Press) **[PF]**.

Kierkegaard, Søren (1962) *Works of Love*, tr. H.V & E.H. Hong (Harper & Row) **[WL]**.

Kierkegaard, Søren (1975) *Søren Kierkegaard's Journals and Papers (Volume 3)*, tr. H.V Hong, E.H. Hong & G. Malantschuk (Indiana University Press).

Kierkegaard, Søren (1978) *Two Ages: The Age of Revolution and the Present Age: A Literary Review*, tr. H.V & E.H. Hong (Princeton University Press).

Kierkegaard, Søren (1980) *The Concept of Anxiety*, tr. R. Thomte & A. B. Anderson (Princeton University Press) **[CA]**.

Kierkegaard, Søren (1988) *Either/Or, Part II*, tr. H.V & E.H. Hong (Princeton University Press).

Kierkegaard, Søren (1989) *The Sickness Unto Death*, tr. A. Hannay (Penguin) **[SD]**.

Kierkegaard, Søren (1992) *Either/Or: A Fragment of Life*, tr. A. Hannay (Penguin) **[EO]**.

Kierkegaard, Søren (1996) *Papers and Journals: A Selection*, tr. Alistair Hannay (Penguin) **[PJ]**.

Kierkegaard, Søren (2006) *Fear and Trembling*, tr. S. Walsh (Cambridge University Press) **[FT]**.

Kierkegaard, Søren (2007) *Kierkegaard's Journals and Notebooks, Vol. 1*, eds. N. Cappelorn, A. Hannay, D. Kangas, B. Kirmmse, G. Pattison, J. Rasmussen, V. Rumble & K. Söderquist (Princeton University Press).

Kierkegaard, Søren (2008) *Kierkegaard's Journals and Notebooks, Vol. 2*, eds. N. Cappelorn, A. Hannay, D. Kangas, B. Kirmmse, G. Pattison, J. Rasmussen, V. Rumble & K. Söderquist (Princeton University Press).

Kierkegaard, Søren (2009) *The Point of View*, tr. H.V & E.H. Hong (Princeton University Press).

Kierkegaard, Søren (2011) *Kierkegaard's Journals and Notebooks, Vol. 4*, eds. N. Cappelorn, A. Hannay, D. Kangas, B. Kirmmse, G. Pattison, J. Rasmussen, V. Rumble & K. Söderquist (Princeton University Press).

Kierkegaard, Søren (2012) *Kierkegaard's Journals and Notebooks, Vol. 5*, eds. N. Cappelorn, A. Hannay, D. Kangas, B. Kirmmse, G. Pattison, J. Rasmussen, V. Rumble & K. Söderquist (Princeton University Press).

Kierkegaard, Søren (2013) *Kierkegaard's Journals and Notebooks, Vol. 6*, eds. N. Cappelorn, A. Hannay, D. Kangas, B. Kirmmse, G. Pattison, J. Rasmussen, V. Rumble & K. Söderquist (Princeton University Press).

Kierkegaard, Søren (2016) *The Lily of the Field and the Bird of the Air: Three Godly Discourses*, tr. B. Kirmmse (Princeton University Press).

Marcel, Gabriel (1925) "Existence et objectivité," *Revue de métaphysique et de morale, 32:2*, pp. 175–195 **[EO]**.

Marcel, Gabriel (1949) *The Philosophy of Existence* (Philosophical Library) **[PE]**.

Marcel, Gabriel (1950) "What Is a Free Person?" *Der Monat*, no. 24.

Marcel, Gabriel (1951) *Homo Viator: Introduction to a Metaphysic of Hope* (Victor Gollancz) **[HV]**.

Marcel, Gabriel (1956a) *The Mystery of Being, 2 Vols*, tr. G.S. Fraser (Gateway) **[MB]**.

Marcel, Gabriel (1956b) *The Philosophy of Existentialism*, tr. R. Rosthal (Philosophical Library) **[PEX]**.

Marcel, Gabriel (1963) *Existential Background of Human Dignity* (Harvard University Press) **[EB]**.

Marcel, Gabriel (1965) *Being and Having* (Harper & Row) **[BH]**.

Marcel, Gabriel (1967) *Essai de philosophie concrète* (Gallimard) **[EPC]**.

Marcel, Gabriel (1973) *Tragic Wisdom and Beyond*, tr. S. Jolin & P. McCormick (Northwestern University Press) **[TW]**.

Marcel, Gabriel (2002a) *Awakenings* (Marquette University Press) **[AW]**.

Marcel, Gabriel (2002b) *Creative Fidelity*, tr. R. Rosthal (Fordham University Press) **[CF]**.

Marcel, Gabriel (2005) *Music and Philosophy*, tr. S. Maddux & R.E. Wood (Marquette University Press) **[MP]**.

Merleau-Ponty, Maurice (1962) *Phenomenology of Perception*, tr. C. Smith (Humanities Press) [PP].

Merleau-Ponty, Maurice (1964a) *Sense and Non-Sense*, tr. H. & P. Dreyfus (Northwestern University Press) [SNS].

Merleau-Ponty, Maurice (1964b) *Signs*, tr. R. McCleary (Northwestern University Press) [S].

Merleau-Ponty, Maurice (1968) *The Visible and the Invisible*, tr. A. Lingis (Northwestern University Press) [VI].

Merleau-Ponty, Maurice (1969) *Humanism and Terror*, tr. J. O'Neill (Beacon Press) [HT].

Merleau-Ponty, Maurice (1973) *Adventures of the Dialectic*, tr. J. Bien (Northwestern University Press) [AD].

Merleau-Ponty, Maurice (1973) *The Prose of the World*, tr. J. O'Neill (Northwestern University Press) [PW].

Merleau-Ponty, Maurice (1975) "Philosophie et Non-Philosophie depuis Hegel (II). Notes de cours," ed. C. Lefort, *Textures,* No. 10–11, Belgium.

Merleau-Ponty, Maurice (1993) *The Merleau-Ponty Aesthetics Reader*, tr. M. Smith (Northwestern University Press).

Merleau-Ponty, Maurice (2004) *The World of Perception*, tr. O. Davis (Routledge).

Nietzsche, Friedrich (1911) "The Greek State" in *The Complete Works of Friedrich Nietzsche, Vol.* 2, ed. O. Levy, tr. M. Mügge (T.A. Foulis) **[G.S]**.
Nietzsche, Friedrich (1911) "Philosophy in the Tragic Age of the Greeks" in *The Complete Works of Friedrich Nietzsche, Vol.* 2, ed. O. Levy, tr. M. Mügge (T.A. Foulis) **[PTAG]**.
Nietzsche, Friedrich (1967) *The Birth of Tragedy and the Case of Wagner*, tr. W. Kaufmann (Vintage) **[BT]**, **[CW]**.
Nietzsche, Friedrich (1967) Ecce Homo, tr. W. Kaufmann (Random House) **[EH]**.
Nietzsche, Friedrich (1967) *On the Genealogy of Morals*, tr. R. J. Hollingdale & W. Kaufmann (Random House) **[GM]**.
Nietzsche, Friedrich (1967) *The Will to Power*, tr. R. J. Hollingdale & W. Kaufmann (Random House) **[WP]**.
Nietzsche, Friedrich (1968) The Antichrist, tr. R. J. Hollingdale (Penguin) **[A]**.
Nietzsche, Friedrich (1968) *Twilight of the Idols*, tr. R. J.Hollingdale (Penguin) **[TI]**.
Nietzsche, Friedrich (1969) *Selected Letters of Friedrich Nietzsche*, ed. & tr. C. Middleton (University of Chicago Press).
Nietzsche, Friedrich (1969) *Thus Spoke Zarathustra*, tr. R. J.Hollingdale (Penguin) **[Z]**.
Nietzsche, Friedrich (1973) *Beyond Good and Evil*, tr. R. J.Hollingdale (Penguin) **[BGE]**.
Nietzsche, Friedrich (1980) *Sämtliche Werke, Kritische Studienausgabe, 15 vols*, eds. G. Colli & M. Montinari (Walter de Gruyter) **[KSW]**.
Nietzsche, Friedrich (1982) *Daybreak*, tr. R. J. Hollingdale (Cambridge University Press) **[D]**.
Nietzsche, Friedrich (1986) "Assorted Maxims and Opinions" in *Human, All Too Human*, tr. R. J. Hollingdale (Cambridge University Press) **[AOM]**.
Nietzsche, Friedrich (1986) *Human, All Too Human*, tr. R. J. Hollingdale (Cambridge University Press) **[HH]**.
Nietzsche, Friedrich (1986) *Sämtliche Briefe, Kritische Studienausgabe, 8 vols*, eds. G. Colli & M. Montinari (Walter de Gruyter) **[KSB]**.
Nietzsche, Friedrich (1986) *The Wanderer and His Shadow*, tr. R. J. Hollingdale (Cambridge University Press) **[WS]**.
Nietzsche, Friedrich (1997) *Untimely Meditations*, tr. R.J. Hollingdale (Cambridge University Press) **[UM]**.
Nietzsche, Friedrich (2003) *Writings from the Late Notebooks*, tr. K. Sturge (Cambridge University Press) **[LN]**.
Nietzsche, Friedrich (2006) "On Truth and Lies in a Nonmoral Sense" in *The Nietzsche Reader*, eds. K. Ansell-Pearson & D. Large (Blackwell), pp. 114–123.
Nietzsche, Friedrich (2018) *The Joyous Science*, tr. R. Kevin Hill (Penguin) **[JS]**.
Ortega Y Gasset, Jose (1962) *History as a System and Other Essays Towards a Philosophy of History* (W.W. Norton & Co.).
Sartre, Jean-Paul (1939) *Le Mur* (Gallimard).
Sartre, Jean-Paul (1947) *Situations I* (Gallimard).
Sartre, Jean-Paul (1949) *Situations III* (Gallimard).
Sartre, Jean-Paul (1957) *The Transcendence of the Ego*, tr. F. Williams & R. Kirkpatrick (Noonday Press) **[TE]**.
Sartre, Jean-Paul(1965) Nausea, tr. R. Baldick (Penguin) **[N]**.
Sartre, Jean-Paul (1965) *What Is Literature?*, tr. B. Frechtman (Harper & Row) **[WL]**.
Sartre, Jean-Paul (1966) "Jean-Paul Sartre répond," *L'Arc*, *30*, pp. 87–96.

Sartre, Jean-Paul (1968) *Search for a Method*, tr. H. Barnes (Vintage Books) **[SM]**.
Sartre, Jean-Paul (1969) "Itinerary of a Thought: Interview with Jean-Paul Sartre," *New Left Review*, *58*, pp. 43–66 **[IT]**.
Sartre, Jean-Paul (1970) "Intentionality: A Fundamental Idea of Husserl's Phenomenology," *Journal of the British Society for Phenomenology*, *1:2*, pp. 4–5.
Sartre, Jean-Paul (1972) *Words*, tr.I. Clephane (Penguin) **[W]**.
Sartre, Jean-Paul (1974) *L'idiot de la famille, Vol. 3* (NRF/Gallimard) **[IF3]**.
Sartre, Jean-Paul (1974) *The Writings of Jean-Paul Sartre* (with Contat, Michel & Rybalka, Michel), tr. R. McCleary (Northwestern University Press).
Sartre, Jean-Paul (1976) *Black Orpheus*, tr. S. Allen (Présence Africaine) **[BO]**.
Sartre, Jean-Paul (1976) *Critique of Dialectical Reason: Theory of Practical Ensembles, Vol. 1*, tr. A. Sheridan-Smith (New Left Books) **[CDR]**.
Sartre, Jean-Paul (1977a) *Life/Situations: Essays Written and Spoken*, tr. P. Auster & L. Davis (Pantheon).
Sartre, Jean-Paul (1977b) *Situations 1–10* (Gallimard).
Sartre, Jean-Paul (1979a) "Entretien avec Jean-Paul Sartre" (with Catherine Clément & Bernard Pingaud), *L'Arc*, *November*, pp. 33–37.
Sartre, Jean-Paul (1979b) "La Gauche, désespoir et Espoir" (with Catherine Clément), *Le Matin*, *November 10*.
Sartre, Jean-Paul (1980) *Situations VIII* (Gallimard).
Sartre, Jean-Paul (1981) *The Family Idiot, Vol. 1*, tr. C. Cosman (University of Chicago Press) **[FI]**.
Sartre, Jean-Paul (1981a) "An Interview with Jean-Paul Sartre" in *The Philosophy of Jean-Paul Sartre*, ed. P.A. Schilpp (La Salle).
Sartre, Jean-Paul (1981b) *Oeuvres Romanesques*, eds. M. Contat & M. Rybalka (Gallimard).
Sartre, Jean-Paul (1982) *Three Plays* (Penguin).
Sartre, Jean-Paul (1983) *Cahiers pour une morale* (Gallimard) **[CM]**.
Sartre, Jean-Paul (1983) *Lettres au castor et á quelques autres* (Gallimard).
Sartre, Jean-Paul (1984) *The War Diaries of Jean-Paul Sartre, November 1939–March 1940*, tr. Q. Hoare (Pantheon) **[WD]**.
Sartre, Jean-Paul (1985) *Existentialism and Human Emotions*, tr. B. Frechtman (Citadel Press) **[EH]**.
Sartre, Jean-Paul (1987) *The Family Idiot: Gustave Flaubert 1821–1857, Vol. 2*, tr. C. Cosman (University of Chicago Press) **[FI2]**.
Sartre, Jean-Paul (1987) *The Family Idiot: Gustave Flaubert 1821–1857, Vol. 3*, tr. C. Cosman (University of Chicago Press) **[FI3]**.
Sartre, Jean-Paul (1988) *Mallarmé, or the Poet of Nothingness*, tr. E. Sturm (Pennsylvania State University Press).
Sartre, Jean-Paul (1990) *Ecrits de jeunesse*, eds. M. Contat & M. Rybalka (Gallimard) **[EJ]**.
Sartre, Jean-Paul (1991) *Critique of Dialectical Reason: The Intelligibility of History, Vol. 2*, tr. A. Sheridan-Smith (Verso) **[CDR2]**.
Sartre, Jean-Paul (1991) *The Family Idiot: Gustave Flaubert 1821–1857, Vol. 4*, tr. C. Cosman (University of Chicago Press) **[FI4]**.

Sartre, Jean-Paul (1991) *L'espoir maintenant: les entretiens de 1980* (Verdier) **[EM]**.
Sartre, Jean-Paul (1993) *The Family Idiot: Gustave Flaubert 1821–1857, Vol. 5*, tr. C. Cosman (University of Chicago Press) **[FI5]**.
Sartre, Jean-Paul (1993) *Quiet Moments in a War: The Letters of Jean-Paul Sartre to Simone de Beauvoir, 1940–1963*, ed. S. de Beauvoir (Charles Scribner's Sons).
Sartre, Jean-Paul (1995) *Literary and Philosophical Essays* (Criterion Books).
Sartre, Jean-Paul (1996) *Hope Now* (with B. Lévy) (Gallimard) **[HN]**.
Sartre, Jean-Paul (2001) *Colonialism and Neo-Colonialism*, tr. A. Haddow, S. Brewer & T. McWilliams (Routledge).
Sartre, Jean-Paul (2002) *Sketch for a Theory of the Emotions*, tr. P. Mairet (Routledge) **[STE]**.
Sartre, Jean-Paul (2003) "About Munich," tr. E. Bowman, *Sartre Studies International*, *9:2*, pp. 7–8.
Sartre, Jean-Paul (2004) *The Imaginary: A Phenomenological Psychology of the Imagination*, tr. J. Webber (Routledge) **[IM]**.
Sartre, Jean-Paul (2008) *Between Existentialism and Marxism*, tr. J. Mathews (Verso).
Sartre, Jean-Paul (2010) "A New Mystic" in *Critical Essays*, tr. C. Turner (Seagull Book).
Sartre, Jean-Paul (2012) *The Imagination*, tr. K. Williford & D. Rudrauf (Routledge) **[I]**.
Sartre, Jean-Paul (2012) *Saint Genet: Actor and Martyr*, tr. B. Frechtman (University of Minnesota Press) **[SG]**.
Sartre, Jean-Paul (2014) "Lettre à Gabriel Marcel de Jean-Paul Sartre," *BNF Revue* 248 (Paris).
Sartre, Jean-Paul (2018) *Being and Nothingness: An Essay in Phenomenological Ontology*, tr. S. Richmond (Routledge) **[BN]**.
Tillich, Paul (1952) *The Courage to Be* (William Collins Sons).
Tillich, Paul (1956) "The Nature and the Significance of Existentialist Thought," *The Journal of Philosophy*, *53:23*, pp. 739–748.

# FURTHER READING

## *Chapter 1*

Gillespie, John (2021) "The Death of God" in *Agamben and the Existentialists* (Edinburgh University Press).

Kirkpatrick, Kate (2017) *Sartre and Theology* (Bloomsbury).

Pattison, George (2024) "Existentialism and Religion" in *The Bloomsbury Handbook of Existentialism* (Bloomsbury).

Westphal, Merold (2012) "Existentialism and Religion" in *The Cambridge Companion to Existentialism* (Cambridge University Press).

Woodward, Ashley (2011) *Understanding Nietzscheanism* (Acumen).

## *Chapter 2*

Cannon, Betty (2013) "Psychoanalysis and Existential Psychoanalysis" in *Jean-Paul Sartre: Key Concepts* (Acumen).

Detmer, David (2013) "Bad Faith" in *Jean-Paul Sartre: Key Concepts* (Acumen).

Edwards, Mary L. (2023) *Sartre's Existential Psychoanalysis: Knowing Others* (Bloomsbury).

Kirsner, Douglas (2024) "Existentialism, Psychoanalysis and Psychotherapy" in *The Bloomsbury Handbook of Existentialism* (Bloomsbury).

Stolorow, Robert D. (2016) "Heidegger and Post-Cartesian Psychoanalysis" in *The Bloomsbury Companion to Heidegger* (Bloomsbury).

## *Chapter 3*

Abram, David (1997) *The Spell of the Sensuous* (Vintage Books).

Ally, Matthew (2017) *Ecology and Existence: Bringing Sartre in from the Water's Edge* (Lexington Books).

Bennett, Jane (2010) *Vibrant Matter: A Political Ecology of Things* (Duke University Press).

Glazebrook, Trish (2016) "Heidegger and Environmental Philosophy" in *The Bloomsbury Companion to Heidegger* (Bloomsbury).

Manschot, Henk (2021) *Nietzsche and the Earth: Biography, Ecology, Politics* (Bloomsbury).

## *Chapter 4*

Belle, Kathryn Sophia (2024) *Beauvoir and Belle: A Black Feminist Critique of the Second Sex* (Oxford University Press).

Boulé, Jean-Pierre (2005) *Sartre, Self-Formation and Masculinities* (Berghahn).

Kirkpatrick, Kate (2022) *Becoming Beauvoir* (Bloomsbury).

Oliver, Karen (1995) *Womanizing Nietzsche: Philosophy's Relation to the "Feminine"* (Routledge).
Stendera, Marilyn (2024) "Existentialism and Gender" in *The Bloomsbury Handbook of Existentialism* (Bloomsbury).

## *Chapter 5*

Bernasconi, Robert (2023) *Critical Philosophy of Race* (Oxford University Press).
Gordon, Lewis, R. (2015) *What Fanon Said* (Hurst).
Macey, David (2012) *Frantz Fanon: A Biography* (Verso).
Ngo, Helen (2024) "Existentialism and Racism" in *The Bloomsbury Handbook of Existentialism* (Bloomsbury).
Wolin, Richard (2022) *Heidegger in Ruins: Between Philosophy and Ideology* (Yale University Press).

## *Chapter 6*

Cummings, Naomi (2000) *The Sonic Self: Musical Subjectivity and Signification*, (Indiana University Press).
Marcel, Gabriel (2005) *Music and Philosophy* (Marquette University Press).
Noudelmann, François (2012) *The Philosopher's Touch: Sartre, Nietzsche and Barthes at the Piano* (Columbia University Press).
Wicks, Robert, L. (2020) *Introduction to Existentialism: From Kierkegaard to The Seventh Seal* (Bloomsbury).
Wittmann, Heine (2009) *Aesthetics in Sartre and Camus: The Challenge of Freedom* (Peter Lang).

## *Chapter 7*

Abram, David (1997) *The Spell of the Sensuous* (Vintage Books).
Ally, Matthew C. (2017) *Ecology and Existence: Bringing Sartre to the Water's Edge* (Lexington Books).
O'Shiel, Daniel (2019) *Sartre and Magic: Being, Emotion and Philosophy* (Bloomsbury).
Wild, John D. (1962) "The New Empiricism" in *Sartre: A Collection of Critical Essays* (Prentice Hall).
Wolin, Richard (1992) *The Terms of Cultural Criticism: The Frankfurt School, Existentialism, Poststructuralism* (Columbia University Press).

## *Chapter 8*

Ansell-Pearson, Keith (ed.) (2015) *Nietzsche and Political Thought* (Bloomsbury).
Kruks, Sonia (1981) *The Political Philosophy of Merleau-Ponty* (Harvester Wheatsheaf).
Remley, William (2018) *Jean-Paul Sartre's Anarchist Philosophy* (Bloomsbury).
Sherman, David (2024) "Existentialism and Politics" in *The Bloomsbury Handbook to Existentialism* (Bloomsbury).
Wolin, Richard (1990) *The Politics of Being: The Political Thought of Martin Heidegger* (Columbia University Press).

## *Chapter 9*

Davis, Colin (2024) "Existentialism and Literature" in *The Bloomsbury Handbook of Existentialism* (Bloomsbury).
Eshleman, Matthew C. (2009) 'Beauvoir and Sartre on Freedom, Intersubjectivity, and Normative Justification' in *Beauvoir and Sartre: The Riddle of Influence* (Indiana University Press).
Kaufman, Eleanor (2024) "Existentialism as Literature" in *The Oxford Handbook of Modern French Philosophy* (Oxford University Press).
McCumber, John (2016) "Language" in *The Bloomsbury Companion to Heidegger* (Bloomsbury).
Schrift, Alan (1990) *Nietzsche and The Question of Interpretation* (Routledge).
Vasey, Craig (2020) "Sartre's Fiction" in *The Sartrean Mind* (Routledge).

## *Chapter 10*

Ansell-Pearson, Keith (1997) *Viroid Life: Perspectives on Nietzsche and the Transhuman Condition* (Routledge).
Ruin, Hans (2016) "Technology" in *The Bloomsbury Companion to Heidegger* (Bloomsbury).
Sheehan, Thomas J. (2015) *Making Sense of Heidegger* (Rowman & Littlefield).
Siegler, Marcel (2023) *Needful Structures: The Dialectics of Action, Technology, and Society in Sartre's Later Philosophy* (Transcript Publishing).
Smith, Dominic (2024) "Existentialism and Technology" in *The Bloomsbury Handbook of Existentialism* (Bloomsbury).

## *Chapter 11*

Aho, Kevin (2016) "The Body" in *The Bloomsbury Companion to Heidegger* (Bloomsbury).
Carman, Taylor (2012) "Merleau-Ponty on body, flesh, and visibility" in *The Cambridge Companion to Existentialism* (Cambridge University Press).
Daigle, Christine (2021) *Nietzsche as Phenomenologist: Becoming What One Is* (Edinburgh University Press).
Jaarsma, Ada (2024) "Existentialism and (Dis)ability" in *The Bloomsbury Handbook of Existentialism* (Bloomsbury).
Morris, Katherine (2020) "Sartre on the Body" in *The Sartrean Mind* (Routledge).

## *Chapter 12*

Caws, Peter (2013) "Sartre's Theory of Groups" in *Jean-Paul Sartre: Key Concepts* (Acumen).
Kruks, Sonia (1990) *Situation and Human Existence: Freedom, Subjectivity and Society* (Unwin Hyman).
Warren, Mark (1991) *Nietzsche and Political Thought* (MIT Press).
Webber, Jonathan (2018) *Rethinking Existentialism* (Routledge).
Wolin, Richard (1990) *The Politics of Being* (Columbia University Press).

## *Chapter 13*

Kirkpatrick, Kate (2022) *Becoming Beauvoir: A Life* (Bloomsbury).
Kruks, Sonia (1990) *Situation and Human Existence* (Unwin Hyman).

Macquarrie, John (1973) *Existentialism* (Penguin).
Webber, Jonathan (2018) *Rethinking Existentialism* (Routledge).

## *Chapter 14*

Bell, Linda (1989) *Sartre's Ethics of Authenticity* (University of Alabama Press).
Daigle, Christine (2021) *Nietzsche as Phenomenologist: Becoming What One Is* (University of Edinburgh Press).
Farrell Fox, Nik (2023) *The Parallel Philosophies of Sartre and Nietzsche: Ethics, Ontology and the Self* (Bloomsbury).
Gosetti-Ferencei, Jennifer Anna (2021) *On Being and Becoming: An Existentialist Approach to Life* (Oxford University Press).
Webber, Jonathan (2018) *Rethinking Existentialism* (Oxford University Press).

## *Chapter 15*

Derrida, Jacques (2001) *The Work of Mourning* (University of Chicago Press).
Howells, Christina (2011) *Mortal Subjects: Passions of the Soul in Late Twentieth-Century Thought* (Polity Press).
Marovich, Beatrice (2021) "Death and the Negative in Agamben and Beauvoir" in *Agamben and the Existentialists* (University of Edinburgh Press).
O'Byrne, Anne (2016) "Heidegger and Death" in *The Bloomsbury Companion to Heidegger* (Bloomsbury).
Welch, Andrew (2021) "Endless Ontology: Agamben and Sartre on Death" in *Agamben and the Existentialists* (University of Edinburgh Press).

## *Chapter 16*

Ferrando, Francesca (2020) *Philosophical Posthumanism* (Bloomsbury).
Flynn, Thomas R. (1984) *Sartre and Marxist Existentialism* (University of Chicago Press).
Meyer, Matthew (2018) "Nietzsche's Ontic Structural Realism?" in *The Nietzschean Mind* (Routledege).
Mitchell, Andrew, J. (2016) "The Fourfold" in *The Bloomsbury Companion to Heidegger* (Bloomsbury).
Plank, William (1998) *The Quantum Nietzsche: The Will to Power and the Nature of Dissipative Systems* (Writers Club Press).

## *Chapter 17*

Fleming, Michael (2020) "Political Violence" in *The Sartrean Mind* (Routledge).
Gloag, Oliver (2020) "Sartre and Imperialism" in *The Sartrean Mind* (Routledge).
Gordon, Lewis (2015) *What Fanon Said: A Philosophical Introduction to His Life and Thought* (Hurst & Co.).
Sheikh, Shela (2021) "Violence" in *A Posthuman Glossary* (Bloomsbury).
Wolin, Richard (2022) *Heidegger in Ruins: Between Philosophy and Ideology* (Yale University Press).

## *Chapter 18*

Boulé, Jean-Pierre (2005) *Sartre, Self-Formation and Masculinities* (London: Berghahn).
Cleary, Skye (2015) *Existentialism and Romantic Love* (Palgrave Macmillan).
Corriero, Emilio Carlo (2023) *"The Gift" in Nietzsche's Zarathustra: Affirmative Love and Friendship* (Bloomsbury).
Gosetti-Ferencei, Jennifer Anna (2021) *On Being and Becoming: An Existentialist Approach to Life* (Oxford University Press).
Verkerk, Willow (2020) *Nietzsche and Friendship* (Bloomsbury).

## *Chapter 19*

Ally, Matthew, C. (2020) "The logics of the *Critique*" in *The Sartrean Mind* (Routledge).
Arp, Kristana (2012) "Simone de Beauvoir's Existentialism: Freedom and Ambiguity in the Human World" in *The Cambridge Companion to Existentialism* (Cambridge University Press).
Dreyfus, Hubert, L. (2012) "'What a Monster Then Is Man': Pascal and Kierkegaard on Being a Contradictory Self and What to Do about It" in *The Cambridge Companion to Existentialism* (Cambridge University Press).
Farrell Fox, Nik (2022) "Nietzsche and Sartre: Twin Philosophers of Paradox" in *Nietzsche und der französische Existenzialismus* (De Gruyter).
Richardson, John (2020) *Nietzsche's Values* (Oxford University Press).

## *Chapter 20*

Ansell-Pearson, Keith (1997) *Viroid Life: Perspectives on Nietzsche and the Transhuman Condition* (Routledge).
Butterfield, Elizabeth (2012) *Sartre and Posthumanist Humanism* (Peter Lang).
Gordon, Lewis R. (2015) *What Fanon Said: A Philosophical Introduction to His Life and Thought* (Hurst & Co.).
Kruks, Sonia (1990) *Situation and Human Existence: Freedom, Subjectivity, and Society* (Unwin Hyman).
Sheehan, Thomas (2015) *Making Sense of Heidegger: A Paradigm Shift* (Rowman & Littlefield)

## *Chapter 21*

Ally, Matthew C. (2017) *Ecology and Existence: Bringing Sartre to the Water's Edge* (Lexington Books).
Ansell-Pearson, Keith (1997) *Viroid Life: Perspectives on Nietzsche and the Transhuman Condition* (Routledge).
Boria, Damon (2022) "Reading Nietzsche and Sartre toward an Eco-Existentialism" in *Nietzsche und der französische Existenzialismus* (De Gruyter).
Glazebrook, Trish (2016) "Heidegger and Environmental Philosophy" in *The Bloomsbury Companion to Heidegger* (Bloomsbury).
Manschot, Henk (2021) *Nietzsche and the Earth: Biography, Ecology, Politics* (Bloomsbury).

# INDEX